RICHARD ALDINGTON

An Autobiography

in Letters

RICHARD ALDINGTON

An Autobiography

in Letters

Edited by

Norman T. Gates

The Pennsylvania State University Press

University Park, Pennsylvania

Frontispiece photograph of Richard Aldington
courtesy of the *Literary Gazette*, Moscow.

Library of Congress Cataloging-in-Publication Data

Aldington, Richard, 1892–1962.
    [Correspondence. Selections]
    Richard Aldington, an autobiography in letters / edited by Norman
T. Gates.

        p.   cm.
    Includes bibliographical references and index.
    ISBN 0-271-00832-6 (acid-free paper)
    1. Aldington, Richard, 1892–1962—Correspondence. 2. Authors,
English—20th century—Correspondence. I. Gates, Norman T.
II. Title.
PR6001.L4Z48   1992
821'.912—dc20
[B]   91–33992
                                                                            CIP

It is the policy of The Pennsylvania State University Press to use acid-free paper
for the first printing of all clothbound books. Publications on uncoated stock
satisfy the minimum requirements of American National Standard for Information Sciences—Permanence of Paper for Printed Library Materials, ANSI
Z39.48–1984.

Dedicated to

the New Canterbury Literary Society
and to the Memory of These Former Members

Netta Aldington

Miriam J. Benkovitz

Denison Deasey

Lawrence Durrell

Margery Lyon Gilbert

Selwyn Kittredge

Harry T. Moore

Norman Holmes Pearson

Dilyara Zhantieva

ALSO BY NORMAN T. GATES

The Poetry of Richard Aldington: A Critical Evaluation and an Anthology of Uncollected Poems

A Checklist of the Letters of Richard Aldington

Contents

ACKNOWLEDGMENTS

More than ten years have passed since I first wrote Miriam J. Benkovitz that Alister Kershaw had suggested publishing a selection of RA's letters. Miriam had just finished editing the Richard Aldington–Alan Bird letters, *A Passionate Prodigality* (1975); my own *Checklist of the Letters of Richard Aldington* (1977) was in press.

Originally Miriam and I had hoped to compile such a collection together. Although the pressure of her other commitments prevented our collaboration then, I felt sure we would have the opportunity to complete this present work, but Miriam died on 12 June 1986. By the time of her death, we had planned a general format and selected letters we wished to include. Many of Miriam's notes as well as the listings in the index for the letters she had edited were completed although none of the introductory apparatus had been written. During the past five years, however, this selection has undergone considerable change. The general arrangement has been revised; the letters are no longer grouped by recipient, but are now in strictly chronological order. This new format required additional letters to new recipients to ensure a more uniform representation of RA's writing over the fifty years covered; these additions also required new notes and new biographical data. The typescript in this arrangement proved so long that many of the letters originally included had to be dropped. The present book represents the fourth compléte revision of the original plan.

Even with these substantial changes made over the past five years, I owe a great deal to Miriam Benkovitz: she helped launch the original project and wrote a good number of the footnotes and glossary entries for many of the letters finally included. I deeply appreciate the help she gave me and acknowledge it gratefully.

For much more recent help, I wish to thank Fred D. Crawford and acknowledge the assistance he gave me putting this work in its final form. He made hundreds of helpful suggestions, exposed many hidden errors, and suggested additional letters that increased the value of this book.

No work such as this could be completed without help from many quarters. I thank the institutions and individuals concerned. Permission to publish these letters was granted by the copyright holder, Catherine Aldington, Richard Aldington's literary executor, Alister Kershaw, and their respective owners: The British Library (letters to Netta Aldington); the Department of Rare Books, Cornell University (letter to James Joyce); Patricia Frere (letters to A. S. and Patricia Frere); Houghton Library, Harvard University (letters to Amy Lowell, John Cournos, and T. S. Eliot); New York Public Library, Henry W. and Albert A. Berg Collection (letters to Alan Bird); the Poetry/Rare Books Collection, University Libraries, State University of New York at Buffalo (letter to James Joyce); Temple University (letters to Alison Palmer); Department of Special Collections, University Research Library, UCLA (letters to Harold Monro and Lawrence Powell); Special Collections, Southern Illinois University at Carbondale (letters to P.A.G. Aldington, Margery Lyon Gilbert, Harry T. Moore, Geoffrey Potocki, Henry Slonimsky, and Eric Warman); Henry Ransom Humanities Research Center, University of Texas at Austin (letters to Pascal Covici, F. S. Flint, Babette Hughes, Glenn Hughes, and Brigit Patmore); Mikhail Urnov (letter to Mikhail Urnov); Yale Collection of American Literature, Beinecke Rare Book and Manuscript Library, Yale University (letters to Leonard Bacon, Winifred Bryher, H.D., and Ezra Pound); Stanley Weintraub (letter to Stanley Weintraub). Thanks also to Catherine Aldington Guillaume and Alister Kershaw and to the staffs of the libraries of the repositories given above as well as to Valerie Eliot, Patricia Frere, Alex Frere, Mikhail Urnov, and Stanley Weintraub for their additional help.

I thank also the following libraries and their staffs for their assistance: BBC Data Enquiry Service, Bibliothèque Nationale, Canton (Ohio) Public Library, Columbia University Library, Glassboro State College Library, Kenyon College Library, Library of Congress, Los Angeles Public Library, National Library of Australia, National Library of Ireland, New York Public Library, Philadelphia Free Library, Princeton University Library, Rider College Library, Rutgers University Library, Seton Library, Skidmore College Library, Temple University Library, University of Chicago Library, University of Colorado Library, University of Michigan Library, University of Mississippi Library, University of Pennsylvania Library, and University of South Carolina Library.

Many individuals and institutions have also assisted during the years these letters were in preparation. Thanks are extended to Peter Aberger, Romaine Ahlstrom, Patricia Aldington, Charlotte Atkinson, Helen H. Bacon, Betsey Barofski, Carol Bean, Robert H. Bertholf, Barry Bufton, Benjamin Burck, W. J. Charlotte, Don A. Cook, Shelley Cox, Fred D. Crawford, Rodney Dennis, Charles Doyle, Ellen S. Dunlap, Carol Evans, Miriam Feinberg, C. J. Fox, Donald Gallup, Margery Lyon Gilbert, Alexander M. Gilchrist, Eunice Gluckman, Thomas B. Greenslade, James Guimond, Henry Halpern, Frank Harrington, David Holmes, Judith Johnston, Stephen C. Jones, Janet Jurist, Idulis Kepars, David V. Koch, Andrée Lheritier, Katherine Lockwood-Vogel, Jean McKenzie, Ian Mac-Niven, Rhoda Martin, Francis O. Mattson, Lori Misura, Harry T. Moore, John Morris, Ohio Department of Health, Alison Palmer, Lawrence C. Powell, Jennie Rathbun, R. T. Risk, Sherrie Sam, Alfred W. Satterthwaite, Stacy Schiff, Paul Schlueter, Paul C. Sherr, Denise M. Shorey, George Sims, Marie-Brunette Spire, F.-J. Temple, Jerry Thornton, Hope Tillman, Suzanne Tocyski, James Tyler, Cassandra M. Volpe, Eric Warman, Samuel Weigh, K. J. Westmancoat, Thomas Whitehead, David Wilkinson, Henry Williamson Society, Patricia Willis, Robert J. Winter, Marjorie G. Wynne, and Caroline Zilboorg.

I wish also to thank Stanley Weintraub and the editorial board of the Penn State Press for their helpful suggestions and Philip Winsor, senior editor, Cherene Holland, managing editor, and the staff at Penn State Press for guiding this work through the intricacies of publication. Special thanks are also due to Andrew B. Lewis, whose careful copyediting has surely saved me from much future chagrin.

Special thanks are due to the Rider College Faculty Research Program for grants given during the years this work was under way, and to the Rider College Educational Support Center. Thanks also to Meredith Gates Hart for her excellent proofreading of the typescript.

And, finally, my thanks for the loving support of my family over these long years, and especially for that given by my wife who suffered through countless hours of proofreading with me.

INTRODUCTION

Richard Aldington loved life and lived it fully. His three score and ten bridged the Victorian and Atomic ages, and he scorned those aspects of each that opposed the only gods that to him were real—those hidden in the beauty of the natural world. Paradoxically, he was a pagan possessed by a Puritan drive to accomplishment. Without benefit of a university degree, he became learned in the languages and literatures of classical and modern times. A true man of letters, he could honestly say that, except for his soldier's pay, he had earned his livelihood by his writing—hundreds of his books are listed in the catalogue of the British Library, and he wrote thousands of articles, essays, and reviews for scores of periodicals.

In his old age, Aldington himself said he did not believe a writer could do then what he had done, given the changed times. But in the 1920s, in letters to Herbert Read, he argued that a writer should be "fertile," and surely Aldington was: one of the original Imagists, in his twenties an editor of the *Egoist*, a translator some of whose work is still the standard, a critic and reviewer for the *Times*, a novelist whose scathing satire of those responsible for World War I still burns, and a biographer who saw the greatness of one Lawrence and exposed the sham of another.

For Aldington told the truth—when others might have seen wisdom in silence, he insisted (writing about his own letters), "publish and be damned to everybody." This candor, which was not, as some of his detractors suggest, motivated by spite but rather by stubborn British honesty, hurt him badly in his last years. Friends of Norman Douglas could not forgive him for deflating Douglas's image. And worse, neither the friends of T. E. Lawrence nor the English reading public could forgive him for exposing the deceit of one of the heroes of a war that had produced so few at such fearful cost. Aldington's books, which were in a very real sense his only "savings" for his old age, went out of print, and only the kindness of a few old friends (and help from an unexpected quarter) made his last years reasonably happy.

At the very end of his life, Aldington's gods were good to him. When, in the late 1950s, his writings were still doing poorly in England, and not much better in the United States, he received cheery news from Russia where his fiction was being published in huge editions. In 1962, therefore, when the Soviet Writers' Union invited him and his daughter Catherine to their celebration of his seventieth birthday, he accepted. The outpourings of admiration, affection, and love he found in Russia surprised and moved him.

An intense appreciation of nature that he shared with his friend D. H. Lawrence, a fierce independence that would let him follow no banner but his own, a need to rebel against conformity and cant, a recognition that love is man's only weapon against the void—all these qualities of Aldington's literary work are present in his letters. Happily, Richard Aldington, a quarter of a century after his death, is beginning to receive recognition as the important literary figure he is. These letters, a mere hundred and fifty-four of the ten thousand extant, will go far to show him worthy of that recognition, for they are surely among the most interesting by any figure of his era. And this is not simply because he moved in the most important literary circles of his time, but also because his own consummate skill polishes every sentence he writes. Richard Aldington was one of the last of the "good Europeans" with the sort of mind and world view that term implies. You may not always agree with what he says but you will not find him dull!

Following the advice he gave "in the unlikely event of a book of letters," I have tried to reproduce the selections exactly as RA wrote them, silently correcting only misspellings, omissions of accents, or typographical errors; since RA was a careful writer, there were few of these. Occasionally, when an error was significant or seemed intended, I have let it stand.

RA usually dated his letters and gave an address. When a date or place had to be deduced from a postmark or internal evidence, I have placed it within brackets. Place names have been made uniform following the list of "Aldington's Principal Addresses" in *A Checklist of the Letters of Richard Aldington* (1977). The full address is given on first letters with abbreviation thereafter. Letters written when RA was traveling or with a poste restante or forwarding address are given as they were written with any added information in brackets. The holder of each letter is identified following the recipient's name as well as under "Acknowledgments."

I

POET-SOLDIER: 1912–1918. LETTERS 1–24

1892–1912

Edward Godfrey Aldington, who early in life adopted the name Richard, was born 8 July 1892, at Portsea, near Portsmouth, Hampshire, England. His mother, Jessie May, was of Kentish peasant stock. Strong-willed and emotional, she herself authored five novels and two books of poetry between 1905 and 1917. Albert Edward Aldington, his father, was a clerk articled to a local solicitor when RA was born; he continued his career in law without great success. Albert Edward traced his family to solid pre–Norman Conquest Saxon landowners. Harbington, an early seventeenth-century historian, says of the family, "The male line, the more it worketh the better it lyveth."

When RA was still a child, his parents came to Dover; and although his family later moved into the country, he spent many of his early years on the seacoast attending the preparatory schools at Walmar and St. Margaret's Bay and studying four years at Dover College. RA's poem "Childhood" tells us of his dislike for Dover. He was happier with his family in the country of the South Foreland. Both RA and his sister Margery write of the pleasures of the chalk-cliff beaches, prawning, hunting for fossils on the cliffs, and endless summer days of sea bathing. Here, too, RA began collecting butterflies, an interest he later pursued in many parts of the world and from which he derived the chrysalis imagery used in his poetry and fiction. The great ships that passed by in the English Channel, the fearful wrecks on Goodwin Sands he saw through his telescope, the trips to Calais and Brussels with his family all contributed to the wanderlust of his later years.

When RA was seventeen, however, his family moved away from the Channel coast of his boyhood and into greater London. For a few months he lived in suburban Harrow where, used to the spectacular beauty of the South Foreland, he was desperately unhappy; a further move to Teddington and enrollment at University College, London, changed his outlook. His new home was in a less city-like area and close to the Thames, Bushy Park, and Hampton Court where the country boy who wrote lovingly many years later of the long walks he took over rural roads inland from St. Margaret's Bay could enjoy the more formal beauty of lawns, terraces, and gardens. He was also able to visit in comparative solitude the buildings and art galleries of Hampton Court.

RA's selective reading in his father's fine library, together with eclectic education provided him by Dudley Grey, an older friend of his boyhood days in Dover and a world traveler and classical scholar, may have prejudiced him against the more formal education he received at University College. He became displeased with both the architecture, "the rusty skeleton of a Greek temple," and the scholastic standards, "designed to turn out . . . ten thousand pedants for one poet," although he had good things to say about many of his professors, particularly the classical dons. Curiously, RA objected to the University's being coeducational as "a mistake in practice however desirable in theory." Whether this youthful rebellion against organized learning would have been overcome in time and RA would have fulfilled the early promise of academic achievement some of his teachers had seen in him was to remain unknown—his father, never astute in financial matters, suffered such losses through unwise speculation that RA was forced to withdraw from University College. RA tried later to minimize the value of the degree he lost and emphasize the freedom he felt, but, despite his scholarship when older, he often seemed defensive about lacking this official stamp of academic approval.

1912–1918

Writing his autobiography, RA saw a pleasing symbolism in his last walk from the philistine world of the university down Gower Street toward bohemian Bloomsbury, but at the time he faced some difficult alternatives. The accepted careers normally open to a young man of his social standing were closed to him without a degree; he was forced to consider clerking in the City. A well-meaning friend recommended that he do this for the next twenty-five or thirty years and then retire to a life of literature. RA decided, instead, to see whether he could earn a living as a writer. He accepted the offer of the sports editor of one of the big London dailies to share a Bloomsbury flat, provided that RA would cover the sporting events he could not attend himself. RA's friend also gave him letters of introduction to newspaper editors who occasionally bought poetry; to RA's surprise one editor bought several poems. With youthful optimism, RA decided that by devoting part of his time to reporting and the rest to selling a few poems he could earn a Spartan living; he turned his back on the City forever.

After a few months of this ascetic life RA was introduced to London literary society at the home of Mrs. Deighton (Brigit) Patmore and for the first time met avant-garde writers such as Ford Madox Hueffer (later Ford), Harold Monro, W. B. Yeats, and Ezra Pound. At the Patmores' he also met H.D. (Hilda Doolittle) with whom Pound had been close when he was a student at the University of Pennsylvania where Hilda's father was the astronomer in charge of the Flower Observatory. The two young poets, RA and "Dooley," as he later called her affectionately, were soon attracted to each other when they found they shared a fervent love of classical Greece and its literature. In the spring of 1912 RA went to Paris—"Ezra and H.D. were there, so I didn't lack companionship." The decision to visit Paris cost RA his newspaper work, but a small monthly allowance from his parents and his income from the sale of poems and articles to newspapers helped to offset this. RA fell in love with Paris. He wrote a few poems and made some translations, but most of his time was spent seeing the city and living its special rhythm. He also began his lifelong friendship with the philosopher Henry Slonimsky, whom both he and H.D. admired greatly and who talked to them of Hellas and the beauties of Hellenism.

When RA returned to London that summer he accepted a part-time job with the Garton Peace Foundation. His work there did not last long, for he quickly became disillusioned with the Foundation's ideas. Moreover, other important opportunities were opening to the young poet. Sometime later in 1912, after Pound, H.D., and RA had all returned from Paris to London, Pound conceived and brought to life his school of Imagism, nominating RA, H.D., and himself as the three original Imagists. By this time, Pound had become "European Correspondent" of Harriet Monroe's new *Poetry Magazine* in Chicago. RA credits Pound with arranging for his poems and H.D.'s to be printed there as examples of the new "Imagisme." The payment for these (forty dollars), a postcard from Italy showing almond trees in bloom, and the promise of A. R.

Orage, editor of *New Age,* to take a series of articles on Italy prompted the youthful writer to buy a ticket for Rome.

RA reached Rome in December intending to stay for two months, but he stayed for seven and, besides Rome, where he spent most of his time, visited Capri, Naples, Florence, Venice, Amalfi, and elsewhere. H.D. was in Italy too and, looking back, RA remembered this first visit to Italy as "the good time" when they read Sophocles in Rome, Theocritus and the *Greek Anthology* in Capri. RA wrote many of his early poems then, and his lack of money did nothing to mar the joy of being young, alive, and in love.

When RA returned to London after a stop in Paris in July, he found Ezra Pound planning the first Imagist anthology, *Des Imagistes.* It was published the next year in New York and London and included poems by both RA and H.D. On 18 October the two young poets were married. At about this time, through Pound's influence, RA became the literary editor of the *New Freewoman,* soon to be renamed the *Egoist.* This position enabled him to promote Imagism and to review and include the work of contemporary English, French, and American writers. He also continued to write poetry and contribute to other literary journals.

In 1914 Amy Lowell made her second trip to London to visit her fellow contributors to *Des Imagistes.* Since Pound seemed occupied with Vorticism and Wyndham Lewis's *Blast,* Lowell was able to interest the Aldingtons in continuing the Imagist anthologies, which she promised to promote and have published. Pound was disturbed to see someone replace him as leader of the movement and refused to contribute, but Amy Lowell was able to persuade D. H. Lawrence to join the new group. Three anthologies entitled *Some Imagist Poets* were published in 1915, 1916, and 1917. Also in 1915, Harold Monro's Poetry Bookshop published RA's first individual volume of poetry, *Images 1910–1915,* which was followed in 1916 by an American edition, *Images Old and New,* published by the Four Seas Company in Boston.

RA was well along the way he had planned for himself the day he left University College, but his literary career was soon to be disrupted by the Great War. Later he was to write that he never recovered from his participation in the trench warfare of World War I. In the early days of the war, RA tried to volunteer, but the military rejected him because of a hernia operation he had undergone in 1910. For the present, then, he continued his literary career, even acting, for a short time, as secretary to Ford Madox Hueffer (Ford). In 1915 a personal tragedy added to the general tragedy of the war: on 21 May RA wrote Amy Lowell, "Hilda was delivered of a little girl still-born, about 2:00 a.m. this morning." In September of 1915 the Aldingtons moved to Devon with their friend

John Cournos, renting a cottage Cournos had located near Carl Fallas and J. M. Whitham. As the war continued, the military relaxed its restrictions. Fallas and RA left for military service 24 June 1916 and managed to stay together even when RA was sent to France that December, following military training at Verne Citadel, Portland, Dorset.

RA fictionalized his wartime experiences (June 1916 to February 1919) in *Death of a Hero,* one of the best novels about World War I and a savage satire of the society that RA felt was responsible for it. Although his novel was not completed until ten years after the war, RA was able to do a considerable amount of writing while a soldier, some of which, with the help of H.D. and various friends, including Amy Lowell, was also published during this time. Many of the images that RA used in his war poetry published in 1919 reappeared in *Death of a Hero.*

Eventually the war disrupted RA's marriage as well as his career: during his leaves he was seeing not only H.D., but also John Cournos's friend Dorothy Yorke, or Arabella as she was called. Possibly H.D.'s fear of pregnancy after the loss of her child the year or two before may have inhibited her so that the soldier-husband home infrequently on short leaves looked elsewhere, and the attractive Arabella was at this time living just above the Aldingtons at 44 Mecklenburgh Square. In any event, RA's love split into a spiritual union with H.D. and a physical one with Arabella.

1. To Harold Monro* (UCLA)

Jesmond
London Road [1912][1]
Twickenham, England

My dear fellow,

Your rebuke was perfectly just and justifiable, and argues an interest flattering to me.

The real answer is this: If I am so feeble-minded as to remain permanently under Pound's influence, God help me, I'm not worth bothering about. If I am so dull and stertorous-minded as not to be influenced by a man of Pound's intellect—then also God help me. I know I am extremely susceptible to other people's influences, especially when they are congenial folk, but I think they always simmer down and become absorbed in the Kosmic RA!

I don't accept any emendations to my *verse,* unless after thought I conceive them as improved expression of my own thought; and not always then.

I don't give a damn for my prose; anyone can alter it to please himself.

Of course, I am always delighted to review books for you—send along anything you want. I've tinkered up the Angel review;[2] here it is. Did I show anger in it? No. Irritation and some humourous contempt perhaps.

Yrs,

Richard A.

P.S. I see from your announcement at the end of P.R. you are fixed up till July; when do you propose to use my stuff, if at all?[3]

---

*Harold Monro (1879–1932), poet, critic, editor, anthologist, and publisher, is best remembered for his Poetry Bookshop, opened in 1913 and continued until his death. Not a great poet or even a good one, Monro was a devoted servant of poetry. To him Aldington owed the publication of his first book of poetry, *Images (1910–1915)*; Monro also published the English edition of the anthology *Des Imagistes* (1914) and was editor-publisher of *Poetry and Drama* and the *Monthly Chapbook*, to both of which Aldington contributed. "The Marshall Joffre of contemporary poetry," Aldington called him, "always ten minutes late and two divisions short," but he contributed greatly to English poetry and to Aldington's career. (See also the Annotated Index.)

1. Dated from internal evidence.

2. The unsigned review of *Angel at the Loom* by Helen A. Green and *Home Strange* in *Poetry Review*, April 1912, p. 184.

3. RA's only contribution to *Poetry Review*, other than short reviews and notices that were either initialed or unsigned, was a "Prefatory Note" to the poems of James Stephens in the issue of June 1912, pp. 264–65.

2. To Harold Monro (UCLA)

[1912][1]   Twickenham

Dear Monro,

I enclose criticism of the last book you sent me. I am sorry to be so damning time after time, but alas, it must be so. Doing these little reviews makes one crystallise vague ideas. This is what I found myself doing with McClymont,[2] & which on reflection I find I did with Walt Whitman,[3] arriving at totally different results by the same lines of thought.

What struck me first on a cursory glance, was McC's inadequacy of expression; he writes bad grammar & leaves out definite and indefinite articles because he can't fit them into his line. Weakness I. With Walt it was different; I was extremely amused by his expression, but occasionally found phrases which "smote like driven spears." Note the difference at this stage.

Then, as I read deeper, I found all McC's stuff reminiscent of somebody else; he imitates Theocritus; his one justification for doing so would be a conviction that he could write in the manner of Theocritus better than the Sicilian himself; I got down Δαφνις, & compared the lovely music with McC's lame ass of a Pegasus (mixed metaphor, never mind)—he was hopelessly wanting. In Walt, at this stage, I found all was new, hot from the oven of thought, even when he palpably imitates the Bible.

Next I read some of McC's aloud, & the incongruity of his pretensions & his attainments were irresistably funny; W.W. when read aloud is also funny, when you begin to read him.

I am at this stage, then, that, beginning with a prejudice in favour of McC (for he loves poets that I love) & a prejudice against W.W., I find myself forced to condemn the former & trying hard to find fresh arguments against the latter. But when it comes to the question, what have I got from them? W.W. must win. From McC I get annoyance, ignoble amusement, a sense of pity; from Walt new ideas & sensations—& *noble* new ideas, or developments of old ones—expressions, struck straight away, or patiently carved out, which I shall not forget, & newer, fuller harmonies in the use of language, where the discordant notes of the parts are blended harmoniously in the whole, & a sense of the man being a pioneer, not claiming to have caught "the final lilt of songs," but having accomplished something, leaving other men to choose other paths & reach him or go beyond him.

You may argue that I have not necessarily proved W.W. a poet, or McC not to be a poet, but I feel it myself, though realizing the difficulty of expressing it.

How did you like The Hymn at Night;[4] I like it; two other people don't, which seems rather hopeless.

Yrs sincerely,
Richard Aldington.

1. Dated from internal evidence.
2. Unsigned review of *Metrical Romances and Ballads* by J. R. McClymont in *Poetry Review,* April 1912, p. 185.
3. Not traced; RA may be writing in general terms.
4. See "Night Piece," in *Images (1910–1915)*, London, 1915, p. 28.

3. To Harold Monro (UCLA)

8 Holland Place Chambers,
25 May 1914   Kensington, London, England
Dear Monro,

Arriet has kept only two of my pomes[1]—two dance pieces, which have touched her soul.[2] I have stuck in two new pomes—Under a Tree,[3] and

Daisy,[4] which brings the number up to six.[5] All of these are in the ms of my book[6] except the Tree one, which I did about a week ago.

Will you hustle some and let me have em back soon if you don't like them?

Have there been any more reviews except the Westminster? I saw acknowledgments in the Sphere and the PMG.[7]

I have done a long idiotic article on Imagisme and the book in the Egoist.[8]

Are you going to Marinetti's lecture? I am preparing a costoom of violent green orange and blue for the occasion.[9]

Yours,

Richard Aldington.

1. Harriet Monroe, for her *Poetry: A Magazine of Verse.*
2. See "Dancers: Palace Music Hall [and] Interlude," *Poetry,* February 1915, pp. 221–22.
3. Not traced.
4. See Amy Lowell, ed., *Some Imagist Poets: An Anthology,* Boston, 1915, pp. 13–14.
5. For Monro's periodical *Poetry and Drama.*
6. Of the six, only "Interlude" appeared in *Images (1910–1915),* RA's first book publication.
7. RA very likely refers to a review of *Des Imagistes: An Anthology,* published by Monro's Poetry Bookshop in April 1914. Neither the review nor the acknowledgments have been traced.
8. See RA, "Modern Poetry and the Imagists," *Egoist,* 1 June 1914, pp. 201–3.
9. The "costoom," which H.D. and Dorothy Shakespear helped design, had trousers of green billiard cloth, an orange shirt, and a blue coat. Ezra Pound and RA wore such suits to a lecture on futurist clothing when Marinetti advocated a "drably utilitarian . . . single suit fastened by a zipper." Marinetti observed the two men and "denounced young Passéists in the audience." In a letter of 1960, RA placed this event in 1910 (RA to Charles Norman, 5 November 1960 [Texas]).

4. To F. S. Flint* (Texas)

[4 July 1914]   [Kensington]

Dear Frankie,

Don't curse me for ever for not answering your invitation. Hilda[1] has not been well—nothing much, largely mental strain through working too hard with Hueffer on his novel.[2] And the heat always oppresses her too. So you will see that I have had my time occupied.

When shall we come? I think she will be all right next week. Though it might be easier if you and Madame could come to us for this time and leave the visit to you until a later date. What do you say?

I wonder if you have anything you can't sell that you'd like to publish in the Egoist. I would rather have your stuff than almost anyone's. Apropos—and for God's sake *don't* tell Ezra—Cournos has got a man coming over from America in a week or so who is founding a new paper.[3] He has money and wants new stuff. Cournos has put you and me on the head of the list of people he is going to recommend. Can you bring some poetry and prose—if you have any—with you when you come so that Cournos can show him?

In haste, with "all the titles of good fellowship,"

Richard

P.S. Lewis intended to ask your permission to put your name on the Blast manifesto.[4] He wants some of your stuff for next number.

*Frank Stuart Flint (1885–1960) and RA met as young men adventuring in literature. Flint, who was self-educated, entered the civil service at nineteen. In 1908 he became the regular poetry reviewer for the *New Age*. Flint wrote a number of books of poetry between 1909 and 1920, and was one of the poets who contributed to the original Imagist anthology, *Des Imagistes*. His literary reputation, however, rests on his criticism, which introduced the work of the modern French poets to his British contemporaries. RA's lifelong attachment to French literature and to France, important in his position as reviewer of French literature for the *Times Literary Supplement*, and his excellent translations of French classics can all, to some extent, be traced to his "best friend" Frank Flint. (See also the Annotated Index.)

1. Hilda Doolittle Aldington, who signed herself H.D.

2. Ford Madox Hueffer, who changed his name to Ford, began *The Good Soldier* in December 1913.

3. Alfred Kreymbourg, whose *Others: A Magazine of the New Verse* commenced publication in July 1915.

4. A review edited by Wyndham Lewis. *Blast* No. 1 was dated 20 June 1914. RA reviewed this first issue in the *Egoist*, 15 July 1914: "Its editor, Mr. Wyndham Lewis, has carefully and wittily compiled a series of manifestos [e.g. 'We only want tragedy if it can clench its side-muscles like hands on its belly, and bring to the surface a laugh like a bomb.']—to which we have all gleefully set our names—in which the distressing and cow-like qualities of this nation are successfully blasted, and the admirable, unique and dominating characteristics piously blessed" (p. 272). See Letter 48 n. 1.

5. To Harold Monro (UCLA)

22 October 1914   Kensington.
Strictly confidential
Dear Monro,

I received last night a letter from Remy de Gourmont in which he says that he has been absolutely ruined by the war, can get no payment for work in Paris and foresees "des temps durs." He asks me to try and get him some work over here and I thought perhaps you could squeeze an article by him into your next number. He suggests that he should send a sort of Parisian letter, but I think it would be more in accordance with the plan of P. & D. if he did something on modern literature. On vers libre; on the Symbolist movement; on the tradition des libres esprits as opposed to the Prussia system of repression; on literature in general. What do you say? Gourmont is a writer who cannot possibly be considered as doing anything but honour to any paper. And you would be helping a man whom I, at least, consider to be one of the most distinguished intelligences in Europe.

If you think favourably of this proposition could you advance him say, two pounds, to tide him over present difficulties? And if you can't do anything can you give me a helping hand towards getting him something? Of course, I will do the translation of any article myself without payment.[1]

I'm sure I can rely on you not to mention what I have told you here.

I would have come to see you but unfortunately I shall be out of town until Tuesday in connection with some work I am doing for the government.[2]

Yours ever,
R.A.

1. Monro advanced £2.10.0; see Remy de Gourmont, "French Literature and the War," trans. Richard Aldington, *Poetry and Drama,* December 1914, pp. 335–41.

2. Alec Randall and RA were hired to do research for Ford Madox Ford's *Between St. Denis and St. George,* London, 1915. The book was written as propaganda at the request of C.F.G. Masterman, head of the government office for propaganda.

6. To Amy Lowell* (Harvard)

5 April 1915   7 Christchurch Place
                                          Hampstead, London, England

My dear Amy/

The Imagist review "marche toujours." Flint's article is in; quite good. I am hoping to get a better poem from him. My chief difficulty is Lawrence; he has sent in a 3 page poem on the war, & he has not yet replied to my note asking for a shorter one.[1] Space, in this venture is the great bother. I am fighting a battle-royal with Miss Weaver to get Dora Marsden out of it. I am afraid that the best we can do is to push her into "Notes & Queries." You see, someone has just given £50 to the paper, *because he admired D. Marsden;* that enabled me to get the special Imagist number, but it also tied my hands in any manoeuvre against Dora.[2] If possible, I shall print your long poem & Fletcher's; but I may have to print Fletcher's Japanese thing & your "Maladie de L'après-midi," which I like best of the 3 smaller ones. Monro has asked for 2000 words; Flint has about 1500; Fletcher on you about the same;[3] there are three or four more articles of uncertain length to come in; and the poetry, as it is now, will take up two columns & a half. If I have to defer your long poems, I will have a notice inserted in the May number, saying that they will appear along with Lawrence's war poem in the June number. I hope you'll think I did the right thing by you.

The poetry titles now run:

In the Tube	Richard Aldington
Mid-day	H.D.
Chicago or Japanese Print	J. G. Fletcher
Springs or ?	F. S. Flint
War or ?	D. H. Lawrence
Spring day or Maladie & c.	Amy Lowell
To W. B. Yeats on Tagore	Marianne Moore
After the Retreat	May Sinclair

You, Flint, Hilda & I, are, therefore all that is left of the old guard![4] I wrote Ezra again & asked him for a poem, & also asked him to get one from Bill Williams.[5] He has not replied! Which is really *absurd*, considering how long & how intimately I have known him. I can get on a damn sight better without him than with him; I am only too glad to have him out of things; & he imagines that I want his poetry because of his "great reputation." Tiens, tiens! By the way, Flint tells me that James Stephens had a perfectly slamming letter about Ezra in the New Age. It appears that Ezra said something patronisingly praising about Stephens (in parentheses, he [Ezra] is getting out a "new" anthology, & has asked— *Monro*!! to contribute);[6] Stephens was riled & wrote that he begged the world to take notice that *he* had not asked Mr. Pound to mention him, that he did not like Mr. Pound's mentioning him, that he agreed with everyone else in London, for they were wishing that Mr. Pound would shut up & go back to America, that we have discovered a new use for policemen's feet—in Mr. Pound's verse—& many more pleasantries of a like nature.[7] I haven't heard that Ezra has replied, but I guess he's "some" surprised!

Ferris Greenslet writes that he has got the Boston Transcript to take Remy's articles[8]—so that's all right. I wish, by the way, that you would swipe my article on Remy[9] back from those niggers on the Noo Republic & send it to little Miss Margaret of Little Review reputation.[10] Name of a name, can't some one save that che-ild from Powys & Mrs Havelock Ellis e tutte queste brutte gente who inhabit her pages? I am very glad about the Remy articles because now I can push our claims in the Mercure.[11] The April 1st number is here; it is absolutely war, war, war.

I now see what Remy means by "il faut rattacher votre Imagism à la guerre." I think it would be better to wait a month or so, until *after* the great offensive in the west; probably after that date they will admit non-war material. In this number the only unwarlike thing is a poem by Verhaeren. Meanwhile, I will write a short article on Anglo-French friendship—jut to keep our name before the Mercure—eh? I wish you & Greenslet could arrange to print some[where] an article or so on ruined Belgium, by my little Belgian friend, Jean de Bosschère. He is translating my articles for the Mercure & also will probably translate some Imagist poems in French reviews after the war, or during, if they are revived. Conditions in France are pretty bad just now. I have also a woman who will write about us & translate us into Russian.[12] I wonder if Greenslet could make his 6 copies to me, 12? I can do a good deal for the "movement" by judicious distributing of copies, but am hampered every moment by my accursed poverty. I have given away all my copies of the first Imagist anthology & could give more to useful people if I had 'em. Our Russian friend is just now translating Synge; I think she'll turn her attention to us next.

More & more, my dear Amy & Fletcher, I see the necessity for our having a review for ourselves. Time & again I hear of people who would buy the Egoist, were it not for our friend;[13] similarly we annoy *her* admirers by the triviality of our interests in belles lettres! Plank & I have been slaving away, trying to get things clear, to get a little money, to get some enthusiasm. We are rather discouraged; I can find no one here with any enthusiasm except Anna Wickham, & she has no taste, no conception of our ambitions. She wanted to call the paper "The New Columbus" (o Christ!!), to mix it up with social reform, with lectures on English dancing & English opera (of all things!) & finally to beat the big drum before the mob. She would have got me £200, I think, in fact I'm sure, probably £500. But what's the good; such an enterprise is doomed to ignominious failure, unless you have at least £10,000 at your back. Even then it's doubtful.

Your offer of £100 was splendid; but I will ask you just to keep it in reserve; perhaps we shall need it, but I would like to make the thing go without tapping the pocket of any *artist*. If no member of this over-wealthy British Empire cares enough to finance a review to save his country from intellectual damnation & stagnation—if no such person can be found, dammee, I'll emigrate & let my light so shine before America that England shall be shamed!

I am sorry you aren't coming over this year. Can't you after all? It is very interesting & in essentials unchanged. By June or July when you would normally come there will be great things doing. If I were you, I would go to France & Germany & have a look around. (I was going to make a joke, but forbear, lest the censor should take it seriously. They have no sense of humour, those johnnies.)

I am having the 50 copies of the Imagist Egoist sent you. I wanted Miss Weaver to stamp the head "Special Imagist Number" in red ink. Not she; it might injure the fame of the beloved Dora!

Well, mes frères, I've done my bally rd [?] best, & can only hope that our united boosts & wits will send the new anthologia through a dozen editions. When you get this it will be out; *do* send me unfavourable press cuttings. The others don't matter. I will subscribe to Durant's here. (press cutting agency)

Au revoir, mes braves. Hilda sends her love to you & Mrs Russell.

Richard

---

*Amy Lowell (1874–1925) visited London in 1913 to investigate the new "imagisme" she had seen promoted by Ezra Pound in Harriet Monroe's *Poetry* magazine. She met RA, Pound, H.D., and Fletcher at a dinner party she gave. As Flint helped direct the course of English poetry by transmitting the influence of the new French poets, Lowell influenced American poetry by supporting Imagism. The center of the movement transferred to America when she organized the anthologies *Some Imagist Poets* in 1915, 1916, and 1917. Although Amy Lowell and RA often held contrary literary views, the American poet was an important influence on RA's life and career. With her help and encouragement his work became known in America; indeed, RA might have visited America then if World War I had not prevented him. (See also the Annotated Index.)

1. See D. H. Lawrence, "Eloi, Eloi, Lama Sabachthani?" *Egoist*, 1 May 1915, pp. 75–76.

2. Marsden, founder of the *Freewoman*, 1911, renamed the *Egoist*, continued as its editor until July 1914, when she became contributing editor with Harriet Shaw Weaver as editor and RA as assistant editor.

3. See the following in the *Egoist*, 1 May 1915: Amy Lowell, "Spring Day," pp. 76–77; John Gould Fletcher, "Chicago," pp. 74–75; Harold Monro, "The Imagists Discussed," pp. 77–80; F. S. Flint, "The History of Imagism," pp. 70–71; and John Gould Fletcher, "The Poetry of Amy Lowell," pp. 81–82.

4. Poets represented in the original Imagist anthology, *Des Imagistes*, New York, 1914.

5. Neither Pound nor Williams contributed to the "Special Imagist Number" of the *Egoist*.

6. See Harold Monro, "Hearthstone," pp. 56–57; "Suburbs," pp. 57–58; "Milk for the Cat," pp. 59–61; and "Strange Companion," pp. 61–64, in Ezra Pound, ed., *Catholic Anthology*, London, 1915.

7. See James Stephens, "Affirmations," *New Age*, 18 March 1915, p. 551, which concludes: "And he made policemen's feet to beat in the verse of Ezra Pound."

8. See Remy de Gourmont, "Paris as Canonized by Conflict," *Boston Evening Transcript*, 3 April 1915, part 3, p. 4; and "Another of De Gourmont's War Sketches," *Boston Evening Transcript*, 7 April 1915, part 3, p. 2.

9. See RA, "Remy de Gourmont," *Little Review*, May 1915, pp. 10–13.

10. Margaret C. Anderson founded and edited the *Little Review*, which specialized in experimental writing.

11. De Gourmont was not able to get the Imagist article published in *Mercure*.

12. Not identified.

13. Dora Marsden, whose long philosophical essays were at odds with the literary pages of the *Egoist*.

7. To Amy Lowell (Harvard)

21 May 1915
My dear Amy/   Hampstead.

After some negotiation, I have managed to get a little space to defend you & Fletcher in this number.[1] Miss Sinclair has done a charming article on H.D. & the Imagists in general,[2] so I was leaving you & Fletcher till July, thinking you might get an American champion. Miss Sinclair's article more or less covers me, so I think your article might do more good in say, The Little Review. I should be awfully pleased if you would do it.[3]

Please forgive my delay in cabling you & the feebleness of my defence; I have been rather distressed, because Hilda was delivered of a little girl still-born, about 2 a.m. this morning. She (Hilda) was in a good nursing home & had an obstetrical specialist. I haven't seen the doctor, but the nurse said it was a beautiful child & they can't think why it didn't live. It was very strong but wouldn't breathe.[4] Poor Hilda is very distressed, but is recovering physically. I don't think there is any danger.

That will explain the briefness of this note & the badness of my defence, which I must try to write to-day.

With much love

Richard.

1. See "The Poetry of Amy Lowell," *Egoist*, 1 July 1915, pp. 109–10. RA evidently was not able to get any space in the June issue. This essay does not mention Fletcher.

2. See "Two Notes: I on H.D., II on Imagism," *Egoist*, 1 June 1915, pp. 88–89.

3. See May Sinclair, "Richard Aldington's Poetry," *Little Review*, September 1915, pp. 11–16.

4. It is possible that RA wrote "couldn't" rather than "wouldn't."

8. To F. S. Flint (Texas)

11 August 1915   Hampstead.
Dear Franky,

Of course, there is lots of talent. All that is needed is enthusiasm and a little organisation. I have already more stuff than I can print in the Egoist. Unfortunately, it is the Americans and not we who have the enthusiasm; nearly all new contributions and subscribers come from U.S.A.

It is practically impossible to get English people to work for love of the thing—witness yourself. And then, there is a stone wall of opposition from the press and from the commercial booksellers and from the public! The Mercure fellows had 1. a press which at least gave them publicity—we haven't; no English paper ever dreams of mentioning the Egoist; 2. Valette, who got round the booksellers and had a genius for organisation; 3. a small but efficient public, which bought instead of borrowing the Mercure and its productions.[1] Very many people, considerably more than a thousand see and crib from the Egoist, but they all try and get it for nothing, or else borrow it off somebody else who does.

These things, though, do not discourage me and I thoroughly agree with your proposals. Unfortunately, it isn't so much good translators and people with a knowledge of languages that we need; it is original contributions. Then lack of funds often cause us to display a fine piece of work badly. Take Joyce's serial[2]—that ought to have been printed in very much larger chunks, and the paper ought to have been increased in size so as to keep the same amount of other contributions.

After next number, Joyce will be gone and we shall have 5 to 6 extra columns at our disposal. November will, I hope, be a special Russian number.[3] Will you help me to make October and December good numbers, really good ones? I should be darned glad if you would, for the Egoist means a lot of work without much thanks. I am agitating for 20 pages again. I have recently got them a full-page ad. in an American paper. &c. &c. Is there any possibility of getting exchange ads. in England? I don't know of any.

As to people accreting, I know they would. Only a few days ago a man promised me to do a series of woodcuts for nothing and to give us the block so that we could print originals in the paper.[4]

Come over sometime and we'll talk about things.

Yours.
Richard

1. *Mercure de France.*

2. James Joyce's *A Portrait of the Artist as a Young Man* was serialized in twenty-six issues of *Egoist*, beginning 2 February 1914 and ending 1 September 1915.

3. The 1 January 1916 issue contains an article by John Cournos, "Feodore Sologub," which includes a woodcut of Sologub, pp. 4–5, Cournos's translation of Sologub's "Little Tales," pp. 8–9, and the translation of the Chekhov story, "A Drama," by Natalie Andronikoff and John Hilton, pp. 12–13.

4. Eleven woodcuts by Roald Kristian appeared in the *Egoist* between 1 September 1915 and 1 March 1916.

9. *To F. S. Flint (Texas)*

Oakley House,

14 September 1915   Bloomsbury Street, London, England

(*The Egoist*)

Dear Franky,

Let us come before the Lord with a noise of timbrels, let us praise him with a loud voice! For he hath harkened the desires of his children, & out of the shop of an Israelite hath raised us up a copy of Ausonius![1]

It is a Cologne edition, printed by Iacopus Stoer in 1608 with notes by Scaliger & Vinetus. It is bound in vellum 16°, & will fit your pocket nicely. The type is a little small & dark, but it will be easier, anyhow, for you to type it from this than from my m.s.s. There is *no* English translation of Ausonius Mosella in the British Museum, so you have the field clear. There is a magnificent variorum edition, published by M. de la Ville de Mirmont in 1889, with notes & a French translation. This text is, of course, an improvement on this little pocket volume, but you can compare them & note variations. There are several versions in French & German, but none in English, or any other language that I could discover. However, the B.M. is rather poor in editions of lesser known classics.

At the same shop where I got the Ausonius, I found a fine copy of that Amsterdam edition of Sannazaro[2] which Ezra had. I got it for 2/–, while his cost 5/–! It is priced at "8–12 francs" in Burnet's Bibliography.[3] I also got cheap a Giunta edition of Claudius,[4] so we'll have plenty of stuff for further translations. Total gross takings for the Series[5] is now £2.15.6, with several shillings more promised. One person writes from Ireland to say she has my pamphlet & likes it so much, she is subscribing for the whole series!

Do I know anything of the raid? My God, we had shrapnel bursting over head for 15 minutes, & saw the Zeppelin wondering where it would plant its next bomb! The Post Office was just missed; Wood St., Cheapside is burnt to the ground; an immense warehouse in Farringdon Road is smashed & every window for a hundred yards around broken; Queen's Square has a bomb in the middle of it, every window in the Square smashed, frames & doors broken—one window of the Poetry Book Shop smashed![6] Lamb's Conduit St. has a couple of houses down, & a bomb went through the Penny Bank![7] That's what I've seen myself—there's lots more. It was the biggest raid up to date. They've been every night since, but were driven off, so we hear.

Have a good time—thine

Richard

P.S.: Important

Korshune[8] says Constable's are quite keen for you to do a book on modern French poetry. You are to see Hutton when you get back & *are not to be too damned modest.* Understand? No swank about poverty, now. I'll do your dirty work at the B.M. & buy any bloody books you want, but you're not to shirk this job. Cournos seems to think you can fix up a contract almost immediately—they will give you plenty of time.[9]

R.

1. Decimus Magnus Ausonius, *Mosella*, trans. F. S. Flint, London, 1916.

2. *Actii Synerci Sannazarii . . . Opera Omnia*, Amsterodami, 1648, is the earliest of four Amsterdam edition.

3. H. Mattingly and I. A. K. Burnett, *List of Catalogues of English Book Sales, 1676–1900*, London, 1915.

4. A.W.G. Randall translated *De Raptu Proserpinae* by Claudius Claudianus as *Carrying-off Persephone*, London, 1919, for the Poet's Translation Series, second set, but no Guinta edition of this work was located.

5. The Poets' Translation Series, inaugurated in 1915 with *The Poems of Anyte of Tegra*, trans. Richard Aldington, London, 1915. The series was sponsored by the *Egoist*.

6. Harold Monro's Poetry Bookshop.

7. Yorkshire Penny Bank. Lamb's Conduit runs between Guilford Street and Theobald's Road.

8. John Cournos.

9. Flint did not write the book, but later he produced two articles. See "Some Modern French Poets," *Monthly Chapbook,* October 1919, pp. 1–40; "The Younger French Poets," *Chapbook,* November 1920, pp. 3–32.

10. *To F. S. Flint (Texas)*

8 February 1916   Hampstead

Dear Franky/

The Daily News review had, up to yesterday, not affected the sales at all, but Monro said it might have sold out the copies Simpkin Marshall took.[1]

I have your ed. de luxe copies but those imbecile printers have put "price 6^d net" at the beginning. Otherwise it is the handsomest of the lot. Unfortunately, I gave no direct order to remove the price, only "advertising matter" so technically I am wrong. It is a nuisance, but doesn't really make any difference. But I do curse printers; they are ensanguined imbeciles.

There is so much I want to see you about. Can you come to Whitall's, 217 King's Road, Chelsea, S.W., at 5.30–6.00 on Thursday? I want to discuss with you & W. the future of the Series.[2] As things stand, we may have to postpone it, unless he will do some of the work & we can get some people, including ourselves to take shares, like the Mercure people did. I suggest 30/– shares, payable 5/– monthly. If we could get people to take 10 or 15 such shares, I should worry less, but we have only about £5.10.0 towards the expenses of the new series, which will be heavy, to judge by the recent estimates I have received.

Come to W.'s if you can & then we can come on here & you can sign your ed. de luxe. There will be at W.'s a person who has bt. your Ausonius, so you can sign it there.[3]

Monro has a review of us from the Southport Guardian, calling us "Futurists"! Merdre de bougre, bougre de Merdre! (Ubu Roi.) The rest of the article is made up of quotes from us & immeasurably stupid remarks thereon.[4]

Saw Yeats last night & gave him your Ausonius. He likes H.D.'s Euripides,[5] & also my poem "Kensington Church Yard."[6] Why don't you send him your poems? W.B.Y. also suggests that we send our work & translations to Poet Laureate[7] who is very sympathetic. I will send off P.T.S.[8] to-day, & we can send our poems together. I have an extra copy of yours which I bought—you can buy mine—touching reciprocity.

What price enclosed cutting in re "Entente Cordiale"??? Don't lose it whatever you do. C'est précieux![9]

Thine

R.

1. See J. C. Squire, "Recent Verse," *Daily News and Leader,* 4 February 1916, p. 4, which reviews Flint's *Cadences,* London, 1915, and RA's *Images (1910–1915),* London. 1915. Simpkin, Marshall & Company was a leading London wholesale bookseller.
2. The Poets' Translation Series; see Letter 9 n. 5.
3. See Letter 9 and n. 1.
4. "Poets—Minor and Modern," *Southport Guardian,* 2 February 1916, p. 11.
5. Euripides, *Choruses from Iphigeneia in Aulis,* trans. H.D., London, 1915.
6. RA, "Church Walk, Kensington," *Little Review,* December 1914, p. 2.
7. Robert Bridges.
8. Poets' Translation Series.
9. Not retained with RA's letter.

11. To John Cournos* (Harvard)[1]

Monday/ [14 August 1916]   24965—Pte R. Aldington
                                            Comp: "E" Hut 8,
                                            11th Devons, Wareham, Dorset

My dear Korshune/

I have "gone sick" this morning with diarrhoea, so have a few minutes off. You must try to forgive my silence. On week-days I have so little energy after work that I can only write one letter & that nearly always goes to H.D.; & on Saturday afternoon & Sunday I just sleep!

I wish I could tell you how much I appreciate your devotion & that of Frank & Alec.[2] H.D. and you three seem to be all that are really left to me of my world; other people fade, become phantoms, vanish from one's life. Little May[3] is very sweet, and seems to understand in a way, but her sense of duty is too ever-present!

Dear boy, whatever sneers & unpleasantness may be your lot, don't, *don't* let yourself be shoved into this. Better retire to U.S. for 6 months or so, than get this soul-destroying mechanism on to you. With your sensitiveness & physique you could never stand the heavy marching in full marching order. I often wonder how Manning[4] has stood it. You know I am pretty strong, yet I often feel ready to drop down & I can see from the faces of the others that they are too. Yet we keep on. Why? Heaven knows, the machine just pushes & you have to go on.

It is a great pity I don't know German, because they have been through the camp for men who knew German to act as interpreters. Can you find out from Alex what this new "Training Reserve" scheme is? I understand we are to be transferred from this regiment to the general Training Reserve & then sent to any Regiment needing recruits.

I hope I shall see you during my 6 days war leave before going abroad. I am uncertain whether to come to London & say good-bye or to stay & rest at Corfe. It would be good to see everyone again, but then I shall need a rest badly. If you & Alec could come to Swanage for a couple of days during my leave it would solve the problem. I would supply you with funds from the £30 from Drama[5] if you would come—ask Alec if he could get leave. There is really no one else I want to see, as Franky will be at Swanage.

Well good-bye; remember if I don't write that I'm thinking of you just the same; try to send me a line occasionally.

Affectionately
Richard

---

*John Cournos (Johann Gregorievich Korshune) (1881–1966), Russian-born naturalized American citizen, went to England in 1912, where he became friends with the literary group that included Pound, H.D., and Aldington. Cournos proposed marriage to Dorothy "Arabella" Yorke, an American he had known before both traveled separately to Europe. In 1917, Cournos was invited to join an Anglo-Russian commission sent to Petrograd. He left Arabella with H.D. at 44 Mecklenburgh Square, London. RA and Arabella began an affair that lasted until 1928. Cournos, novelist, journalist, translator, describes these years in his *Autobiography* and his novel *Miranda Masters*. (See also the Annotated Index.)

1. This letter was published in *The Dearest Friend: A Selection from the Letters of Richard Aldington to John Cournos*, intro. R. T. Risk, Francestown, N.H., 1978.

2. F. S. Flint and Alec Randall.

3. Possibly May Sinclair.
4. Frederic Manning.
5. Probably for his translation of two of Remy de Gourmont's plays, *Theodat* and *The Old King,* which appeared with a lengthy introduction in *The Drama: A Quarterly,* May 1916.

12. To F. S. Flint *(Texas)*

20455. L/Cpl R.A.
"D." Company
44 T.R.B.
Verne Citadel
Portland, Dorset.[1]

[22 November 1916]

Dear Franky/

It is quite possible that I may "go across" in a week or so.[2] I don't know anything definite of course, but I believe an Army Order is coming out soon for all trained N.C.O.'s & officers to proceed to France. Anyhow, there is another "push" coming off soon on the Somme.[3] I believe the bombardment has already started. And they need reinforcements. Unfortunately, L/Cpls have to go as privates, so my "stripe" is no particular good, except for the extra training.[4] Don't tell H.D. this, because it may be a myth, & I don't want to worry her uselessly. But you might see her & try to find out if she has made any preparations for such an eventuality. Personally I still favour the U.S. trip[5]—I don't mind betting that all women under 30 without children are industrially conscripted within 6 months. You are all a lot of kids—you don't realize what's impending: frightful battles, huge casualty lists, diminishing trade & production, famine prices, forced labour—each follows from the other.

I know you think I'm mad on this—but contrast the state of affairs now with Nov 1915. What do you think things will be like in Nov. 1917 & Nov. 1918? Remember things will get worse more rapidly. If H.D. *is* industrially conscripted I shall never forgive you people who have persuaded her to stay. You and Alec,[6] don't forget, were among the omniscient gentry who *knew* we should never have forced Military Service.

I don't want to be unkind, but we mustn't shirk facing things as they are—& they're damned bad. Think it over, talk it over once more with Alec & H.D., & let me know if you still think it wise for her to stay.

All affectionate greetings, dear boy, & cordiale poignée de mains.

R.

1. Site of RA's military training.
2. RA, with Carl Fallas, novelist, had volunteered for the infantry and on 26 June was called up; in 1914 RA had been refused because of a hernia operation.

3. The first Battle of the Somme began on 1 July 1916; the last important operation took place 13 November 1916.

4. The "stripe" denoted the rank of lance corporal.

5. A U.S. citizen, H.D. could have returned home.

6. Alec Randall.

13. To F. S. Flint (Texas)

22 January 1917   [B.E.F., France]

Dear Franky/

Why on earth send me all that piffle of Wilkinson's?—it rather annoys me, because obviously the thing is inspired by his wife, who has always detested me with that woeful detestation of wh. only women are capable. Apropos, the character of Eunice has been adulterated—I use the word advisedly—with many of the qualities of Mrs W. But there is something rather repellent about reading these descriptions of other people making love to one's wife; even in a novel! I think I will put a Mills bomb in Wilkinson's pocket after the war. Damn his silly novel.[1]

By the way, you remember some time ago the Times issued a series of pamphlets for soldiers, extracts from English classics? I wish you'd get hold of some for me—I'd like something to read & chuck away.[2]

To speak the honest truth: I worry very little about all these literary squabbles—how can one trouble in the face of so much human misery?

Here is a real Bairnsfather[3] incident that happened the other night. We were going through a village wh. has been absolutely battered out of existence by bombardment. We were passing what had once been a row of shops. Everyone was tired & trudging along in silence; even the guns were silent: then a broad midland voice remarked: "Bill, business don't seem to be very brisk these parts." Perhaps it doesn't sound so very funny, but it seemed so to us.

Are you writing anything? Your literary idleness is really a disgrace. You've done nothing recently except that Katt book,[4] wh. you did for filthy money. Why don't you plug away at the book on modern Frenchmen? You needn't be a blooming encyclopaedia! Why not do a series of portraits, impressions, memories of authors, with an introductory essay?[5] For Heaven's sake do something! Are we all to be "wash-outs"? You are too comfortable. Try sleeping on the floor with two blankets & an overcoat, or spend a frosty night in a hole in the back garden with your wife letting off Roman candles & Ianthe[6] throwing bricks at you! You might hire de Bosschère to knock a hammer rapidly on a table (like Marinetti) for a machine-gun, & if you make the hole over a drain you can wear an anti-gas helmet! That would stir you up a bit—I don't think.

I haven't any particular ruling passion—just "carry on" from day to day with a kind of bored pertinacity. You dear people seem tremendously far away, like demi-gods in a smoky Elysium. For the Lord's sake don't interrupt H.D. if she is having a good time with any one—when I said "look after H.D." I meant help her to have a good time & not bother about me. I didn't want to make you a kind of Argus! Take H.D. out, if you can, to theatres, & get her to meet new & amusing people. And if you can devise any sort of an "affaire" pour passer le temps, so much the better.[7] She'll be a grass widow a while longer yet.

Every day I go by the grave of a French soldier, named Jean Viguelle. And—don't laugh—I say an "Ave" for the repose of his soul! Not that I've become religious, but I have a mysterious feeling that he'd like it, even from an infidel like me. Let's hope it shortens his time in Purgatory.

There also are the graves of two little girls, killed by the same German shell. I often go & stand by them & think many things.[8]

Perhaps you can see now why Wilkinson annoys me?

All luck, old man, and work, get going, pro-dooce.

Thine
Richard.

1. See Louis Umfreville Wilkinson, *The Buffoon*, London, 1916; Mrs. Wilkinson was H.D.'s girlhood friend, Frances Gregg. The Mills bomb was a grenade developed by the British Army during World War I.
2. In 1915 the *Times* provided pocket literature in the form of broadsheets for soldiers in the trenches.
3. I.e., the type of situation that Bairnsfather (see the Annotated Index) depicted in his cartoons of the war.
4. *Frederick the Great, The Memoirs of His Reader, Henri de Catt (1758–1760)*, London, 1916.
5. See Letter 9 n. 9.
6. Flint's daughter.
7. See Letters 22 and 23. RA advocated sexual freedom within their marriage for himself and H.D.
8. Cf. RA, "Three Little Girls," in *The Complete Poems of Richard Aldington*, London, 1948, p. 94.

14. To F. S. Flint (Texas)

29 January 1917   [B.E.F., France]

My good, (to be as French as we can!),

I have well receive your letter so fair and blackguardly . . . It's no good! I need the fantasies of language of Huysmans & Rabelais to write well in a letter. I can't handle the epistolary style in English somehow.

Excellent that you've found an ex-soldier in your department who knows the Pioneers—but the latrine yarn is a libel! All the rest is perfectly accurate. You know how my days are spent now! Convey your knowledge to H.D.

Yes, I received your Wilkinson letter,[1] which rather depressed me. I hope I didn't slay you in my reply—I forget what I said; I forget everything, but I felt just as affectionate as of yore.

Dear boy, oh for one hour in either of our dens, with books & wine & smokes and the talk half French, half English rolling from the latest Parisian poetaster to Meleager & from Marinetti to Folgore da San Gemignano! Apropos, H.D. has sent Bubb[2] my translation of Folgore[3]—the best Italian work I've done—as well as the Konallis poems.[4] So with the Imagist anthology & a possible small collection of prose poems,[5] 1917 won't be altogether a blank for me. Every day in which one begins nothing, every week in which one writes nothing, every year in which one publishes nothing, is lost! How I yearn for the dear, musty smell of old vellum & the crisp rustle—like unto bank notes, yet how much more precious!—of those unreadable Aldines[6] I collected with such gusto. You make me long to read all those seven—or eight is it?—volumes of Verlaine—& I would most willingly exchange my rifle for a set of Mardrus! When oh when this armed strife is o'er I shall retire to Rome for a season, grow hyacinths in my shrapnel helmet—which I intend to purchase or abduct as a "*souveneer*"—and mess about in the Vatican library. Also wander about that city with H.D. whose gusto for antiquities fits in gloriously with mine. There is a little church on the Aventine, dedicated to Santa Sabina, where I hope to sit one whole morning & listen to the silence. It has some fine Byzantius mosaics if I remember rightly, but hang them! Can you imagine the pleasure of listening to the silence, while the sunlight runs over the worn flag stones? What a place to think in! Perhaps you will abandon respectability & a government job & come with me. There's nothing like vagabondage, freedom, the arts, starving & feasting together as luck turns. Then life has a tang where it is now insipid. Then one can dream great things besides one's best friend—you know whom I mean[7]—& be content if the year ends with nothing done. One's art, looked at selfishly, is less important for what it produces for others, than for what it adds to one's own life making things poignant & strange & beautiful where otherwise they would be "just ordinary."

Never feel angry or grievedabout me—a prophet is not without honour!—and whatever happens I have something that cannot be destroyed. I had a talk with a field-mouse in the trenches the other day—we got on splendidly! And there are hawks & crows and chaffinches & sparrows & owls & starlings & grey crows to look at & understand. They are so delightfully unorganized, such vagabonds! So you see I have found friends.

Au revoir, dear boy; forgive all this babble. But my mind is becoming vegetable through disuse.

Thine
R.

P.S. I've even forgotten your address so must send this via H.D. Couldn't send Almanac—against regulations. Send your poem when finished.

1. See Letter 13.
2. That is, The Clerk's Press.
3. Folgore da San Gemignano, *The Garland of Months*, trans. Richard Aldington, Cleveland, 1917.
4. *The Love Poems of Myrrhine and Konallis*, Cleveland, 1917.
5. *Reverie. A Little Book of Poems for H.D.*, Cleveland, 1917; see also *Some Imagist Poets, 1917, An Annual Anthology*, Boston, 1917, pp. 3–16, where ten poems by RA appeared.
6. Books published by the Aldine Press, founded at Venice in 1490 by Aldo Manuzio.
7. In his poem "The Walk (for F.S.F.)," RA writes of his deep friendship for Flint. See Norman T. Gates, "Richard Aldington and F. S. Flint: Poets' Dialogue," *Papers on Language and Literature*, Winter 1972, pp. 64–65.

15. To Amy Lowell (Harvard)

20[?] November 1917   [B.E.F., England]
My dear Amy/

You must forgive my not having written you. All my time is taken up at the Officers' Training School,[1] and the week-end, when I do get away, is too delightfully lazy for me to spoil with writing. Indeed, all writing is distasteful if one is without leisure—for one must have time to live.

I am exceedingly happy to know how very greatly you have succeeded in the last three years—for both your talents and your enthusiasm plainly have deserved for you the recognition—and more—which you have received. Your influence upon literature in America should be decisive, creating there something of that pungent enjoyment of the things of the mind which one admires so much in the French. You remember how de Gourmont just before he died bequeathed to me the care for the "tradition des libres esprits"? I feel that you have kept alive this tradition while I have been plunged in more sordid confusions, in an ordeal which has perhaps strengthened my character but only at the expense of imagination. My "thanes fly from me"! I cannot write as I could once, though I have recaptured a certain stern ideality, have regained a serenity by leaving any kind of journalism or publicity for the anonymity of my present life. After all in the general futility of things it matters very little whether I use my superfluous energies to write poems or to make stories and tales & jokes for the soldiers ("rough men" as the Little Review in its daintiness calls them) who are my companions.

But don't think that I haven't ambition or the desire to make beautiful things. I have lost a great deal, I am handicapped in ways you cannot imagine, but this abrupt withdrawal from the rapid current of my life into something alien & painful may, perhaps, be as salutary for me as prison for the author of De Profundis![2] One sees the unimportance of the "literary life" and the supreme importance of literature, the one imperishable record of the human soul, the means of multiplying personality, the expression of destiny.

Most of the things I thought about poetry two years ago I still think; but in the present pause in my intellectual life I am not sure whether it is the final pause or a period preceding intense creation. In any case I do not complain. Why should I?

Hilda tells me you want some facts about my life. I can't think that anyone else would be interested, but here they are just for you to know.

My father's family is an old one—Saxon in origin—and though not noble, "respectable" as the 18th century people say. There are two Aldingtons (i.e. villages) in England; one in Kent, one in Worchestershire. My father comes from the Worchestershire branch, of which there are a good many records in the British museum. They were yeomen & owned land in Worchester according to a survey made in 1503.

My mother comes also from an old Kentish stock. Her father was an Army Doctor.

I was born on 8th July 1892 in Hampshire. My father had literary ambitions & published a novel of Elizabethan life[3] wh. had some measure of success. He practiced as a lawyer in Dover, Kent. His library which contained some 2000 volumes, & much poets, especially Elizabethan, was my "home university." He taught me my letters at the age of two, & got me any book I wanted, as I grew up. I hated Dover, which is the place meant in "Childhood."[4] Even now the place depresses me unutterably & fills me with nostalgia for the south. When I was seven I went to school at a "Seminary for Young Gentlemen" at St. Margaret's Bay, a little fishing village; here I was immensely happy and here also I developed a sort of mystic enthusiasm for life. I can remember when I was about ten, leaning from my bedroom window to listen to the thrushes singing on an April evening with feelings of such intense aesthetic pleasure that one's finest emotions now seem blunt & coarse by comparison. I had a sort of scientific period—from 11 to 15—when I collected & classified insects & read books on geology, zoology & kindred sciences. At 12 I went to Dover College, where I was extremely unhappy. I hated the discipline, disliked the futility of the boys, & was nearly disgusted from learning by the unimaginative way it was presented to me! The only thing I enjoyed was Rugby football, which, in some ways, still appears to me the sole raison d'être for many of the educational establishments of my country.

Later I lived at Sandwich, a town of immense antiquity, the great port of England in the reign of Edward III. I loved its great circle of walls, its Barbican and turreted gates, its old winding grass-grown streets, and air of immemorial languor.

My people had some few acres of land there, and I loved to wander about by myself under the shadow of a line of vast poplars which bordered one side. Near this place too were a Roman town & the site of a Saxon temple to Woden, which gave reality to my dreams of "old far-off unhappy things."[5]

Here I wrote a good deal, from about my 15th year, poetry of all sorts, reading a great deal & getting familiar with French & Latin. All this stuff was rhymed & pretty poor, the mere echo of things read, though always with a strong Hellenic tinge I caught from my father's Elizabethans. At 17 I came to London. My first poem was printed in some obscure journal when I was 16. By the time I was eighteen I had printed quite a number of poems & translations in papers like the Evening Standard, the Westminster Gazette, the Pall Mall, etc.[6] I got half a guinea each for them & was delighted!

I began to write vers libre about the early part of 1911, partly because I was fatigued with rhyme & partly because of the interest I had in poetic experiment. I didn't know Heine or Patmore's "Unknown Eros"[7] & never suspected the existence of the French vers libristes. I got the idea from a chorus in the Hippolytus of Euripides. In fact the cadence of Choricos and the Greek Marble—the earliest of my poems in Images,[8] written when I was just 18—is very similar to that of Hippolytus' invocation to Artemis, though, of course, the subject is very different.

I met Ezra Pound through our mutual friend Mrs Deighton Patmore early in 1912. I showed him my *vers libre* poems over a beef-steak in Kensington & he said: "Well, I don't think you need any help from me!" We were great friends, very great friends, and I cannot forget how much his knowledge & sympathy meant to me, after many years of spiritual isolation and almost morbid sensitiveness to general misunderstanding. I met H.D. at Mrs Patmore's about the same time.

Is there much more to be said? I went to Paris & to Italy, as you know. From Italy I sent back the "Letters from Italy" published in the New Age.[9] (I omitted to say that I met Monro before I met Ezra; Flint just a little afterwards.) Hueffer, Yeats, & Lawrence have all taught me something, but, apart from any personal feelings, H.D.'s poetry is the only modern English poetry I really care for. Its austerity, its aloofness, its profound passion for that beauty which only Platonists know, make it precisely the kind of work I would like to do myself, had I the talent.

This all seems very inadequate and perhaps a little foolish. Someday perhaps I will be able to tell you more, but after all whatever is interesting in me should be in what I write and not in what I do.

I leave the school in about a fortnight & hope to be gazetted in about a month. What happens to me then depends upon the gods & the War Office.

All good wishes & affection to you.

from
Richard.

1. On the recommendation of his commanding officer in France, RA had been sent back to England for officers' training; he returned to France in April as a second lieutenant.

2. See Oscar Wilde, *De Profundis*, London, 1905.

3. See A. E. Aldington, *The Queen's Preferment*, London [1896].

4. See RA, "Childhood," *Egoist*, 15 December 1914, pp. 453–54.

5. RA, from memory, has misquoted this line from Wordsworth's "The Solitary Reaper," which reads: "For old, unhappy, far-off things."

6. The earliest published poem traced dates from 1910, when RA was eighteen. See "Song of Freedom," *Justice*, 29 October 1910, p. 5. This and poems from the *Evening Standard*, *Westminster Gazette*, and *Pall Mall* are collected in Norman T. Gates, *The Poetry of Richard Aldington*, University Park, Pa., 1974.

7. See Coventry Patmore, *The Unknown Eros*, London, 1877.

8. *Images (1910–1915)*, pp. 9–11.

9. See RA, "Letters from Italy," *New Age*, 1913. Twenty-two letters were published between 13 February and 10 July 1913.

16. To Amy Lowell (Harvard)

2 January 1918   44 Mecklenburgh Square,
                                                         London, England.

My dear Amy/

Hilda sent me on your charming letter this morning and I was most happy to get it. We had your cheery cable on Christmas day—I was at home—and were delighted that you had thought of us.

After I passed my examinations[1] I had nearly a month's leave. It was a wonderful time, so much was compressed into those few weeks. It was marvellous after those other days.

I have my commission now and am expecting to be back in the trenches in a month or six weeks. So probably I'll be gone before I can hear from you again. I will try and send you just a word before I go.

Unhappily, I feel I mustn't send you any details about my military life—the rules are very stringent and I don't want to say anything I shouldn't. I got my commission for "services in the field," whatever that may be, for I did nothing extraordinary. However my company officer in France was good enough to say that he thought I'd earned it!

I'm afraid that's all I can tell you—after the war I'll spin you more soldier's yarns than you'll care to hear!

I am thinking of collecting all my war poems—I have about 60 or 70—into a book. Do you think the U.S.A. would care for them? They are not popular—I mean they are bitter, anguish-stricken, realistic, not like Brooke or Noyes or anybody like that. They are stern truth, and I have hesitated about publishing them. But I would like to get rid of them— they cling to me and if I could publish them & forget them it would be a relief. I think perhaps I will submit them to Constable.[2]

There is a sort of anthology of verse, prose and pictures being brought out in the Spring—Hilda & I have been asked to contribute 2 poems each, which we are doing.[3] Sadler is connected with it. Perhaps you don't know that no one is allowed to start a new periodical now? So this will be just a book. I have my suspicions, though, that further orders in respect to paper may prevent its publication.

Mr Bubb has two or three things of mine he is printing.[4] I know he will send you copies if he has your address. I will ask him next time I write. I am translating Anacreon[5] in camp—I find I can't do really good work in a camp, so I am doing these light Greek things, just to keep the "feel" of literature. Great poetry—Shelley and Euripides and Dante— moves me so terribly that I cannot bear it. I feel choked. For this reason I had to give up those burning passionate poems of Meleager.[6] They left me unnerved & unstrung. I am reading a little Dante, but only a very, very little each day—it exhausts me with emotion. He understands so wonderfully the piercing passion of love—the mystic exaltation which is prolonged beyond the contact of the flesh. Do you remember the two cantos towards the end of the Purgatorio where he meets Bia after those years of absence and where Virgil leaves him?[7] It seems to me to put most modern poetry utterly out of count. It is like Plato's Symposium, but more tortured, more like ourselves in its bitterness & intensity.

Indeed I like your prose book very much.[8] You have presented your poets in quite the right way—I mean that you have achieved the result of making one wish to read the poets. And that after all is the chief object of appreciation.

I think as a matter of fact that Hilda's work has now outgrown your just charge of narrowness—just, I mean, at the time it was written. Un- fortunately, she has burned some most poignant lyrics and a long poem of about 10,000 words. I can't forgive her for it, but she said she thought them inadequate! The long poem—such as I saw of it—had beautiful passages. But she is so relentless. I think she has grown very much spiritually. Everything she writes has now that sure touch which seems to me immortal—the arrangement of simple poignant words in an absolutely original way yet perfectly inevitable, so that one wonders why one has not thought of it oneself. But she is frightfully reserved—I had to beseech her for hours to prevent her burning a lot more!

Are you bringing out anything fresh soon? I hope you will send Hilda anything you do so that I can have the pleasure of reading you in the trenches! Did you know that the one copy of our 1916 anthology[9] I had in France is buried in the ruins of a house? I lent it to my platoon officer & his billet was blown down by a shell—fortunately in his absence—before he'd had time to read a word! I didn't tempt fate & Fritz again!

Au revoir, dear Amy; it is up to you to carry on the tradition.

Ever yours
Richard.

1. For his commission as second lieutenant.
2. Constable did not publish RA's "war poems," but see *Images of War: A Book of Poems*, Westminster, 1919; *Images of War*, London, 1919; *War and Love (1915–1918)*, Boston, 1919; and *Images of War*, Boston, 1921.
3. RA's, "The Blood of Young Men" and "Soliloquy" appeared in *New Paths . . . 1917–1918*, London, 1918, pp. 22–24; no poems by H.D. are included.
4. See Letter 14 n. 2–5.
5. See *Greek Songs in the Manner of Anacreon*, trans. Richard Aldington, London, 1919.
6. See *The Poems of Meleager of Gardara*, trans. Richard Aldington, London, 1920.
7. Cantos 30 and 31.
8. Amy Lowell, *Tendencies in Modern American Poetry*, New York, 1917.
9. *Some Imagist Poets, 1916, An Annual Anthology*, Boston, 1916.

17. To John Cournos (Harvard)[1]

6 April 1918   Tunbridge Wells
Dear Korshune/

Of course you are angry and indignant with me.[2] I foresaw that. It seems rather odd that we should be quarrelling, but naturally it's up to you to take any line you choose & to dictate what our future relations shall be.

Now, my dear boy—for whatever you say or do I shall think of you affectionately—please allow me to say that it was at Arabella's request that you were not informed sooner. I am not trying to shelter myself behind her, but am merely telling you this to exculpate myself from the obvious charge of trying to deceive you since you returned. You will admit that I had no choice.

That is really the main point wh. I desire to make clear; for I held that you had a right to know immediately what had happened.

You ask for an "explanation"—what exactly does that mean? I suppose it really means that you want to say bitter things, perhaps contemptuous things to me. Yes, I suppose you want to work off your feelings on me, perhaps even to make a permanent break. Well, I don't know why I should give an "explanation," nor why you should expect one from me. Isn't it a matter between yourself and Arabella? I am not ashamed of anything I have done; I regret nothing. If I told you that I have suffered through this—suffered for you too—you would not believe me. It doesn't matter.

What chiefly hurts you, I know, is that you feel I took advantage of your absence[3]—but would your presence have altered things? I don't know; there are events which are stronger than we are; there seems a kind of fatality about it, a bitter irony some ways.

I am not excusing myself, Korshune, because there is nothing to excuse—we fell in love with each other, that is all. Of course, I know you well enough to know that you will reserve your displeasure for me and will spare Arabella any pain that you can. I accept full responsibility. But is there really anything to be gained by our writing or talking bitterly and acrimoniously to each other?

No, dear Korshune, I shall not quarrel with you unless you force me to do so; indeed whatever happens I shall think kindly of you; but, and this is final, you cannot expect me to alter the relationship between Arabella & myself, not only from my own standpoint but chiefly because she tells me that she has found a sanction & a sweetness in life that she had lacked before.[4]

I shall try to get up to town next week-end; if I do get permission it rests entirely with you how we meet or if we meet at all.

Yrs
Richard

P.S. You really ought not to have written me a letter like that, Korshune. It is—how shall I say?—unworthy of you. Let us hate each other if necessary, but let us keep our dignity.

I realise the inadequacy of this letter—but I am ready to answer anything you wish to ask.

1. This letter was published in *The Dearest Friend: A Selection from the Letters of Richard Aldington to John Cournos*, intro. R. T. Risk, Francestown, N.H., 1978.
2. Arabella had told Cournos that she and RA were to be married. Actually, RA remained married to H.D. until 1938, a decade after RA and Arabella parted.
3. Cournos was in Russia for the British government when the affair between Arabella and RA began.
4. RA and Arabella lived together until 1928, when he left her to live with Brigit Patmore.

18. To H.D.* (Yale)

20 May 1918   [B.E.F., France]

It is more difficult not to love you when I am away from you than when I am with you. Really, it is true that one has many lovers but only one love. And I gave you everything, so that I have only desire and consideration to give to others. But I wonder if I was your love or just one of the lovers?

To-day I have looked at whole trees all green with spring and fields and I have seen an old French woman I used to know out here who nearly wept over me & gave me tea & cognac!

But still, though things are kind, I am terribly indifferent. The truth is: I love you & I desire —l'autre.[1] Really I can never be happy without you; and very often it seems I couldn't be happy without her. Folly to talk of happiness when this horror goes on. But on remâche ses idées in the long nights of watching. The stars are very powerful instillers of truth. Somehow, Dooley, I have made a great mess of my life. But I would have ben content if I hadn't made you suffer so much. And then, and then, I must look after A.[2] C'est de la démence. I find it hard to write to her. Do you realise what that means? It is a psychological point which gives me distress.

Out here I really don't know what one lives for. I don't pretend it is all misery and horror; there are moments of rest, compensation, gaiety even. But there is a constant wear—& having lost somehow the pearl & essence of life there seems no point in keeping on. Je vis en bête. Do you think there is any point of keeping on? Twice last week I tried to get killed—and was unlucky or lucky, whichever you like.

Isn't this folly?

Do be happy with Cecil.[3] I shall get over this someday.

R.

*Hilda Doolittle (1886–1961), better known as H.D., came to London from Philadelphia in 1911, probably expecting to marry Ezra Pound but instead becoming the first wife of RA. Before their marriage in 1913, H.D. and RA visited France and Italy with Pound, who promoted the three of them as the original Imagists. When RA joined the British army in 1916, H.D. carried on his literary affairs. A stillborn daughter effectively ended their marital relationship. RA began seeing Dorothy Yorke, whose friend John Cournos had left her with the Aldingtons when he was sent to Russia by the War Office, and H.D. left RA for a liaison with Cecil Gray, by whom she had a child. Befriended during these troubled times by Winifred Ellerman (Bryher), H.D. lived and traveled with her. RA and H.D. were not divorced until 1938 and remained good friends until H.D.'s death. Of the four women most important to RA's life, surely H.D., who is recognized today as a major poet of the modern period, was the most influential. (See also the Annotated Index.)

1. Dorothy Yorke, called Arabella.

2. Arabella.

3. Cecil Gray, whom H.D. met through D. H. Lawrence in the latter part of 1917, while she lived at 44 Mecklenburgh Square. Shortly thereafter, RA returned to London on leave from military service. According to H.D., he was certain that he would be killed when he returned to the front and determined to "get every ounce of pleasure out of life while he had the chance." That included sex. Meanwhile Arabella (Dorothy Yorke) had moved into 44 Mecklenburgh Square, and she and RA began an affair. That they had was impressed on H.D. during two air raid warnings. At the first they appeared together in "pajamas"; the second she found them in bed together. H.D.'s unhappiness and dismay were so apparent to Cecil Gray that he took her to his home at Bosigran, Zennor, near St. Ives, Cornwall. See *Petitioner's Statement* In the High Court of Justice Probate Divorce & Admiralty Division Between Hilda Aldington Petitioner and Edward Godfree [Richard] Aldington Respondent (Yale).

19. To H.D. (Yale)

1 June 1918   [B.E.F., France]
11:30 p.m.
Dearest Dooley/

I have just sent you a little note[1] saying how glad your letter made me; I wanted to get it off at once in case anything should happen to prevent my writing to you later.

Ah yes, I do think of our days together. What strange, despised creatures we were & yet what a treasure we had. At times I think of some statue we looked at together or remember some book we both cared for. How could there ever be anyone but you?

Maupin.[2] It was in London, I think, that we read it. But how far, far away that time is. In such a way people spoke of the Golden Age. I wonder what is gained through this deprivation & suffering? After all we have scarcely known each other for two years. It is a lot.

"Friends" you say. Not verse now, only prose? Once when I threw myself at your feet I felt your heart beat so wildly I was frightened. Friends—I would like you to kiss me passionately just for one night, to realise once with you, my Beatrice, the great frisson, with the woman I love best.

Oh, I know the world is a queer place, & those who love each other best hurt each other most. Perhaps it will be only "friends," but I cannot bear to think it yet; I shall think "lovers" until you tell me "no" with your own lips. But, as I told you I have changed, through misery, through routine, through the strain of things. Perhaps I may get back equilibrium, some sort of life, even write again, but "never glad confident morning again." One acquiesces in the death of a flower but it is hard to admit that the flower of one's unique life dies as surely & nearly as quickly as the Summer lilac.

Isn't it strange. I know the date & what time it is; but none of us knows which day of the week it is. All days are alike. I think it is Friday or Saturday.[3] But, really now, aren't days of the week a superfluity?

Do you get enough money, enough to eat & buy clothes & books? Won't you let me give you "of my scant pittance"? (You can see, can't you, how hard I'm trying to "make up" to you!) Ah, but I'm nearly crying as I write, my wife, my Dooley. I am so proud that you have my name—please, won't you keep it, whatever happens, in memoriam as it were.[4]

I shall go on writing until dawn, if I don't stop. For a while thinking of you I forget the horror. I never forget you.

Richard.

1. See RA to H.D., 1 June 1918: "Darling, . . . Your letter melted much bitterness of heart. I thought you did not write because you did not care. And I wanted you to care so much. It is horrible here—you probably know where I am. But yet I have not forgotten to love you. You write sweetly & I pardon your reserve. If only I had more than myself to give. My sweet, you seem so beautiful & tranquil—any flower makes me think of you."
2. Théophile Gautier, *Mlle de Maupin*, Paris, 1835.
3. It was Saturday.
4. Even after their divorce in 1938, H.D. kept her married name.

20. To H.D. (Yale)

2 June 1918   [B.E.F., France]
My dear Dooley/

I hope you don't mind my writing to you so often. You must tell me if it causes any difficulty in your new ménage[1] and I will then abridge my correspondence. But I shan't stop writing until you tell me you don't want to hear—& perhaps not even then!

On the day after to-morrow I am being sent down the line for a five weeks course. It may not last anything like that time as I should be sent for if reinforcements were badly needed. But at least for a little I shall be back of the line. Better keep the same address if you write—letters will be sent after me. I don't particularly want to go—I'm more or less at home now with this battalion, but as it's an order I can't refuse. It makes a change anyhow, though I am more or less indifferent.

I think of you perhaps too much and wonder if I shall ever see you again. Arabella sends me very kind letters & seems genuinely grieved to have me gone. But I can't tell. In any event I don't really care, but sometimes I would give everything just to touch your little finger as I did that first day at Brigit's.[2] It's queer to be living in memories so early in life.

I can't quite give up the idea that we shall be together again. There is of course the complication of Cecil & Arabella, but they seem—to me at least—to fade into the arrière-plan where we two are concerned. Ah, Dooley, we have not been as happy as we might—somehow I have failed. Of course it makes no difference that we have had other lovers—though sometimes it hurts, hurts. But out of this present utter darkness of mine, this confusion & complete lack of direction & interest, there is one thing that seems to matter—you.

The little less & what miles away! Why didn't you love me passionately *before* Arabella & not after? Don't you know that it's you, you I wanted & want life, everything with? The bitter irony of it! Like St Augustine I repeat to myself bitterly: "too late have I loved thee o pulchritudinem antiquam!"

Infinite problems circle about us, but, dear Dooley, let us at least keep a certain tolerance, a certain tenderness for each other. Here I am in this wretched dug-out & there you are in Cornwall. What the next year will do for us, god knows. Perhaps it is very wrong of me to write you loveletters—perhaps I ought not to disturb you. You are very reticent—you do not tell me if you are happy with Gray. It is a great consolation to me to know that there is someone to look after you now & in the future, if by chance I should not be able to do so.

How one wanders in words—half expressing half one's thoughts. I write rather my meditations than a letter—chiefly writing because for a time I concentrate on the memory of you, all I seem to possess now. Why should one agonise with hope? I won't ask anything of you, anything of some things I was going to ask. I'll just finish & go up & listen to the guns a bit.

Richard.

1. That is, with Gray in Cornwall.
2. Brigit Patmore, who had introduced H.D. and RA.

21. To H.D. (Yale)

28 July 1918   [B.E.F., France]
Dear wild Dryad/

I'm so glad to know that you're going to "the isles,"[1] though I'm afraid this rain and rough wind will have spoiled a little the lilies of all kinds you were to live with. Two days ago I had a very sad little note from you but instead of answering it I just sent you a Faun poem.[2] I'm so glad I did because I know now that the Faun & Dryad will always live & always love each other. You see sometimes the Faun kids himself he's dead & sometimes the Dryad kids herself *she's* dead—& then, like Toddy, they wake up from the "burn-down-dead" and find themselves good & alive again. I hope you'll like the Faun song anyhow.

I wish I'd known you were going earlier—it would have cheered me up lots. Are you staying with the little girl who learns H.D. by heart?[3] Or have you just got rooms? As you speak of Alec[4] & Amy[5] coming down that way I suppose you are not staying with yr: amie.[6] I wish you were in some pleasant house. (Apropos, will you remember I always keep a small balance for you in Cox's? You have only to mention that you need it and I'll send a cheque by return. Don't be proud about this, for I get more pay than I need & I can't use it more pleasurably than for you.)

Amy Lowell's letter strikes me as about the most offensive thing that was ever penned—she in her fat Boston drawing-room having the impertinence to lecture me in the front line! It takes my breath away. She is absolutely past all decency—and that talking that rot about wishing she were in the trenches. She'd get so stuck in the mud she'd never shift. Amen!

Ah, my dear, how sweet and beautiful you are. Of course I will come to you after the war and we will be "wild & free," and happy "in the unploughed lands no foot oppresses, the lands that are free being free of man." I love you, best beloved and dearest among all the daughters of the half-gods; you knew that though you forgot that Fauns are queer & wild, with "maggots in their brains" sometimes! Dooley birds get maggots sometimes, only they just trail their wings & look kind of doleful— but it's the same thing in the end!

You must tell me more about this new admirer of H.D. She must be very wise since she can love your poems so much. Has she a name or is she just some belle anonyme? Is she truly of the sacred race or merely one to whom it is given to recognize the gods yet not be of them?

I would like so very hard to kiss you again—that dear small mouth that was made to speak exquisite things just as your curved ears were made to hear "the music of the spheres." But perhaps I should not say this, for silence is most noble to the end. And yet I tremble with pleasure when I think that on the very day of my leaving this prison I shall kiss again the cool fragrant petals of your pale hands and hold against me the tiny points of your sterile breasts.

Over me have swept great waves, yet the great ninth wave has so far missed me; perhaps in the end I shall win through. But, like you, I have been a wanderer upon foreign seas and yearn only to return to "the isles" that are mine by right.

R.

9th R. Sx. B.E.F. is correct address.

1. Scilly Isles as guest of Winifred Ellerman (Bryher); see n. 3.
2. See "The Faun Captive," in RA to H.D. [26 August 1918] (Yale); cf. "The Captive Faun," *Nation*, 31 May 1919, p. 265. Both H.D. and Ezra Pound often referred to RA by the nickname "Faun."
3. Winifred Ellerman, who adopted the name Winifred Bryher. She had committed H.D.'s *Sea Garden*, London, 1916, to memory some time before meeting H.D. on 17 July 1918.
4. Alec Randall.
5. Amy Randall.
6. Cecil Gray.

22. To H.D. (Yale)

3 August 1918   [B.E.F., France]
My dear girl/

Mail, which had been delayed several days, has just reached me. You seem to be in rather a devilish mess, and in a way I am responsible. Distinctly unfortunate that this should happen now as I have been nearly four months in France & haven't much hope of getting back before November! There is the faintest possible chance of my getting back on duty before then and if so I could of course see you & possibly establish your "alibi."[1]

However, the chief point is yourself, your own health and well-being. Do this:

1. Stay in Cornwall until you know whether Gray is going to be enlisted.[2] (I think he will—most Grade III men are now.)

2. When you are sure of your condition—which, by the way, you should establish at once by consulting a doctor—you must tell Brigit[3] and get her advice & assistance.

3. You must then leave Cornwall. If you stay where you are there may be all sorts of unpleasantness.

4. I don't quite know where to suggest your going—Brigit can help here.

5. You must not worry about the situation—I will accept the child as mine, if you wish, or follow any other course wh: seems desirable to you.

6. I enclose £5. I will send you as much of my pay as I can. Try & keep it by you for doctors etc. You will need it.

Of course I won't tell Arabella. I can see you must be feeling pretty rotten about things, but you must just feel that this is one more strange experience and not feel badly about it. Cheer up and eat lots—I expect you are frightfully hungry?

Can you give a guess at the date of conception? You see, the devil is that I've been corresponding with Gilbert[4] & he knows I haven't been out of France! I wrote grousing about it only a few days ago. That's rather a blow isn't it? But perhaps that can be arranged—I can tell him I managed to wangle a couple of days from the Corps School & that I didn't write it to him because of the censor, as I'd been asked to keep it quiet. Let me have as soon as possible the date on which you want me to have been in England.

I really don't know what else to suggest. I am pretty powerless here, as you know. But I will do anything I can.

Brigit is the only trustworthy woman friend you have.

The money question is the most difficult. You can have any cheques that come for me. And perhaps I can borrow some. If necessary I can refuse leave & send you the money I would have spent on that.

Anyway, you must keep on keeping on and not get hysterical or anything. These little matters are not really as grievous as they seem.

With love
Richard.

Address: 9th Royal Sussex. B.E.F.

1. For her pregnancy by making himself appear to be the father.
2. When Gray volunteered for service in 1914, he was rejected. Some time after the introduction of conscription in 1916, he was classified C.3, the lowest military category. Gray was called up for service in late August 1918, but he "absented" himself (that is, failed to report for duty) and left Cornwall for London, where he lived until early 1919. He then went to Italy.
3. Brigit Patmore.
4. Probably Gilbert Cannan.

23. To H.D. (Yale)

5 August 1918   [B.E.F., France]
My dear/

Your letter postmarked Aug 1st has just come. I don't understand at all. Please see a doctor at once. I've been living hell these last 48 hours, thinking of your anguish & distress, thinking that this strange event has separated us perhaps for years. Please, *please,* please find out & let me know. I can stand the truth—I've faced the whole problem for us both. But I'm just grasping at the hope you may be mistaken.

You will wonder why I seem to lay so great a stress on you having a child with G,[1] when I approve of your being his mistress. My dear, no man can take you from me by being your lover & I'm only too happy for you to have a pleasant companion, a lover, to keep you gay & well and interested while I'm here. But I do lose you if you become a mother, naturally & inevitably. It was for precisely that reason I stifled my desire to have a child with A. That desire was very great but it was madness—it meant binding A. very closely to me or else behaving very cruelly. Am I right? You must really get this affair put straight. One way or the other. I'll face *everything* with you & stick by you, dear. Don't have any doubt of that. I spent terrible hours thinking how confused you must be feeling. Have this child if you are pregnant—we will arrange things somehow. Do get my attitude correctly—I'm not angry or jealous or "honourable" or any such bilge, but only profoundly grieved because I suddenly realised that your maternity would naturally & inevitably cut you away from me & join you closer to G. And I don't want to lose my Astraea— queer wonderful creature that she is! You've just got to understand me properly here or you will be making a bad blunder in psychology. I love you & I want you to be happy & hav lovers & girl-lovers if you want, but I don't want to lose you as I should if this happened. Gray would be a worm if he let you go when you had his child in your womb. Now wouldn't he? You know he wouldn't do such a thing; he would want to have you with him. And you & I would just be friends or lovers, not imperishable sweet comrades as we have been.

O my dear, I pray I don't hurt you by what I say. I want to be so tender, so all-embracingly compassionate—but while this thing is in doubt I haven't the right.

Your
Richard

P.S. Shorter's article[2] need not worry you. Why change H.D.? You are bound to get that sort of thing. Let them print your photograph—you don't care. What the devil do these people matter?

1. Gray.
2. Nothing on H.D. by Shorter has been traced. He wrote a weekly article for the *Sphere*.

24. To H.D. (Yale)

27 September 1918   [B.E.F., France]
My dear Astraea/

Your plans seem to me excellent and sensible, and you should pass a fairly comfortable winter I think. Take exercise & kp normal. The arrangements for food and warmth seem O.K. It is not precisely the ideal existence one formulates but it is the best you can do under the circumstances.[1]

Will you note that after Oct. 4, letters should be addressed 9th Royal, Sussex, and the "Signal School 8th Corps" discontinued. I go up the line on the 8th.

I am very glad to find that you are cheerful and, as you say, "without resentment." Yet, when you say that, I wonder if you have completely "got" my attitude. God forbid that I should re-touch new wounds, but as I was categorically definite with Arabella, so must I be with you. I want you to understand that in the actions & determinations I have taken I have been moved by affection for you rather than any bourgeois sense of duty. That is clear, isn't it? But I want you to understand also that this affection is purely that of friendship. Your friendship seems very valuable to me & I am anxious to retain it, but on no misapprehension. So far as you & I ever being lovers again or living together as husband and wife, you must understand that it is fini, fini, fini. Now I am not trying to force you into anything. I am proud that you should bear my name; glad if you correspond with me on matters of art & literature & life; happy to meet you as one meets an old friend. You are quite free to make any kind of "liaison" you choose, providing some sort of elementary social camouflage is used; I don't wish to interfere with you in any way. Be as "free" as you can in a world of slaves. If you care to give & accept friendship upon these terms, I am only too happy. It is purely up to you. But I cannot have you being pleasant to me if I feel there is any idea in your mind of the old relationship being renewed. Because that is now impossible. You may think me idiotic and affirming more than I carry out. But women are not so essential to life as they imagine; and in any case—well, there's no need to be offensive, is there?

I think I've made my point clear, and made it so with as much consideration as is consistent with precision.

It is no use our being humbugs, my dear. Things can't ever be the same again, so why carry on with something patched-up, a makeshift? I have at last "sorti mon beau tranchant," as you see & cut the Gordian knot of this affair. Arabella knows precisely how I stand & we have now ceased to correspond except at rare intervals. But there is no necessity for you & I to adopt this severity, unless you are anxious to eliminate so eccentric a person from your circle. We have many points of common interest not at all affected by the state of our hearts. You don't need any reiteration of my admiration for your work (though, since we are being so devilish frank, it wouldn't hurt for you to improve your spelling & punctuation!) or for your personality and fine mind. So, as I have said, if you care to carry on, on this purely friendly basis, I am delighted. If not, it is up to you.

Now then; I believe this is really the last postscript to this almost year-old affair. I am conscious of being less pleased with myself than I could wish, yet on the whole I have been fairly frank & not altogether inconsistent. Your going off with Gray was of course a mistake—never, in future, have an affair with a man if you are not both in love with each other. If you had been in love passionately with G, all right; but just slipping off like that—wrong, dead wrong. Probably you will now write & say that you *were* passionately in love with G. In which case I shall just note down that all men are liars, especially women.

For myself, as I wrote you, there seems to be no particularly brilliant future. There is nothing I particularly want, and that is very dull. Yet I have gained a certain balance, a certain possession of myself, and a measure of certainty that no person in the world is essential to me. That is a great gain, for to put one's happiness into the hands of another is indeed a handing of hostages to fortune.

You will, I hope, pardon the frankness and perhaps offensiveness of this letter—it is for the truth's sake. I hope to hear from you.[2]

Ever yours
Richard.

1. Many years later H.D. said that although Gray suggested that she marry him after divorcing RA, she left Cornwall at RA's urging. She was currently living at 3 Christchurch Place, Hampstead. See *Petitioner's Statement* In the High Court of Justice Probate Divorce & Admiralty Division Between Hilda Aldington Petitioner and Edward Godfree [Richard] Aldington Respondent (Yale).

2. The tone and intent of this letter are in sharp contrast with that of 21 August 1918 (Yale) where RA wrote "I seem to bring unhappiness to everyone I care for—it drives me mad to think of such unhappiness falling on the little girl I saw in Brigit's room six years ago. I feel very angry with Gray sometimes—because it's just like a sloppy musician not to be precise and careful. God, I feel deadly sick to think what you are going through—poor dear, my dear little girl Astraea. You have suffered too much already that this should come on you. . . . It is perhaps wea selfishness for me to regret that your child is not ours. But 'no man escapeth his fate by lamentation,' and I must accept this, the bitterest thing that has ever happened to me. Between you & me as always there is great love, a perfect love. I do not see the future clearly, yet I do know I shall never love anyone but you inevitably. Though we be oceans apart I never forget you. Be brave, be strong, have your child and I will try to care for it for your sake—if you want. Sleep, dear; don't think; just be a happy mother."

H.D.'s pregnancy was a difficult one. She had left Cornwall to live at Speen, Prince's Risborough in Buckinghamshire by December 1918 and at the end of January went to London, where she lived at 2 Hanger Lane, Ealing. There she contracted pneumonia and was forced to go to a nursing home. She remained there until the birth of her child. Throughout this difficult period, H.D. was nursed by her new friend Bryher.

II

Editor-Translator: 1919–1928. Letters 25–49

When RA returned from Belgium, where he had been instructing troops, to London in February 1919, he had to rebuild both his personal and his literary life. H.D. had left London for Cornwall with the music critic, Cecil Gray. While there, she met Bryher (Winifred Ellerman), an early admirer of RA and the other Imagists and the daughter of the immensely wealthy and powerful shipowner and financier Sir John Ellerman. Bryher befriended H.D., saw her through her illness and pregnancy, and became a second mother to her little daughter Frances Perdita. Thereafter, the two were intimate friends, living and traveling together much of the time. RA, meanwhile, not being able to find living quarters to his liking, stayed only a short time in London before leaving with Arabella for a cottage in Hermitage (a village in Berkshire, near Newbury) that D. H. Lawrence turned over to them when the Lawrences left England after the war.

Before RA left London to settle again in the placid countryside that recalled the rural area inland from his boyhood home, he was able to make important literary connections that were to provide for him for the decade ahead. Some of these were made possible by Sir John Ellerman. RA says that during the summer of 1918 he received a letter at the front expressing an interest in the Imagist poets. The letter was from Bryher; RA answered and "put the lady in touch with H.D." After he returned to London, RA received a dinner invitation from the Ellermans and, subsequently, letters of introduction to the editors of the *Times* and the *Sphere*. With this help and his own efforts RA was able to place poems and articles in the *English Review*, the *Anglo-French Review*, *To-day*, the *Sphere*, and most important of all, the *Times Literary Supplement*, for which he eventually became the regular reviewer of French literature. He also became, in 1921, assistant editor of T. S. Eliot's newly established *Criterion*. During this period RA also was able to arrange for the publication of five books of his poetry in England and the United States.

The eight years RA spent in Berkshire with Arabella provided the time he needed to cope with the physical and mental damage that the war had inflicted on him. Like many soldiers who survived World War I, he suffered from the effects of being gassed and shell-shocked. By 1922 RA had moved from Hermitage to a cottage about fifteen miles away in the valley of the Kennet. Malthouse Cottage, built against the end wall of an old malthouse, provided exactly the seclusion and tranquil setting that he longed for. The peaceful English countryside of the Kennet and the three-day walks he took along the ancient Ridge Way helped to heal the scars of his wartime experiences. In his poems "The Berkshire Kennet" and "A Winter Night" and in the novel *The Colonel's Daughter* RA recaptures something of the spirit of this time and place.

During the early part of these years RA took seriously his position as reviewer of French literature for the *Times Literary Supplement* by polishing and perfecting his command of Old French and Italian and by reading widely in these literatures. He also read a good deal in the classics; after his father's death, in 1921, his mother gave RA many of the books from his father's library. Through the kindness of May Sinclair he also became a life member of the London Library and, in addition, built up a library of five or six thousand volumes by judicious purchasing. The intensive work RA did included not only two books of poetry and a great amount of literary journalism (some of which was reprinted in book form as *Literary Studies and Reviews* [1924] and *French Studies and Reviews* [1926]), but also more than a dozen volumes of translations and the editorship of an excellent translation series. RA's work in this area provided the basis of a lifelong career in translation that eventually produced some thirty titles in all.

The 1920s saw RA establishing his position as an important critic and enjoying an influential friendship with the greatest literary critic of the period, T. S. Eliot, who visited Malthouse Cottage and accompanied RA on some of his long walks. Although he remained close to his cottage during these years, he needed to visit London occasionally, if only to see Bruce Richmond of the *Times Literary Supplement*. On one of these visits in 1919, RA had introduced Eliot to Richmond; later, Eliot became a leader-writer for the *Times Literary Supplement*. Also, after the first quiet years, RA was able to repeat his 1912 visit to Italy. A check from *Poetry* had paid for his first trip, and a check from the publishers of his Cyrano translation (*Voyages to the Moon and the Sun*) made possible his second visit ten years later. Of his time there he wrote later, "There are many periods of my life I would gladly live again, but few periods so willingly as those two months of 1922." Later visits followed in the spring of 1924 and 1926; on both trips he stopped off in Paris.

These trips to the continent and the visit of an old friend opened new vistas for RA. Among those people who genuinely affected his life, none looms larger than D. H. Lawrence, whom RA called "a remarkable man, the most interesting human being I have known." In 1917, D. H. and Frieda Lawrence had shared H.D.'s flat at Mecklenburgh Square. In 1926 Lawrence and Frieda returned to Europe from their ranch in New Mexico and visited RA at Malthouse Cottage. Their private conversations about contemporary England—"something had gone wrong"—and Lawrence's descriptions of his adventurous wanderings—"wholly facinating and rewarding"—prompted RA to look more closely at his own life. He concluded, he wrote later, that he was irritated by the people with whom he worked, his literary journalism was trivial compared to real writing, and he was becoming obsessed with the desire to get away from England permanently. Even if he may have distorted past feelings to suit present circumstances when he wrote of this period of his life some fifteen years later in his autobiography, the contrast between these views and his position as he saw it when he wrote Glenn Hughes on 26 November 1925 is astonishing. Possibly Lawrence's visit convinced him that somewhere he had taken a wrong turn on the road that led from University College. He may now have felt that his life at Malthouse Cottage, his journalism, his translations, and all his efforts to fit himself into the London literary elite constituted exactly the same bonds of society that he thought he had once cast off.

In any event, although RA still kept his Berkshire cottage and returned there occasionally until 1928, by the spring of 1927 he was in Paris staying in a small apartment near the Luxembourg. He and Arabella lived part of that winter in London, but this only served to strengthen his resolution to leave England permanently. Bruce Richmond did not object to his living much of the year in Paris, and a handsome payment for the anthology *Fifty Romance Lyric Poems* (1928) from Crosby Gaige, who had looked up RA at Padworth with John Squire as guide, helped to implement his decision. According to John Cournos, RA declared his intentions at a pub gathering of the *New Criterion* group of which he was a member. This occasioned considerable shock since it was generally assumed that he had been marked for the editorship of the *Times Literary Supplement* on Bruce Richmond's retirement.

April 1928 found RA and Arabella again in Paris where they stayed first in an apartment belonging to his friends Walter and Lillian

Lowenfels and later in quarters they found for themselves. They remained through the summer, but in September went to Florence and then to Naples to travel by boat to Marseilles and the island of Port-Cros where Jean Paulhan, editor of the *Nouvelle Revue Française,* had rented the *vigie* (an old observation fortress), and then offered it to RA for October and November. Since room for guests was available, RA asked the Lawrences and Brigit Patmore, an old friend from RA's early London days, to join them. The Lawrences left in November when the weather turned too cold for D. H.'s tubercular lungs; he also disapproved of RA's obviously growing attachment to Brigit and of his disloyalty to Arabella. RA said goodbye in Toulon to the man he most admired of his contemporaries and never saw him again. Lawrence died in Vence (near Nice) less then sixteen months later. Arabella left to travel alone to Paris while RA and Brigit Patmore returned to Paris together. Passionately in love, RA saw Brigit frequently in Paris before the cold weather drove them south to Italy and the beginning of their eight and a half years together.

25. To Amy Lowell (Harvard)

31 March 1919

The Authors' Club,
2 Whitehall Court,
London, England.

My Dear Amy,

I am absolutely in agreement with most of what you write and I am deeply appreciative of your offer to help in spite of your own doubt. The attempt to get out the series[1] was provoked first because I wanted to get back the "feel" of literature again after so an absence & secondly because Miss Bryher & Mr. Shorter were so keen on it. I have talked it over with them both & with Hilda & I am coming over to your opinion: that the attempt is ill-advised at present & probably beyond my power to carry to a successful conclusion. Hilda, W.B.,[2] & I will therefore probably publish our translations as individuals though, if possible, with the same publisher.

There is a bigger interest in our classical translations in England than in U.S. & it seems to me a useful bit of propaganda for us all. Since people admit that our translations are well done, then gradually we shall force them to admit our own work. The "Nation" has published or is publishing Miss B's Zonas & Callimachus, my Anacreontia & Hilda's Hippolytus. Holbrook Jackson is also bringing out my Anacreontia in To-Day (which has only a circulation of 3000 it is true). I shall also be doing some more for other papers.[3]

So you see, dear Amy, it isn't altogether a "wash-out," though I agree with you that the whole project would be more trouble than it is worth. I see that quite well now. I didn't see it in Belgium because I was in such a condition of wrecked nerves then *any* sort of hard slogging work seemed desirable.

As to my books: As you know Beaumont is publishing a limited edition of "Images of War" on vellum at 30/–, fine paper 21/– & ordinary paper 12/–. I only get about £15, but as I get back the copyright in 6 months it seems worth while, for one can then get out a cheap edition.

Images of Desire, added to & carefully revised & castigated is coming out with Elkin Mathews. He gave me £5 advance royalties & 15%. He's doing a first edition of 1000.

I have the following projects.
1. A reprint of Images plus the poems in the anthologies, plus a number from periodicals.[4]
2. Anacreon.
3. Meleager.
4. A collection of prose.[5]
5. A collection of prose poems.[6]

The position with Brown is certainly *very* unsatisfactory.[7] But you see, my dear Amy, when the war was on & one might have been slain any moment such things didn't matter. I only wanted to get the book printed to please someone else.

Mr. Shorter has promised to give me an introduction to Lane over this new, enlarged edition of Images. If Brown has sold out could I get it away from him & have a better publisher take it? Lane would probably be unwilling to sell to Four Seas, but would to another more reputable firm. I will write you further about this; meanwhile if you could sound Brown it would be useful.

I think in some ways you aren't quite fair to me, Amy. Of course I don't expect non-combatants to understand; they can't. But you see I'm not at all well; my nerves have got in such a state that I have a sort of "sympathetic" neuralgia in my neck & arms; I sleep badly; I have a "trench throat" & cough; I have ague directly I get cold. This sounds a devil of a grouse, but it's true; only for Heaven's sake don't mention it to Hilda.

I'd like to go away & lie in the grass & rest & sleep for a month or two; but of course I can't. I'm grateful enough to be back free with all my limbs; but I can't help a feeling of listlessness. Still I'm working. I'm "critic of poetry" for the Pall Mall Gazette; I have got reviewing for the Anglo-French Review & I'm doing a series of articles on French poets for them; I'm doing 6 articles on life in France for the Sphere.[8] Jackson has promised to use my work regularly in To-Day & Harrison has promised to give me a show in the English Review. As I've only been home six weeks I think I've done very well.[9] Unfortunately London is so full I can't find a flat, & have to live in a small room in a Soho restaurant. It's amusing but uncomfortable & I can't feel settled down at all.

Your Chinese work[10] sounds "exciting" as Winifred says. I shall be happy to see it. Apropos, your book[11] has at last arrived after pursuing me to the Expeditionary Force via two or three other addresses back here. I read it in the train going to see Hilda. No, I haven't any objection to polyphonic prose, but I must tell you that I read the four poems as I should have read four interesting stories. I think I like the Nelson one best, though "The Coaches" have also that flavour of romance you so well impart.[12] I feel you have the gift of "interest," the power I mean to compel reading, in a great degree. Personally I found I had to read the whole book straight off, & the hour's journey seemed like five minutes. I enjoyed the whole book immensely and congratulate you on its vividness & picturesqueness. And I am proud of possessing your autographed copy.

Everybody is very kind to me. I think they realize that I suffered quite a bit during the war & are anxious to help me on. Every editor I have been to has received me courteously & no one has refused my work. It is probably only a temporary thing but I'm very much touched by it, & of course it enables me to live a little more comfortably.

You are very good about everything and I hope that the Transcript will take me on. I'm not sanguine about it. It's C.K.S.'s[13] idea & he insisted on it.

Forgive this fragmentary note. I think I must quit as I feel tired. *Please* don't let Hilda know I feel ill; she has more than enough worries. I tell you just to explain things.

Yours affectionately,
Richard

1. Poets' Translation Series.

2. Winifred Bryher.

3. See Bryher, "The Nine Epigrams of Zonas," *Nation and Athenaeum*, 22 February 1919, p. 615; RA, "From *Anacreon*": "The Winecup," "Love the Slave," "Portrait of a Lady," "A Lover's Wishes," "Love the Pursuer," and "The Hedonist," *Nation and Athenaeum*, 1 March 1919, p. 644; H.D., "Hippolytus" (lines 199–233), *Nation and Athenaeum*, 19 April 1919, pp. 80–81. See also RA, "Anacreontics": "The Vision of Anacreon," "The Singer," "The Painter," "The Wine-Cup," "On Love," "Gaiety of Wine," "The Wine-Bibber," "The Swallow," and "Love," *To-Day*, July 1919, pp. 183–85.

4. See *Images*, London, 1919.

5. RA's first prose collection was *Literary Studies and Reviews*, London, 1924.

6. See *The Love of Myrrhine and Konallis, and Other Prose Poems*, Chicago, 1926.

7. The Four Seas Company, Boston.

8. See the following by RA in the *Sphere:* "Books in the Line," 5 April 1919, p. 2; "The Bookshop at Grenay," 12 April 1919, p. 26; "Crosses," 26 April 1919, p. 70; "Culture in the Army," 3 May 1919, p. 96; "War Poetry," 10 May 1919, p. 114; and "Preferences in French Literature," 17 May 1919, p. 140.

9. RA was discharged from the British army on 31 January 1919 and went at once to London.

10. See *Fir-Flower Tablets* (with Florence Ayscough, translations of ancient Chinese poetry), New York, 1921.

11. *Can Grande's Castle,* New York, 1918.

12. The "Nelson one" is "Sea-blue and Blood-red," pp. 3–46.

13. C. K. Shorter suggested the *Boston Evening Transcript* for RA's work.

26. To James Joyce* (Cornell)

6 May 1919   Authors' Club

Dear Mr. Joyce/

I am very sorry for what has happened, & am doing my small best for you.[1] I saw Mr. Sturge Moore on receipt of your letter & he advised my going to Mr. H. G. Wells, who, unhappily, is not a personal friend. However, I sent a letter to him through a mutual friend, Miss May Sinclair, asking her to forward another letter to Mr. H. G. Wells. Unfortunately, she has sent it to his country address & I've not yet heard from him. Will communicate with him immediately.

I was considerably handicapped at first by not precisely knowing what was up. But your statement—which arrived about half an hour ago—clears things up & I will put it before Mr. Wells as soon as I can get in direct communication with him.

I fear all this is poor satisfaction for you, but I thought it best to get at Mr. Wells through another friend rather than bluntly introduce myself. To-morrow I hope to be able to say things are going all right.

I will do all I can, believe me. And pray accept my sincere sympathy for the rotten position you are in. Cheer up!

Yours very truly

R. Aldington.

*James Joyce (1882–1941), had left Ireland by the time that RA entered University College, London. The first installment of Joyce's *Portrait of the Artist as a Young Man* appeared in the *Egoist* when RA was assistant editor, and during that year (1914) Joyce and RA appeared together in *Des Imagists: An Anthology*—later their poems were published in the final *Imagist Anthology, 1930*. In a letter dated 25 February 1919, Joyce wrote that he had asked a Zurich friend to convey his thanks to RA, not specifying a reason. The two did not meet, however, until RA moved from Padworth to Paris. RA was certainly aware very early of Joyce's importance, having selected him in an article for *Outlook* in 1919 as one of the current group of young writers most likely to make a name for themselves. He also wrote "The Influence of Mr. James Joyce," which appeared in the April 1921 *English*

Review following an agreement with Eliot to review *Ulysses* from opposite points for view. Furthermore, as the letters in this collection show, RA commented frequently on Joyce's work. However, RA regarded Joyce as an individual genius whose writing style was not likely to be imitated successfully by others, and he did not admire *Finnegans Wake*. (See also the Annotated Index.)

1. While it is difficult to determine the exact nature of the "rotten position" Joyce was in and what RA was doing to help him, it probably involves Joyce's litigation with Henry Carr of the British consulate in Zurich. Joyce had nominated Carr to play the leading role in *The Importance of Being Earnest* for a production that Joyce was supporting to enhance British prestige in Zurich, but he subsequently quarreled with Carr. Joyce refused to pay costs and damages assessed against him as the result of a countersuit filed by Carr, and instead resolved to make his plight known. In late April and early May he mailed copies of a long statement about the affair to various people; this is probably the "statement" RA refers to in his letter. Without asking directly for financial help, he made it clear that 10,000 francs was at stake. About a week after RA's letter, Joyce was informed that an unknown benefactor (Harriet Weaver) had settled 5,000 pounds on him; he also received money from Scofield Thayer and from a friend of Thayer's, which ended his worries about the Carr case. What exactly RA sought from H. G. Wells or what, if anything, Wells did is not known.

27. To T. S. Eliot* (Harvard)

18 July 1919   Authors' Club
Dear Eliot/

I have several times recently felt impelled to write you my admiration for your critical articles and put it off in the hope of meeting you.[1] Your article in the current Egoist[2] again stirs my admiration and (I admit) my envy. You have a power of apprehension, of analysis, of the dissociation of ideas, with a humour and ease of expression which make you not the best but the only modern writer of prose criticism in English. I read your essays in the Athenaeum[3] with the greatest pleasure; I hope that someday you will collect these & other essays into book form.[4]

Having said this much, with complete sincerity, I feel compelled to add that I dislike your poetry very much; it is over-intellectual & afraid of those essential emotions which make poetry.[5]

Excuse the impertinence of all this and its rather heavy style, due to a sort of pious terror.

Yrs
Richard Aldington

*T. S. Eliot (1888–1965), replaced RA as assistant editor of the *Egoist* beginning with the June 1917 issue. They first met at about this time, but they were most closely associated from 1919 to 1928. As his letters to Eliot and to others about him show, RA admired Eliot's critical writing, but found his poetry, as he writes above, "over-intellectual." How much RA contributed to Eliot's selection as his successor on the *Egoist* is unclear, but RA un- questionably helped to advance Eliot's career in many ways. Among other things, he introduced him to Bruce Richmond of the *Times Literary Supplement* and participated in efforts to raise funds to free Eliot from working at Lloyd's Bank. During the early 1920s, the two were fast friends: RA visited Eliot for dinners and met him at parties in London, and Eliot spent time with RA at Malthouse Cottage, accompanying him on long walks about the countryside. In 1923, RA became assistant editor of Eliot's *Criterion*, and it was there that their first disagreements arose. In 1925, RA's feelings toward Eliot deteriorated further when Faber & Gwyer, where Eliot was a director, planned a series of monographs on foreign men of letters that RA thought subverted similar plans he had made earlier with Routledge. The real break between the two men came, however, with the publication in 1931 of RA's *Stepping Heavenward*, a sharp lampoon of Eliot and his first wife. In *Richard Aldington: An Intimate Portrait* (1965), Eliot wrote, "We were on the same side for a long time and I was the first to give offence, although unintentionally, which made a breach between us." (See also the Annotated Index.)

1. In *Life for Life's Sake*, RA says of Eliot, "I met him once when on leave during the war." Eliot confirms this in *An Intimate Portrait*.

2. "Reflections of Contemporary Poetry," *Egoist*, July 1919, pp. 39–40.

3. Eliot began to write for *Athenaeum* in April 1919.

4. In the following year, Eliot's essays on Swinburne and *Hamlet* that had first appeared in the *Athenaeum* were collected in *The Sacred Wood*.

5. In "Tradition and the Individual Talent," first published in the *Egoist* (September and December 1919), Eliot wrote the following: "Poetry is not a turning loose of emotion, but an escape from emotion; it is not the expression of personality, but an escape from personality. But, of course, only those who have personality and emotions know what it means to want to escape from these things." Could RA's references to Eliot's fear of "essential emotions which make poetry" have inspired Eliot's oft-quoted exclusion of emotion from poetry?

28. To T. S. Eliot (Harvard)

Tuesday 23rd [23 September 1919][1]   15 Noon St., W
My dear Eliot/

   I hope when you read this letter that you won't think me guilty of an impertinence!

   Briefly, Mr. Richmond, the editor of the Literary Supplement, has a great admiration for your critical prose and, I think, would be willing to publish a leading article by you, if you cared to write it. I had some conversation with him about you & he expressed two scruples, which forbade his approaching you directly: the first was that you would consider the Times too old-fashioned to write for; the second, that you were rather the property of the Athenaeum.[2] I told him that I thought he was wrong in both & offered to approach you & take on myself the consequences if it turned out that I was wrong. I told him also that you were a student of Elizabethan literature, and I believe, if you are willing, that he would offer you the chance of writing a leader on the new edition of Ben Jonson wh. is being issued. Would you undertake it, and if so could you be at the Times office (Queen Victoria St. entrance) at 11:30 a.m. on

Monday next so that I could introduce you? I hope *very* much that you will consent, because I think your criticism so excellent that it should have many readers and also (if I may add the sordid detail) because you will find writing for the Supplement remunerative.[3] May I add that Richmond leaves his contributors as free in their expression of opinion as Miss Weaver leaves hers?[4]

Will you let me know if you will undertake this & if you can come at the time mentioned? If not perhaps you can fix another time of day more suitable.

I hope you won't think that I've been indiscreet in this; I think you'll know I acted "with good intent."

Yrs
Richard Aldington

1. In a letter to Eliot dated 21 December 1919, RA wrote, "Richmond said he was delighted with your essay on 'Ben.'" In 1919, the only month prior to December with a "Tuesday 23rd" is September.

2. See Letter 27 nn. 3 and 4.

3. See "Ben Jonson," *Times Literary Supplement*, 13 November 1919, pp. 637–38, which reviewed G. Gregory Smith's *Ben Jonson* (English Men of Letters), London, 1919.

4. Harriet Shaw Weaver was editor of the *Egoist*. RA served as assistant editor from the journal's inception in 1914 until June 1917, when Eliot replaced him. Both writers were also contributors to the *Egoist*. For a listing of more than one hundred essays, poems, reviews, and translations by RA that were published in the *Egoist* and its predecessor, the *New Freewomen*, see the *New Canterbury Literary Society Newsletter*, beginning with vol. 19, no. 1 (Spring 1991).

29. To Amy Lowell (Harvard)

11 October 1919   Authors' Club.

My dear Amy/

It has been a pleasure to hear from you again and I hope that next year we shall have the pleasure (for me at least) of meeting again. I have to thank you for subscribing to the translations,[1] for the cheque for royalties,[2] and for your book.[3] Reading over that book I realized how enormously you have progressed in your art since 1914 and that you have conquered a place in contemporary English-written literature. I feel sure your work will be appreciated here later; the prejudice against the Imagists is slowly dying down. Unhappily a lot of our American imitators have seriously damaged our prestige with the best critics, but Flint, H.D., you & I are slowly emerging. There is a very laudatory article on my poems by young Alex Waugh in this month's To-Day & my recent reviews have been much more sympathetic.[4] I mention this to show that the tide is turning here & that you may take advantage of it. Our association with Pound, Hueffer & Lawrence has harmed us; personally I don't care, especially in the case of Lawrence who I still think is a great writer.

I am taking your poems round personally. The reason I have not done so earlier is because in September I had to go away. I had no holiday after demobilization, the Govt. did not pay me my gratuity for three months & I had to work like a slave just to keep going. The result was I nearly broke down mentally, though my physical health is excellent. Since I got back I have only been able to work three days a week; if I work more I get horrible pains in my head, due, people say, to a sort of deferred shell-shock. But I am rapidly getting better & shall be able to attend to things.[5] My troubles are increased by the impossibility of finding any-where to live except a room in a Soho restaurant. Hilda is living with the Ellerman's.[6] There are thousands upon thousands of ex-soldiers in a sim-ilar predicament, while large houses in Mayfair & Kensington stand empty for years, because the owners won't let them out in flats! Discon-tent is wide-spread here, due to disillusion over the war which is now proved a piece of murderous humbug, to the famine prices, to labour struggles & to a kind of general demoralization. You will be shocked at England when you see it; the honesty & rough courtesy has given place to greed & open rudeness. The general state of things reacts violently on the individual, especially on the artist. Rationing is not serious, espe-cially if one can afford more expensive foods; we are probably better off than any other combatant European country, but of course far worse off than U.S., Holland etc. It will be at least five years before we approxi-mate to normal conditions, if we escape a revolution.

There is something I must mention, unwillingly as I fear it will pain you. Hueffer has published an article in the English Review on Gautier,[7] & he begins by describing that dinner you gave some years ago.[8] He does not mention you by name, but he says the most appalling things about all of us. The insult is obvious and complete. I've talked it over with Flint & we thought at first we would write a letter of protest. Then I thought it would be best—as you were the person chiefly insulted—to find out if you intended to ignore it or to take any action. I consider the article to be the worst piece of ill-nature and bad manners I have ever seen. To write of a woman so is incredibly disgusting. Let me know your inten-tions. Probably the best would be to ignore it.[9]

Thanks for your offer about poems—I will try to send some. I more or less realised that Brown was hopeless. His contract promsed 50 dollars on the publication of "Love & War."[10] I only accepted his offer because I was going back to France & no one else would have taken the trouble to get the book published. I can only hope that he will pay up some day. I have never had an account for Images[11] & no money except the amount you made him disgorge. It's hard luck, but I suppose I must put up with it.

Do you think if I made a fuss about the broken contracts, he would yield up the two books to some reputable publisher? The English edition of Images[12] is now published by the Egoist; of Images of Desire by Mathews, & of Images of War by George Allen & Unwin. Boni & Liveright are probably taking sheets of the Translation Series;[13] do you think they would approach Brown for the American rights of the other books? After all as he has broken his contract he could be forced either to give them up or to pay what he owes. If you think it possible I will write to O'Brien about it.

My Times work is great fun—I enjoy it immensely. If I had a flat to live in I'd be comparatively happy!

With best wishes, my dear Amy, and congratulations on the new book whose success is certain with your name on it,

Ever yours
Richard.

1. The Poets' Translation Series, second set.
2. Royalties for *Some Imagist Poets, 1917, An Annual Anthology,* Boston, 1917.
3. *Pictures of the Floating World,* New York, 1919.
4. See Alec Waugh, "Richard Aldington," *To-Day,* October 1919, pp. 61–65.
5. RA suffered a nervous breakdown as a result of his army experiences.
6. Sir John Reeves Ellerman and Hannah Glover Ellerman, parents of Bryher.
7. See Ford Madox Ford, "Henri Gautier, the Story of a Low Tea-Shop," *English Review,* October 1919, pp. 297–304.
8. Amy Lowell gave a dinner during her 1914 visit to London at the Dieudonne to celebrate the publication of *Des Imagists;* all the contributors were present.
9. Lowell did ignore the Ford article. In an earlier letter [11 June 1915] (Harvard), RA had warned Lowell of Ford's feelings toward her.
10. RA frequently reversed the title of *War and Love.*
11. *Images Old and New,* Boston, 1916.
12. *Images,* London, 1919.
13. The Poets' Translation Series was not published by Boni & Liveright.

30. To Ezra Pound* (Yale)

29 December 1919

Chapel Farm Cottage,
Hermitage, Newbury,
Berkshire, England

Dear Ezra,

I'm glad you found the war book not too hopeless.[1] I should like very much to have your detailed criticisms, so that in the event of another edition I can make corrections. The trouble with writing in France was that time was very limited and then exposed to frequent interruptions; and to alter things long after the mood has evaporated is only a botch very often.

You will observe I have retired from London, to get the rest I wanted.[2] I shall write as little as possible for a few months, just enough to keep living.

American mail! I have already experienced the bitterness of that ungodly invention. Harriet[3] has the absurd idea that the views of London must coincide with those of Chicago. However, I am keeping my temper and trying what can be done.

What are you going to do about "Coterie"?[4] They have put Lewis, Eliot, Huxley & myself on their editorial committee; it seems we might use that majority against the Squire party.[5] I am getting things from Fred & H.D. & F.S.F.[6] I've also suggested that they exclude proposed articles on Bridges, De La Mare & Hardy and substitute Joyce, Lawrence & yourself. I've written to T.S.E.[7] to find if he is going to support the rag, for I think it's well worth it. The spontaneous demonstration against the Gosse-Squire-Times attitude is instructive.

Have a look at the last number—mostly bilge I admit—but I think you ought to be in it. If they don't get anyone to do an article on you for the next number, I'll write one myself for the subsequent issue.[8]

The enclosed is my contribution to them![9]

I am convinced that fairly soon there will be a reaction in our favour; you will, I think, get a boost. Old Waugh[10] invited me to lunch the other day & extended olive and laurel boughs!

Ever yrs
R.

*Ezra Pound (1885–1971), the American poet who was a strong influence on the poetry and poets of his century, met RA in 1912. Until Pound left London in 1920 he and RA were both friends and associates. During these years, especially before World War I, Pound was of considerable assistance in advancing RA's literary career. After the war and Pound's departure for Paris, RA was able to help Pound in London literary matters. The two met again in Paris in the late 1920s, and later still RA visited Pound in Rapallo. Despite what he considered Pound's eccentricities, RA and "Unkil EZ," as the younger writer often addressed him, continued to correspond with each other. Even during the years of his confinement in St. Elizabeth's and after World War II, when Pound's reputation was low, although the two often disagreed vehemently, RA was one of his few early friends who remained loyal. (See also the Annotated Index.)

1. *Images of War. A Book of Poems,* Westminster, 1919, published by C. W. Beaumont. An expanded edition was published in the same year by George Allen and Unwin, London, and by The Four Seas Co., Boston, 1921.

2. Before D. H. Lawrence left for Italy in mid-November, RA had agreed to take over his lease of Chapel Farm Cottage in Hermitage near Newbury.

3. Harriet Monroe, editor of *Poetry: A Magazine of Verse*, which was published in Chicago.

4. *Coterie*, published in Oxford, survived only until the Winter 1920–21 issue.

5. J. C. Squire edited *Georgian Poets*, which published the work of the group of poets most opposed in technique and spirit to the Imagists.

6. Frederic Manning, H.D., and F. S. Flint.

7. T. S. Eliot.

8. *Coterie* did not publish an essay on Pound by RA.

9. RA encloses a holograph copy of his unpublished poem "Any Georgian (In Memoriam E.M.)," which mocks Georgian poetry and poets. "E.M." is probably Edward Marsh, editor of *Georgian Poetry*.

10. Arthur Waugh.

31. To Amy Lowell (Harvard)

17 June 1920   Hermitage
My dear Amy,

I was awfully glad to get your letter. I didn't know what to think as you didn't answer. Sometimes I feared you might be very ill and sometimes I thought perhaps you were angry with me and sometimes I thought you were perhaps too busy to write. Well, I'm glad to know that you're still intellectually vigorous as ever though it must be infuriating to you to be laid up like this. I'm afraid you'll have to be more careful than you seem to be from your letter because hernia can be dangerous. It can also be darned painful as I well remember.[1]

Tiens! I am not really surprised about Shorter and Co, only very amused. I took your letter out on the lawn and just laughed to think of things happening. Of course you were dead right not to let Shorter preface your book[2]—why it would have queered you *instanter* and people would have thought you were a Jew! No, no, be careful of him. Even be careful what you let him babble about you in the Sphere. He can be the most blundering old imbecile in creation though I know he means well. Or does he mean well? I ask myself sometimes. Isn't his stupidity really malignity? I suppose you know that he had a big finger in suppressing the Rainbow?[3] That work, by the way, is being re-issued by Martin Secker and there's going to be a hell of a row if the old fogies try to step in this time. It will probably make Lawrence the most talked of writer in England for a bit.

Ah, you still underestimate Eliot. As a literary personality he is fascinating. His manners are charming and ironical, his conversation really witty, his point of view always finished and sometimes profound; he is a really polished American and I know of no greater praise to give a man. His influence as a critic is much greater than as a poet, though there he is exceedingly admired and attacked, but his critical articles have given him great prestige. I will try to send you a volume of his prose which is being issued by the Egoist;[4] I know that you with your French training will delight in his easy style and unique point of view. He reminds me a little of dear old Gourmont. By the way, it's singular that none of the French notices ever mentioned the part we played in Gourmont's latter years. Do you know I have a large bundle of letters from him which prove some nice things about you and me?[5] Sometime when you are in England, I will let you look over them. He speaks with great gratitude of "la dame Americaine." You must feel happy sometimes to think that you lightened so considerably the last year of a man like Gourmont.

Well! H.D. and Winifred seem pretty potty. They both wrote from Greece that you were to have the mss. of H.D.'s book.[6] But really such a mess! I leave it to them to disentangle it. I know H.D. still thinks you have it!

Apropos the Dial. I suppose you know E.P.[7] is Foreign Correspondent? I think he'll do well as he has great energy and discrimination. Don't forget he discovered us whatever he may have said afterwards! Personally I take him humourously; he amuses me mightily when I see him and I do my best to give him a shove up occasionally. It's rather galling for him to have me get ahead of him—into the Times and almost anywhere else I want now. This month I have articles in the English Review[8] and To-Day,[9] poems in Art & Letters,[10] the Nation[11] and Coterie[12] and of course almost weekly articles in the Times.[13] By unremitting hard work I have made exactly £200 since January 1st this year; it is not wealth, I know, but it is what the 18th century called "a competence" and it's the first time I ever had one. I'm grateful to whatever gods may be for it and I've not "written down" one particle. Of course I know you must make more as your reputation in America is so very much higher but you must remember that I lost three whole important years. But (please forget all my boasting, won't you) I didn't let the grass grow under my feet when I got home. I left Belgium Feb 8th, '19, arrived in London Feb 11th after a hellish journey, slept and washed myself on the 12th and started work on the 13th! The first month I did rank journalism for papers like the Express and the Pall Mall—articles on the Army and Belgium and so on,[14] but I dropped all that as soon as other and better things came along. I am deeply grateful to Sir John Ellerman who made Shorter take some articles[15] and introduced me to the Times; that gave me the breathing space and the opportunity and though I've had a few times when things went badly they've been very much better recently. So, in a sense I feel I've begun to "make good" and can feel a little more tranquil about things.

I ought to tell you that I sent two articles to the Dial which they accepted and paid for at once;[16] I've also, at E.P.'s request, been sending them stuff from other people, and as our relations are cordial I think I'd better not trouble them about that odd 30 dollars. If you've already mentioned it, so much the better—they ought to pay old debts.[17] But if you haven't, don't now; it might look a bit mean after their kindness. Curiously enough Brown has also stumped up that 50 dollars he owed me; according to his statement, which I've no means of checking he has sold 291 Images and 211 Love and War. This seems a little queer to me since over here, in spite of long opposition, I have sold 650 first edition of Images and 100 or more of the second edition; moreover Images of Desire (English edition of part of War & Love) sold 300 copies in the first six months and more since I know. These are not grand, but how do you account for the American sales being so small?

Well, I don't want to be ungraceful about American criticism since most English is pretty dud. Still, they don't seem to me at all profound in their critical remarks. Naturally they aren't up to the French standard; no one is; but they might try. Hagedorn had a shot, but when I read some of it published nowadays, I feel kind of weary. Apropos there was an article by Harriet Monroe on contemporary English periodicals which I did admire;[18] I don't say it had any of the graces and profoundities but for honest sound judgment it struck me as excellent. She put her finger on every one of the vices of current English poetry and, writing quite without malice, she made out an excellent case for American poetry.

I don't know who wrote the article on American poetry for the Times; Eliot and I both tried to discover but failed; he was a damn fool whoever he was and I wrote and told the editor so.[19] I also sent a copy of the article to Miss Monroe and asked her to reply to it. In my opinion, and I'm not really "up" in American poetry, it was a very ignorant and supercilious article, which put Fletcher above everyone else and never mentioned H.D., Ezra, Eliot, Wallace Stevens, and several more; patronized you and put Lindsay above Sandburg!

Looking at your letter I see you say French criticism is "too long, too meticulous and too dull in the way of expressing itself." Nenni, ma soeur! Do you read La Nouvelle Revue Française regularly? There have been some fascinating articles by Marcel Proust,[20] Thibaudet[21] and Valèry Larbaud,[22] which made one's hair stand on end with envy. They get at the writer's very vitals, they illuminate the whole work of art and send you scurrying back to it to compare your view with theirs. It is real criticism because it makes you understand more and enjoy more. And as to dullness of expression, you will find no more graceful books about books than those of France,[23] Gourmont[24] and Lemaître.[25] There is a book by a man called Vanderèm, not exquisite stuff, but a kind of mirror of contemporary literature.[26] I read it with great pleasure because he does know what he's doing and he has got definite standards. Standards may be a nuisance to the creator but you can't have criticism without them.

Of course I agree Coterie and Voices especially are pretty punk; Art & Letters was better; but the best critical work does appear in papers like the Nation, Athenaeum and (if I may say so!) the Times. The Times is horribly uneven because so many people write for it, but there are several really excellent critics on it. There was a slap-up article on Huxley the other day which was a delightful piece of clever "placing."[27] I have seen the first few numbers of the new Dial—the whole lot of prose in it didn't come near that one little anonymous article. As to poetry, isn't America getting a little "Dada"?[28] I'm damned if I understand half the stuff that's supposed to be the latest effort.

I am sending you a few poems, most of which have been published or will be published here, more for you to read yourself and for your candid and severe criticism than to avail myself of your offer of placing some. Of course if you can, I shall be very glad of it. I attach a slip to them to show what is happening to them here.

Au revoir, my dear Amy, come and see us as soon as you are well. England is settling down slowly and seems to be prospering again. So you won't have civil disturbances to fear.

Affectionately,
Richard.

Poems enclosed and disposal in England
Meditations
No. 1 Pub Art & Letters. 1920 second quarter.[29]
Nos 2, 3, 4, to be published Monthly Chapbook, July.[30]
The Walk. Nowhere.[31]
Nightingale. Voices not yet published, but proof passed.[32]
Night Fancies. Nowhere.[33]
Note: Harriet Monroe has two poems, one of which I forget (I think Nightingale) and one not here "Eumenides."[34] These she may send you if she don't want them.

R.A.

1. Earlier in the year, Amy Lowell had undergone a series of unsuccessful hernia operations. RA had also been operated on for hernia; see Letter 12 n. 2.
2. *Can Grande's Castle*, Oxford, 1920.
3. D. H. Lawrence's novel, *The Rainbow*, was suppressed by Scotland Yard in November 1915.
4. T. S. Eliot, "The Art of Poetry," promised in the *Egoist*, December 1919, p. 71, for early spring 1920 was not published by the Egoist Press. Material for this volume was presumably included in *The Sacred Wood*.

5. Published as an appendix to vol. 1 of *Remy de Gourmont. Selections from All His Works*, Chicago, 1928. Amy Lowell and RA helped de Gourmont with money during the war; see Letter 5.

6. See H.D., *Hymen*, London, 1921.

7. See Ezra Pound, "The Island of Paris: A Letter," *Dial*, October 1920, pp. 406–11, but this was Pound's only contribution during 1920.

8. See RA, "The Approach to M. Marcel Proust," *English Review*, June 1920, 35488–93.

9. See RA, "Of Literary Success (An Imaginary Discourse of Mr. Abraham Cowley), " *To-day*, June 1920, pp. 132–35.

10. See RA, "Meditation," *Art and Letters*, Spring 1920, pp. 1–2.

11. See "Two Poems by Meleager of Gadara. Love at Auction. He Threatens Love," trans. Richard Aldington, *Nation*, 26 June 1920, p. 404.

12. See RA, "Le Maudit," p. 14; and "On Frederic Manning," pp. 15–16, *Coterie*, Easter, 1920.

13. Although unsigned, "New Foreign Books" appeared in the *Times Literary Supplement*, 3 June 1920, p. 353; 17 June 1920, p. 384; and 24 June 1920, p. 404.

14. No articles signed by RA appear in the *Pall Mall Gazette* for January, February, March, or April 1919, but see "Belgium Today: A Scene of Desolation," 26 February 1919, p. 4, and "Revive the 'Terriers': Training Demobilized Men," 26 March 1919, p. 6, both signed "Infantryman." No articles signed by RA appear in the London *Daily Express* for January, February, March, or April 1919, but see "The Professor's Class," 28 March 1919, p. 4, and "Liaison Officers," 11 April 1919, p. 4, both signed "Frontiersman."

15. See Letter 25 n. 8.

16. See RA, "The Approach to M. Marcel Proust," *Dial*, October 1920, pp. 341–46 (same article as in note 8 above); RA, "The Art of Poetry," *Dial*, August 1920, pp. 166–80.

17. See RA, "Letters to Unknown Women: The Amaryllis of Theocritus," *Dial*, 22 February 1919, p. 183; and "Letters to Unknown Women: La Gross Margot," *Dial*, 17 May 1919, p. 510.

18. See Harriet Monroe, "Our Contemporaries: New English Magazines," *Poetry: A Magazine of Verse*, April 1920, pp. 54–56.

19. See "Modern American Poetry," *Times Literary Supplement*, 6 May 1920, which reviews *The Little Book of Modern Verse: A Selection from the Work of Contemporaneous American Poets*, Boston, 1917, and *The Second Book of Modern Verse: A Selection from the Work of Contemporaneous American Poets*, Boston, 1920, both edited by Jessie B. Rittenhouse. The letter RA wrote to the editor was not published.

20. See, for instance, Marcel Proust, "A Propos du 'Style' de Flaubert," *Nouvelle Revue Française*, January 1920, pp. 72–90.

21. See, for instance, Albert Thibaudet, "Réflexions sur la littérature: Autour de Jean Giraudoux," *Nouvelle Revue Française*, December 1919, pp. 1064–76.

22. See, for instance, Valéry Larbaud, "Lettres Anglaises: Jeunes Poètes et Jeunes Revues," *Nouvelle Revue Française*, December 1919, pp. 1108–13.

23. See, for instance, Anatole France, *La Vie Littéraire*, 4th ser., Paris, 1888–92.

24. See, for instance, Remy de Gourmont, *Henri de Regnier et son oeuvre*, Paris [1908].

25. See, for instance, Jules Lemaître, *Chateaubriand*, Paris, 1912.

26. See Fernand Vanderèm, *Le Miroir des Lettres*, published in Paris as an annual series, beginning in 1918 and ending with the eighth number, 1925–26.

27. See "The Old Grimace," *Times Literary Supplement*, 27 May 1920, p. 327, which reviews Huxley's volume of poems, *Leda*, London, 1920.

28. Dadaism was a literary and artistic movement, international in scope and nihilist in character, which lasted from 1915 until 1922.

29. See RA, "Meditation," *Art and Letters*, Spring 1920, p. 1.

30. See "Meditation [2]," *Chapbook*, July 1920, p. 16; see "Meditations 3" and "Meditations 4," in Norman T. Gates, *The Poetry of Richard Aldington*, University Park, 1974, pp. 195–96 and pp. 196–97.

31. See "The Walk (For F.S.F.)" in Norman T. Gates, "Richard Aldington and F. S. Flint; Poets' Dialogue," *Papers on Language and Literature* (Edwardsville, Ill.), Winter 1972, pp. 62–69.

32. See RA, "Nightingale," *Voices in Poetry and Prose*, June 1920, pp. 239–40.

33. See "Night Fancies," *The Poetry of Richard Aldington*, pp. 200–202.

34. See "Eumenides," *Exile and Other Poems*, London, 1923, pp. 15–17.

32. To Amy Lowell (Harvard)

12 October 1920   Hermitage.

Dear Amy,

I am sorry to hear this news. I can't understand how it is you have had so much trouble unless it is that it occurred when you were fully grown whereas mine was fixed when I was a kid.[1] I feel sure that it can be fixed for you—do you know I've carried a 100 pound weight of equipment etc for days in and out of the trenches and felt nothing but a slight dragging pain when I was very tired? That makes me feel certain that the good surgeon you have now gone to will put you right. One thing—don't let your natural activity get you up too soon. Stay in bed an extra week and give it every opportunity to heal firmly. I wish you hadn't got to have this done; the shock to your nerves after each of these operations must be bad for you. It is rotten bad luck.

Your remarks on Joyce interest me. I was a little surprised at your saying there was no interest in his work in America, since the Dial has a long article on him this month[2] and all the Little Review writers are under his influence. I don't agree with you in your judgment on Joyce—I think he is an amazing writer, a kind of modern Tertullian plus Rabelais. I don't mind his obscenity because it is intellectual. As to the Watch and Ward Society I will willingly subscribe to any body whose purpose is to extirpate them, preferably in as painful a manner as possible. It isn't Joyce we should object to, but Rodker, Bodenheim, Elsa von Freytag-Whatshername[3] et hoc genus omne. They who have plagiarised Joyce's dirtiness, without his genius to support it, must be sat on. Hence my article. I think in a year's time you'll regret it wasn't published because the influence is going to be a big one. However it will appear in the English Review and I must be content with that.[4]

I note what you say about poems and articles in America. Since that is so, I fear my contributions to America will be mighty small. Naturally I prefer to print my things in England and I can usually achieve this, but since American periodicals are perfectly content to print duplicates of Arnold Bennett, Clutton Brock and the rest I don't see why I should place myself on an inferior footing. If it is merely a question of more or less notoriety I am content to wait until my degree is sufficient to ensure simultaneous publication!

I loved your article on the Georgians and wished there had been more of it.[5] Of course Eddy Marsh is a fool, and you said so as plainly as print and decency will allow. But Georgian Poetry is going down fast—the latest volume was severely sat on by several English critics, including old Waugh on the Telegraph.[6]

I shall try to send you off a letter about once a fortnight while you are in bed. Don't trouble to answer. And good luck to you!

Ever yours,
Richard

1. Reference to surgery for hernia. See Letter 31.
2. See Evelyn Scott, "A Contemporary of the Future," *Dial*, October 1920, pp. 353–67.
3. Baroness Elsa von Freytag-Lovinghoven.
4. See RA, "The Influence of Mr. James Joyce," *English Review*, April 1921, pp. 333–41.
5. See Amy Lowell, "Weary Verse," *Dial*, October 1920, pp. 424–31.
6. See Arthur Waugh, "Current Literature: Georgian Poetry (1918–1919)," *Daily Telegraph*, 17 December 1919, p. 14.

33. To Harold Monro (UCLA)

24 October 1920   Hermitage.
Dear Harold,

It will not be said in your biography that you were a satisfactory & punctual correspondent and you ought to reflect that as I am about ten years younger that sad task may fall to me. However I suppose I must forgive you.

If you have any time this week, perhaps you could return me the ms of my dialogue,[1] as I want to show it to Manning for his criticism & advice. The objection I feel to writing of that sort is that one is merely talking commonplace to thoughtful people and at the same time being too profound for the ignorant. You do not need me to tell you that the universe is limitless, that men make their gods, that society is founded on humbug, that truth is merely relative; on the other hand that elusive creature, the man in the street, like Gallio,[2] cares for none of these things.

I have been collecting material for an essay on prose poetry and need some "objective" to force me to use it; do you think a chapbook might be made out of it? What I thought of making is an enquiry into the nature of prose poetry, with "divers illustrations," and a discussion of its value or otherwise. I have no desire to write the usual English *plaidoyer* but to try and get at the truth of the matter. One might start some useful reflections. Perhaps you could get Eliot and Manningto write something on the same subject.[3] Eliot's views I know; he is rather against prose poetry for highly respectable & subtle reasons. Manning's I don't know; he is himself a fine prose poet—as witness his "Scenes & Portraits"[4]—and as very few people do know he is an admirable critic. His letters are "full of meat" and the unsigned articles he publishes are admirable. You ought not to neglect him in collecting critical material; both he & Eliot have critical capacities far above Flint's, for Frank never gets beyond the state of giving information about new writers; he is just incapable of writing an interesting essay on Keats or Lamartine, whereas Eliot & Manning are really profound, their intelligence is constantly at play. Don't tell Frank I wrote this; he would be hurt and it would not help him; no man can acquire facilities merely by knowing he does not possess them. Moreover, he might not even admit that he was at fault!

I have found no cottages![5] That is a poor confession to make, when I was so certain I would find some. But the shortage is far more acute than I had thought. It is really peculiar that remote country villages, losing steadily population to the towns, should be in an even worse state than towns themselves. But speculation is rife; and a 3/6 a week cottage, if empty, is put up for sale at a fabulous price which up to now it has obtained. I can't help thinking that the most absurd incompetence has directed these building problems—the Govt. has refused to allow an economic rent wh. would have permitted private enterprise & has completely failed to erect houses. Yet the Germans, we hear, have built enormous quantities of new houses and small houses. We might have done the same. If I decided to come to town for a bit, could you let me a room at the book shop? Not the small room upstairs, but the other wh. you needed before? I ask tentatively, as I may decide to go to a place in Devonshire instead. I am in a state of great dubiety!

Yrs
Richard.

1. Cf. RA to H.D., 24 December 1918 (Yale), where RA wrote, " I want to write 'critical dialogues' about books. I have actually done: (1) The Tenderness of Dante. (2) Les Chevaux de Diomède. (3) A Soldier's Library. (4) The Scholar's Italian Book. . . . I have planned tentatively these: (5) Anacreon. (6) Fologore de San Gemignano. (7) Scenes & Portraits (8) La Double Maitresse (9) Rimbaud (10) Landor's Classical Dialogues (11) Campion &

Quantity in English (12) Sea Garden (13) Villon (14) Alciphron's Love Letters. Of course I might not do all or any of these but I shall do some."

2. See Acts 18:14–16, where Gallio, deputy of Achaia, is indifferent to "a question of words."

3. See T. S. Eliot, "Prose and Verse," pp. 3–10, Frederic Manning, "Poetry in Prose," pp. 10–15, and RA, "A Note on Poetry in Prose," pp. 16–24, *Chapbook*, April 1921.

4. 1909.

5. That is, for Monro to rent. Despite considerable correspondence on the matter and the fact that Monro rented a number of country cottages, he rented none in Berkshire.

34. To Harold Monro (UCLA)

Malthouse Cottage,
Padworth, near Reading,
Berkshire, England.

12 January 1921

Dear Harold,

I though the article in the Times—the only note on your book[1] I've read—ignorant and incompetent. You are quite absurd to say that you "haven't learning enough"—unless you mean it ironically, as I suppose you do. There is no one else who knows the subject so well as you know it. I think that, as a Baedeker to modern English poets, you could hardly have written anything more just & succinct. Your judgments—and that (judgment) is half criticism—are pondered, logical & just. Inevitably a strictly personal judgment, which ignores reputation & notoriety, will irritate reviewers who have created both. You must pay no attention whatever to comments of reviewers, many of whom will be the very people who will take your impersonal judgments as a personal insult. I myself read the book closely and felt I'd learned something from it; I knew of course that there was no humbug about it, that you were writing from a great reserve fund of knowledge.

My objections to the book are: 1. That you seem to despise your subject; 2. That you are so afraid to praise that when you do, you splash into hyperbole (Bridges, Hodgson, Huxley). 3. That you did not have nearly enough space. 4. That you have not been able to achieve a synthesis, a critical synthesis. 5. That hasty or perturbed writing has meant a colourless, conventional prose. 6. You have let your "pungent" satirical mood run away with you & satirized where a critic should ignore.

The grand defect to me is the hasty & undistinguished prose:

"In this form the poems already gained that popularity they so well deserved, & the precedent was again established of placing verse on the market, at first, in some cheap edition, testing, in fact, its selling potentialities by offering the public initial samples of the quality."[2]

That seems to me very detestable!

By the way, *why* do you & other people talk of Mallarmé as a *vers libre* poet?[3] He only wrote one *vers libre* poem—"Jamais un coup de dés &"—and that is quite unlike the *vers libre* of Kahn, Régnier, Duhamel, Vildrac, Ghèon et hoc genus omne. Most of Mallarmé's poetry is Parnassian.

I should say that your book is two-thirds successful & that you hadn't time & leisure to make it wholly so. On more than one occasion you have sunk to the level of the people you were discussing.

I will undertake the number as you wish, if I may be relieved of the mechanical part of press-work, dove-tailing, mutilation, & other editorial abominations.[4] I will arrange with Manning, drum up Eliot & get going myself. Will you give me a letter of introduction to Aldous Huxley or write him that I am about to do this thing.[5] My idea will be not to aim at any uniformity of judgment, but uniformity of subject-matter. Huxley must not be allowed his irrelevances. You will find that the four of us probably hold fairly similar views as to what *is* prose-poetry, but very divergent views of its legitimacy as an art form. Huxley & I will be for it, Manning & Eliot against it; any highly trained mind is revolted by a suspicion of mixed *genre* in art. However, that's neither here nor there. Get in touch with Huxley and I'll arrange the rest—do *not* let Huxley know the date of the number; I shall alert him! My reservations about "mechanical duties" is simply because I can't afford to come to London—it cost me £50 to fix this place up, so I'm broke for a couple of months.

O.K. about the dialogue etc. It is as I said, above the mob & below the intelligent. It amused me to write it.

By the way, has your trip to America been abandoned? Or are you going later?[6]

Reverting to the Prose Poetry number—I will take all the compilation completely off your hands. All you have to do is to put me in touch with Huxley.

No need to write if you are busy. I'm afraid I shan't be in town before you leave.

Ever yours,
Richard.

1. *Some Contemporary Poets,* London, 1920. RA may refer to the review "Originality and Poetry," *Times Literary Supplement,* 30 December 1920, p. 889.
2. See *Some Contemporary Poets,* pp. 68–69.
3. Ibid., p. 22.
4. That is, production of the issue of the *Chapbook,* April 1921. See Letter 33.

5. Huxley was not solicited.
6. Monro did not go to America.

35. To Amy Lowell (Harvard)

1 April 1922   Padworth.

My dear Amy,

I have to acknowledge receipt of the cheques for 12/5 for Flint and my-self. It is always a surprise to receive these continued royalties, for one would think the anthologies were out of date by now.[1]

It is a disappointment to hear that you are unable to visit England this year.[2] Things are very much more agreeable and cheerful than they were and a Conservative government is always more comfortable than a Liberal one which upsets people with experiments. I see very little of literary London; I only go up to see Richmond on the Times, to give an occasional reading or to attend some foolish dinner I have been unable to escape. I suppose I am rather lazy for after I've polished off my weekly article I prefer to read Elizabethans than to do anything else. I am more and more realising the immense riches and beauty of English literature of the late 16th, 17th and early 18th centuries. I believe old Saintsbury is right when he says that the 'Elzabethan" is the greatest period in poetry since the Attic drama.[3] On the other hand the more I read French Poetry the less I like it, though I see its value; French prose is immensely stimulating and from the days of Amyot and Montaigne has outclassed English prose. This I know is the conventional view but three years hard reading confirms me in it.

I cannot accept your view in the matter of James Joyce. Of course I don't expect him to have yet the influence of Lawrence, because the ordinary periodical is so many years behind the artist. But I have the evidence of my own senses to prove that some of the youngest American prose writers are studying and imitating Joyce.[4] There is also an editorial in the Literary Review admitting that I am right and stating that a novel showing the very influence I deplored had just been published.[5] Of course my article was written for England and was published here about two years ago,[6] but there are not many pseudo-Joyces here. Moreover, imitation of some superficial eccentricity is rather an American than an English vice—look at the deplorable result of vers libre in America! It makes one blush with shame.

I admire Joyce very much and consider him a most original mind, so original that few people have yet perceived its ability. I want to prevent, if possible, his being made ridiculous by imitators.

The new development here is getting very "metaphysical" and incomprehensible. The influence of Eliot has been limited but intense and the movement is entirely in accordance with his philosophic and satirical poetry and against our poetry of impression and emotion. (Of course I put the Mercury Georgian poetry coalition nowhere—though they appear to be the only English poets who manage to cross the Atlantic.)[7] I have just seen an Ms of Herbert Read's[8] which I must say is pretty heavy reading—modern philosophy of the school of Whitehead and Berty Russell in the manner of Donne and the "Phoenix and the Turtle." There is quite a craze for the "Phoenix and the Turtle" just now and I am very much looked down upon because I suggest that it is only the divine William[9] making fun of Donne.

You have a great opportunity in your Keats[10] book to correct popular misrepresentations and exaggerations of his talent. I hope you will attack the curious illusion that Keats is "classic" and "Greek," since his classicism is merely a reflection of the Jacobeans. Have you read Chamberlayne's "Pharonnida"?[11] It is supposed to be one of the sources of Endymion,[12] I believe.

Yours affectionately
Richard.

1. *Some Imagist Poets*, the annual anthology published in Boston, 1915, 1916, and 1917.
2. Amy Lowell did not visit England again; she died on 12 May 1925.
3. Not traced.
4. See RA, "The Influence of Mr. James Joyce," *Literary Review*, 11 March 1922, p. 491.
5. See "Literary Pioneers" (editorial), *Literary Review*, 18 March 1922, p. 501.
6. See Letter 32 n. 4.
7. Poets contributing to *Georgian Poetry*, ed. Edward Marsh, in 1912, 1915, 1917, 1919, and 1922; see also Letter 32.
8. Not identified, but see Herbert Read, *Reason and Romanticism*, London, 1926, which includes eleven "Essays in Literary Criticism."
9. William Shakespeare.
10. See Amy Lowell, *John Keats*, Boston, 1925.
11. William Chamberlayne, *Pharonnida*, London, 1659.
12. John Keats, *Endymion*, London, 1818.

36. To Amy Lowell (Harvard)

Padworth.

Private and Confidential.
5 May 1922
Dear Amy,

This is an official begging letter!

T. S. Eliot is very ill, will die if he doesn't get proper & complete rest for a long time.

A scheme[1] is on foot to raise the money by asking a selected number of people to contribute £10 a year towards the nucleus of an income for him. About £80 has been promised already in England & more is hoped for; also I have a guarantee from the Literary Supplement that they will take at least £100 a year's worth of articles from him.

It is hoped to get at least 25 people. Since Eliot is American-born I thought I might venture to ask you.

No payment is to be made until a proper committee of responsible people is formed. But if you could privately become the American representative of the fund I would of course see that you were a member of the committee. I should not feel justified in putting this to you, were it not that I have the strong support of the editor of the Literary Supplement[2] whose name is I think a guarantee that the scheme is a serious and necessary one.

I know you are too generous-minded to allow any possible differences of opinion between yourself and Eliot to prejudice you.[3] And since he is a compatriot in distress—and in my opinion a very distinguished one—I think you would not like to feel that he had to rely entirely upon his English friends.

Forgive me, dear Amy, if I seem importunate.

Yours always
Richard.

1. This "scheme" preceded the so-called "Bel Esprit" plan; see Letter 37.
2. Bruce Richmond, to whom RA had introduced Eliot in 1919.
3. Eliot had called Lowell a "demon salesman"; Lowell said *The Waste Land* had "interesting pages" in it, but the work as a whole left her cool, "cooler than Ezra's *Cantos*."

37. To Amy Lowell (Harvard)

7 July 1922   Padworth.
My dear Amy,

I was very glad to get your letter this morning since it allows me to clear up a situation which has become at least embarrassing. I have sent a public statement to the Literary Review which I hope will be enough without my having to write more.[1] What has happened is simply this: A scheme which I intended to be absolutely private has been made public by Ezra and my name has been attached to it though I have repeatedly told him that I would have nothing to do with his "Bel Esprit." [See Figure 1.] When he formed this crack-brained project, which traversed my own plans for Eliot, I tolerated it for a time (as I think one might lawfully do under the circumstances) but when upon reflection I perceived how foolish his idea was, when I found that he was making it public (for the sake of *réclame*) then I disassociated myself from it and I have now entirely severed any lingering acquaintance I had with him.

My grief in the matter is simply that Eliot is made to look foolish and ignominious; you are right in supposing that he knew nothing of the scheme and, if my advice had been followed by Ezra, it would never have been made public. My idea was simply to ask a few people who really care for Eliot's work to make a small annual subscription each to free him from economic slavery. Whether he would have accepted the offer is another matter; he would very probably have refused it; but, in that case, my conscience would have been clear for I should have done my utmost to save his life from the effects of continual over-work at the Bank. After what has happened I now see this is impossible. After Ezra published his article in the New Age[2] I had a long talk with Eliot, who pointed out that we were all being made ridiculous and that he could not possibly accept such hare-brained propositions as Ezra's scheme involved. I quite agreed with him, but I still thought then that my private scheme might have worked out independent of Ezra. I now see that he has compromised the whole thing, for he has written to everybody I know with *his* scheme (thus traversing me) and the publicity he has created (revolting to the last degree) makes the whole thing impossible. Your blunt refusal to co-operate practically confirms me in this opinion. I had roughly £100 a year promised, with some additional possibilities; but I find that the Americans with whom I have communicated are either quite unwilling to do anything or else regard the matter as something which should immediately be communicated to the press "with photographs." Neither of these is helpful. I propose therefore to inform Eliot that my scheme has failed; to release my correspondents from their promises; and to rely upon my statement in the Literary Review to correct as far as possible the misstatements emanating from Ezra and perhaps to clear Eliot and myself from the inevitable ridicule and odium. I don't mind very much myself—though I am very angry with Ezra—but I do mind for Eliot's sake.

I don't propose to argue about your views of Eliot's abilities by letter. De gustibus . . . you know what I think and I know what you think; we are probably both equally amazed that the other should be so obtuse. Yet I can't help saying that the two adjectives you choose as descriptive of the "Sacred Wood"[3] are remarkably inappropriate. "Jejune" implies a lack of matter and thought, whereas Eliot's prose is filled with matter and drenched with thought. Again "pedantic" implies a pre-occupation with the mere husk or machinery of literature, whereas Eliot is constantly directing his readers' attention to its spirit and significance. But the mere fact that a book which has made so profound an impression upon me and upon people so different as Professor Saintsbury, Augustine Birrell, Lord Balfour, Lady Rothermere, Holbrook Jackson, Julien Benda and André Gide, should also be so profoundly disliked by you and Robert Lynd, Clutton Brock, Tomlinson, and several other very able and acute people—this fact is not only interesting in itself, but an indication that the work itself is not wholly negligible. In such matters each side exaggerates; for myself I cannot conceive how any artist can read the two essays "The Perfect Critic" and "Tradition and the Individual Talent"[4] without being immensely interested and stimulated.

I send you under another cover a copy of the Times with one of my articles.[5] I don't know whether you see the Supplement regularly or not at all; in any case I shall be interested to hear your opinion.

Yours always
Richard

1. See RA's letter, "A Protest," under "Correspondence," *Literary Review,* 8 July 1922, p. 798.
2. See Ezra Pound, "Credit and the Fine Arts," *New Age,* 20 March 1922, pp. 284–85.
3. T. S. Eliot, *The Sacred Wood,* London, 1920.
4. See pp. 1–16 and 47–59 in *The Sacred Wood.*
5. Not traced.

38. To Harold Monro (UCLA)

23 June 1923   Padworth.[1]
Dear Harold,

I was glad to have your letter this morning. It is awfully good of you to do this for the Criterion.[2] I need hardly say that help of this kind is extremely valuable.

I know Eliot is counting on your Wordsworth article,[3] for he wrote me about it and said he was glad to have you do it. I will jog his memory about the book.[4]

I don't see that the Criterion and Chapbook clash at all. The Chapbook is now almost entirely new poetry, isn't it? The Criterion is almost wholly critical. I am urging Eliot to use poetry as rarely as possible, though this time we have a huge wad by Ezra Pound,[5] which by the way I can make nothing of.

Early in July we are taking a holiday, but I expect to be in London on Weds the 4th. Would it suit if I called in about one? Make your own time.

It may interest you to have the present list of people who are contributing to the second year of the Criterion beginning October: W. P. Ker,

I HEREBY pledge myself to contribute £........yearly

$........ yearly

for........years

to (*a*) T. S. Eliot.

(*b*) To Bel Esprit for T. S. Eliot (in which case a treasurer of Bel Esprit, R. ALDINGTON, Malthouse Cottage, Padworth, Reading, Berks, acting in England. Or—EZRA POUND, 70 bis rue Notre Dame des Champs, Paris, acting in France, stands personally responsible for the transmission of funds to Mr. Eliot).

This money is given on the understanding that Mr. Eliot shall devote his entire time to literary work. No restriction is placed on the nature of that work, and I, the present donor, will make no effort to influence either the subject-matter or the manner of his writing save by such literary criticism as any critic of literature might indulge in.

I will pay this money { annually / semi-annually } beginning

................date.

(Signature)..........................

Fig. 1. "Bel Esprit" Subscription form. RA enclosed a copy of this in his 7 July 1922 letter to Amy Lowell.

J. M. Robertson, F. M. Ford, Hugo von Hofmannsthal, Harold Monro, May Sinclair, C. Whibley, Professors A. B. Keith, G. Elliot Smith, Lévy-Bruhl (de l'Institut), Guignebert, Miss Jane Harrison, Sir J. Frazer, G. Saintsbury, Marcel Proust (inédit), and H. H. Joachim. I think people like the paper and feel there is a need for it; at all events they all reply with contributions or promises of contributions. The number which is now in the press is not quite so good; it has Yeats, Barfield, Jacques Rivière, Whibley, Pound, Rice, E. M. Forster, Richard Aldington. I should like to increase the size, so that we can have ten contributors to each number as well as notes. As a matter of fact this number will be 122 pages, and I hope to get that fixed as a minimum.

Yours
Richard.

1. Written on the letterhead of the *Criterion*. Solicited by T. S. Eliot to "take charge and organise the foreign section," RA had joined the *Criterion*'s staff between May 20 and June 16.
2. Perhaps RA refers to Monro's decision to "drop criticism" in the *Chapbook* and concentrate on the "representation of Poetry and of Design." See the *Chapbook*, June 1923, p. 3.
3. See Harold Monro, "Wordsworth Revisited," *Criterion*, July 1924, pp. 468–76.
4. Not identified.
5. See "Malatesta Cantos (Cantos IX to XII of a Long Poem)," *Criterion*, July 1923, pp. 366–84.

39. To Harold Monro (UCLA)

8 May 1924   Padworth.
My dear Harold/
    I've only just got over the results of your hock! But I had a very good time & enjoyed your party.
    It is still miserable weather here, but I like it; perhaps I am becoming permanently bumpkinized.
    You are getting awfully virtuous in your ardent love of civic & matrimonial respectability; I do not despair of seeing you, in another decade, return to the bosom of the One True Church.
    I am against the "Grandfather Wordsworth"[1] title; people won't take it seriously. I don't see why you should blackguard me about the Criterion.[2] I did a hell of a lot of work for it, gave suggestions, procured authors, acted as secretary, tried to get subscriptions, got people interested in it, and all for a pound a week! I had continually to put aside other work to answer Eliot's letters for him; I found him difficult to work with and I also found I was absolutely paralysed mentally by the

snobbish attitude of the "Criterion." My reward was a piffling little "attack" on something I said about Joyce, and the growing realisation that I was a "useful hack journalist" whose plodding habits might be of use to the superior intellectuals with whom I was graciously permitted to come in contact. I have no doubt, my dear Harold, that I am a vulgar, uneducated and not thoroughly respectable person, but that is only one more reason for not eing a philanthropist on behalf of immature & amateur literary schemes.

We are both [3] looking forward to seeing you on the 31st.

Yours always,
Richard.

No man who is an intellectual snob can retain people's admiration indefinitely.

No man who despises his subordinates will ever inspire confidence, or obtain good results.

No man can win people's minds by negation and despair.

The greatest intellectual gifts are rendered sterile by selfishness and excessive intellectual pride.

1. The published title was "Wordsworth Revisited"; see Letter 38 n. 3.
2. RA served T. S. Eliot as an assistant editor of the *Criterion* for about a year, commencing in late May or early June 1923; see Letter 38 n. 1. No editor or adviser other than Eliot, however, was named as such in the *Criterion*.
3. That is, RA and Dorothy Yorke ("Arabella").

40. To Glenn Hughes* (Texas)

5 October 1925   Padworth.
Dear Hughes,

By letter you are exactly 17 days from Malthouse Cottage, for your epistle arrived this morning and gave us great pleasure. I am sorry you had such a tedious passage, but remember your 17th century ancestors were three months on board and then had to sleep with the cows and agricultural implements in the hold! In the matter of transport we certainly have the bulge on the pilgrim fathers.

Yes, I should greatly like to see the natural beauties of your great West and to meet some of the friends I know only by post, but I have only risen to be (I hope) one of Nietzsche's good Europeans. I confess that I prefer European civilization to that of the Orient and that all I hope to do is to pass my life among the wrecks of our dying culture. For you it is different, you look forward and hope to build something in the future. I think we are a bit sceptical about that, but in any case our instinct is rather to enjoy what has been created in the last thirty centuries than to harry our-selves with ambition to create more. But that only makes us the more interested in watching your effort to turn the vast energies of America into the creation of beauty. It must be fascinating for you—every one of you, perhaps, Petrarchs to a new Renaissance.

It was a great pleasure to us to see you and to exchange talk with you both, and we are very glad indeed to know that you were not bored by our quiet retirement. Recently we spent a few days with my mother and were horrified by this awful English habit of Golf, Motors, Horses, Ten-nis, Mah-Jong and all the rest of it. Our principal trouble was to keep sober among the "flow of cocktails and the feast of gin."[1] It is certainly up to those of us who have any sense not to get caught in this inane waste—it isn't luxury, luxury is artistic, but mere senseless waste, a quelling of the mind under the natural man.

Glad to have the explanation about Littell and to know he is not a quitter, as I unjustly suspected. Get into touch with Canby if you are able; he has promised to take some things of mine.[2] Make him pay you.

You certainly cut it rather fine by arriving home with only five dollars, but I think we can beat you. We once got back to London from Italy with only 7/9. I couldn't sleep on the boat for wondering what I'd do if the customs discovered anything dutiable. You will find that the various art things you collected on your travels will give you very great pleasure. Our Florentine plates are a daily reminder of pleasant days. Next time you come you will be hardened travellers and will take more of the con-tinent. England is small beer compared with Italy, Provence, Spain and the old Austrian Empire. Somehow we'll have to see those 80,000 Italian churches.

The French are rampaging with fury at the U.S. and I hear it is very unpleasant for both English and Americans in Paris at the moment.[3] However they'll boil down soon. I can't help wishing that the original proposal for the cancelling of all war debts had been carried out. These enormous and apparently endless foreign debts are the greatest encour-agement to the Communists in the poorer countries. I wish we may not live to regret the whole business of exacting payment.

Let me hear from you sometimes. With all good wishes to you both,

Richard Aldington

*Glenn A. Hughes (1894–1964), traveling in Europe on vacation from teaching at the Uni-versity of Washington where he had been since 1919, met RA during the summer of 1925. In September 1928, Hughes, having received a Guggenheim Fellowship, left Seattle for a nine-month visit to Europe to study the Imagist poets. The result was *Imagism and the Imagists* (1931), the first book-length work on the subject. In 1927 Hughes had started a series of publications, *University of Washington Chapbooks; RAs D. H. Lawrence: An In-*

discretion was no. 6 in the series, and during the following year his *Remy de Gourmont* became no. 13. The fourth publication linking RA and Hughes is the *Imagist Anthology, 1930: New Poetry by the Imagists,* which RA edited and to which Hughes contributed a foreword. The chapbooks became forerunners of more important books by RA on Lawrence and de Gourmont while the two Imagist works closed a period for him.

1. Cf. Alexander Pope, *The First Satire of the Second Book of Horace,* line 127, which RA parodies here.

2. Canby was editor of the *Saturday Review of Literature;* see RA, "D. H. Lawrence as Poet," 1 May 1926, pp. 749–50; review of *Essays in Biography* by Bonamy Dobrée, 26 June 1926, p. 882; and review of *The Art of Being Ruled* by Wyndham Lewis, 31 July 1926, p. 4.

3. France was dissatisfied with the Dawes Plan for reorganizing German finances and with the United States's insistence on collecting Allied war debts.

41. To Harold Monro (UCLA)

CONFIDENTIAL   Padworth.
26 November 1925
Dear Harold,

Routledge have appointed me editor of a new complete section of their Broadway series of translations and joint editor of their series of literary monographs, the Republic of Letters.[1] They will make the announcement later on, but meanwhile I am communicating with two or three friends in confidence.

It seems to me that the least I can do in return for the many kind things you have done for me is to offer you some share in these enterprises. My position is that of advisor rather than of complete editor; that is to say, I am to prepare lists of books for each series and Routledge will have the last say in the matter. But, of course, they will consider all recommendations favourably. (I say this to avoid promising too much.)

Of course, I know you have other work and might not want the bore of doing a monograph, still less a translation. But the Republic of Letters series ought to be a big thing and Routledge are prepared to put money and energy into it. I suggest you ought to help me, as I can make these a certain counterpoise to the Gang.[2] I wish you would suggest any monographs you would like to do yourself and suggest the names of any people who ought to be given a chance in such a series. I expect the first 12 vols will be followed up by a programme of about 50, so there will be plenty of room.[3]

If you would undertake a translation I should be delighted.[4]

There will be another Vogue article[5] next week, but these women are exasperating to deal with. It needs a lot of patience, I assure you.

I feel sure you will give me your assistance with these Routledge affairs, because it is an important thing and a chance to put forward the people whose work is good and who have been held back. I ought to say that the monographs will nearly always be of "historical figures" and therefore will not cut across Tom Eliot's series[6] which will be contemporaries. I think the most "modern" in our series is Symons on Verlaine.[7] What about your doing a book on Daddy Wordsworth? You could have all sorts of fun with it, and bring in plenty of remarks on contemporary poetry. Do say you will, and I will make a special point of it with Routledge. But suggest anything not too modern, English or foreign.

I will send you the terms of agreement when I hear that you are prepared to consider the affair seriously. And don't forget to give me the names of promising people.

Yours ever

R.

1. In 1923, Routledge had asked RA to collaborate in a series of critical biographies to be edited by William Rose and to be called "The Republic of Letters." RA invited Herbert Read and T. S. Eliot to contribute, but both refused. Then, Eliot, as a director of Faber & Gwyer, initiated a similar scheme called "The Poets on The Poets," and Routledge, after consulting RA, proposed to combine the two series under the joint imprint of the two publishing houses and the joint editorship of Rose and Eliot. Although Routledge tried to ease the situation by making RA editor of the French section of their Broadway Translations, RA resented the "set-back" in his efforts to lift himself "out of the mire of journalism and poverty" and blamed Eliot's about-face. (See "Richard Aldington's Letters to Herbert Read," ed. David S. Thatcher, *Malahat Review,* July 1970, pp. 7–8.)

2. That is, the group associated with Eliot and the publishing firm Faber & Gwyer. See n. 1.

3. Eight volumes only were published in the "Republic of Letters" series. Nothing by Monro was included in this series.

4. Harold Monro has written two notes on this letter. The first reads: "Wrote 29/12/25 promising answer shortly." The second reads: "Wrote 8/2/26 asking if he wanted a translation for *Mdme de Stansky's Memoirs.* Could do a few pp. possibly on appro[val]."

5. See "Modern Free Verse. Article II: The International Characteristics of the Earlier Free Verse Writers," *Vogue,* early December 1925, pp. 95, 130. The first article of this series was included in the late September 1925 *Vogue.* See Letter 131 n. 11.

6. "The Poets on the Poets"; see n. 1.

7. No such book has been traced. Symons first published a discussion of Verlaine in *Studies in Two Literatures,* London, 1897. A second study appeared in *North American Review,* May 1915, pp. 743–48.

42. To Glenn Hughes (Texas)

26 November 1925   Padworth.

Dear Hughes,

I am both touched and honoured by your very friendly letter and the spirit of good-fellowship which prompted you to take so much trouble on my behalf. The experience, the travelling, the pleasure of seeing you again, the chance of touching new audiences and new people, are all most attractive; and if your offer or one like had been made to me when I was demobilised from the army I should have accepted it. As it is, I do not reject but postpone it, for I should like to see the West and circumstances may be such in a few years time that I might be able to go away. But let me explain the position which I know will convince you that I should be foolish to go away now.

First I should make a sacrifice of income and of a position laboriously built up by several years of hard work. The year's income would not matter, but I should have to abandon my reviewing in England and the influential (behind-the-throne) position it gives me here and some other affairs of which I will tell you. What I shall say will be entirely in confidence and I trust you and Mrs Hughes with it.

Now, I review regularly for the Times, the Nation and the Spectator, and this brings me in roughly 2500 dollars a year. If I went away for nine months, I should lose those jobs and other people would get them. They are the three best and most solid literary papers in England and if I stick to them, they will stick to me. This connection with these three papers is of the greatest importance, because they touch the whole or nearly the whole of the cultured classes throughout the Empire. You must remember that my interests are as much literary as poetic. I send you a cutting about the Republic of Letters. I am offered and shall probably accept the joint editorship of this very important series, and this will not only increase my income, but provide me with an almost unlimited outlet for literary monographs. Further, the same publishers have offered me the sole editorship of a series of translations from 18th century French literature; I shall do some of the translations myself and arrange others.[1] This work cannot possibly be done except with complete leisure and the proximity of great public libraries and a constant close communication with Paris. The books I am doing and shall do will all be published in the United States, but they could not be produced there.

You see I am playing for a fairly big thing—nothing less than the position of the accepted English authority on French literature. The two acknowledged authorities, Dr Saintsbury and Sir Edmund Gosse, are both very old men. Dr Whibley has other fish to fry. I don't fear any of my contemporaries: those who know more about French than I do cannot write so well, and those who can write better, do not know so much.

Within the next six months I am bringing out a monograph of Voltaire, a collection of essays on French literature from the 12th to the 19th centuries and a translation of the 15th century Quinze Joyes de Mariage.[2] I have contracts or proposals for contracts for something like ten books. Within the next five years I consider that I can bring out at least fifteen more books, translations, monographs, essays, new editions of French literature. I have already put in six years strenuous work on these lines and it would be madness to abandon it in mid career. If all goes as I hope—and there's many a slip—another six years should see me well on the way to what I want.

Only last week I sent to Paris for 200 francs worth of books and yesterday for another 600 francs worth for these various plans. I am preparing lists of books and authors for the two series, and lists of translators and scholars to undertake the work.

There, I need not labour the point further. Your very generous offer comes to me at a time when I have already laid the foundations of a decent literary career in mine own country and I think you would be among the first to advise me not to abandon it. Only last month I spoke to my publisher about going to Italy for three months and he gave me a fearful lecture about wasting opportunities and forbade me to go for more than a month. As events have turned out, I shall now not be able to go at all this year. But if you and Mrs Hughes are going there next year, I would certainly make an effort to try to meet you either in Italy or in Paris. You will both adore Italy when you get used to the difference of customs and language. Make your wife learn Italian—if one of you can speak the language you will halve your bills. I envy you the pleasure of the first weeks in Italy. I think the seven months I spent there in 1912 were the happiest of my life.

I am sorry the chest got smashed. What a fool the man was to pack it so badly—but you ought to have insured it. If you have a good working carpenter, with a taste for fine old work, you will find that he will be able to restore it for you, unless it is hopelessly smashed.

Thank you very much for the two books of poetry which arrived safely.[3] It was most kind of you to send them.

The way to treat your Scotsman is to praise everything Scotch—whiskey, Bobbie Burns, heather, golf, grouse, Edinburgh, Mary Stuart, Sir Walter, the Highlands, &c &c—speak affectingly of Bannockburn and Pinkie[4] and say what confounded rascals the English are.

Our love to you both.

Richard Aldington

---

1. RA edited "Broadway Translations" and did nine of these translations himself.

2. *The Fifteen Joys of Marriage, Ascribed to Antoine de la Sale*, London, 1926. *Voltaire*, London, 1925, was the first volume of "The Republic of Letters" series; see Letter 41 n. 1.

3. Not identified.

4. Pinkie (1547) and Bannockburn (1314) are famous battles between England and Scotland.

43. To James Joyce (State University of New York, Buffalo)

10 March 1927   Padworth
Dear Mr. Joyce,

I have received the final printed form of protest against the pirating of Ulysses.[1] I wish I could feel that this would achieve the end that every decent person must desire, i.e. the confounding and suppression of Mr. Roth.[2] But the skin of the commercial person is hard, and he does not mind scorn if he can collect money.

Two ideas have occurred to me and these I submit to you for you to see if you think they might usefully be put into practice.

(1) Considerable portions of Ulysses were published by the Little Review.[3] In spite of suppression, does this not give them copyright in those portions? Therefore, if Roth reproduces any of these, could not the Little Review and you combine to bring an action?

(2) Since the damage of a mutilated version has occurred and is irreparable, would it not be wise for you to issue immediately in book form with honest American and English publishers your own bowdlerised edition of Ulysses? The horrid work of expurgation could be carried out by the publishers and you could write a short foreward explaining why you were driven to this action. I don't think it would interfere with the sale of the complete Paris edition[4] which, by the way, is now comparatively easy to obtain in England. No work of genius has ever been suppressed by any government, so you need have no fears for the future. Meanwhile, I don't see why you should not torpedo Mr. Roth in the way I suggest.[5] I imagine you would have no difficulty in finding a publisher, but, if you have, I can (I think) arrange the whole thing for you with Routledge[6] in London and some equally respectable firm in America. Let me know if I can serve you here.

Please accept my sincere admiration for your genius,

Yours very truly,
Richard Aldington

1. In an effort to stop the unauthorized publication of *Ulysses* in the United States in Samuel Roth's *Two Worlds Monthly,* Joyce conceived the idea of an International Protest, which he had drawn up by Ludwig Lewisohn and Archibald MacLeish. Copies of the protest were sent to principal writers all over the world for their signatures. RA was one of those who signed.

2. Samuel Roth first wrote Joyce in 1922, expressing regret that *Ulysses* was not available in America. In September 1925, Roth began reprinting fragments of *Work in Progress* in his *Two Worlds Monthly,* sending Joyce $200 and promising more, which he never sent. In July 1927, Roth published in slightly expurgated form the first three episodes of *Ulysses.*

3. Before *Ulysses* was suppressed, the *Little Review* had published the first fourteen episodes. Publication began in March 1918, and "Oxen of the Sun" was published September–December 1920.

4. The first copies of this edition were delivered to Sylvia Beach, its publisher, in Paris on Joyce's birthday, 2 February 1922.

5. The protest had no effect on Roth, who continued to print *Ulysses* through October 1927. He was forced to suspend publication 27 December 1928 when he was enjoined by the Supreme Court of the State of New York from using Joyce's name in any way. A consent decree without damages was entered.

6. RA was closely connected with Routledge at this time. See Letter 41 n. 1.

44. To Ezra Pound (Yale)

22 August 1927   Padworth
Dear Ezra,

I got a letter from Valette[1] this morning, from which I gather (1) That there is no exclusive copyright in Remy in U.S., and (2) That only Ransom's Luxembourg[2] is copyright[ed] in England exclusively.

I do not want to use anyone else's translation, but am making my own. If no one has exclusive rights—and I don't believe they have—alors, ils ourront se faire foutre, 's'pas?

Further, Boni &c and I have paid the Mercure for illusory rights!! Remains to be seen whether we cannot all take action against the Mercure and J. de G.[3] Odd position. I will let you know what happens, as I am being advised by an English publisher of one of Remy's works, who is anxious to get to the bottom of the matter. I am informing Covici[4] of the present state of affairs.

Now, as touching yourself and your works in England—you can depend on support from Tom Eliot and me as certainties. (To the best of my slight ability, I have kept your flag flying by occasional references in Times reviews (especially Provençal) and I quoted you in Literary Studies and Reviews, unless it was in French Studies.[5] Not much, but well meant.) The crowd which was hostile to you has disintegrated; Nichols has vanished; Squire is heavily in debt and anxious to be friendly to anyone, moreover his stock is low; Bloomsbury is the powerful clique and they are more or less hostile to us both, but I have got some of their "jeunes" by giving them translations;[6] Gosse is exceedingly friendly to me (!!). Consequently, I think your dramatic re-appearance might be a success. Wyndham Lewis's article on you in his new periodical certainly did you harm.[7] If I might offer you advice, I would suggest this: That you will do yourself infinitely more good by issuing your collected poems, re-issuing old books, and producing some new work, than by engaging in polemics. We are neither of us much good at polemics, and you manage to hit yourself and your friends more than your adversaries when you wield your Excalibur. Leave the polemics to Tom Eliot, who has a genius for it. After all, mon vieux, polemics are distinctly a sideline; our business is to get on with the job, and leave others to squabble over what we do. I feel very hopeful about the chances of your collected poems in England, and I'm very glad to hear they have gone well in U.S.[8] I did not know they had been issued.

Now, if you come to England, what is it you want? And what would you like me to do?

It is unfortunate, but the senior partner in Routledge is rather disgruntled with you. He bought the translation of the Physique de l'Amour from Rodker,[9] and told me that it was full of scientific mistranslations and that he had to pay to have it revised. I don't know whether this is true or not. Routledge would be the people to re-issue your translations and possibly the Spirit of Romance.[10]

What copyrights do you possess both in Eng. and U.S.? I mean that if Routledge do a book, they like to be able to sell sheets to U.S.

What I should like to suggest and try to arrange is this: You to revise the Spirit of Romance, correct any minor errors and generally tidy it up; you also to collect your Guido, Arnaut[11] and other Romance translations in one volume. I would then go to Routledge and make it a personal matter, and make them republish the two books. Perhaps I could induce them to put the translations into the medieval section of the Broadway.[12] Eileen Power is the effective editor, and I think she would back us up. See what you think of this, and find out if you have the copyright in both countries.

How do you stand with Tom Eliot? I have withdrawn from the Criterion on what I consider excellent grounds, i.e. that T.S.E. is employing that Ghetto guttersnipe Cournos.[13] I have told Tom that I won't appear in the same periodical with said C. However, T. and I are still on perfectly friendly terms otherwise. Together we might be able to leg you into the Supplement[14] (if you want?) after a lunch with B.L.R.[15] Tom does much gallivanting to parties which I haven't time or inclination for, so he can be of much more use to you than I.

Covici is a bold lad—I hope we don't ruin him too soon. I am writing Hughes to-day to get in touch with you.[16] Yes, he is a Prof. at the University, and feeds us as pap to his Sophs. But Washington University[17] is a one-horse affair.

Adieu, yours
R.

1. Alfred Valette was the director of the *Mercure de France,* Remy de Gourmont's publisher.

2. Remy de Gourmont, *A Night in the Luxembourg*, trans. Arthur Ransome, Boston, 1912.

3. Jean de Gourmont.

4. Pascal Covici of Covici, Fried who published RA's *Remy de Gourmont. Selections from All His Works*, Chicago, 1928.

5. RA refers to Pound in *Literary Studies and Reviews*, London, 1924, in the essay "Mr. James Joyce's 'Ulysses,' " p. 199, and in *French Studies and Reviews*, London, 1926, in the essay "Two Troubadours," p. 41.

6. Routledge had appointed RA editor of their Broadway series of translations; see Letter 41 and *passim*.

7. See "The Revolutionary Simpleton," chapter 9, "Ezra Pound, etc.," *Enemy*, premiere issue, 1927, pp. 61–70.

8. See *Personae, The Collected Poems of Ezra Pound*, New York, 1926.

9. John Rodker established the Ovid Press and was associated with the Egoist Ltd.

10. See *The Spirit of Romance*, London and New York, 1910.

11. Guido Cavalcanti and Arnaut Daniel.

12. See n. 6.

13. See the notes to Letter 11, and see Letter 17 for probable reasons for this ill feeling toward Cournos.

14. The *Times Literary Supplement* where RA was the regular reviewer for French literature and Eliot a leader-writer.

15. Bruce L. Richmond, editor of the *Times Literary Supplement*.

16. See Letter 40 and notes. *University of Washington Chapbooks* published Pound's *Ta Hio: The Great Learning* in 1928.

17. Hughes was at the University of Washington (Seattle), not at Washington University (St. Louis).

45. *To Glenn Hughes (Texas)*

Armistice Day, 1927   Padworth.

I think your Guggenheim idea A.1.[1] Now, I have this morning written to (1) Bruce Richmond, editor of Times Literary Supplement, (2) T. S. Eliot, editor Monthly Criterion, (3) J. C. Squire, editor London Mercury; asking them if they will support your application and give references. I shall hear from them within a few days, and as soon as I do, I shall at once write you. If they consent, you can put them as extra references. If we can get the Times to back you, all should be well. I have made a personal matter of it, and am very hopeful.

I am sorry to say that I have had no success with the Chapbooks.[2] The bigger publishers say that they are too small to be worth their while. Monro got jealous, because you used the word Chapbook, which he likes to think is his own property.[3] Remains Beaumont and a bookseller called Neumayer, whom I will write to. But the great difficulty is this: Such pamphlets would be published in England for a shilling at the outside; and your price makes them come to about 3/6. You will see that this is a grievous snag. Now, I think the following might help. Will you send a complete set of the Chapbooks to date for review to (1) Times Literary Supplement, Printing House Square, London E.C.4. (2) J. C. Squire, The London Mercury, 229 Strand, London, W.C.2. (3) T. S. Eliot, the Monthly Criterion, Messrs Faber and Gwyer, 24 Russell Square, London, W.C.1. In with each set, put a short note written on University paper, saying that you have edited this series, and asking in each case if they could find room for a review, even though they are small, since you are anxious to have the Chapbooks brought to the notice of English readers. (In writing to English editors, always adopt the modest tack.) This will kill two birds with one stone, i.e. It may get the Chapbooks reviewed, and will introduce you to the people whose support I am trying to get for your application. If the Times reviews the Chapbooks, I can then go straight to Beaumont, and ask him to take the agency in England. As you know, or perhaps don't know, a favourable review from the Times, produces great respect in England. Meanwhile, I will pull a wire at the Times, and since my name is among the crowd of contributors, they will certainly notice the series. (I rather wish I hadn't said so much about the Prince of Wales and the golf champion on the Times!) However, I said it was an indiscretion.[4]

Many thanks for the 25 dollars draft. I am glad you like the Gourmont.[5] Try to bring out the essay before Covici issues the Gourmont anthology.[6] He now has the complete MSS, and I should be receiving proofs shortly. (My introduction to the Anthology is almost a complete contradiction of what I say in the essay you have—thus, in one way or another, I am almost bound to be right!)

I am delighted to hear that the Lawrence pamphlet[7] has already been reprinted. You remember that at first you did not expect to reprint until Christmas, but your letter (Oct 27) shows that we were well ahead of scheduled time.

Your Pound experiences amuse me.[8] He is quite bughouse. I shall send you and Babette a copy of an American "quarter" periodical, published in Paris, to which E.P. contributes under the name of Abraham Lincoln Gillespie.[9] Any doctor would certify insanity on such a document. As I prophesied (only no one believed me) James Joyce and Gertrude Stein have sent a whole generation of jeunes Americans off the rails. "transition," the periodical, is as bughouse a production as you would wish to see. One Sam Putnam, from Chicago, came to see me recently, and said that Covici had an awful time reading Pound's letters. I know him so well that I know what he means when he doesn't know himself. Apropos, I have recently reviewed his Collected Poems for the Times. I must get an extra copy and send you. It will make Ezra mad as a hatter.[10]

I greatly deplore your view that the Imagists are dead, especially at the moment when I am about to produce my collected poems.[11] Come over here, you scoundrel, and I'll show you I'm alive! I'll dog's-nose you![12]

You can put in my name at once as a Gug reference. I hope I can write you that the others will come along. I might try to get the Poet Laureate? Hopeless I fear; he was born before Seattle was founded![13]

Apparently, we have at least another year certain tenancy here. The rest is in the laps of the gods.

Our love to you both, and our respectful compliments to Mary Anne.[14]

Ever yours,
Richard Aldington

1. Turned down for a Guggenheim Fellowship earlier, Hughes was invited to apply again; this time he proposed a study of Imagism.
2. *University of Washington Chapbooks*.
3. Harold Monro edited the *Monthly Chapbook* from 1919 to 1925.
4. See RA, *D. H. Lawrence: An Indiscretion*, Seattle, 1927, p. 22, where RA depreciates golf and the Prince of Wales.
5. See RA, *Remy de Gourmont: A Modern Man of Letters*, Seattle, 1928.
6. See RA, *Remy de Gourmont: Selections from All His Works*, Chicago, 1928.
7. See n. 4.
8. See Glenn Hughes to RA, 27 October 1927 (Texas): "Have a couple of letters from Pound. Where the hell does he get that wd. and shd. stuff? Such spelling gives me the jim-jams. I never saw a man who could think of so many annoying things to do."
9. See A. Lincoln Gillespie, Jr., "Music Starts a Geometry," *transition*, November 1927, pp. 166–69.
10. See "Reprints," *Times Literary Supplement*, 29 September 1927, p. 671.
11. See *Collected Poems*, New York, 1928.
12. A "dog's nose" is a mixed drink of malt liquor and spirits.
13. Robert Bridges was born in 1844.
14. Mary Anne Hughes, now Mrs. W. G. Mauerman.

46. *To Glenn Hughes (Texas)*

c/o A.W.G. Randall,
16 Via Nicole Porpora,
22 September 1928   Roma 36 [Italy]
My dear Hughes,

We are delighted to know that you and Babette and Mary Anne are "pretty comferable" in that poor old English cottage.[1] You seem from what you say and from what Mrs Capper tells us to have made very good arrangements, and we hope you will enjoy yourselves thoroughly. Your purchases of drink (wish we could share it with you!) sound like what Mrs Hood, down at the Hare and Hounds calls "an orghie."

I hope you find the tradesmen bring you decent food? I have never found that English tradesmen try to cheat in the abominable Italian manner—i.e. sticking up price to foreigner and giving short change. But the English tradesman may think you don't know quality, especially in meat. If you pay for English beef or mutton, show it to Mrs Stacey and see that you have it. Tom Hann's fellow is quite honest, I think. Mr Ford at the post-office or the butcher will cash cheques for you, if you say you are a friend of mine.[2]

As to rent—my dear fellow! Never let me hear you utter the sound again.

Don't you bother too much about that Imagist book. Get out as much of the bookish part as you can at Malthouse. But, in my opinion, you would do well to make the book as popular and personal as possible. My idea of the book would be to begin with a short but pithy account of modern Anglo-American poetry from 1909 until today, with a really accurate history of Imagism. Then, I should proceed to devote a separate chapter of various length to each of the relevant poets, dividing this into two sections. Section 1 should be a light and amusing personal impression of the poet, what he looks like, where he lives (with a photograph), and your reactions to him; section 2 should be an analysis of his work, with plenty of quotation. I should also be inclined to compose a questionnaire to submit to each man for his opinion. If you can make a well-documented and amusing book, you ought to get a considerable sale. But don't be in too great a hurry to write the book. Wait till you've had time to consolidate impressions. Pound is collecting a whole mass of early Imagist data for you at Rapallo, where you'll certainly have to go visit him. I'm seeing him here next week, and will try to find out where and when he can see you.

Your selections ought to be carefully made so as to form an "anthology of the Imagist movement," which will look well in the book's blurb.

If you want any books not at Malthouse, why not use the London Library, of which I am a life member? I enclose three blank letters to the Librarian, signed by me. Don't, of course, tell him that you are getting the books, but write in the blank space the names of the books you require—best type them in. You are allowed up to 15 books at a time, which they will send by post. If you get them a few at a time they'll often give you more than fifteen. When you've finished with them, wrap them up, stick on one of their labels (which they always send) and post. You can get Amy Lowell that way—I fear I sold all my Amy Lowells for 150 dollars. As to my own books—if you will note any you would like, I will tell you if I want to sell them, and no doubt we shall not quarrel about the price. I should be glad for you to have the Italian comedy book.

Amy Lowell's lecture on me is in typed MS somewhere in that cupboard of old periodicals and junk under the stairs. If you can't find it, I'll have a hunt for you. It is an amusing bit of bunk—begins by describing me as a dyed-in-the-wool Englishman, which I certainly ain't.[3]

But, my dear chap, Loving is very hard up indeed, and if you possibly can, you ought to pay him. But—a word of warning—he is so hard up that he is not wholly scrupulous. Do not give him a chance to borrow from you, and above all, do not let him introduce you to any publisher. I can assure you from personal knowledge that he does this, and then tries to strap the person he introduces for a 10% commission! So look out.

(Yes, I believe Amy's lecture would make a Chapbook. Try to find it in that mass of junk.)

As to your STORY OF THE THEATRE—herewith a letter to my publisher, Mr Stallybrass.[4] If he turns down the book, I will give you another letter to a very nice agent man in London, who will do his best to place it for you. But try Stallybrass first.

By the way, may I ask as a favour that you will be very vague to the Cappers about my plans of leaving Malthouse and staying in Paris this spring? Just say, you don't know exactly what I'm doing.

It is beautiful weather here. Yesterday we went out on the Appian Way, and to-day we are being motored to Frascati. We went to Ostia the other day and bathed. We leave here on the 30th for Naples, then take a boat (two days across the Mediterranean) for Marseilles, where we meet Mrs Patmore. After that we proceed to Port-Cros. The address (I think) is: La Vigie, Ile de Port-Cros, (Var) France. If the Lawrences come to the island, I do hope you both will manage to run down and see us all. Mrs Patmore, by the way, has some part in the history of Imagism, since she used to bat around London every day with E.P., H.D., and me, and certainly stimulated us by her personality.

Keep in touch with us. Letters sent here will be forwarded, and those addressed to the island will certainly be delivered to us.

Our love to you both,
R.A.

---

1. Although RA and the Hugheses had long awaited their visit together, a last-minute telegram from Alec Randall's wife asking RA to stay with her convalescent husband sent RA rushing to Italy. RA turned Malthouse Cottage over to the Hugheses.
2. Mrs. Capper, Hood, and Stacey and Messrs. Hann and Ford were Padworth people.
3. Not traced.
4. See Glenn Hughes, *Story of the Theatre*, London, 1928.

47. To Brigit Patmore* (Texas)

Monday
3 [December 1928]

The Select,
Place de la Sorbonne,
Paris, France.

I half hoped there would be a letter from Darling today, but on re-flection I see that the hope was absurd. You could not have written until Sunday at earliest, and the letter would not reach Paris until Tuesday, even if you had written this address, instead of to the Bank. By the way, it is exactly: Select Hotel, 1 Place de La Sorbonne, Paris (5 ième). If you put the arrondissement number, the letter arrives a post earlier. So much news & gossip for you, dearest love, and I still haven't described this room to you, so that you can see how comfortably I am arranged. But that must wait until the end of the letter, or for another.

Well, I went out and posted the pencil note to you about Nancy,[1] then had dinner, & returned here & "did" Boccaccio.[2] I felt a bit annoyed with Nancy for bolting off at once, but then thought she was justified, since I hadn't made love to her. However, at 10:30 just as I was finishing a page, & thinking of bed, comes a tap at the door, & enter Nancy lit-erally clothed in cloth of gold (wouldn't Lorenzo[3] rub in the "talis-man"!). She insisted that I get into evening clothes & come to Montmartre. I didn't particularly want to go, since I'd been up since 7:30, & was tired. However, out we went, sat in a café and talked for an hour, and agreed to be good friends & not lovers. (Naturally, I didn't mention you or even say that I am in love with someone else, but left everything vague.) Well, that important point settled, we went off to Montmartre chattering vigorously, we taxied to Montmartre & went to a most amusing nigger cabaret.[4] (Between ourselves, I deduce that Nancy has now passed to the culte des nègres & is no longer interested in poor white trash.) The dancing room was decorated in style moderne with fanciful patterns in blue & silver of no particular shape or meaning; there was an alcove with a large picture of a Mississippi steamboat seen in oblique perspective from the prow; the walls had a number of black panels rather like school blackboards, with very clever sketches of ne-groes in white outline. There were wall seats of pinkish velvet, and tables with red & white check tablecloths. The nigger orchestra was good, but I didn't think it very extra; but I was introduced to "Henry,"[5] the nigger pianist & he turned out to be one of Jelly Roll Morton's Red Hot Pep-pers! Such a thrill! There were some tunes, a nigger songstress whom Nancy thought marvellous & I thought rather bad, a nigger lady, clothed only in a red cache-sex & silver breast-containers, who danced with remarkable undulations of her lumber regions; & a negro man who cut double shuffles with unusual celerity.

We met Aragon,[6] Dolly Wilde, "Victor" & "Edward" (?Cunarders?)[7] and Nancy danced with Victor & Dolly with Edward while I watched or talked to Henry & Aragon. I like Aragon very much, he has a very beautiful & sensitive face, and a charming manner. But he is jealous as a million devils, & made a frightful scene with Nancy about 3 a.m. *apropos* a girl whom he said Nancy had taken away from him, and also apropos the "Henry." Nancy was furious, & they went and had a row in the street, & then came back & rowed over supper like husband & wife—quite a "vigie"[8] scene in fact. We four all gazed at our plates and said nothing. Then Nancy jumped up & took Louis away in a taxi, saying she was going back to Chapelle-Réanville at once; but whispered us to stay, & returned in half an hour! The others then left & Nancy & I went back to the dance room & discussed the unfortunate Louis until 4:30. I tried to persuade her to "make it up," but she wouldn't, & I left her to Henry at 4:30, & returned home. I didn't drink much—1 sherry cobbler, and ½ bottle of white wine, but O Lord, these scenes of midnight dissipation are not for me! I woke at 10:30, and felt very nasty. After this, if I ever go again, I shall ask Nancy to let me leave early. Getting to bed at 5 a.m. is not for old gentlemen like me!

I said to Nancy that the scenes with Arabella at the Vigie had been too much, and she said: "Never mind, darling, you'll solve those complications by getting into others!" which is cheerful. I asked Dolly Wilde to tell Natalie Barney I have left Arabella, & Dolly says the news has already travelled far! Nancy says that "Janet" (?)[9] told her that a few days ago she saw a pile of letters addressed to "M. et Mme Aldington" at the Hotel Saint-Germaine des Près! So apparently Arabella is not there. With Joseph?[10] The grand secret Louise Theis told Nancy about H.D. & Bryher is not much—only they had apparently a furious row because they both fell in love with Nancy. Do you believe it? In any case, I don't see that is any reason why Louise shouldn't want to know Bryher—I think Nancy invented that on the spur of the moment because she didn't want to tell me.

Today I have lived wholly on cafe crème, but shall go & dine early, and go to bed early. I felt too beastly after a night up to work, so went to an English tailor Henry Church told me about; and also bought a new overcoat ready-made. The tailor is to make me a lounge suit for £10.10.0, cut of English material, cut in the English style. I asked about a dress suit, but that comes to 1500 fr; so I have decided only to get a new white waistcoat, & wait until I go to America[11] (if I go) for the dress suit. I hope Darling will see about her coat, hat & shoes at once, & get good ones such as she really wants. Please, my lovely one, do this for me, & tell me what you get.

Did you have any trouble with the Customs? Did you find the key? I went out from the Gare du Nord with the intention of wiring Derek[12] but then thought you might feel it was officious. I am simply yearning for a letter from my sweet Brigit. It is going to be very hard to live 350 miles away from you. I want you so very much, sweet love, want to mingle my body with yours, & lie with you in my arms, and have your companionship. I feel I would do anything & go anywhere to be near you— but I must not bother you with this. Tell me as much as you wish of what you are doing and feeling. Brigit dear, I love you and yearn for you. I adore you and my whole body burns when I remember you said "I love you" to me.

Richard

Do you remember you said at the Henri IV that you would always like the smell of French cigarettes? Brigit, that made me very happy.

---

*Brigit Patmore (1882–1965), married to a grandson of the Victorian poet Coventry Patmore was considered by contemporaries a beautiful and charming woman. She was RA's lover—"you who first held my body"—in late 1910 or early 1911 when he was eighteen and she ten years older. Brigit, who moved in the social circles of Alice Meynell and later of Violet Hunt and Ford Madox Ford, introduced RA to London literary society and to H.D. who was to become his first wife. Mrs. Patmore was herself a novelist and translator. In 1928, RA and Dorothy "Arabella" Yorke entertained D. H. Lawrence, Frieda Lawrence, and Brigit Patmore at Port-Cros. Here RA began anew his liaison with Brigit and they spent a happy eight years together (Brigit wrote of them in *My Friends When Young* [1968]) before he left her for her daughter-in-law, Netta, wife of Michael Patmore. (See also the Annotated Index.)

1. Nancy Cunard.
2. See *The Decameron of Giovanni Boccaccio*, trans. Richard Aldington, New York, 1930.
3. D. H. Lawrence.
4. Plantation Club.
5. Henry Crowder.
6. Louis Aragon.
7. Victor and Edward Cunard, cousins of each other and of Nancy.
8. The fort made into a residence at Port-Cros. The rows originated when Dorothy Yorke—"Arabella," his mistress of some ten years—objected to RA's attentions to Brigit.
9. Janet Flanner.
10. In an interview with Walter and Lillian Lowenfels in 1964, Arabella said, "[W]e had a servant named Joseph—an Italian—who consoled me at Port Cros." RA probably refers to this "Joseph."
11. For a lecture tour. RA did not go.
12. Derek Patmore.

48. To Brigit Patmore (Texas)

Thursday evening　　　　　　　　　　　　　　　　Chapelle-Réanville.
[6 December 1928]

I had to post off the letter I wrote this morning in the train in a great hurry, because I found the mail left here at 12, & I hadn't time to add anything. I am writing this in the few minutes before dinner, & I shall add (if possible) more on the train going back to Paris. I don't get there until nearly midnight, so I shall wait until I see whether there is a letter from Darling, & post tomorrow morning. Always, always, so much to say to my own beautiful love, for whom I yearn!

Oh first—Nancy is sweet & charming & kind but I find I do not love her *at all*. I am so filled and, as it were, perfumed with your presence, that there is not the least touch of desire in me for anyone else. I want Brigit, Brigit. Just now I opened a copy of Wyndham Lewis's "Blast" & the first words I read were: "Bless Bridget"![1] Do you know who put that in? Can you guess? I remember so well saying to Lewis: "Put Brigit, put Brigit." But was it not strange to find that after 14 years? I had quite forgotten it. And probably you never saw it. Bless Brigit indeed! O my perfect love, my woman, I want you almost every hour of the day & at night I sleep & wake with memories of you. We must indeed "give life a trial," & it must be life together.

Dinner bell already! I must go, & hide this book under my coat. Will try to continue in train, certainly to-morrow morning. I adore, adore, love, desire, worship, Brigit, Brigit, Brigit!

Later. In the train. Oof! Such a rush, and only 1 minute to spare at the station! Taxi late & roads bad &c. (Darn this joggly train!) Very late— shan't be in until one. Will finish this & post tomorrow (Friday) morning. Also, try to describe Nancy's charming house. (Can't write—train too woggly!)

Friday morning—Went to bed very late, after reading & re-reading and kissing Darling's letter; and another this morning. Bless Brigit, bless Brigit! (How strange & how lovely it was, to come on that in "Blast", and to think & feel you intensely for a moment. My Brigit!)

Had to rush out—it is 10 a.m.—to send a letter by aeroplane to Michel Sevier from a girl named Marjorie Craigie who is staying with Nancy. Love letter, I *hope*—otherwise should regret derangement.

Well, Nancy has a very charming place in the country. An old French farm & barn converted into the charming English country house. The printing place & library are in separate buildings in the garden. The house has two storeys & you go up rough stone or new wood stairs. There is a big hall–drawing room with a stove, couches, chairs, & quantities of amusing African fetishes and one or two Mexican heads in stone. Excellent taste everywhere. Dining room, with Lord Cunard's[2] large desk at which Nancy writes & pretends to keep accounts & be business-like. Then the kitchen & servant's bedrooms. The last ground-floor room is Nancy's bedroom, rather luxurious, with masses of those wooden bracelets she wears on rails. Rather *too* many. But also lots of books. There are other bedrooms & a bathroom—all very comfortable, but she says it is very difficult to run. The "Press" is getting on her nerves, & she is tired of it before the first book is out! Wants to go to Germany for 6 months! I know she is dying to ask me to take it over, but doesn't dare. And I don't want to, because it would take all my time, chain me down, & keep me from my own work.

Darling, I find I like Nancy very much, but I'm not the least little particle in love with her. We kiss each other on meeting and parting, but it is almost perfunctory. You are sweet and right to say "take any consolation," but the plain truth is that my body is yours and at least now does not feel anything for other women. I am filled with desire—for you, and think so much of your naked body and the love ecstasies and minglings between us; but I have no feeling of desire for Nancy or any other woman. Marjorie Craigie is a beautiful girl with very lovely eyes, but I looked at her dispassionately as at a charming & animated work of art. (But I was flattered that she entrusted me with a letter for her lover!)

What Nancy is going to do about the Press, I don't know. I hope it doesn't collapse too soon. She began with a long thing of George Moore's,[3] & is bored with it. And the hand-press *is* a bore. I set up a couple of lines of type, & helped pull off a few sheets of G.M.—& it takes *ages*. Also, Nancy has only just begun to realise what publishing means—i.e. sending out circulars, correspondence, filing letters, acknowledging cheques, designing ads, keeping day book, Press accounts & authors' accounts, despatching parcels &c &c. She is horrified—&, I can see, wants someone to do it for her. I can see she wants *me* to do it, but after the Egoist & the Criterion,[4] I have had enough of that sort of thing. If you were here, we *might* perhaps do it together, since I can systematize things, & it would give us another £3 or £4 a week. But I doubt even then if it would be worth it. I think we can *both* make more by writing.

I enclose a letter from Times—so that's all right. Shall write Richmond today, & send in an article I have done. When I see Paulhan this afternoon I shall try to get some more novels, & send two to Darling. In any case shall send her a funny diary of 1820 by a parson (already reviewed for T.L.S. by me) but which *might* give Darling an idea for an amusing little article.[5] The edition is very limited & almost certainly unknown in England.

(How I love you, Brigit my sweet. When I am writing about other things, my "subconscious" is saying: "I love Brigit, I love Brigit.")

Don't be surprised if you hear I am "living with Nancy Cunard"! John Mavrogordato turned up at Puits Carré yesterday with Norman Douglas's very amusing book of Limericks,[6] over which we shrieked with mirth. But Nancy and I were greatly amused that Mavro had a discreet attitude of complicity & seemed to assume I was living at Puits Carré!

Letter from my Bank—they have credited me 100 *too much* in the sale of my Oil Shares!! Tempting devils! Of course, they'll find it out, so I may as well get the credit of being honest!

I return to Darling's letters. The Hungarian Restaurant sounds great fun, and how amusing of Darling to "get off" with a decadent lady. (I must certainly learn to dance—but how, when? Time, time, time. One runs a losing race with time. A week, a century, since you went—and Oh, I am sick at heart with longing for you.)

Thursday's letter here already—I hope mine yesterday from Puits Carré was not too much delayed.

How exquisitely lovely for me to think of Darling running down with Boots to find my morning letter and "good-day" kiss and touch for her. I shall think of you sitting in bed & reading "me." All yours, my woman possessor. How much I love your "man who possesses me"—ah Brigit. And it is true, *true.* Sometimes I have that feeling of incredulity and wonder—can it be true, is it not a dream that Brigit and I have found each other, are lovers, lovers and more than lovers, mouth to mouth & body to body and spirit to spirit, lovers, can it be true? And, like sunlight, "It *is* true, and *isn't* a dream. And soon we shall have each other again." Oh, I am faint with desire and my blood runs quicker when I think of holding you again, naked, divine, & desirous. And still I say to you: The love ecstasy will grow more beautiful, more intense, more prolonged. I am certain of it. I want to fill your body with mine, to attune to the utmost intensity of sensation until all *all* that a woman can feel & be & experience is yours.

How I run on & run off! Do you mind this curving movement of thought, which always returns to you and our love, & the pain of separation, & the joy of loving you, & the ecstasy of our love-making, and the eager awaiting you? Ah! Yes, to work, when it is for "us." My darling, if I could tell you the inexpressible joy of working & "doing without things"—for you! The triumph of denying myself something—for you! My life is almost too full of happiness, when nearly everything I do can be done (so it seems) for you.

Indeed, I have not forgotten how to laugh, but I need my Brigit to laugh with freely & happily. Darling irreverent strumpet! I shall always love the memory of our two meals at the Arles buffet.

O damn Lorenzo. I haven't written him & shan't. He is a life-killer, for all he says, and he is sick of self-love, a very Malvolio of letters. *Of course,* Lorenzo will try to find out. All I fear is that he and/or Frieda came to my bedroom & found me not there![7]

It is hard for me to write about Stephen,[8] because I am your real lover. I must not let myself be ungenerous to him. And yet I must not let my feeling of wanting to stand aside & leave you both absolutely free, make me ungenerous to you in a negative way. I *must* tell you that I think it ungenerous bullying & grabbing to *threaten* suicide. If one loves to that extent, and if love somehow eludes, one kills oneself perhaps, but does not talk about it. Don't let him bully you with pathos, Darling. I know it is easy for me to talk—j'ai le beau rôle. And I was so weak & cowardly with Arabella! And if you tell him *why* now, he will immediately guess *who*—and for the first time in my life I feel the sweetness & rightness of keeping love secret, because (I think) I know how the "world" tries to separate lovers. But Darling will do what is right & keep her little Lamb of God flag flying! O my sweet, if I could take that & all other worries from you—& yet life is better when we are most human, & it is good that we can both speak out to each other & be certain of understanding and sympathy. I *do* see your difficulty. It is so easy for me with Nancy, because we have never been lovers, but so hard for you. I hope to God Stephen doesn't get into "states" and make "scenes"—*too* much, after Port-Cros. Yet a woman "knowing love in her heart" can surely deal patiently and justly & finally. I worry just a little bit about this, and beg you to tell me from time to time how it goes on—if you say nothing, trying to spare me, I shall feel the more worried.

Yes, I can acquiesce in this temporary parting, because it is made so that we may be nearer. I had to get free, to build up a new life, and make some money for us both. You have greater difficulties & responsibilities to battle. You must always be with your boys, Darling, whenever & as much as you want. Don't ever have a feeling that I am jealous of them—I shall never call you "Lot's wife" because you look back at your children! So put that out of your mind if it has troubled you.

By the way, will Derek look me up if he has time when passing through Paris? Thanks for the Bookman address, and, yes, I would like those other poems. Bad ones, but *might* be sold to periodicals. How pleasant to think of Derek in Toulon!

Tell me what you are doing when you get to work again. My last jobs were a Times article & another careful revision of Chapter 1 of my novel—wish I felt less *disgraced* by this novel![9] As you see from Richmond's letter he is eager for stuff, so we must send in as much as we can. Oh, how much I feel I can work; and I am sure you do also. What delicious fun, what happiness to be doing things together, for each other. O my loved woman, how happy I am that we are both alive. Take care of yourself. Crossing streets & things! I tremble for that fragile Venetian cup of life. I have often thought the most beautiful expression of profound love is Donne's, "God give me grace to *survive* thee," i.e. give me & not her the agony of outliving. It would be so easy, so beautiful to die in your arms, so unendurable, so unexpressible an agony to survive you. Why these images of gloom? Because I am so happy, because I am so much alive, I can dare to look at these things. Oh, Brigit, a man is no more than a man, but what a man can give to a woman, spontaneously, happily, eagerly, desirously—all, all is yours.

Will Darling think now that my lips are on hers and our two naked bodies touching? Ah, my love!

Richard

1. See Letter 4 no. 4; Brigit Patmore was one of those blessed.
2. Sir Bache Cunard, Nancy's father.
3. *Perronik The Fool* by George Moore, published in December 1928. The first book printed at the Hours Press, however, was Norman Douglas's *Report on the Pumice-Stone Industry of the Lipari Island* sent as a present to the author in June 1928.
4. RA was assistant editor of the *Egoist* when he went to war in 1916. In 1923 and part of 1924 he acted as T. S. Eliot's assistant at the *Criterion*. In both positions, RA felt that he was not properly rewarded for his efforts. He also resented the treatment Eliot (who succeeded him on the *Egoist*) accorded him on the *Criterion*.
5. Thomas Jessop, *Journal d'un Voyage à Paris en Septembre–Octobre, 1820*, ed. F.C.W. Hiley, Paris, 1928. For the review see "An Englishman in Paris," *Times Literary Supplement*, 17 January 1929, p. 38.
6. *Some Limericks . . .* [Florence], 1928.
7. At the Vigie, Port-Cros.
8. Haden-Guest.
9. *Death of a Hero*.

49. To Brigit Patmore (Texas)

Weds. evening   Chope Latine. [Paris]
[19 December 1928]

My love, my beautiful, My Brigit—I have just discovered that nice Marcel Jouhandeau has written a book called "Brigitte, ou la Belle au Bois Dormant."[1] Alas, it is out of print, but I shall try to get a copy. Qui est cette belle qui ressemble si étrangement à mon amour?

Well, Louis having an appointment at 2:30, turned up at 5, bringing proofs of my Xmas poem[2] from Nancy[3] (not a mistake in it), but arrived

confusedly at the same moment as Ezra's friend, Bill Bird. Bill may be a
hell of a chap, for all I know, but he struck me as pretty or'nary. However, he took me up to the bar of the Café du Dôme (where my reputation fell to minus infinity because I utterly & fiercely refused to take
more than one drink!) and there met—Bob McAlmon. Well, Kid, he
strikes me as a bit of a rough-neck, kinder unkulchered, and a bit more
uster prairies an' cocktail bars than the West End—but ... The point
is—and this rather exciting—Darling, isn't it mean of me to keep you
waiting?—well, as I was saying,
    BOB SAYS

        THAT both H.D. & Bryher[4] want a divorce!?!!
        Does Darling believe it?

Bob says Bryher hates me so much she would like to cut off any
shadow of hold I have on Hilda; that they would have both had the divorce years ago, but they thought I'd be mean about the child (my
God!)[5] and he advises me to write to H.D., through Sylvia Beach, & ask
her (H.D.) to divorce me. Now I'm not going to do anything without
Darling's advice. What does she think? Hadn't I better see Haynes before
doing anything?
    Bob says: "Tell her (H.D.) you want to marry someone."
    I *wonder*? Perhaps better wait until Darling comes, & we can both see
Bob? At any rate, I shall say & do nothing until I hear from Darling.

Apropos, these "quarter" types here leave me a bit staggered, & feeling rather 1880. They seem to have killed all beauty, all poetry, all sen-
sibility, all feelings, all love, with drink, cynicism and unlimited
promiscuity! You ask what it is that Nancy misses—well, it's just *that*.
Only there is a fineness in her which rebels against this squalid sodden-
ness; her only hope is her misery. But these people up at the Dôme &
Coupole haven't even the grace to be miserable. Ah! Les *crapules*! I'll
take you up there to see them—it's an odd sensation. Why, Darling, you
and I have more happiness in one meal together than they get out of
months of intoxication & not remembering next morning who they
"went" with the night before!

I hope Darling had a peaceful day to-day (Weds.) This will reach her
Thursday evening, &, I hope, be a help. Sweet girl, don't let Stephen
bully & hurt you. That little flag, you know, it's so worth fighting for!
I mustn't interfere, must I? But I don't shirk, Brigit—remember, I'll
come to you by aeroplane whenever you care to wire me.

And bless your two wires to-day! How greedily I pounce on every word that comes from Darling! I feel that for the present at least your "brain-storm" is over. It must have been pretty bad, for I felt it heavily. I *can* feel your moods even from here, you know. But to-day Darling is happy, & so is her love.

And it'll all come right o' Sunday! You *see?* I wish I could kiss you here & now—I am so very happy through & in you. And, oh, for love's sake, don't let us get into this awful drinking—cynical—promiscuous Montparnasse life! It rather scares me. I value so much all the delicacies of love with you.

I am happy that you liked my love-toy calendar of hours. The columns are beginning to get black. Christmas will soon pass, & then life begin.

Ah! when I speak calmly of "twenty years," it is the calmness of despair that I have so little to offer you. Why, what are 20 years to speak one's love in? But have no fear—you shall be free. If I "lose" you, it will be my own fault.

Yes, you know the eternal things, and you have much to teach me. You see, I feel a kind of limitlessness, an unbounded horizon to us—I do not know what strange new beauties of living we may discover together. But I *feel* the sense of immense possibilities. How much we had in that brief fortnight![6] How much! But I feel there is so much to come, so much more.

To-day, I spoke to the Select again about our rooms: "Mais oui, monsieur, vous pouvez absolument y compter—deux chambres sur le même étage." You *see!*

How happy I was & am that you refused to allow yourself to be bullied out of our plans!

I may see Barney[7] on Friday; we'll go there together when you want. Do you "know" her, by the bye? I suppose I'll have to put up with her falling in love with Darling. O these frivolous strumpets—how they twead wecklessly on our hearts!

Sent you two more novels to-day, my sweet, but don't let them bother you. Only to show I remember. Have *piles* more for you here! But I want you to rest & amuse yourself for your first few weeks (ahem!) in Paris. *Then* you can work afterwards, if you want. Tell me either by wire or letter if you need more cash before leaving, & I'll send. Don't hesitate, & for love's sake, don't go without.

And tell me what you think about the McAlmon-H.D.-divorce business. Odd if we both had to appear in the same court!

I love you more deeply, more tenderly, more passionately, more affectionately every day; & life's going to be *good*, Sister!

Your own love,
Richard.

1. Paris, 1925.
2. *Hark the Herald*, Chapelle-Réanville, Eure, France, 1928.
3. *Hark the Herald* was the third publication issued by Nancy Cunard's Hours Press.
4. Bryher and McAlmon had been divorced in 1927, and she promptly married Kenneth Macpherson. That marriage, too, ended in divorce some years later.
5. The child, Perdita, was H.D.'s by Cecil Gray, not RA, although she was given the name Aldington. See Letter 22 and *passim*.
6. At Toulon, after leaving Port-Cros.
7. Natalie Barney.

III

NOVELIST-TRAVELER: 1929–1938. LETTERS 50–80

In his memoirs RA speaks of 1928 as "a year of activity and change, a watershed year which sent me moving in another direction." Not only did his personal life change at Port-Cros, but also while he was there he began to write the long book that had been simmering in his head since the war—the novel that was to become *Death of a Hero*. He had encouragement from Frieda Lawrence and Brigit but none from Lawrence, who told him to destroy what he had written if he wished to preserve what little reputation he had. Thrice before, RA had begun to write out the memories of his wartime experiences and the hatred and disgust he felt for an age and its people who could permit this holocaust to happen. He had begun his narrative in 1919 at Taintignies following the Armistice, but put it aside when he was demobilized the following February. In 1925 and 1927, he again took up the project only to realize he had made further false starts. This time, once he had written the first sentence, the beginning of the novel came quickly. He took a substantial piece of work to Paris with him that fall when he left Port-Cros, the Lawrences, and Arabella forever.

Back in Paris early in 1929 after having been chased to Italy by the cold and spending time in Rapallo with Pound and Yeats, RA met his American publisher Donald Friede to discuss various plans for books. When Freide asked about any other work he had done, RA gave him the unfinished manuscript of his war novel. A few days later Friede called from London expressing interest in the novel, offering an advance, and urging RA to finish it. This he did in May. When the novel was accepted, RA waited in Paris to correct proofs and then set off for the south of

France for the summer, finally settling in La Seyne near Toulon from July to September. While there he translated the *Alcestis* and wrote the short stories collected in *Roads to Glory,* which he considered "a kind of hangover from *Death of a Hero.*"

That September RA returned to Paris to await the British reception of the British edition of *Death of a Hero,* scheduled two weeks after the American edition, which was already being reprinted. The news from England was as good as from America, and that autumn in Paris RA, not yet forty, tasted the success most authors only dream of. The reception of his novel brought more than relief from financial worry, for RA made many new friends in and out of literary circles, and many new doors were open to him.

RA and Brigit Patmore now began a life of adventurous wandering that Lawrence had made sound so attractive when he visited Malthouse Cottage in 1926. Leaving Paris in the late autumn, RA first went to Rome and Naples and then stayed some time at Amalfi before going on to Palermo and Sorrento. He spent January and February of 1930 in Tunisia and Algeria. "Henry Davray gave me introductions to the governors of Tunis, Algeria, and Morocco."

During 1930 RA wrote his second novel, *The Colonel's Daughter,* while living on the French Riviera, in Venice, and in southern Italy. If RA had a permanent address in the 1930s, it was the Villa Koeclin, Le Canadel, Var, France. In *The Colonel's Daughter,* RA switched his satiric attack entirely to the home front, taking aim at the middle-class English villager. He felt this novel a natural sequel to his first since its heroine was not only frustrated by the society around her, but also left an old maid because the war had destroyed so many of the men of her generation.

From the French Riviera RA took long trips to Spain, Portugal, and Austria as well as to his favored Italy. He was in Florence when he began to write his third novel, which he later described as a "romantic idyll." Feeling the need to finish his romance in a proper setting, he retreated to Anacapri where he rented rooms in the same little restaurant where he had stayed in 1912. At Capri RA found things sadly changed from prewar days, and he welcomed the excuse of a telegram from Frere to leave Italy and return to the French Riviera, where he finished his novel, *All Men Are Enemies.*

In 1934, after he had completed the manuscript of a fourth novel, *Women Must Work,* which again attacked the society responsible for the conditions in England that had led to war, RA decided to visit Vienna and Budapest, partly in hope of collecting blocked royalty accruals on his work, which was by then being published in Hungary, Czechoslovakia, Poland, and Russia. He brought an American car from London to

Lisbon and spent two months in Portugal, Spain, and France before driving through Switzerland and crossing into Austria early in June. An automobile accident near Feldkirch in which his knee was broken prevented RA from reaching Hungary. He remained in Feldkirch until that September, part of the time in the local hospital and the rest in the hamlet of Fontanella.

When his leg had healed sufficiently for him to drive again, RA prepared to leave for France, intending to take a villa on the Riviera for the winter, but the increasingly unsettled conditions in Europe prompted him to return to London for the winter. On his way up the coast to London, RA stopped to see his old friends Hal and Etta Glover in Sussex. While there he slipped and broke his knee again. Another operation followed, and during his convalescence he had time to take up his writing. He finished some essays and his third long poem, *Life Quest*, an important poem to an understanding of RA since it so clearly expresses his idea of "life for life's sake," repeating the message of all his postwar poetry: love while there is time.

While RA was recovering from this second accident, his wanderlust returned. He had been in every province of Italy, France, Portugal, and Spain; knew Paris and Rome as well as London; and had seen Belgium, Switzerland, the Rhine, the Schwarzwald, Bavaria, and Austria; but he had not yet visited the New World, and he still felt the longing of the schoolboy looking at Calais from the cliffs of Dover. At first he considered Brazil and the Amazon, an adventure he had dreamed of since reading Bates's *The Naturalist on the Amazon* as a boy, but, instead, he decided to try Tobago and boarded a banana boat in February 1935 en route to Barbados and Trinidad.

In Tobago, RA found an old plantation house high above the island's beaches and overlooking a broad vista to the Caribbean. He remained there until May 1935, writing most of the essays collected in *Artifex* and selecting the anthology of Lawrence's prose that was published as *The Spirit of Place*. He soon "fell into the easy rhythm of life in the tropics varied only by excursions about the very beautiful island and bathing picnics," but, in the end, the same urge to work that had kept him from the café life in Paris ten years earlier drove him from his island paradise. He booked passage to New York.

Reaching New York, RA was met by his old friend and publisher Pascal Covici. He was able to rent a house on the Connecticut River at Old Lyme through the kindness of a reader of his books. Although RA would spend 1939 to 1946 in the United States and in 1940 said that he now considered it his "headquarters," he was not yet ready to stay there. He was back in London in October 1935, remaining until March. In April he was in Portugal and Spain, and by June had reached Austria, where he stayed until early September to complete the novel *Very Heaven*. RA was back at Le Lavandou the same month, driving from Austria via Switzerland, Alsace, and then up to Boulogne and right across France. In October he returned to London and in December sailed to New York on the S.S *Normandie*.

Like 1928, the year 1937 was an important one in RA's life. He had fallen in love with Brigit Patmore's daughter-in-law Netta, then Mrs. Michael Patmore. When he returned to London after his short trip to New York, the two left for Italy, where RA had traveled with H.D. in 1912 and with Arabella and Brigit in the 1920s. RA and Netta were in Le Canadel by April and stayed there until October; RA had finished his last long poem, *The Crystal World*, and was working on the novel *Seven Against Reeves*. *The Crystal World* was for Netta as *Love in the Luxembourg* had been for Brigit, many of the poems of *Images of Desire* for Arabella, and *Reverie* (among many others) for H.D.

As RA wrote Eric Warman, his honeymoon with Netta was "occasionally disturbed by legal rumbles from the divorce court." In the fall of 1937 RA had to go to London to attempt to resolve the matter of Netta's divorce; he had already asked and received H.D.'s consent to dissolve their marriage of almost twenty-five years. But RA's elopement with Netta had embittered Brigit and her son so that the legal problems with the Patmores were not easily settled, and Netta's divorce was not granted. By December, Netta and RA were back at the Villa Koeclin where they lived until May 1938.

After a visit to Switzerland, where they stayed at Pully, Lausanne, Netta and RA returned to London and were married on Saturday, 25 June 1938. "My daughter [Catherine] was born between 5 and 6 a.m. on 6th July, 1938, in Wigmore St., London." Netta's divorce had come through none too soon, and the settlement RA had made to obtain it would create problems for him in the future, but for now all was well. The new family spent the summer in a cottage in Liphook, Hants, returning to the Villa Koeclin in September.

50. To Glenn Hughes (Texas)

6 May 1929   Select.
Dear Glenn,

I got the cabled acceptance of Imagist anthology from New York at noon to-day.[1]

Have you got the address of William Carlos Williams? If you have, please give it to me, so's I can write him. I've asked Flint to write to Ford, and I guess H.D. would be the best person to write to Lawrence.[2]

Brigit has gone to London. Michael rather hastily chucked up his job in the City and has gotten another better one which he thinks he'll like better, at Maidstone.[3] He's got a couple of weeks vacation, and asked Brigit to come over and help him get fixed in his new quarters. I've just got back from seeing her off. She'll be back before the end of the month at latest.

When are you two coming to town?[4] I've nearly finished the novel, and would like you to take the MS and read it. Of course, let Bab read it, but don't show it anyone else. Friede cabled me to send a blurb about it, and I sent 500 words last week.[5]

Ever yours,
R.A.

P.S. Will you bring up the MS of your Imagist book, first part?[6] I'd like to see it, if you can spare it.

1. Taunted by Walter Lowenfels that the Imagists were hopelessly out of date, RA put together *Imagist Anthology, 1930: New Poetry of the Imagists*, New York, 1930.
2. Williams, Flint, Ford, and Lawrence contributed to *Imagist Anthology, 1930*.
3. Michael Patmore, Brigit's younger son.
4. The Hughes were staying in Saint-Cloud, a suburb of Paris.
5. *Death of a Hero*, New York, 1929.
6. *Imagism and the Imagists: A Study of Modern Poetry*, Stanford, 1931.

51. To Brigit Patmore (Texas)

Monday   Select.
[13 May 1929]
My adored Brigit,

I was happy to get your very sweet & generous telegram to-day. It was very dear of you to offer to return. But I want you to stay & do all you have to do.

After I finished the novel,[1] I sort of collapsed nervously.[2] I worked the last day from 10 to 2:30, and took it straight round to Walter's. Walter made me eat eggs & drink one of his infamous cocktails, & I felt better. But I was very nervous as you probably guessed. Everything became portentous—"you know"! But after a few days' rest I am perfectly O.K. and shall be *completely* all right. So please don't worry, and forgive me for getting into a "state." It wasn't *any* feeling about you—only the tiredness following the desperate effort to finish, and then staying up too late the night following. I'm drinking nothing & going to bed early.

Just had a wire from Prentice: "Last three chapters received hope wire decision tomorrow or Wednesday."

That looks *slightly* encouraging. If he hadn't liked the part he has read, he wouldn't have troubled to wire. I wrote him a "stampede" letter & it seems to have worked.

I got a good hunch this morning. Re-named "A Dream in the Luxembourg" as "Love and the Luxembourg; A Novel in Free Verse,"[3] and wrote an Introduction against over-subtle high-brow poetry—directed against Tom,[4] but not mentioning him. I took it around to Walter, & he thought it a first-class idea. Lilian[5] is going to type it at once, & I have written Friede about it. If Friede "sees" it, he can issue it soon after "Death of a Hero," and maybe "put over" my poems too. Walter says that there is a sudden revival in U.S. of the "story in verse," and that the poem is "just right." You know how shrewd he is! He got "terr'bly" excited about it.

After gassing to Walter, Lilian & I went out & bought me a new hat, & then walked along the quais. The Seine is most lovely now with the trees covered with fresh green leaves, & such warm spring sunlight. I wear no overcoat & no pull-over, & I am perfectly warm.

To-night I dine with Janet[6]—& it'll be good to see her. The women at Steve Green's party were awful hard boiled New Yorkers, drank like fish, and were unpleasant. We went to an awful hole call "The Palermo," filled with tarts. I left at 11:30—couldn't stand it.

My darling, I say again "don't worry" and again "forgive me if I worried you." I am *quite* all right. My life is filled with happiness because of you. It is Brigit & Brigit only who is the perfect lover, the perfect companion and the perfect woman. I am completely happy with you, dear, and want only you. There is nothing so lovely as you in the world. You mean all happy things to me now. So long as you are you I shall be happy. Our love delights me—I like the idea of us.

I must tell you what Mrs. Church said. "I'm so sorry Mrs. Patmore left to-day, since the luncheon was planned in her honour." She thinks you very lovely, and admires you greatly. Liked the way you "pass among all those Montparnasse people and they cannot touch her."

Lilian (!) asks me to send you her love. So did Nancy. N. & H. have gone back to Puits Carré.[7] They are going to Brussels & then back to Paris.

Brigit—can you feel how "Brigit" means all the beauty & tenderness and passion of life? Be happy, & when you return, you will find me waiting for you, & so happy to have you back again. Good-night, my adorable one.

Your
Richard

1. *Death of a Hero*. RA had completed the novel by 10 May 1929 and on the following day sent the last three chapters to Charles Prentice at Chatto & Windus.

2. Cf. RA to Brigit Patmore, 11 May 1929 (Texas), where he wrote, "I am rather 'all-overish' to-day, what with the emotions of the past weeks, the strain of working at the

novel, and staying up late." In the same letter RA recorded his "awful depression and physical illness" at the thought of being away from Brigit for three months owing to a suggestion from Donald Friede, his American publisher, that RA spend that time in America
lecturing and publicizing *Death of a Hero*.

3. See RA, *Love and the Luxembourg*, New York, 1930; limited to 475 numbered copies
signed by Frederic Warde, the book's designer, and RA. Cf. RA, *A Dream in the Luxembourg*, London, 1930. RA had been at work intermittently on the poem for some time.
Within the past year, he had sent extracts to Nancy Cunard with an unsigned, typed note,
designated as from RA in Nancy Cunard's hand: "This poem really exists and occupies
twenty-four closely typed sheets, or considerably more than a thousand lines. It was an
attempt to recapture for poetry some of the thunder filched from it by the novel. Either
because I worked over it too long, or for other reasons, I decided it was verbose and flabby.
Perhaps some day I may change my mind and publish it. Meanwhile, the extracts here given
may be thought sufficient evidence to warrant the suppression of the whole." Obviously
sent to Cunard for her literary evaluation, the extracts lack the introduction and differ in
several other ways from the published versions.

4. T. S. Eliot.

5. Walter and Lilian Lowenfels.

6. Janet Flanner.

7. Nancy Cunard and Henry Crowder.

52. To Babette and Glen Hughes (Texas)

7 August 1929   c/o Barclays Bank,
                                       33 Rue du Quatre Septembre, Paris.

Dear Bab and Glenn,

I should have written much sooner if I had known your address is still
Seattle. I sent you a telegram the night before you left asking for your
new address, but I guess you never got it.[1]

We hiked it from Paris the same day you left. I was beginning to feel
a bit restless. So we went to Chartres, which I liked very much indeed.
Then back in Paris again to see H.D., and left for La Rochelle. La
Rochelle is fun, Bab. There is a square built-in old harbour, with rows of
old houses, an avenue of clipped limes and a statue to an admiral. The
harbour narrows to about thirty yards wide, and is defended by two old
towers, including the famous Chain Tower of the siege. There are also
the Lantern Tower and the Clock Tower, both very beautiful late medieval. The streets in the town are flanked on both sides by arcades. But the
greatest fun is the colour and movement of the little port. The sail boats
are painted red and blue and yellow, with yellow and blue masts, and
red, brown and white sails, usually patched in some other colour. The
fishermen's nets are dyed bright blue and hang in festoons. The sailors
themselves wear blouses and pants (much patched) of blue or marron or
various shades of red, and sabots.[2] I bought myself a marron outfit for
70 francs, and wear the pants all the times—too hot for the blouse.

Then we went about ten miles south to a little place called Chatelail-lon Plage, from which we visited Rochefort, a rather dreary mushroom town artificially created by Colbert in 1660. There was a wide sand at Chatelaillon, but a casino and side-shows, and the Atlantic always makes disturbed weather. So once more we hit the trail—to Toulouse via Bor-deaux. The country there is as beautiful as South Italy, and you must cer-tainly make the trip when next in Europe. And such marvellous towns, mostly old Roman towns rebuilt in the middle ages. Carcassonne is a dream. I want to go back and see them properly. From Toulouse to Tou-lon, via Sète, Montpellier, Nîmes, Arles and Tarascon and Marseilles. Gee, how Roman all that country is, and the people are Roman looking. We had several days in Toulon, which I like more and more. There is an old harbour as well as new ones for the big modern ships. We stayed right in the center of the old part on the Quai de Crondstadt. Toulon harbour is a wonderful affair with all its wooded islands—looks exactly like a set of Hokusai prints at dawn.

I write this from a little bay called Fabregas, about ten miles from Tou-lon, a very quiet little place between two promontories covered with pines, while the valley is vineyards, olives, cypress, palms and tamarisks. All the eucalyptus trees were killed by that awful cold last year. We have rooms looking over the sea, and bathe twice a day. It is too hot for much walking, but I sometimes get up at dawn and walk along the cliff paths. The country west is very rugged and has no roads, only paths, for about ten miles. It is Cap Cicié, the only place left of the Riviera which isn't tourist haunted. We can see the Ile de Port-Cros far away to the south-east.[3] I hope to stay here for some weeks, and haven't formed any other plans, except vague ones which hover between Athens and New York. Maybe it'll be New York.

Many thanks for the Introduction, Glenn. It is excellent, and just what I wanted.[4] The usual difficulties have cropped up, of course! Joyce has bad eyes and Ezra refuses point blank to come in. However, Williams is dealing with Joyce, and tells me Ford promises some poems. Flint hasn't written anything, in spite of his enthusiasm when the anthology was first started. But I guess we'll get something done eventually. I've got good chunks of poems from Fletcher, Williams and H.D. I'm sorry Flint hasn't anything—if he could have produced even two good poems, it would have given us a chance to boost him.[5]

Any news of your Imagist book in N.Y., Glenn? And what of the nov-els, plays, stories, Bab? Friede cables me that preliminary copies of my novel are on the way to Europe, and that he is publishing on September 6th. Chattos will publish soon afterwards.[6] I think it was after you left that Friede wrote enthusiastically accepting a long poem, "Love and the

Luxembourg,"[7] which I was always going to show you, and didn't. Chattos will publish it in London "if the novel goes," which I doubt it will. I have finished the Nerval book[8] for the Aquila Press, and am now writing a book of short stories.[9] Prentice of Chattos likes them very well, and has promised to try to place some in London periodicals.[10] I am sending copies to Friede as I do them, but haven't had time to hear from him yet. That seems about all my "lit'ry" news, except that I'm working on the Alkestis now.[11] Brigit's novel is due out in N.Y. sometime in September,[12] and she's writing another book here.[13] It's supposed to be funny, but I'm not allowed to see it!

Let us have news of all you are doing. It was great seeing you in Paris, and I shall not forget our happy times together. Nancy and Henry have been to London, and were a GREAT SUCCESS!! Nancy is alleged to be taking a house in Craven St. The Lowenfels are in the country near Dieppe. Church has gone to Germany. Walter's book is out in London.[14] If he didn't send you a copy, I have an extra one I can send you. H.D. is in London. I don't know where Ezra is—he doesn't love me any more since the anthology.[15] I hear from Flint, Monro and Read. Herbert[16] dislikes my novel very much—which rather pleases me, for he seems to me to be getting a bit rigid in his judgments. Derek[17] is coming to see us here soon, and we hear of various people in neighboring villages whom I suppose we'll have to see. Lawrence's pictures in London were removed by the cops as obscene. Poor old England![18]

Here's all good luck to you, and our love to you both,

Richard

And greetings to Mary Anne![19]

1. Hughes received RA's telegram.
2. Cf. "La Rochelle," *Poetry: A Magazine of Verse*, May 1931, pp. 80–81.
3. See Letter 46.
4. See Glenn Hughes, "Foreword," in *Imagist Anthology 1930*, New York, 1930, pp. xvii–xviii.
5. Flint contributed a dramatic poem, "The Making of Lilith," pp. 97–114.
6. *Death of a Hero: A Novel*, New York, 1929.
7. See RA, *Love and the Luxembourg*, New York, 1930, and Letter 51 n. 3.
8. See Gerard de Nerval, *Aurelia*, trans. Richard Aldington, London, 1932.
9. See RA, *Roads to Glory*, London, 1930.
10. Not traced.
11. See *Alcestis*, trans. Richard Aldington, London, 1930.
12. See Brigit Patmore, *No Tomorrow*, New York, 1929.
13. No other "book" was published at this time.
14. See Walter Lowenfels, *Finale of Seem, A Lyrical Narrative*, London, 1929.
15. *Imagist Anthology, 1930*.
16. Herbert Read.
17. Derek Patmore, Brigit's elder son.

18. Thirteen of Lawrence's paintings were removed from the exhibition held at the Warren Galleries, and the exhibition closed.
19. See Letter 45 n. 14.

53. To H.D. (Yale)

10 January 1930   c/o Cooks
                                                   Tunis
                                                   Tunisie.

Dear Dooley,

I was very glad indeed to get your letter. I was wondering whether you were ill or had eloped!

Herewith some snapshots of Palermo and Agrigentum (Akragas). Sicily is a bit bleak in winter, but there were most lovely purple iris in the short grass. Italy is now rather foul. I went up to Anacapri, and drank some wine at the Pensione del Lauro. The Signorina Maria del Tommaso was still there, considerably increased in girth and with two large children. She did not recognise me. I thought very tenderly over old times.

Tunis is really fun. The French have left the old town quite untouched. Consequently, you live in (comparative) European comfort, while you can visit the souks[1] in the daytime. It is really very "picturesque," and I think you would love it. I have an introduction to the director of Tourisme here, and when we get tired of Tunis, I shall go to him, and get railway passes to the interior. I should like to go right into equatorial Africa, but I'm afraid there isn't time, since I have so many articles to do.

Yesterday I finished the translation of "Alkestis,"[2] and begin the "Medea"[3] soon. It is great fun.

Chattos are publishing the Imagist Anthology in England, and will pay us "accrued royalties" on publication. I don't suppose this will amount to much, but it will be something. I feel an unholy glee in that book. It will be: Mr and Mrs Aldington first, the rest also ran.[4] Prentice of Chattos was most enthusiastic about your contributions.

Of course, dear Dooley, I will always do anything I can to arrange for profitable publication of your work. Just tell me what you want, and I will try to do it. I am now "critic in chief" (don't laugh!) of the Sunday Referee,[5] and can be of some help there.

On second thoughts Tunis is no place for you! Those veils!

You'll be amused to know that the English printers Spottiswoode have refused to set up and print a poem of mine called "A Dream in the Luxembourg," which Chatto and Windus are publishing.[6] I really think some of England has gone puritan-mad. Chattos think it is a great joke, and say they will easily get someone else to print it.

"Death of a Hero" passed 10,000 in England before the end of December. Chattos are going to start a fresh advertising campaign this year. It is now being translated into French,[7] Swedish,[8], German,[9] Spanish,[10] and Russian.[11] It is also being serialised in England.[12]

I enclose a Tunisian beauty.[13]

With all love to you, dear Dooley,

Richard

1. Market places.
2. Euripides, *Alcestis*, trans. Richard Aldington, London, 1930. The first publication was part of Chatto & Windus's Dolphin Series.
3. Not published.
4. See Letter 50 n. 1.
5. RA began a series of weekly articles in the *Sunday Referee*, 24 November 1929. See C. J. Fox, "On the Line: Aldington of the *Referee*," *London Magazine*, December 1985/January 1986, pp. 72–81.
6. After producing two proof-copies, Eyre & Spottiswoode refused to proceed with the printing. T. and A. Constable at the University Press, Edinburgh, printed Chatto & Windus's first edition. See Letter 51 and *passim*.
7. 1931.
8. 1930.
9. 1930.
10. The earliest date given for a Spanish translation is 1946.
11. 1932.
12. Not traced.
13. Not with letter.

54. To Brigit Patmore (Texas)

Weds evening   [Paris]
[19 March 1930]

My beautiful love, my wife, my Soukie!

I had rather a broken day, chiefly, I think, because Walter came and worried me at the Voltaire[1] after lunch about that absurd award,[2] and interrupted my letter to you. I wish I had never done anything about the beastly Award. The very idea of it now bores me stiff. I went & saw Tom & talked "cultchah" with him, & he agreed with me that Walter is a bit dotty. I felt so furious with him for breaking in on my privacy.

I slept late, & so was very late getting to work on my story, but got something done. Among press-cuttings was a notice from Tit-Bits (!!!) announcing on the 29th "short stories by modern masters" including Alec Waugh, Arnold Bennett & R.A. I have written to Pinker to ask what this means. I hope it doesn't mean that Tit-Bits have acquired the right to reproduce Nash stories for nothing.[3]

My new story[4] is getting quite good, darling; I think perhaps it is better to do a little bit at a time.

I want to get enough work done to be able to take a holiday when I get to London. I have been reading more books for review, & hope to do 3 more Referee articles[5] before the end of the month.

A letter from Wyn[6] to-night about the proofs,[7] & a cable from Friede about those "limit pages"[8] which still have not arrived!

I am writing this in bed because I seem to need rest. I don't sleep very well, because I terribly miss our love-making and holding my lovely one in my arms afterwards. I have plenty to do & am quite cheerful, but I miss you dreadfully, especially at night. Sweetheart of mine!

I hope you had a good time with Michie[9] today, & a pleasant dinner when you got back. I dined alone, after Tom (who is still in bed)[10] had refused to let me send him in anything. He is pleasant, but has the conceit which seems inseparable from bachelors over 30. He hasn't learned that the only way to be happy, is to give oneself wholly to Brigit!

How much I love you! I simply live for you & for loving you. I don't know that life would have much interest for me without you.

I have a row of four Soukies on the mantlepiece. It is comforting to look at my beautiful love.

I hope you can read this dreadful script!

Sweetie girl, I long for you day & night, & live for the hour when I shall hold your lovely body naked in my arms again and be joined to you in the lovely ecstasy. I want you so much.

Good night, my beauty. Don't worry. I am all right & quite content— cold better—but it will be good to have you again.

Your husband,
Richard

1. Restaurant Voltaire at 1 Place de l'Odéon.
2. An award established in 1929 with proceeds from *Death of a Hero*. RA's plan was to make an award of 2500 francs each year for at least three years to an American poet whose work had appeared during the year prior to the award in *This Quarter*, a review published in Paris by Edward Titus. Early in 1930 the value of the prize was raised to 10,000 francs, thanks to outside support that RA had secured. Walter Lowenfels was determined to receive the award. Cf. RA to Brigit Patmore, 21 [March 1930] (Texas): "I was just in the most important scene of my new story, when in comes a tragic Lilian [Lowenfels]—'I *must* see you.' Then amid tears & protestations came out the most amazing piece of Jew American blackmail I have ever heard of! Briefly: Walter feels I have 'betrayed' him, he also feels it is now 'dishonourable' for other poets to be sending in poems when the award is already made & so—he proposes this afternoon to collect the American journalists & announce the Award himself & thus expose my machinations!!

My answer was: 'Publish & be damned—I shall immediately deny & prosecute.' "

Meanwhile *This Quarter* designated E. E. Cummings as the winner. RA called him an "unimpeachable" choice but insisted that Lowenfels share in the prize because his poetry "excluded" emotion and consisted "in an imaginative treatment of entirely intellectual material." *This Quarter* denied RA's right to name Lowenfels but at last agreed to the division of the prize between Cummings and Lowenfels when the award was made in September 1931. No subsequent award was made.

3. Through March 1930, *Nash's Pall-Mall Magazine* had published three of RA's writings: "Meditation on a German Grave" [story], January 1930, pp. 10–13, 82–88;"Victory" [article], February 1930, pp. 26–29; and "Killed in Action" [story], March 1930, pp. 42–45. Subsequently, two articles, two stories, and a poem appeared in the April, June, July, August, and September issues. See "Killed in Action," *Tit-Bits*, 29 March 1930, pp. 102–4; this was the only short story by RA traced in *Tit-Bits*.

4. Possibly *At All Costs*, London, 1930, or *Stepping Heavenward, A Record*, Florence, 1931.

5. See Letter 53 n. 5.

6. Wyn Henderson, by that time associated with Nancy Cunard's Hours Press.

7. For *Last Straws*, Paris, 1930.

8. For *Love and the Luxembourg*.

9. Michael Patmore.

10. McGreevy, who changed the spelling of his name to MacGreevy in later years. Cf. RA to BP [18 March 1930] (Texas), where RA tells of going to see McGreevy and finding him "almost comically distressed having had a 'seizure,' and commending his spirit to our Lord. [Samuel] Beckett devotedly went & got hot tea in bottles for him, & we made him comfortable."

55. To Brigit Patmore (Texas)

30 March 1930   Voltaire [Paris]

My own lovely Soukie/

This morning I was lying awake after coffee & thinking of you. Darling, I wonder if it is really not possible for us to marry?[1] I think Hilda[2] would have to consent, after all she said & wrote. Could you see Tony,[3] and find out from him if anything could be done about Deighton?[4] You could convey to D. that all expenses would be paid, & that he would be relieved of all future liability about you. After all, we are really married, Soukie dear. I mean that we love, not only as lovers, but as lovers who want to spend their lives together. Don't you feel we ought to be married? The point is—I won't get divorced from Hilda unless you'll marry me. Not that I want *her* in any way, but because of the damned annoyance of other women! I love you so much that I resent other women trying to flirt with me—which is perhaps puritan but a feeling I can't get over.

Good news from little Prentice! 300 signed copies of Luxembourg sold. Subscriptions so good that they have bound all the first impression of 1500, and ordered a second impression of 1000.[5] A second impression of a poem before publication is almost unique in England since I've known it. I know you and Derek will be pleased. If this reaches you before you lunch with Prentice, could you—if opportunity offers—try to find out how he is advertising the book? He ought to advertise:

---

300 Signed Copies at 15/-. (Sold Out.)
First impression nearly exhausted.
   Second impression Printing.

I will write him about it to-day. But it really is good news, don't you think?

I have written to Benét, making alternative appointments. I have lunch & dinner appointments to-morrow.

Walter came round this morning & made quite humble apologies.[6] Norman Douglas has sent him £25, & Frere some money, too, so he feels better about things.

Apropos, did I tell you Titus offered me £100 for a long-short story?[7] What a pity it is that I have no real talent for fiction.

Soukie dear, I have been sort of crazy without you. I didn't know that a woman could mean all life, as you mean to me. It is lucky that you love to be loved, otherwise you might get tired! Everything I can give you shall be yours. I often think that I really live *positively*, only for you. You are my life and my happiness, my beauty and my desire. We shall be very, very happy together, because I know you love me, and I know I love you. And that is happiness—to love more and more the person who loves you. Do you remember how you once reproved me for writing to you about 16 months ago that we had twenty years of happiness at least before us?[8] Do you still feel so reproving? I don't doubt that we have. O my Brigit, in love one wants to mortgage everything, every possibility, for the beloved.

And, don't mind my saying this. If you have some passing "pash" for someone else, but still feel you love me best & want to live with me— don't tell me. I have to admit—very humbly & regretfully—that I should be hurt if I knew, though I should love you just as much. (I can't help loving you.) This is *not* an indication of "suspicion," but a precaution. At first, I thought it wouldn't matter, but now when I examine my feelings in solitude, I see it should. So—feel utterly free, but don't tell me! Only if you want to go away for always, you must tell.

This is rather gloomy! Not really, for I don't & can't believe that you would want anyone else.

Your telegram came in with my coffee this morning, and was such a sweet "good morning, phillipschen"[9]—is that how it's spelled? It was sweet of you to send it, because a day without word from you is a blank day.

Sweetie, it is almost too lovely to think of having you in my arms again. That will be indescribable happiness. Do you know what Frere said in his last letter? "Brigit was looking very lovely to-day." And I saw you, looking happy and well and gay, and felt such a warm feeling of love for you, and so much pride that I had done something towards making you "look lovely." You know how one sometimes looks at one's love and the beauty of it all makes you catch your breath? Often I look at you and think—how lovely she is, my God, how lovely! To parody the famous Bishop—doubtless God could have made a better woman, but doubtless God never did![10]

Lovely one, there are only 3 more complete days! To-morrow I shall buy my ticket and that will be a comfort! The most impatient part of all will be the journey. Don't bother to come to the station, my loved one. But let us dine together on Thursday evening. I will ring you up from the hotel, or else come round to Millman Street after I have washed. I will write you to-morrow which way I am coming.

I want to go on talking to you, but, loveliest, I must go & finish an article, & I don't want to weary you. I adore you, wife of my flesh and life,

Your husband.

P.S. Did you see the announcement of Brigit Patmore's "Marmontel" in the Times Lit. Supp.?[11]

1. Brigit Patmore agreed at this time to marry RA despite reservations owing to her age and current state of health. Cf. RA to BP [1 April 1930] (Texas). Brigit and Richard never married, however, because her husband Deighton would not permit a divorce.

2. Hilda Doolittle (H.D.), married to RA since 1913. They were divorced in 1938. See the *Petitioner's Statement* In the High Court of Justice Probate Divorce & Admiralty Division Between Hilda Aldington Petitioner and Edward Godfree [Richard] Aldington Respondent (Yale).

3. P.A.G. Aldington, RA's younger brother, who practiced law.

4. Patmore.

5. The book published by Covici, Friede in America as *Love and the Luxembourg*, 1930, appeared in England the same year with Chatto & Windus's imprint as *A Dream in the Luxembourg*. One attempt at English publication failed when the printers refused to proceed owing to the supposed indecency of the book. The publishers eventually prevailed and brought out a special edition of 308 copies (300 for sale) plus an ordinary edition of an unknown number. See Letter 51 n. 3.

6. For his determined effort to secure RA's literary prize offered through *This Quarter;* see Letter 54 n. 2.

7. Titus published nothing by RA.

8. RA rebutted Brigit's awareness of her seniority more than once. See, for example, RA to Brigit Patmore [1 April 1930] (Texas) where he wrote: "[I]f you are ill, who should tend you but the husband who loves all your body so tenderly? And as to age—first, the War blokes like me and Tom & Frere, are pretty 'battered' (!) to start with: then, a man gets old

sexually much sooner than a woman." His first wife, H.D., was four years younger than Brigit, and six years older than RA.

9. Possibly a private endearment.

10. Cf. Isaac Walton, *The Compleat Angler,* Oxford, 1915, part 1, chap. 5, p. 120, where William Butler is quoted as saying of strawberries: "Doubtless God could have made a better berry, but doubtless God never did."

11. Jean François Marmontel, *Memoirs of Marmontel,* trans. Brigit Patmore, London, 1930.

56. To H.D. (Yale)

2 May 1930   14 Rue des Ursulines,
                                                             Paris, France.

Very glad to have news from you again, dear Dooley. I have been intending to write daily, but life has been a scramble. Early in April I went over to England to arrange some contracts and got involved in all kinds of parties and invitations. Among other people saw Malcolm Hilbery (you remember him?) who is now a K.C., and Recorder of Margate. Then returned to Paris and took this small furnished flat. It has only three rooms, but they are sunny, and there is a bath.

Ezra[1] is here. We dined with him and Olga[2] the other night, and he was very sweet and charming. I wish so much that you also were in Paris. In fact, why aren't you? I suppose Territet is very lovely just now— Versailles last Monday was very nearly perfect. It is unlucky that one can't be everywhere during the three perfect months.

Who do you think is coming to tea to-day? Harriet Weaver! I ran across her in Sylvia Beach's shop. She looks exactly as of old, and was altogether nice. We shall speak of you to-day.

Under separate cover I am sending you a "Heldentod"[3] and an "Imagist Anthology."[4] I must apologise for the printer's errors in this American edition—they omitted sending proofs. The English edition, which I have carefully corrected myself, will be out about the end of this month. Chatto's are publishing at 6/–, and will probably do much better with the book than Friede. His first edition is only 1000 and priced too high. He should have made it 2500 at 1.50. Chatto will tell me the subscription sales on publication day, and I'll send them along to you. The Luxembourg was 1215, and is now past 1500. I think they should do even better with the Anthology.

I hope you will like my pamphlet on Lawrence,[5] which should be out this month too. On my suggestion, Chattos have arranged for two large window displays in Nottingham.[6] I think Nottingham might wake up to the fact that Lorenzo is the greatest honour that ever happened to it. The English press was foul about him. I did my little best with a couple of very "pro" articles and the pamphlet mentioned, and I see Arnold Bennett has come out very strong for him. But in general the attitude is lamentable. The English are senile adolescents.

I haven't written to Frieda,[7] though I should like to; but I expect she is much occupied. Did you know that Barbey[8] is ill? They are both at Vence, I believe. Herbert Read, who has just been there, is passing back through Paris, and I hope to get news of Frieda from him.

Nancy has been at Chapelle-Réanville, "doin' de doors" with Henry, she says. Returns to-day, and I lunch with her on Saturday. She is a lovely creature, and I think grows more beautiful. She says she hates Paris, but I notice she stays on! Henry has a brand new car, and the last time I saw them they each had a little bow tie of different colours but the same pattern.

We haven't done much in the way of Bacchanals. These night excursions are trying to the health, and I have a lot of work to do these days. So much, in fact, that I am a bit scared at what I have undertaken. London was pleasant in a way, but cold and gloomy, and I wasn't sorry to get away.

I hope all is well with you. Do tell me about the film.[9] We saw Le Diable Blanc, which was illustrated in Close-Up,[10] and like it very much. That Russo-German combination is good.

Brigit joins with me in love,

Richard

1. Pound.
2. Olga Rudge.
3. The German edition of *Death of a Hero*, translated by Dagobert von Mikusch and published by Paul List Verlag.
4. See Letter 50 n. 1.
5. *D. H. Lawrence*, London, 1930. This essay is a revision of *D. H. Lawrence: An Indiscretion* (1927), and the basis for *D. H. Lawrence: An Appreciation* (1950).
6. D. H. Lawrence's birthplace was Eastwood, a village less than nine miles from Nottingham.
7. Lawrence.
8. Barbara Weekley Barr.
9. Possibly *Borderline*, in which H.D. played a prominent part opposite Paul Robeson. The film was directed by Bryher's second husband, Kenneth Macpherson.
10. Film review published by Bryher and Macpherson.

57. To A. S. Frere* (privately held)

24 November 1930   c/o Barclays Bank,
                                                                Paris.

Dear Frere,

Tetelestai, as Jesus said, it is finished. In other words I wrote The End to Georgie just before dinner, and this is the first letter I have written since. I must also drop a note to Charles[1] to tell him the "gel" (as Alvina would say) is entirely at his disposition. Mr. Judd is silent for ever,

Purfleet has burbled his last, the Colonel is dead and buried (and they didn't even blow the last post over him), Coz has B.Oed, the last lover (Geoffrey) has done a bunk with Margy, and Georgie has biked her last trip. So there we are. I don't know if Charles will forgive me for two episodes he hasn't seen, (1) where Georgie is offered a rape by a cocktail-blottoed gent, and (2) where she discovers the Colonel's French letters and bawdy books after he's dead. Afraid to burn the latter, in case Alvina finds suspicious ashes and denounces her to the executors, Georgie makes a large parcel of them, and writes on it: "Strictly Private. To be destroyed unopened after my death. Georgina Smithers." Could filial piety go further?

I feel a little melancholy. Would God you were here to on the blind withal.

Lecce is quite a bon little hole, but as soon as MS of Georgie is finally revised and posted to her fiancé,[2] I think we shall push off somewhere. First, though, I want to explore some villages near here, said to contain the only uncontaminated descendents of the Byzantine Greeks. Then I suppose one ought to take a look at Otranto. After that, I think perhaps Taormina might be pleasant. I don't know. Or Corfu. Anyhow, write to Barclays—I wire them of any change of address.

Nelson Doubleday sent me his revised wrapper,[3] which arrived yesterday. It is pretty bloody, but I shan't bother about it, for the simple reason that now it would delay the publication of Roads. But we must get something better for next time. I shall write him at length to-morrow, and try to make all pleasant and serene. The wrapper really doesn't matter in this case. We must meet before Georgie goes over the top in U.S., and try to think up some stunt for a cover.

About old Tom.[4] He got a hell of a kick out of Venice, and went off full of beans and good intentions. One idea is to get him the offer of a sort of second leader on the Referee. Charles has seen Pinker about this, and Pinker has sounded Hayter Preston, who is interested but unable to do anything definite. It appears that the Ref is re-organising and (?) trying to raise more capital. At all events, so far as I am concerned, the present contract is renewed for two months only, to give the Referee people time to make their new arrangements. After that, they've got to come up to the new terms or I shall be looking for a job elsewhere. Pinker says 600 is by no means too much to ask, and I suppose he knows. For Tom, this reorganisation may be a good thing, because Preston may be able to work him in. I have sent a letter cracking up Tom's abilities which can be showed as a testimonial if required. I think Tom is determined to get away from his present scratch as scratch can existence, but we shall have to keep him up to it. It seems to me that he must see it's better to make

8 pounds a week on three days a week journalism, than 4 pounds a week on six days a week translating of bilge. He'll be in a better position when Charles publishes that essay[5] of his. Which will be in January.

Thanks very much for the books you have sent me. You know I'll always use any I can for Referee articles.

Poor Eliot! Cambridge made him—Cambridge will kill him with much cherishing. The first straws are already blowing in the wind. I prophecy that in a year, the reaction will have set in full speed, and by 1933 we shall be defending him again!

Au revoir, and keep the pennon of C.L.S.[6] flying.

Always yours,

Richard

*A. S. Frere (1892–1984) was with William Heinemann Ltd for almost forty years and was chairman from 1945 to 1961. Frere, whose name was originally Frere-Reeves, like RA, fought in World War I. He was at Gallipoli in 1915 and with the Royal Flying Corps in 1916. When Charles Prentice retired from Chatto & Windus, RA, as he says in *Life for Life's Sake*, "transferred lock, stock, and barrel to Heinemann's," since he considered Frere "the only man in England" who for him could take Prentice's place. Frere attracted authors to his publishing house; indeed, many became his personal friends—RA was best man at his wedding. RA's 1938 novel, *Seven Against Reeves*, was dedicated to "Pat," Frere's wife. RA also dedicated his 1930 collection of war stories, *Roads to Glory*, "To Frere." In an interview with C. J. Fox a few months before his death at age 91, Frere spoke of the famous authors for whom he had served as editor, "But Aldington," he said, "He was my closest friend." (See also the Annotated Index.)

1. Charles Prentice of Chatto & Windus, RA's publisher at this time. The references that follow are to characters in RA's second novel, *The Colonel's Daughter*, London, 1931. "B.Oed" could mean "buggered off" or "ran away" as Coz did at the end of the novel.

2. Probably a joking reference to Prentice.

3. For the U.S. edition of *Roads of Glory*, New York, 1930.

4. McGreevy.

5. See Letter 58 n. 10.

6. The Canterbury Literary Society, RA's mock society whose purpose was to accept in membership "someone who had been refused membership of an English Literary Society." Today's New Canterbury Literary Society is an association of individuals interested in Aldington and his work.

58. To H.D. (Yale)

16 December 1930   c/o Cooks
                                                         Via Tornabuoni
                                                         Florence.

Dear Dooley,

The letter you speak of must have gone astray, for I should certainly have answered it. But it is not extraordinary considering how we have moved about. Lecce[1] was very charming—such classical Baroque and such gaiety of fancy in the decoration. But it was too remote and, in a way, savage. We went to Rome, and saw Storer, who is still a journalist, but fairly prosperous. Then came on here. Pino Orioli found us a lovely apartment on the Lungarno, just midway between the Trinita and Ponte Vecchio. It is quite a huge suite, complete with bath, and I feel as pleased as punch (or Michael Arlen) as I look down on the Arno and up to San Miniato, having always previously lived in back courts in Florence.

The only drawback is that so many people ask us out, and we want time to write and look at things. I wish one could arrange never to see anybody before five. There is really quite a lot of music here! On Sunday we went to a symphony concert at the Politeama—good orchestra, but rather tasteless audience. Yesterday we heard Thibaud, having joined the Florentine Music Society for the season. They hold their concerts in the Sala Bianca of the Pitti, not a very beautiful room, but excellent for chamber music. To-night Pino[2] is taking us to the opera, Bellini's Son-nambula; and to-morrow night we go to Casals. If that doesn't sound both "gay" and highbrow, what could? You must remember that Lecce has nothing but ancient ancient movies and Sicilian dialect comedies.

Apropos movies, I was very happy to have your essay on Borderline.[3] I think you are right to take your own line entirely, because a new art obviously needs a new form of criticism, a new technique of exposition. Do let us know of any good new films. In Rome we saw an Italian film called "Nerone," a talkie. Part of it quelconque, but the clowning was very amusing in its way—an attempt at acting, and excellent speaking. There was none of the dreadful slow tempo which I hate so much, and which ruins most of the talkies for me.

I forget if I had finished the new novel when I wrote you from Lecce.[4] At any rate, it *is* finished, and the English publishers say they are de-lighted with it. At present, I want to forget about it, for it won't appear until September, and writing a long book with a good many characters is rather a strain. Now, apart from my weekly article,[5] I am not doing anything, except work leisurely at some short stories[6] of a slightly satir-ical or farcical kind. I hope so much that you will keep in touch with Prentice. Under a very shy, almost hold-you-off exterior, he has one of the sweetest natures I have ever known, and quite a flaming enthusiasm for literature. At the same time, a remarkably good business man, who has made Chattos a very sound firm financially. He is doing amazingly well with the Dolphins. I was absolutely surprised when he told me the sales of the first week. Even poor old Alcestis has been bought.[7] I hope and believe that they will extend the series considerably, though without rushing.

Brigit is working hard at something,[8] I don't know what. But for so long she had to creep away into corners to write that she is very shy about it—so I don't say nuffin. However, I observe the exercise books are increasing in number. I hope it's another novel.

I didn't give her your messages, because I wasn't sure how she'd feel about it. For one thing, I was afraid I'd put it clumsily. Perhaps the best thing would be for you to write to her—some time, any time you feel like writing. I can't tell you anything about the other novel,[9] because she begged me not to read it. She is most terribly sensitive about people she cares for seeing what she writes—almost a malady. Perhaps best to say nothing whatever about it. I feel so very sorry that things are not quite "right" between you two.

I am asking Chattos to send you a copy of a Dolphin written by a friend of ours, called Thomas McGreevy—to be published in January.[10] McGreevy is a great dear, one of those charming "Oirish" with an infinite capacity for generous friendship and no common sense about practical affairs. I shall be interested to know what you think of his little book.

Pino has just come to take us out.

With love,
Richard

1. RA, with Brigit Patmore, had been at Lecce in November, having come by boat to Brindisi after five weeks in Venice.
2. Pino Orioli.
3. Not traced. For *Borderline*, see Letter 56 n. 9.
4. On 1 December 1930 (Yale); RA, *The Colonel's Daughter*, London, 1931; see Letter 57.
5. For *Sunday Referee*, commencing 24 November 1929, p. 6., with "A Critical Attitude." See Letter 53 n. 5.
6. *Soft Answers*, London, 1932.
7. Dolphin number 2; see Letter 53 n. 2.
8. Not traced.
9. Brigit Patmore, *No Tomorrow*, London, 1929.
10. *Thomas Stearns Eliot: A Study*, London, 1931; published as the fourth Dolphin.

59. To Brigit Patmore (Texas)

9 February, 1931   Firenze [Italy]
Darling sweetheart love,

I was so happy to find your telegram here when I got back from lunch at Pino's flat. You have been away only 5 days, and it seems like 5 years. However, the days do pass, and you will come back. But don't stay away too long!

Letters from Charles & Tom to-day. I enclose Tom's. Instead of sending him the ticket, I sent him a small cheque, and told him to come here or go to Kerry, as he liked.[1] It is absurd for him to hang about in Paris.

If he came here and learned a little Italian, Pino would give him at least 10,000 lire to translate the Lasca stories[2] which Lorenzo didn't finish.[3] Tom hasn't yet learned that you must take certain risks in life if you want to be happy. Il est vraiment un peu trop paysan. However, I think & hope my letter will stir him to action.

That stupid Nancy sent more propaganda about her silly communist film[4] to Norman & Pino & me. Norman has written to her, on behalf of us all, to say she must *not* send any more to Italy, because it might get people into trouble. Still not a word from her about my story[5] and not a penny of money. Ah! les sales riches! How foully *dishonest!* She goes & spends on niggers & saphs the money she owes me. To hell with her. I'm finished as far as she's concerned. When I get my cheque from her—fini, mais fini. Rotten little beast.[6]

I got a book with a brief note from Louise[7] to-day. She said you had reached London, but had not yet seen you. Purdom and Morrow have got flu! Do be careful, sweetheart, I should be desolated if you got ill.

There is still tramontana here, but not cold. As I went along the Lungarno about noon, there was real warmth in the sun, and the light from the windows in Pino's flat was wonderful. He is very pleased by the way you corrected Lorenzo's proofs,[8] keeps saying "how good was Brigitina." I have your Lorenzo *capretto* here, by the way.

Pino showed me three senseless letters from Frieda. Really, she is idiotic. Wants Pino to go & see the T[9] at Savona, and arrange for them to go to the ranch. Also says she had "an adventure in the train" with a young French soldier, and that she loves Frere! As Pino says, "She is a nymphomaniac." All this mixed up with laments for Lorenzo and business about the estate,[10] Philip Morrell, Pollinger and what-not. Che roba! Fortunately, Pino & Tussell put M.M.[11] off—he was after the money! *Zum!*[12]

Both Charles and Pinker write that it is O.K. about Georgie[13]— Charles is to publish in April & Doubleday in September, as first arranged. This is rather fun, since we get the excitement twice.

As soon as I hear from Charles that Pino may do Cibber,[14] I want Sukie to get a new hat, shoes, and any other clothes she wants. I will write or wire you. As soon as I get the £300, I want you to get all you need.

Don't get worried about me driving the car. I shall be very careful, and feel quite confident. My papers still haven't come from Rome.

I hope you are well and happy. Remember, there is nothing to worry about.

Your own love,
Richard

1. McGreevy returned to Florence.

. 2. A collection of twenty-two mostly comic novellas.

3. See *The Story of Doctor Manente, Being the Tenth and Last Story from the Suppers of A. F. Grazzini Called il Lasca,* trans. and intro. D. H. Lawrence, Florence, 1929. This was the first volume in Orioli's Lungarno series.

4. *L'Age d'Or,* a surrealist film.

5. *Last Straws,* Paris, 1930, issued in January 1931.

6. Nancy Cunard and RA were not as close friends as they had been when both lived in Paris, and in March RA complained to the Authors' Society about her. The breach between them widened when he disparaged Norman Douglas in *Pinorman* (1954) but Nancy remained loyal to Douglas, a friend of long standing. When she was invited to contribute to a memorial volume for RA after his death, she declined.

7. Louise Morgan Theis (Mrs. Otto).

8. For Lawrence's *Apocalypse,* published in June 1931. Lawrence had died on 2 March 1930.

9. Ravagli. The "T" refers to his rank, "tenente" in Italian.

10. D. H. Lawrence's will could not be found, and his family, especially an older brother, demanded a share of his estate. It was considerably larger than Frieda had realized.

11. Middleton Murry; see Letter 61.

12. RA frequently imitated the speaking habits of others in his letters, nowhere so playfully as with Pino. *Zum!* Pah! "ve radiate her!" and "I go against" all derive from Pino's English (his second language). Similarly, "What next!" "My dear, and "Pouf, my dear" parody Norman Douglas.

13. See *The Colonel's Daughter,* London, 1931; Garden City, New York, 1931.

14. Chief character, a caricature of T. S. Eliot, of *Stepping Heavenward: A Record,* Florence, 1931. Orioli published 808 numbered and signed copies (800 for sale) as no. 7 in his Lungarno Series. See also *Stepping Heavenward: A Record,* London, 1931, a Chatto & Windus Dolphin Series book.

60. To H.D. (Yale)

17 August 1931   Villa Koeclin,
                                                          Le Canadel,
                                                          Var, France.

Dear Dooley,

I have just finished the fourth long story for my next book,[1] and have come up to the surface for a short breather. You know how it is when you are possessed with a piece of work—how impossible it is to think of anything else. I have hardly written to anyone, except Charles Prentice. In the midst of it all, I got unwell—nothing serious, but enough to put me back three weeks. I only got back to schedule yesterday.

My God, how difficult it is to write! I've done about 50,000 words this summer, and most of them seem rot. I've one more story to do to complete the plan of the book, and then I hope to start another novel, which I think suits me better than stories. The Colonel's Daughter still plods on, in spite of bans, and slumps and financial panics, and what not. Nearly 9000.

I enclose a circular about the small book which Pino put forth recently. It is rather expensive, so don't get it; I will see that Chattos send you a copy in November,[2] and I'm asking them to send you next month another McGreevy essay.[3] The subject is not worthy of him, but he says some good things on the way.

Life here is very quiet, so there is little to report, except bathings and visits and small excursions in the Ford. We went to see Elizabeth, who now inhabits a Cannes garden,[4] and Noel Coward, whom I liked far more than I expected. There is a vein, a genuine vein of humanity in him.

When is the book of poems coming out with Chattos?[5] I haven't seen their autumn list yet, but I hope you are in it. I think you will do very well with it.

I have just finished re-reading Herodotus, and am now on the Iliad. A slightly militarist poem, but otherwise what the reviewers call a notable achievement.

A few days ago I had a card from Norman, who is in Austria. I re-read South Wind[6] when I was ill, and thought it good piece of work. It was a great feat of the imagination to reconstruct Capri so clearly in Bournemouth.

Let me hear from you some time, when you have a few minutes to spare. What are you writing?

Love from
Richard

1. *Soft Answers*, London, 1932; the story may be "Now Lies She There."
2. *Stepping Heavenward: A Record*, Florence, 1931; Chatto & Windus issued the book as a Dolphin, also in 1931.
3. *Richard Aldington: An Englishman*, London, 1931, Dolphin no. 10.
4. Elizabeth Mary Annette, Countess Russell; see *Elizabeth and Her German Garden*, London, 1898.
5. H. D. *Red Roses for Bronze*, London, 1931. The title poem was published in New York in 1929.
6. 1917.

61. To A. S. Frere (privately held)

Monday
[25 January or 1 February 1932]   Florence [Italy]
Dear Frere,

I feel you ought to be au courant with the Frieda situation, for it does rather involve you. If I'm being a busybody, God forgive me, for I only want to see all quiet on that particular front.

Frieda is in a curious state, and both Pino and I are afraid she will commit some unspeakable folly. F. and the T.[1] came back from the ranch, on receipt of an Italian W.O. telegram forwarded by his wife. The T. is now with his regiment, but writing to F. that he cannot possibly stay there—wants to resign and go back to ranch. That involves F. in responsibility for him, his wife and 3 children.

This is bad enough, but there is a worse possibility. Pino has discovered that J.M.M.[2] (!!!) has been writing smarmy letters to her at the ranch, and that there is a serious possibility (if the T. fails) that F. will go off with Murry. It sounds inconceivable, but remember Shakespeare's Richard III. This would be the crowning cap to Murry's vengeance on Lorenzo. Pino has told her: "If you do that, I vill never more talk to you, none of Lorenzo's friends vill talk to you, and" (comble d'horreur!) "I vill never publish anozer vurd of Lorenzo—prrum, I send zem all to Pollinger."

Frieda is a bit barmy, thinks everyone is in love with her, and that she must make men of us all. I have a sinister feeling that she would thrust greatness upon you.

Further, she denies utterly having signed any agreement assigning L's unpublished MSS to Secker. She vows that only the Letters agreement with you, and Apocalypse and Short Stories[3] with Secker have been signed. She has torn up all other agreements without signing, as Pollinger has sent them. What is one to believe.

Further, George[4] has not carried out his undertaking to pay royalties to Frieda. She says that when she came to leave the ranch, she found nothing had been paid into her account and that Pollinger threatened George with a writ and got £1500 from him. F. is on the warpath against George, and coming to London to start a legal action against him.

Was there ever such a bloody mess?

I have told Pino that I see only three possible courses of action

(1) Throw Frieda in the Arno,

(2) Frighten Murry with threats of physical violence;

(3) Discover another man for Frieda.

Must we be Frieda's pimps to save Lorenzo's fame?

So far this is what I have done:

I have advised Frieda that she should not confide her love affairs to Maria,[5] but keep them within the bounds of the C.L.S.[6]

I have advised strongly against the law suit with George, and urged that he made the renunciation in front of three witnesses, and that therefore he cannot go back on it.

I have pointed out that a law suit with George would be mad, that every possible bit of mud would be thrown at Lorenzo and herself, and she would most probably lose everything.

Officially I know nothing about Murry, but in conversation I have pointed out that he has the envy of the frustrated creator, the anger of the ex-friend lampooned, that he is a carrier of consumption and a necrophile.

As a choice of evils, it is better, that she should squander L's money rather than smirch his fame, for if she goes to M. it is a public acknowledgement that his book[7] is true—which is exactly what M. is playing for. Plus, I suppose, the money. God help us, as Tom says.

So long as she is here, Pino, Norman and I have some control over her, but she'll begin to suspect us of being in league with Pollinger or something soon. I have told her that she should quit writing mad letters to George and Pollinger, and do nothing in London without consulting Michelino[8] and you.

I understand that there are roughly 5,000,000,000 males on this planet. It is annoying of Frieda to get involved with the only one who ought to be absolutely taboo.

The sensible solution of the money problem seems to me this. That £10,000 of the Lawrence estate should be formed into a trustee fund, the interest to Frieda for life, with remainder to the Lawrence family on her death. That the royalties and advances of the future (after providing for the £10,000) go to Frieda absolutely, but all copyright goes to Lawrence family on F.'s death. This should shut up George, and at the same time ensures Frieda £500 a year for life, plus—whatever comes in royalties.

The other problem is far more difficult, for I imagine the T would cost her about £1000 a year. She thinks there is gold on the ranch (!) and that they will become rich beyond the dreams of avarice by dynamiting bits of auriferous rock. Since the whole Rocky mountains have gold in them in non-commercial proportions, this hope is a little delusive. But far better the T than the other bloke.

Now you have the main threads, to which I will only add that F. did not know you had been ill in America, and yet still has complete confidence in you. This is valuable.

I shall send you further situation reports. Will you let me know what you think about it all, or rather if you feel inclined to continue the struggle, and if so what action you think should be taken. You can rely upon me, and to a very large extent on Pino and Norman. It is only necessary to make Pino think he has invented the required solution. I feel the money business can be settled by a Deed of Trusteeship, but the erotic complication baffles me.

There's a good deal of dynamite in this letter, so I'll be glad if you'll destroy it after getting the facts. I'll do the same with yours.

Always
R.

1. Frieda Lawrence and Angelo Ravagli, who was a lieutenant in the Italian army; hence, the W.O. (war office) telegram.
2. John Middleton Murry, see Letter 59 n. 11.
3. See *The Letters of D.H. Lawrence*, ed. Aldous Huxley, London, 1932; *Apocalypse*, London, 1932; and *Tales*, London, 1934.
4. George Lawrence.
5. Maria Huxley.
6. See Letter 57 n. 6.
7. *Son of Woman*, London, 1931.
8. Not identified.

62. To A. S. Frere (privately held)

12 Piazza Santa Croce
21 December 1932   Florence [Italy]
Dear Frere,

Charles tells me you can't find any buggers in the poems. Search the one about the Pilgrim Fathers, and substitute beggars for same, will you? This vicious and filthy locution occurs in line eight of the alleged poem.[1]

I thought from the beginning that Frieda made a great mistake in bringing this law-suit, and I am daily more convinced of it. The costs will be terrific, and she will be worse off than ever. Nor do I see a chance of her winning, and I'm surprised that she has been legally advised to proceed. Pino was very ill-advised to send that letter, as was Norman to confirm it. Consider, her two principal witnesses are (1) the publisher of Lady C. who has been proceeded against in the Italian courts for indecent publication, (2) an author who is not allowed in England.[2] Granted these misdemeanours are nothing to us, but they will make an effect on a Court. How could Pino stand cross-examination? If neither of these crucial witnesses appear, can you imagine any English Court paying attention to their testimony? I can't.

The whole thing has been much in my mind recently since I have been preparing the MSS of Lorenzo's poems for Pino's edition.[3] Coming once more intimately in contact with Lorenzo's thought and feelings, I was utterly convinced that all Frieda's actions since his death have been a complete betrayal of him. I'm damned sorry you're not publishing those poems, old boy. Together we could have made a really good job of it, and I think I can boast it will be the only Lawrence MSS properly edited. I

shall have a struggle with the Italian printers, but I aim at exact reproduction down to the last comma—usually an error of punctuation. Pino
and Frieda haven't the faintest conception of the *respect* due to a MS.
Apocalypse[4] isn't properly edited, though Brigit and I laboured over the
proofs. But we never had the MSS, and I'm pretty certain there exists
among Pino's collection an important variant or rather fragment of a
separate work on the same theme.[5] However, we've done what we could,
and small thanks we'd get from Lorenzo for doing it.

Pino is terrifically bucked by your telling him not to give up his
Lawrence MSS. He thinks, and I agree, that Medley's threatened descent
is partly to collar these MSS, since said gent is also lawyer to C.B.s[6]The
most important thing P. has is Three Separate Versions of Lady C.[7] However, nothing can be done about them.

We look for Charles on Tuesday. I hope we'll be able to get off on
Friday, but I still haven't managed to settle all the blasted formalities
about license renewal. Del Prato, the Italian agent who manages these
things, seems to be away, for I can't get him on the phone. I guess I've got
a hectic week ahead. In addition I've got to do stuff for Referee, and it
bores me. I'm inclined to think that I must chuck journalism, chuck the
present standard of living, and try to find some little cottage where we
can live simply, but at least call our souls our own.

How are you getting along? O.K., I hope. I rely on you to fix the rendezvous in March. You can catch us by writing to Cooks, Palermo. If
you don't know Naples, I think your best plan is to go to the hotel Santa
Lucia on the front. It's not cheap, but not expensive like the Excelsior,
and is moderately comfortable. And we can pick you up there, or wire
you to meet us somewhere else near.

I wish this damned north wind would cease, but it doesn't. The snow
is gradually melting from the hills, but the mountain passes are still
blocked, and as long as the snow lasts on the high ground it's bound to
be chilly. Thank heaven it is sunny, sunny, sunny. In this flat it seems almost hot, but the wind chops your nose off outside.

Always
Richard

1. See "The Power and the Glory," in *Movietones: Invented and Set Down by Richard
Aldington, 1928–1929.* This is RA's rarest book and was privately printed for A. S. Frere;
only ten copies were produced for the Canterbury Literary Society. For a description of this
volume, see *The Poetry of Richard Aldington*, pp. 94–96; the poem referred to, with "buggers" unchanged, is reprinted there on pp. 334–35.
2. Pino Orioli and Norman Douglas; see Letter 61.
3. D. H. Lawrence, *Last Poems*, Florence, 1932.
4. See Letter 61 n. 3.

5. These fragments are included in the Cambridge edition of *Apocalypse* (1980).

6. Not identified.

7. See *Lady Chatterley's Lover*, Florence, 1928 (3d version); *The First Lady Chatterley*, New York, 1944 (1st version); and *Le Tre Lady Chatterley*, Verona, 1954 (2d version).

63. To Eric Warman*(SIUC)

16 March 1933   c/o Ralph Pinker
                                                   Talbot House,
                                                   Arundel Street,
                                                   Strand W.C., London.

Dear Warman,

I'm in the storm-center of packing and seeing people before going off, but, as we had not chance to discuss your idea of a book, I'm sending this note.[1]

If you could turn out the right sort of thing, I would speak to Heinemanns, and they would very likely do it. My idea is that you should write round the subject, so to speak, and include a survey of recent English literature, where it stands, what it needs, and where it is going. That would give the "general interest," of which publishers are so fond. You could use me both as illustration and as a warning.[2]

The essential books are the following:

Collected Poems; Luxembourg; Eaten Heart; Hero; Roads to Glory; Colonel's Daughter; Soft Answers; All Men; Voltaire; Literary Studies; French Studies.[3]

You might find something (not much) in some of the introductions to translations. Among the translations, you need only bother with Fifty Romance Poems, Medallions, Fifteen Joys of Marriage, Cyrano de Bergerac, Remy de Gourmont and Choderlos de Laclos. You will see how each contributed something towards the style of either the poems or the novels. Link Medallions with the early poems, Fifty Romance with Luxembourg and Eaten Heart. You will also see how the War poems and Fool i' the Forest lead up to Death of a Hero.[4]

I think it's advisable to quote pretty freely from both prose and poetry, and of course I'll arrange for the necessary permissions. I should think about 40,000 words would be the right length, unless you want to expand the general part.

If you decide to attempt the job I'll be very glad to give you any information and assistance I can.

The above address will always find me.

                                                   Ever yours,
                                                   Richard Aldington

*Eric Warman (b. 1904) wrote RA in 1932 after reading *Death of a Hero*. RA invited him to tea; from this time until RA's death the two remained friends. RA arranged a membership in the London Library for Warman and wrote to the literary editor of the *Sunday Times* on his behalf. Warman eventually wrote several novels, detective stories, and other books. His great success, however, came when companies he helped to found became the first in England to mass-merchandise books. RA wrote Warman more than two hundred and fifty letters over thirty years. The earlier letters include literary advice; the later ones have the attraction of a shared literary viewpoint; but, finally, Warman became, particularly during the years when RA was in the United States and France, a tie to England. RA wrote as an Englishman far from home reporting on the outside world.

1. RA was leaving for France.

2. Warman did not write this critical study.

3. See RA, *Collected Poems*, London 1929; *The Eaten Heart*, London, 1933; *Death of a Hero*, New York, 1929; *Roads to Glory*, London 1930; *The Colonel's Daughter*, London, 1931; *Love and the Luxembourg*, New York, 1930; *Soft Answers*, London, 1932; *All Men Are Enemies*, London, 1933; *Voltaire*, London, 1925; *Literary Studies and Reviews*, London, 1924; and *French Studies and Reviews*, London, 1926.

4. See these translations by Richard Aldington: *Fifty Romance Lyric Poems*, New York, 1928; *Medallions in Clay*, New York, 1921; *The Fifteen Joys of Marriage, Ascribed to Antoine De La Sale, c.1388–c.1462*, London [1926]; *Voyages to the Moon and the Sun*, London [1923]; *Remy de Gourmont. Selections from All His Works*, New York, 1929; *Dangerous Acquaintances (Les Liaisons dangereuses)*, London [1924]. Also see RA, *War and Love (1915–1918)*, Boston, 1919, and *A Fool i' the Forest*, London, 1924.

64. To Henry Slonimsky* (SIUC)

9 April 1933

Villa Devos,
Pramousquier
par Le Lavandou,
Var, France.

My dear Harry,

I have been slow in writing to you, not because you have been out of my thoughts and affections, but because the agitations of the past six months have made writing so difficult. Let me try to give you a summary.

Soon after you left England, we left for Portugal by car, intending to stay the winter there and to find a little place where I could write. In December I got the proofs of All Men Are Enemies[1] (I showed you the prologue in the nursing home) and found that Chattos had cut the text to pieces in the interests of morality! I tried to argue about the matter by post, but eventually an overwhelming instinctive impulse made me start for England, where I arrived on Christmas Eve. After fretting away a fortnight, while Chattos partners one by one returned leisurely from holidays, I spent most of January arguing and cajoling with them; and finally got all the text restored, except for about 1000 words.

I made the unwelcome discovery that prejudices against me in England were still so strong that there was every chance that this novel too would be boycotted by powerful groups of booksellers and circulating libraries. I determined to counter this so far as was possible. Through the offices of Michael Arlen I wrote for a month the Evening Standard literary article which used to be written by Arnold Bennett;[2] and this frightened the opposition a good deal. I lectured at Oxford; I met people connected with the biggest of the circulating libraries; and I put my case before one or two important independent reviewers (Compton Mackenzie was one) and asked them to support me so far as their literary conscience allowed. Further, extraordinary secrecy was observed as to the contents of the book, which was kept under lock and key until ten days before publication day, which was suddenly shifted forward from April to March 2nd—all this to give no opportunity for concerted reviewers' action against the book, such as happened with the Colonel's Daughter.[3]

This occupied the whole of February, and on publication day my novel was simultaneously attacked with virulence in the Daily Express and warmly praised by the Daily Mail. And this went on almost daily from one paper to another. Meanwhile, I waged a kind of battle against the opposition, giving interviews to papers which were friendly and arranging counter-attack reviews. The opposition were taken by surprise and had not much time to organise, and they did not suppose I should be in London, since hitherto I have always gone away on publication from scruples which were simply exploited against me. Well, I cannot claim that I have battered down the wall of Jericho of British philistinism (if you'll pardon the mixed metaphor) but I achieved something. Booksellers who refused to take more than half a dozen copies have been compelled to order on a bigger scale and to display; one of the big libraries which reported that "this novel is one of the most repulsive we have ever seen" has been compelled by its subscribers to buy quantities of copies almost every day. The book got into the bottom of the best-seller list, into the middle, and finally to the top. By the 4th [of] April (my information goes no later) Chattos had sold 6500 copies, and the book was still going strongly and steadily. It is not exactly a victory, but I have proved that I cannot be suppressed. True, the Australian Customs have hitherto refused to allow the book to be imported, but if they persist I intend to make a formal complaint to the High Commissioner in London, and if possible get a question asked in the Australian parliament.

So you see I've been obliged to fritter away practically six months in the worst kind of literary politics, merely to obtain the free market and access to the public which is granted without question to the most ignominious scribblers. I regret it, but it was necessary. An unquiet saeva indignatio in me refuses to be bullied by these mean methods. The latest line of attack is ingenious but makes me laugh. In January I republished the Eaten Heart with about a dozen short poems.[4] This was utterly ignored by the English press at the time. Well, they can't deny that the novel is a success (it is the success of the season in London) so they dig up these poems, and, while proving at great length that I am not, never was, and never will be a poet, use the reviews for every kind of odious innuendo against my personal character!

Thus much for contemporary literary moeurs in England. I shall be interested to see what the Americans say about All Men Are Enemies when it appears there in the autumn.

We are now settled in to this cottage by the Mediterranean, where there are flowers and the nightingales are beginning to sing, so it is not hard to forget all that waste of time. I even hope that I may be inspired to write something more.

What is your news? Above all, when are you coming to Europe? I hope that you and Mrs. Slonimski will come and stay with us here—it would be lovely to see you. Moreover, I shall be very happy to give you information about the beautiful parts of France, with the addresses of hotels which will treat you well without over-charging. Only let me know, and I will send you an account of what I know. A suggestion—for less than £100 you can buy an almost new Ford car in London. I can get you made a member of the English Automobile Association, and by depositing £50 with them (returnable when the car comes back to England) you will be given a Carnet de Passages en Douane, enabling you to take the car to any European country without payment of Customs duties. This gives you complete freedom of movement and makes you independent of trains. The A.A. will ship the car to a French port for £2.7.6., while your own tickets on the Auto-Carrier amount to 10/– each. I strongly recommend this to you. I can give you the address of an honest automobile dealer in London, while the A.A. will fulfill all the formalities of licenses etcetera for you with a minimum of trouble. On your return to America, you will be able to sell the car for about £50. The running expenses are cheaper than buying second-class tickets, while the enjoyment of freedom, privacy and the open roads is immeasurably greater. Think about it.

I have a nice work room here, looking over the rough garden to the sea, and a long verandah where I can perambulate and meditate on gods and men. We have geraniums and roses, mimosa and irises, marigolds and mesembrianthemums. In the evenings I work off any destructive instincts I may have by weeding the flower beds, and for the rest feel at peace. I don't even see a newspaper—all these atrocities in Germany make me miserable, and I can do nothing to stop them. Obviously Europe is determined on self-destruction. Let it go. Civilisation survived Christianity, and if it can survive that, it can survive anything! But I must say I feel a peculiar sympathy with the Romans of about 398 A.D. But what pinchbeck Attilas and Alarics are Hitler and Mussolini! And what dismal fanatics are these Moscovites!

We shall be here the whole summer, so letters to this address will reach me. Write soon.

Affectionately yours,
Richard

*RA first met Henry Slonimsky (1884–1970) in London in 1912 and by chance encountered him that spring in Paris. Slonimsky (RA spelled his name with a final *i*) was a Polish American who had recently taken his degree as Doctor of Philosophy at Marburg. RA was greatly impressed by him: "As a personality he stands for me alongside Yeats and Lawrence." H.D. and Aldington spent many of their evenings on that first visit to Paris listening "on a bench under the trees in the Petit Luxembourg" to Slonimsky talking of Hellas and Hellenism. Slonimsky became a professor at the Jewish Institute of Religion in New York City; he and R.A. remained lifelong friends. (See also the Annotated Index.)

    1. *All Men Are Enemies. A Romance,* London, 1933.

    2. Following Arnold Bennett's death in 1931, RA wrote this weekly review for a brief time.

    3. *The Colonel's Daughter,* London, 1931; see Letter 57 n. 1.

    4. *The Eaten Heart,* London, 1933.

65. To A. S. Frere (privately held)

25 April 1933   Pramousquier.
Dear Frere,

Walking on the terrace this morning I heard a nightingale say:

"Say to Fre-re, to Fre-re, to Fre-re, that journalists are shitititits. What they say isn't tereu, tereu, tereu. Why, if you believe them you might as well be in jug-jug-jug-jug-jug. So what the he-ell, what the he-ell? Don't be a jug-jug-jug-jug-juggins. Forget it, forget it, and think about your sweet-sweet-sweet-sweet."

If you bring any bloody newspapers here, zum! we throw you violently down a steep place into the sea.

C.L.S.[1] Bye-Law XXXVIII: Journalists Keep out—this means you. Pah!

In re boat—there is not much point in getting one yet, because it is still coolish on the aqua. But I shall sound old Lugon about it. Discuss with him whether we should do better with two canoes. What we really want is a boat to bathe from, and get away from (a) human shits, (b) real shit.

The eye is better, but still not right. However, it does improve slowly. Tomorrow we go to see Dikran,[2] and I hope the drive won't jigger the eye up again.[3]

I hear you have had a cold spell in London. I noticed the air morning and evening was distinctly cooler here, but it's sunny enough, and the roses are wonderful. I wish to god you could see them now, because they'll be over when you come. The one just to the left of my window has between forty and fifty large red blossoms on it, and the other is just starting. There is a Banksia just coming out and three blooms on the large rambler this morning. I was hoping the coolth would keep them back, but the little bastards don't pay any attention to it. Of course, it's warm all through the day.

Did you happen to see Stephen Potter on All Men in your enemy the N. Statesman?[4] His first par. is a nice wipe in the eye for Agate and co. Brigit says Potter used to be one of the fat-arsed 1917 Clubbers, but was much better than most of them, and restive there. I hope it's true. So far the only cutting about A.M. being banned in Australia is a Reuter telegram in Manchester Guardian.[5] The London papers seem to have killed it. They would.

> And blessings on your frosty poll,
> John Rothermere, my jo.

I feel that Calabria trip will be a trial to poor old Charles. Pino will make him drink too much and keep him up at nights, and Norman will walk him off his legs. Did you know MacPherson is with them? Dirty work there. H.D. (my vife) and Bryher (Winnie Ellerman), her sapphic pal, are furious at my being with Chattos and having a bit of reclame. Macpherson is Bryher's "husband" (save the mark! the wrong kind of sod, my dear.) Now for old times sake I got Charl to publish a volume of H.D. (rather a mistake perhaps, but I meant decently) but the idea *there* is to get Macpherson published by Chattos, to do me dirt. (Much I care!) Pino when drunk in Florence let out that Bryher had promised Norman £100 if he could persuade Charl to publish Macpherson. Norman tried damned hard last year, but I was there, and helped to extricate Charles, though Charles is so innocent I don't believe he knew what was up. Now, this Calabria trip is NOT friendship or gratitude to Charles (Norman doesn't like Charles) but a real old Doug plan to get that £100— also expenses of trip paid by Bryher—in order to persuade Charles through Parsons and Pino to issue Macpherson's tripe. I don't know why I should mind, but I do. It just makes me mad for Charles to be got at like that. Fortunately, old Charles is A.1. at refusing books he doesn't want, and I hope and believe he won't get caught. We give him hell if he does. (He won't dare to tell us.) But what if Parsons accepts on behalf of the firm? Frere! It's all as paltry as hell, and perhaps I'm a josser about it. But it gets my goat. Basta.

About the U.S. millionaire and Hero.[6] It was Crosby Gaige. He didn't give me money, but paid me well to do Fifty Romance Poems,[7] which was beautifully printed by Bruce Rogers. The edition didn't sell out, but Gaige gave me 15% on the whole edition and got me £50 out of a bastard who used my translation of Candide[8] without even giving my name (it isn't copyrighted in America, sheets only). With Gaige's money I went to Port-Cros and wrote the first third of the Hero. But that isn't all. If the story is used, in justice, it should be added that I abandoned the novel there in despair of getting anything printed about the War. Donald Friede saw it in Paris and gave me 500 dollars to finish it. Which was decent. And he also mentioned it to Charles. So I owe as much to Friede as to Gaige. But without those two Yanks, I'd probably still be reviewing for the T.L.S. or dead. That's the story, and I'm only too glad to make acknowledgements.

Ever,
Richard

3 Picts & a Florentine![9] Whew!

1. Canterbury Literary Society; see Letter 57 n. 6.
2. Michael Arlen.
3. An infection caused by dust under the eyelid.
4. See Stephen Potter, "Eternal Verities," *New Statesman and Nation*, 15 April 1933, pp. 482–83.
5. Not traced.
6. See *Death of a Hero, A Novel*, New York, 1929.
7. See *Fifty Romance Lyric Poems*, New York, 1928.
8. See Voltaire's *Candide and Other Romances*, trans. Richard Aldington, London [1927].
9. Charles Prentice, Norman Douglas, Kenneth Macpherson, and "Pino" Orioli.

66. To A. S. Frere (privately held)

7 June 1934   Bern [Switzerland]
Dear Frere,

Alt!

Achtung!

KOLOSSALROKOKOBAHNUBERGANGPLATZAUSFAHRT!

How rude! Hier muss mann deutsche gesprachen, und ich kann nicht, ich KANN nicht.

I find a good Weinstube, and ve drink vine.

They have lovely names here—Hugli–Jenni—how sensible!

Have you read Pino book?[1] All that is not Norman is Charl, and all that is not Normancharl iss Pino, yess, yess. Shatto and Vindup sind sehr gaga, yah Senhor, mucho, muito bem, adesso, im Munsterplatz.

Zwei und zwanzig.

I have already applied to Pino for the reward for translating his Italian epitaph. There's nothing difficult about it—only a relative held in suspense through three clauses.

Do admire my invented German word:

KOLOSSALROKOKOBAHNUBERGANGPLATZAUSFAHRT.

If Pat cannot translate it, ve radiate her. Zum!

All boches make me laff. But I did not laff at them at Loos and the Somme.[2] They are not funny always.

I tell you something—R. Macdonald is a shit, a supershit. I go against him. We are soon all in prison for seditionsarbeit, nicht wahr? I sphit on Macdonaldsarseheit. I crappenzummerheit in his teepott. I ausfahrt in his face. I bummelspee on his grave.

Well, soldier, that film[3] sound pretty bum. Charl he womit on it. I find a dozen letters here saying how bum is that film. Yessir. You alone comfort me by saying it does no harm. And you and Charl also comfort me by saying FRAUENARBEITENMUSS is not so bad.

How funny to think of you and Pat at Rye, scène de mes jeunes ébats. When I was four we lived in an arty cottage there and I collected live frogs and stirred them up in a bucket. Also we had doves, and they sat on their eggs and squashed them so they stuck to their arses. I said: "O Mummie! Look! Why do they do that?" and got a clip on the ear. Ainsi fait-on un poète.

As touching that will, it is all a mistake. You and Pat will put roses on my grave. But, will you do something for me? My present will is a scribbled one and perhaps not valid. Could you have a will drawn to this effect: Charl and Frere executors, life interest in "estate" to Brigit, remainder to Frere. If there is some balls (as there may be) about executors being beneficiaries, then make Charl sole executor. I should like Charl to have some souvenirs and any MSS to be shared between you and him. Add that no letters are to be published during life of copyright, except by permission of executors. This is serious, so will you have the document drawn, and I'll sign it, and deposit it with my Bank, so you know where it is.[4]

I do think you mustn't get angry about Manx,[5] not let her spoil your happiness, which is what she wants to do. I suppose if one could take a godseye view, one could understand and pardon it all. She belongs to that immediate post-war generation, who were never any good to us—loathed our guts in fact. I never got over that first dinner at Gatton when she told me she wished she'd married a soldier! Gotterdammerung! You may not believe it, but there is much truth in the old tag: Resist not evil. I know that gets your goat, but there is wisdom in it—in the sense that by making too much of an effort against what is evil, one becomes negative. I have wasted so much time & energy in kicking against the pricks (not to mention cunts) that I want to save you from the same waste.

Outside a band is playing Tannhäuser, and playing it damn well—they are the postmen of Bern! What an awful pack of Philistines we are in England. Imagine England having a composer like Wagner, and postmen able to play him.

I wish you wouldn't go straight south, but take a look at some of that country between Bordeaux and Savoy. It's really wonderful, and so completely unspoiled. Go to Bordeaux, stay at the Chateau-Trompette, then go Libourne-Périgueux-Tulle-Brive-Aurillac-Murat-Gorges d'Alagnon-Le Puy-Tain l'Hermitage, and stop at the Hotel des Negociants. You'll never regret it, and the food at Chateau Trompette and Negociants will make Pat love you for ever. Insist on a back room at Tain—it is on the main Road from Lyon to Marseille. This'll only take you a couple of days extra, and you'll love it.

Pat! Do this. You vill like it! Foi d'animal.

Write me Cooks, Vienna, where you will be (address) in the south. We are going straight on to Buda-Pest now, but shall be coming back. I have found where the Douglashutte[6] is in the Vorarlberg—not far from Bludenz. I go there and send Norman a postcard. He and Pino have gone to St Agata for 3 months, but it would be lovely if you could rendezvous with us someplace in Austria. Keep in touch.

Always
Richard

1. See Giuseppe Orioli, *Moving Along; Just a Diary*, London, 1934.
2. Where RA faced them late in World War I.
3. RA's novel *All Men Are Enemies* was filmed by Hollywood.
4. See Letter 147 for RA's final will; the Freres did survive RA.
5. Frere's first wife.
6. A place where Norman Douglas had lived. On the highway between Feldkirch and Bludenz RA had an automobile accident resulting in a broken kneecap that hospitalized him for six to eight weeks.

67. To A. S. Frere (privately held)

15 August 1934   Edelweiss
                                                  Fontanella im Grosswalsertal
                                                  Vorarlberg [Austria][1]

My dear Frere,

I didn't expect to hear from you so soon (your letter was only 5 days en route!)—imagined you up to your arse in mud in Heine's front line.

> Ein Feste Burg ist unser Gott,
> Ein Bummel und ein Schwankpott.

Here it has been rainy and distinctly cool—snow down to 5500, which must be fairly rare in August. Luckily the rain is mostly at night, and it clears up at intervals during the day. But a little more settled sun would help on the gammy leg. Progress is slow, but not so bad. I can walk out with one stick, Brigit taking the other one for me to use in rough bits, but the bending is the bugger. Two days ago I crawled into the car, but couldn't lift my foot high enough even to get it on the clutch. I can walk up stairs with comparative ease, but have to come down like a crab. However, all this is a terrific improvement on the Spital, and the rest will come in time. The doc says now that the swelling won't finally subside for a year, so I suppose there will be some stiffness for a long time. I can now feel and move the patella with my fingers, so, you see, it has gone down a lot.

You are being very good to Tom,[2] though I shouldn't like to be one of the playwrights on whom he reports! He has been on my conscience too recently, and I wrote Charles about him a day or two ago. What I object to in Tom is that he acts as if his poverty were our fault instead of his own. It is not permissible to blame fate or your friends for your own inability to understand and conform to the inexorable realities. Again, his peculiar attitude and mood make one chary of recommending him. Recently two possibilities came my way for him—one as a writer of advertising copy (now hopeless!) the other to translate a book about Villon's love affairs for Michael Sadleir. I had a vision of Tom finding the book insufficiently catholic and finally refusing to do it after messing about for three months, thereby bringing Sadleir's wrath on me. So I forebore. Also, he never answered a letter of mine in which I suggested his doing L.C.C.[3] extension lectures which can't be so infra dig, since the great T. S. Eliot did them for years. Well, that sort of intellectual snobbery makes me tired, especially when I remember that Lorenzo[4] didn't scorn to write for the Evening News and the Saturday Evening

Post. It's too cheap a superiority. Why, even Willie Yeats got down to the job, and wrote and produced plays. It is sheer Montparnasse cheek to get on the high horse on the strength of one pamphlet of poems, two discursive essays and a few translations. Pardonable at 20, but not at 40. E basta.

Interesting news about Frieda's book.[5] I'm very glad you've got it for England. The title is a bit dangerous, with so many twirps about, but let her stick by it. Better than 'Me and L.' anyway. Lorenzo is dead to the extent that he can live and give no more; and what he did live and give lives on. One mustn't be deceived by words. I think there are several reasons why you and I tend to get worked up about him. First, both in his life and work he most courageously went for most of the essential problems which concern us. Then, we feel he had a particularly dirty deal from his contemporaries—there is an injustice to be atoned for. Admit his imperfections, there was so much of vivid beauty and value both in him and his work which ought to have been recognised, would have been but for the literary and moral shits. That Wells-Bennett gang, for instance, loathed his guts, because they felt instinctively that he was the force which would supersede them. I'm told that Walpole now "admires" Lorenzo—such was not the case in 1913 or in 1919, that I'm prepared to swear. You can see the old bourgeois hatred of L. in Nelson,[6] who can't bear him to be mentioned. That was how people felt about Shelley for many years. Shelley's version of the Plato epigram always makes me think of Lorenzo: Thou wert the morning star . . .

I haven't been thinking or doing very much. I enclose a couple of poems,[7] which strike me as a bit ponderous. And I've done the first of a series of 8 articles for the Referee[8]—on any subject I like. I don't like doing articles, but as I'm not working on a book, there is no excuse for refusing the offer.

Thanks for telling me about Ginsberg.[9] It is always pleasant to hear of such things, particularly from a publisher, since publishers are almost the only people who really know contemporary literature. If they hadn't more gumption than the reviewers they'd soon be bankrupt. Haven't heard much from Nelson recently, an infallible sign that Poems[10] didn't sell much; but he does seem to like the novel.[11] I don't like it much myself. One of these days perhaps I may do something. My ideal conditions for work are to be somewhere in the south, absolutely remote but within an hour's drive of a town, where I should see you and Charles of an evening, with access to a library. Most of these conditions could be satisfied by a cottage in Sussex—which I should loathe, and where I shouldn't be able to write anything. So there we are.

I sent Wallace[12] a bawdy poem about the bride—did she get it? Give her my love.

Always,
Richard

1. RA came here to convalesce following his hospital stay; Frere and his wife, Pat Wallace, visited him in Feldkirk.
2. Thomas McGreevy.
3. London County Council.
4. D. H. Lawrence
5. See Frieda Lawrence, *Not I But the Wind* . . . , London, 1935.
6. Nelson Doubleday.
7. Not with letter.
8. RA began working for the *Referee* November 1929, but stopped in April 1932 to concentrate on *All Men Are Enemies;* starting again in 1933, he wrote several more *Referee* series. See Letter 53 n. 5.
9. Not identified.
10. See *The Poems of Richard Aldington*, New York, 1934.
11. See *Women Must Work. A Novel*, New York, 1934.
12. The maiden name and nickname of Frere's wife, Patricia, who was the daughter of Edgar Wallace, the mystery writer.

68. To A. S. Frere (privately held)

12 January 1935   Georgian House,
                                                     Bury Street, S.W.1.
                                                     [London]
Dear Frere,

It is said in Herodotus that during the period between the crossing of the Hellespont and the battle of Marathon, all Hellas stood upon the razor's edge.

I feel much the same while this question of Lorenzo's work is in the balance. To be frank, I don't much care about Frieda's Lsd,[1] but those books are the soul of Adonais. The situation is as if in 1830 the question of Shelley's copyrights had come up. If the whole position isn't regularised now the Capitano or Monty Weekly[2] will be dictating terms.

This stuff isn't going to die, it's going on and on. Of course, there are weaknesses in L—there are in Shakespeare—but the positive side is tremendous. Last night I re-read several chapters of Sons and Lovers.[3] Nobody else has done it, nobody else can.

Anyone with a sense of literature should read the first section of "Not I, not I, but the wind" (Coll. poems p. 317)[4] and a bit of the "Ship of Death."[5] Then turn to the prose. Read those two bits from the introduction of MM's memoirs (quoted in my pamphlet)[6] and that passage about life from the end of Apocalypse.[7] Read the funeral passages from the White Peacock (pp. 237–242)[8] and that lovely thing about the pregnant girl in The Rainbow (p. 168)[9] Then, to give the other human side, look at pp. 34–37 of Sons and Lovers[10]—the miner getting up and going to work.

There are dozens, scores, hundreds of pages like this in Lawrence—the parrot and dog thing in Mornings in Mexico[11]—isn't this the breath of the gods, the thing which will endure when all our best sellers are one with Babylon and Tyre. To be against L. now is as wrong and *sinful* as to be against Shelley in 1830.

LAWRENCE IS NOT DEAD

They have been announcing that since 1915 and he goes on, and will and will and will. They can't kill him. You can no more stop him than an army can stop the spring. You can no more quench him than you can quench a star.

Aldous[12] and I are not fools and liars like the Fleet street boozers who maligned Lawrence or the cocktail wallopers who try to sneer at the man who despised them or time-servers abashed by his integrity. And yet we, who are so different, and yet have this in common that we try to speak truth without fear, favour or fashion, both agree on this—that, having known all the writers of our time, we think Lawrence the greatest, in spite of his errors, a man so strange and inspired that he seemed to live in a finer, more luminous world than other men.

R.A.

1. Frieda Lawrence's financial situation.
2. Angelo Ravagli, Frieda's lover, or Charles Montague Weekly, her son by her first husband.
3. London, 1913.
4. *The Collected Poems of D. H. Lawrence*, London, 1928.
5. See *Last Poems*, New York, 1933, p. 56.
6. See D. H. Lawrence, London, 1930, pp. 38–41.
7. See *Apocalypse*, London, 1932, pp. 221–24.
8. See *The White Peacock*, London, 1911.
9. See *The Rainbow*, London, 1915.
10. See *Sons and Lovers*, London, 1913.
11. See "Corasmin and the Parrots," in *Mornings in Mexico*, London, 1927.
12. Huxley.

69. to A. S. Frere (privately held)

11 May 1935   Terry Hill
                                                       Tobago

Dear Frere,

Herewith my notes on Ada Clarke's book.[1] I assume that the schoolmaster[2] was responsible for the arrangement of the letters, and a pretty mess he made of it. In excuse it must be said that the Heinemann letters[3] hadn't yet appeared. If you go over these notes you may be able to add further corrections, and confirm or refute conjectures. What is needed is a chronological frame-work of L's life and movements something on the lines of your appendix to Letters, but more a barebones of dates and places. If you see that French bloke[4] who is doing a thesis on L., you might suggest he does it as an appendix.

The letters to Ada and to the Ma-in-Law[5] are important because they fill gaps in your edition. The time for a definitive edition of the Letters is not yet,[6] but you should go on quietly collecting material. I must see if any L letters have survived the various upheavals in my fortunes. There is one letter I should much like to find—one in which he asked me to say or write that "Lady C. is a feather in the cap of the 20th century." You can see, it is not a phrase I should use. But having done this, he then writes Aldous that I had written it to him! But I suspect these letters have been stolen.[7]

The past week has been very damp here—indeed it is the great drawback, because it makes one feel limp.

Curious how in this complete solitude one's past life comes up for review. I have been surprised to find how bitterly I still resent things I thought I had long ago dealt with and forgotten. But no, they are still there. I believe part of the conduct of life should consist in turning one's defeats into victories. For example, the War which for years destroyed me as an artist gave me my revenge with Death of a Hero.

These things being so, I've practically decided to leave here at the end of May and make for N.Y. I've done a good hunk of writing here, but now have come to the end of my energy for the time being. Your remark about the probable heat of N.Y. in July makes me think that it would be better to go a month earlier. For reasons of economy an extra month here would be welcome, but it might easily be false economy, if the damp is going to affect our health and if I can't work. On the other hand, I feel that by going to N.Y. I might be able to place some of these prose pieces and/or get some articles and see about that play[8] and possibly find a more bracing place to work in. We shall have had three months here, which is quite enough to absorb the place. I wish I had heard from Nelson, but he takes no notice of my letters. How I despise this American worship of immediate success—if Women Must Work had sold more he would be très empressé. Never mind. There's a fast boat leaves here on 31st, so we might go on that. In any case, as soon as I can find out I'll cable Harold,[9] and ask him to inform you and Ralph.[10]

Tante belle cose alla Wallace, anche a te.

Richard

1. See *Young Lorenzo, Early Life of D. H. Lawrence,* Florence [1932].
2. Ada Lawrence's coauthor, G. Stuart Gelder.
3. See Letter 61 n. 3.
4. Possibly *La Vie de D. H. Lawrence* by Alfred Fabre-Luce, Paris, 1935.
5. Baronin von Richthofen
6. See *The Letters of D. H. Lawrence,* ed. James T. Boulton, Cambridge, 1979–1989, in five volumes of seven projected.
7. Not all Lawrence's letters to RA were lost. *The Letters of D. H. Lawrence* includes four letters through 1927 (the first five volumes) with many more late letters to be published in the remaining volumes.
8. See *Life of a Lady, A Play by Richard Aldington and Derek Patmore,* New York and London, 1936.
9. Guinzburg of Viking Press.
10. Probably Ralph Pinker.

70. To Henry Slonimsky (SIUC)

23 September 1935   Brockway Manor
                                                     Lyme, Conn. [U.S.]

Dear Harry,

I was glad to have your letter, but sorry indeed that you couldn't come. I suspected you might have to go to Philadelphia, though I hoped you might be able to work us in too.

Yes, we shall certainly arrange to see you before leaving, but I don't know about dinner. You see, we are staying with Doubledays on Long Island, and there is the difficulty of getting back there. Although I have a license I wouldn't attempt to drive in and about New York, and it depends on whether they can let us have the chauffeur. Possibly we could go back by train, and get a taxi from the station.

This beautiful American autumn is slowly burning up the green woods into lovely flames of brilliant colour. Every day winter is a little nearer, and each morning I think how the war flames are drawing a little closer to what is left of the old Europe. To me it has almost ceased to be a tragedy and has become a purposeless biological process. Blessed are the tolerant, for they shall be crushed; blessed are intelligent, for they shall be overcome by force; blessed are they that hunger for justice and peace, for they shall not be fed. Selah.

Well, Harry, you and I have put our money on the wrong horse, as Lord Salisbury said on another occasion. America is the last line of battle, and doesn't know it. But you will salvage something, and about 2,200 . . . but why prophesy? America can never be Athens and Florence, it can only be Babylon. Yet I feel that if anything can be saved, it will be saved here.

We leave here probably on the 4th—sail 11th and the address will be c/o Doubleday Doran Inc. Garden City, N.Y. I will let you know about meeting.

Brigit joins me in love to you both,

Richard

71. To Eric Warman (SIUC)

18 September 1936   chez Monsieur Lugon
                                                              Le Lavandou, Var, France.

Dear Erik,

The next time a Communist calls you "liberal sentimentalist" call him "brutal doctrinaire." You might add that the Liberal is one who tries to submit his passions to the discipline of Reason; whereas the Communist sacrifices reason to hatred, envy and the prejudices of party. Say unto them in the words of O. Cromwell: "My brethren, by the bowels of Christ I beseech you, bethink you that ye may be mistaken."[1]

For us human beings Life is the supreme fact. Communism and Socialism are not facts, nor are they life; they are theories. And they are theories based (in the case of Communism) on the dialectic of Hegel, the imperfect Science of the last century, and a view of political economy which is not even a science. Marx and Engels had never heard of Darwin. Their history and pre-history are worm-eaten. They know nothing of genetics and biology.

Moreover, the supreme objection to both Communism and its inevitable counter-force, Fascism, is that they entirely overlook the human element. The "rightness" or "wrongness" of any particular political economic social theory is a matter of opinion. But its working depends on the kind of people we all are. True progress consists in the substitution of co-operation for hostility, knowledge for ignorance, reason for prejudice, justice for tyranny, richness and variety of life for penury and sameness. The parties of violence forget all this in their vulgar eagerness for power. And so long as they remain cruel, bigoted, vain, dishonest and intolerant, so long will they seek power by any means and abuse power when they have it. The problem of right human organisation is an immense one. And it is merely confused by over-simplifying the issues, by imagining that it can be solved by such puerilities as Nordic blondism or collective ownership of property. The psychological problem still remains.

However, all these things we will discuss at leisure this winter.

You are quite right about the title Bliss Was It Then. Everybody spat on it. In a way I want to keep Very Heaven, as it goes well with the design of the book. But I hope to think of something more appropriate when I re-read the proofs.[2] I wonder if you agree that too ingenious or ostentatious a title is a mistake? People want to read books, not titles. A "good" title is one which hits the attention and sticks in the memory. Death of a Hero did that. But M. Arlen's Hell! Said the Dutchess is bloody bad.[3] The great novels have quite simple titles like War and Peace, Sentimental Education, Madame Bovary, Cousine Bette, Sons and Lovers, and so on.

We had a very fine trip down here from Austria. Went through Switzerland and Alsace and up to Boulogne by way of Compiegne and Amiens. Then right across France, which I still think the most beautiful and varied country in Europe, and far superior to America.

I won't bother with agents yet a while, though as a matter of fact I think Brigit has written to one. For heavens' sake don't waste time on it yourself. Only, if you happen to hear of a flat casually, let me know.

I'll let you have a line when we decide to return. Probably early in October. There have been heavy storms in the Alps, so the sky is rather overcast here. Rather annoying, as we had brilliant sunshine most of the way down. But I think it is clearing. The sea is still very warm.

Our love to you both,

Richard

1. Cf. Oliver Cromwell, "Letter to the General Assembly of the Church of Scotland" [3 August 1650], in Letters and Speeches, New York, 1899, vol. 2, p. 187.
2. See RA, Very Heaven, London, 1937. See also "French Revolution," in The Poetical Works of Wordsworth, London, 1936, pp. 165–66, lines 4–5.
3. Michael Arlen, Hell! Said the Dutchess: A Bedtime Story, London, 1934.

72. To Patricia and A. S. Frere (privately held)

Sat. eve.   Cavendish [Hotel, London]
[? December 1936]

Dearest Pat and Frere,

It's quite impossible to thank you properly for your goodness to me. You are the only real friends I have. I'm all against doing oneself in, but I needed the thought of you two yesterday to get over it.

This situation slightly baffles me. If it were a colonel's daughter or someone of that sort, I'd know the psychology from A to Zee (as the English say). As it happens to be supremely important to me to know it here, I naturally make a balls of it all the time. I'm probably what is known as my own worst enemy.

I'll try to get her[1] to come to lunch with us on Thursday. May I be quite abject, and say that she likes sherry (Oloroso), and then oysters. I shall see her on Monday, and let you know at once about it. Being in a defeatist mood, I'm quite prepared for you to say: "What next?"

This damn pain comes on in regular waves, a yen which would make the New Yorker snigger. I've now had five weeks of it. I'm utterly happy when I'm with her, and an hour or so after leaving it starts up again. I'll tell you what got my goat at Sadler's Wells. She really was looking love into my eyes, and then turned and gazed admiringly at that stinking pansy dancer sticking his arse out. Pouf, my dear, that was no fun. And of course I made a fool of myself.

I can't quite make it out. Does she really care for her "husband"? Or am I merely being too impatient? There are absurd complications. First, those infernal 20 years difference. She was born in the exceptionally warm summer of 1911. Not so good. Then my books have formed her mind. She quite genuinely thinks I'm the greatest poet and novelist in England! (What next, indeed!) But it's rather a handicap. This "great man" rot gets me down. I don't want her to admire my bloody silly books, I want her to love me.

If she's really in love with the pansy,[2] it's a god-awful tragedy. She sometimes says the most moving and beautiful love words. I said: "You have a genius for loving." She said: "And It isn't wanted where I want to give it." I said: "When you love someone utterly, as I love you, it seems impossible that the answer shouldn't be there." She lighted a cigarette, and said: "It is a pity." (Go to, swallow a gooseberry.) I said: "Frere told me I ought to have humility in love." She said: "But you haven't got any." I said: "If pride has been your only line of defence all your life, you can't drop it in a few days!" She didn't answer. I said: "I've been trying all my life to bronze my heart, and now I've merely broken it." She said: "Darling, you're so sweet." (What a crack!) I said: "You mean Noel Coward sweetness?" And then she kissed me, and I took the count. And so it goes on. What do you make of it?

You know how it is when you feel utterly married? It never happened to me before. When I wrote about such things, I imagined them. Now I live them. And what is so agonising is that sometimes the response is (or seems) there and often not. Probably I imagine the response. I seem to make every possible mistake. If I loved her less, I could play games. If I wanted a charming mistress, how easy! But it's just hell to share the only woman I ever loved as a wife. So I seem to spend half my time in heaven, and half hanging on the old barbed wire.

I died in 1916, and came alive again in 1936. And it's damn painful, for I don't know whether I'm coming or going.

Excuse this letter. I've got an idea out of writing it which I think may help. Rather silly of me not to see it before.

Pat dear, try to help me, won't you?
My love to you both and to junior,

Richard

1. Netta Patmore, wife of Michael Patmore, Brigit's younger son; the "situation" is that RA has fallen in love with her.
2. Her husband, Michael.

73. To Patricia and A. S. Frere (privately held)

21 December 1936   [S.S.] Normandie, [at sea]
Dearest Pat and Frere,

There is no way in which I can thank you properly for your sweetness and help during those hellish days in London. Your last telegram was delivered on Saturday morning, and helped at a bad moment. Someday I'll be able to thank you perhaps.

This journey is all rather a dream. To-day is Monday, and we arrive on Weds. In a way I rather dread arriving. Here I have a cabin to myself, and a nice steward who calls me "Monsieur Richard," and was delighted with his 100 francs, and looks after me. On Saturday morning I worked at the proofs, but in the afternoon the delayed shock arrived, and I went to bed and stayed there, sleeping and reading, until this morning. The rest has done me good. I feel calmer, and nearly as cheerful as a Morgue. On avance sur tous les fronts!

Frere, I've corrected up to page 280,[1] so I'll easily get the job done before tomorrow night. The first part of the book is well written; the second part flags badly; the third part picks up again, but isn't so well written as the first. One of the bad defects is the lack of a story. The love scenes with Martha upset me—I was so obviously making love to Netta when I wrote them. What a bloody fool.

I'm going to write to Charlie[2] about the proofs. I think it best for me not to do everything through you. You'll understand this, won't you? Only to keep him good-tempered with us both.

Pat dear, I've thought a lot about what you said—how a woman is suggestible and says things she doesn't mean, and how I might write a calm letter from the ship. And indeed I've spent hour after hour after hour writing letters in my head to her, and getting nowhere. But a calm letter wouldn't be me—my love letters are never calm![3] And I can't find a way to avoid being either denunciatory or abject. I would willingly be abject if it would be successful, but to be unsuccessfully abject is merely inviting contempt. And in this recoil on myself I have a picturesque little vignette of anything I write being eagerly canvassed by a council of three;[4] and that paralyses me. You can understand. I loved, and alas still love that girl more than anyone in my life; for a time I was nearer to her than to any human being; and until Wednesday I trusted her utterly. But how can one go on trusting a woman who allows a dagger to be put into her hands, with careful instructions, and who uses it ruthlessly? She accused me of "pride" when I refused the position of spare-time lover and sugar-daddy. What the hell else has she left me? So I think the only thing is to say nothing and do nothing.

Later. I've now finished the proofs, and shall transfer corrections to the second set tomorrow. The only trouble I find is that my spacing hasn't always been observed. This isn't essential, if it means resetting; but otherwise it's a little tic of mine which seems to matter, though it obviously doesn't.

I've also written a letter to Evans, which I hope you'll approve.

On the whole, Very Heaven isn't such a lousy book. Vun of these days I learn to write a novel—by which time I shall have nothing left to say.

We ran through rather heavy weather for the past 36 hrs, only made 585 knots yesterday. Looks to me as if we can't possibly dock until late on Wednesday night. I don't care, not anxious to arrive, but I don't want that very kindly Malcolm[5] to be delayed on his holiday.

I forgot to say to Evans—I promised the Italian translator a set of revised proofs. Could she have one? She's a poor devil, and she gets some lire out of Mondadori[6] if she can get ahead of the others. Her name is Alessandra Scalero, and Pinker should have her address.

I don't know why I should go on droning about myself, but it seems to help. I've got some comfort out of South Wind[7]—much wisdom in that old boy's cynicism. Has it ever occurred to you that it (South Wind) is his defence against having failed to get the highest in life?

My first business is to re-learn to stand quite alone in life, and for that these five days of solitude at sea are useful. This disaster has been a first class shock. I thought I had found, indeed I had found, someone with whom I was in complete harmony, with whom there was no necessity for defences. That made me so damnably and ridiculously vulnerable. I don't blame her—she knew not what she did. Only it does seem an infernal waste. Had I not been so much in love I shouldn't have made the mistakes I did. Love doesn't calculate. It should. It should be cunning, but I set my ideal too high. I see her point of view entirely. After what she has known, so much passion must have seemed a little unreal, could so easily be misrepresented as "the poet's" quick-passing fancy, etc. I see it all now. And isn't it a measure of how greatly she was attracted that she had to stab so hard and often? Jesus, I didn't think a woman could hurt so much. Tis not so deep as a well or so wide as a church, but twill serve.

Well, this won't buy the baby a new bonnet, though that indeed would be superfluous.

Tuesday. We're in mist and running slow again—can't possibly dock until Thursday morning. I've radioed M. Johnson not to wait, but to wire me where I can find the ticket and I'll follow him. Just as well. Don't feel like Xmas mirth.

All the best to you two—happy days to you, and all my love and gratitude.

Richard

1. See *Very Heaven,* London, 1937, RA's fifth novel.
2. Charles Seddon Evans, chairman and managing director of William Heinemann Ltd.
3. Cf. RA's love letters to Netta's mother-in-law, Brigit.
4. Netta, Brigit, and Michael Patmore.
5. Malcolm Johnson, employed by Doubleday.
6. *Very Heaven* was published in Italian by Mondadori Publishing House, Milan, Italy.
7. See Norman Douglas, *South Wind,* London, 1917.

74. To Patricia and A. S. Frere *(privately held)*

Weds a.m.   M.S. Lafayette [at sea].[1]
[20 January 1937]
Dearest Pat & Frere/

I can't ever thank you for what you've done & are doing. You have literally made this possible, & thereby really saved my life. I'll never forget this.

Everything between us two is *perfect.* I've been hoping for this all my life.

Frere! please don't get to thinking marriage would be a mistake & c. I must have those divorces[2]—if we have to become Yankees & go to Reno. It's a damn crime if we don't have a child.

Bless you both, and thank you—I'll write from Toulon.

Richard

1. Cf. Letter 73 also written aboard ship. Then RA was sailing to the United States convinced that Netta was lost to him; now she is with him as they elope to France.
2. First, a divorce from H.D., about which he had written her five days before, also from the MS *Layfette* en route from America to England, where Netta must have joined him. Second, Netta's divorce from Michael Patmore, which was to occasion considerable difficulty for RA then and in the future. In an effort to mitigate the claims he was sure Brigit would make on him, RA wrote and signed an "Aide-Memoir To Counsel," which he sent to A. S. Frere. In this memoir RA says that he and Brigit first met in 1911, became lovers in 1912, but did not resume "intimate relations" following his return from abroad in 1913 although Brigit remained a friend of RA and H.D., to whom he was married in October of 1913.

The memoir confirms Brigit's relations with Stephen Haden-Guest, which were breaking up when she joined RA in Paris at the end of 1928. RA notes that a letter from Brigit in 1927 saying she was "in very poor circumstances and had been reduced to selling programs in a theatre" elicited help from him in the form of a commission to write a translation of Marmontel for the Broadway Series of which he was editor.

RA adds that when he saw Brigit in 1928, "she was living in a Bloomsbury slum and appeared to be in bad health." He took her to the country for a short stay and then paid her fare to Port-Cros. Following this visit of six or eight weeks, the two lived and traveled together until December 1936.

The memoir accuses the Patmores of selling personal belongings left with Brigit, including a painting by D. H. Lawrence, Lawrence's seal, many books, all RA's clothes, and a trunk containing literary papers, "among them a collection of letters received from all parts of the world about my work."

75. To A. S. Frere (privately held)

11 August 1937   Le Canadel
Dearest Frere,

Herewith cheque for 3.14.11, with the invoice.

I would have written sooner, but I've been having a bit of a tussle with Mason Reeves.[1] The first three chapters are done, completing the exposition of the theme. Then came the problem of the first transition, one of the real difficulties of the novel and the thing that most people go down on. It took me two days and a picnic near Collobrières to work it out. Even so Netta thinks it lousy. However, the action is now moving again, so I shall leave these two pages for the time being and push on. They can always be re-written or cut later.

As this is a roman aux tiroirs in the bad old English tradition, and not on the classical plan like the others, I think I had better adopt the English habit of sub-titles for chapters. Thus the chapters so far written or planned will run thus:

1. First Morning
2. First Evening
3. Cocktail party
4. Of Time and the River-philosopher
5. Mrs. Reeves gives a dinner
6. Mr. Reeves gives a luncheon

I haven't set any definite length, but Mr. Reeves is rather a fragile peg. Mustn't try to hang too much on him. I've now done about 15,000, and with any luck should be finished by Christmas. I then want to start straight away on a more solid novel for which I have the idea. Do wish I could clear up the Patmores[2] and get settled in here somewhere—could get on with the job then and make up arrears.

I meant to ask you here, but think I forgot, whether you favour the idea of making a collection of short prose pieces, like In the South, A

Moment at Sea, Sea Verge, My Immortal Friends, etc, choosing the best ones.[3] I'm all against reprinting journalism, but they were written for their own sake, and merely happen to have been printed in periodicals. I had quite a lot to choose from at the Cavendish, but they've apparently gone west.[4] Also Pino has a lot in a trunk I left with him. I was a mug not to pick them up when I was in Florence. Might get them later.

Looking forward to the proofs of Crystal World. I'll bung them back as soon as I've corrected them. When do you think to publish? And, if you have time, remember to coach one or two reviewers. I think the line should be to link up Crystal W. with Luxembourg[5]—that narrative, this lyric—and to point out that both books go counter to the current intellectualist-political trend in poetry—they are purely poems of la sensibilité, and depend, not on any abstract theory of how poetry should be written, but on the validity, depth and poignancy of the emotions. Instead of seeking the intellectually rare and striking, they accept the obvious, commonplace universal feelings. And they are not written from the attitude of The Bard condescending, but of the ordinary man in and out of a pickle. Gemme? An early article on those lines, would give a hint to the other poops who just parrot. How about not sending it to the Times Li Supp? I'm all in favour of ignoring them. Every book I've published since 1929 has been sent to the same bloke, who always takes a crack at it. So why bother with them?

We loved Pat's wire about Mouser's[6] first tooth. Now you will be spared the horror of knowing how bitterer than a thankless serpent it is to have a toothless child.

Very hot and windless here, with daily grumbles of thunder from the direction of Collobrières. We intended to re-visit the site on Monday, but the driving-band came off and disappeared. So we had our picnic under those chestnut trees, and then coasted down to Hyères for a new band. And then it was too late. I bought a Flaubert in Hyères, and realise once more with pain the difference between novels as novels, and the novel as literature. There is nothing in English to compare with Madame Bovary and L'éducation Sentimentale. The latter (pub 1869) has marvellous portraits of all the Socialist and Communist poops we ever met. Plus ça change . . .

Adios, soldier, our love to you all,

Richard

1. The hero of RA's next novel, *Seven Against Reeves. A Comedy-Farce*, London, 1938. The book is dedicated to "Pat," wife of A. S. Frere (whose name originally was Frere-Reeves).

2. Netta's divorce proceedings; see letter 74.

3. Such a collection was not published. These essays originally were published in the *Sunday Referee, Everyman,* and other periodicals.

4. I.e., were lost or destroyed when RA left Brigit; see Letter 74 n. 2.

5. See *A Dream in The Luxembourg,* London, 1930, and *The Crystal World,* London, 1937; the first is dedicated to Brigit, the second to Netta.

6. "Mouse" was the nickname of the Freres' daughter Elizabeth who was born in 1937; now Elizabeth Jones, she lives in Brooklyn, N.Y., having emigrated to the United States in 1961.

76. To Eric Warman (SIUC)

18 August 1937   Le Canadel.

Dear Erik,

Herewith three of the Bootle cuttings—the others are repeats or shorts. Let me have them back by the end of the month, will you, as I want to show them to a young man from Heinemann who is coming to see us. I'm afraid it won't do a lot of good financially—they'll all buy Penguins. However, it's pleasant to think the old book still has a kick in it after eight years.[1]

We'll like to come and see you when in England. One of Netta's ideas of bliss is bread and cheese, pickles and beer, so you needn't worry about that. You couldn't get a bouillabaisse in London—it isn't even good in Paris. You must have rascasses and other Mediterranean fishes, langouste, herbs, garlic and about a pint of oil. It is delicious. But in England, English food is the best, and darn good too. Aioli is a real peasant dish. You have a big dish of boiled fish, and another of plain boiled vegetables—carrots, potatoes, gourds, turnips, anything—and then a large bowl of mayonnaise with at least two whole heads of garlic pounded in, so you smell it a mile off. Much recommended to fashionables before going to a cocktail party!

I'm very glad to hear your novel is coming into shape.[2] I think myself that one of the great difficulties of the novel is that ideas must be shown in action. It is one of the hardest things to do successfully, i.e. the complete fusion of idea and action. I think Sinclair Lewis's Main Street is an example of its achievement. Point Counter Point, on the other hand, fails continually to "integrate" idea and action.[3] I've found, and I believe you'll find, that directly the novel departs from action and character, it loses interest. The ideas must be contained in them not tacked on to them. Easier said than done!

I wonder very much what you'll think of the novel I'm working on now. It is intended to be comedy, almost farce, the whole way, and is hung on an exceedingly simple plot. Narrative is cut down to a minimum, and almost everything told in dialogue or indirect speech. Netta laughs herself into tears over it, and I must say I find myself grinning like a Cheshire cat as I write it. But whether that great booby called "the public" will see the joke is another matter. However, I feel pretty sure it'll give you some laughs.

We are still in perpetual sunshine here. Unluckily, a lot of other people have discovered this bit of coast, and it is rapidly losing its wild unspoiled quality. What a curse other people are! However, this cottage stands on the edge of a low cliff and is surrounded by about an acre of thick coppice, so the other people bother us not at all. And there is a superb view across the bay and out to the islands. I shall be very sorry to leave the place, but it is in bad repair and lets in the winter rain, and has no real heating defence against the occasional cold winds of January and February. Those are the only two bad winter months here, as you can bathe until December. The sea now near shore must be about 70 degrees, so you can stay in as long as you like without getting cold. The water is so clear it is like having an aquarium. You can stand on the rocks and watch the fishes disporting themselves, from two-foot long monsters called mullets down to tiny little fishes an inch long of a dark glowing gentian blue. Recently there have been queer jellyfish with yellow-brown caps and underneaths of blobby white and purple. What is curious is that little fish live inside them, adventuring out to feed and then dashing inside the jellyfish for safety. A sort of piscatory co-operative society.

I'm having a devil of a time with lawyers, and the whole thing is in a frightful mess, owing to my trying to do what is called the right thing. The Patmores want their pound of flesh, and then some. It is extraordinary how people with highly refined feeling and aristocratic pretentions are so damn keen on money. Not to mention revenge. The idea seems to be to make as big a scandal as possible, to get the case reported if they can, and to cause me as much direct and indirect expense as possible by involving me in a defended suit in which I shall have to pay costs and by claiming fantastic damages, in spite of the fact that Brigit is being paid an income! Directly anything with common-sense in it is suggested to the lawyers, they have expensive conferences, and then say it's illegal.

This is confidence to yourself, of course, but the whole thing seems to be bit thick.

Our love to Vi and yourself.

Ever Yours,
Richard

1. On 7 August 1937 RA wrote Warman: "Apropos, you probably have not heard that the Council of Bootle had a solemn meeting over Death of a Hero, and after they called it vulgar and one of the vilest books ever written, decided by a large majority to remove it

from the Bootle public library. There was about a column report of the proceedings in the Liverpool Daily Post of 29th July, and an editorial making fun of them" (SIUC); see "Bootle Council Ban War Book," p. 4, and "Bootle's Babies" [editorial], p. 6, *Liverpool Daily Post*, 29 July 1937.

2. Eric Warman's next published book was *Relative to Murder*, London, 1940.

3. Sinclair Lewis, *Main Street*, New York, 1920; Aldous Huxley, *Point Counter Point*, London, 1928.

77. *To H.D. (Yale)*

24 February 1938[1]   Le Canadel.

Dear Dooley,

I have just heard that you have been greatly distressed by a rumour which alleges that I have said there was some "trick" in the matter of the deed concerning Perdita.[2] The assertion is too ridiculous, and I'm surprised that you gave it any credit and that you didn't immediately suspect its source.

I don't think I have mentioned the matter three times in the last fifteen years and then only in the strictest confidence. For many years by my silence or in so many words I tacitly admitted paternity[3] in order to spare you in any way possible.

What I said about the deed[4] was this:

(1) That I was at first a little startled by the request to sign it, since I thought it might in law be considered a kind of perjury. As soon as Sir John's[5] lawyer explained the situation, I signed the deed at once without hesitation.

(2) That it suddenly occurred to me at the time (and was subsequently alleged to me) that you had been fearful lest I might use the situation to interfere between you and your child. Upon which my comment was that it had never crossed my mind before that you, who knew me, would think me capable of such baseness; and that, had I known, I should have sent you a reassurance at once.

I am very sorry indeed that you have been troubled by this canard, and I can only assure you that it is self-evidently a lie. What possible "trick" could there have been in a matter of this sort which was put out before me so frankly and openly by Sir John's lawyer?

You may be interested to know that Netta is having a baby about the end of June and that we are coming to Lausanne for this spectacular event.[6] The clinic we looked at there seemed excellent and so much cheaper than London. If you are in Territet at the time, it would be nice to see you.

And do stop worrying about that silly lie.

Ever,
Richard.

1. Only three letters to H.D. from RA written between 17 August 1931 (Letter 60) and this date have been located. They are dated 21 August 1931, 21 February 1932, and 15 January 1937 (Yale). In the one of 15 January 1937, written en route from America to England on board MS *Lafayette*, RA asked H.D. to divorce him.

2. Perdita Aldington Schaffner (Mrs. John), H.D.'s daughter.

3. Cecil Gray was the father. See Letters 22, 23, and passim.

4. By which Bryher adopted Perdita Aldington in 1928.

5. Sir John Ellerman, Bryher's father.

6. Catherine Aldington was born in London.

78. To A. S. Frere (privately held)

5 March 1938   Le Canadel.

Dearest Frere,

You have been an angel in keeping me au fait with the results of S.A.R.,[1] above all since you are so busy. But I can assure you it has been greatly appreciated, and also has prevented me from getting into "states" and worrying. 50, 35 and 97 are not very good, though the 97 on Wednesday looks a bit more hopeful. I've been awfully unlucky in reviewers. Straus, Muggeridge, L. P. Hartley are all ancient hostile ones. Hartley has damned every one of my novels since the Hero; Straus all except the Hero. Muggeridge (what a name!) wrote an almost frenzied attack on Artifex.[2] I don't want to exaggerate the importance of reviews, but it's pretty hard for any reputation to stand up to a continuous gunning like this. Ordinary people who are pretty vague about such things anyway can't help but be influenced. It makes your job twice as hard when you've got most of the reviewers pulling against you.

I've mailed back the dummies to Mac.[3] There seems to be absolutely nothing wrong with them, and I'm "highly delighted."

I don't know if I told you—Cran's taxed costs came to 176 quid, plus 25 Solicitor and Client. I have already paid 100 through Netta's father, and sent Preston another 100 last month. This morning I have one of his incomprehensible letters, but it looks as if this 200 will cover that. Preston himself has had 150, but will need more later he says.[4] No news from H.D.[5]

In spite of this drain of costs and the 5 quid a week to Brigit, the finances are not too bad, owing chiefly to strict economy here. I still have 150 left of the Letter of Credit, plus about 800 frcs in cash, and 180 pounds in the Bank. If *only* S.A.R. could put me straight with Heinemann then I should begin to see real daylight.

After much trouble I've managed to get a drinkable vin ordinaire in "bonbons" of 10 litres for 30 francs. That is about 12 claret bottles, so works out at less than half the Fanning, and less than a third of the

Talbot. I'm hoping eventually to get all costs here down to 4000 frcs a month, I mean for everything, including stamps, cigarettes, car, clothes, wages.

The Encyclopedia has come at last.[6] Many, many thanks. (The bastards made me pay 40 francs Customs Duty!) I am very glad to have it, although it is a damn bourgeois production, for it will be an immense help in mere matters of fact both in articles and books. I'll pay for it as soon as you tell me.

By the way, this month I got 8 quid extra for Albatross royalties.[7] Not much, but it shows some continued sale.

You have been super-patient in not pressing for information about a possible new novel. I haven't yet got a title which pleases me, for the simple reason that I have rather enlarged its scope since I first conceived it. So that the part I have already done will come later in the book.[8]

I find it hard to describe a planned book, no doubt because neat plotting is not one of my strong points. But, as you know, I like to start first with a single character, which shall stand as a symbol of many rather than as an exceptional individual. In this case I thought I would invent the history of one of the children left behind by the troops—a bastard War baby, in fact. (Born in 1915, he would now be 23.) I assume his father was a gent; his mother lower middle class. He is reared by grandparents in a small provincial town—a cross between Folkestone and Reading, say. The First Part of the book is his personal narrative, written in a rather plain realistic style, no fireworks. Genetics authorises me to suppose that if (I provisionally call him David) has upper class genes on one side, he will probably differ from the usual muck-scum of people living in a row of 15/– a week villas. Thus, the first part will show the sufferings of a child with his drawback (I shan't underline the irony of the dead hero's baby), and the *struggle to rise above the class imposed on him*. I want to make him energetic and intelligent, handicapped by growing up with grandparents (kind, but pre-War mentality), by inefficient education. As he grows up, he has almost an idée fixe that, if only he can get among well-bred, cultured people (not social pretenders, but the real thing) he'll be quite happy. All this told in his own words, mind you.

At 18, (say 4 years ago) I propose to put him into an Estate Agent's office, but he will spend all his leisure trying to educate himself; and will have all the excessive respect for learning of the self-educated. I propose, also, to make him a member of a suburban literary society, devoted to the worship of one, Arbuthnot, a literary prophet of the early part of the century, quasi-socialist, quasi-Nature-faking. Arbuthnot is dead, and his idea of an ideal community is being run in the south, here, by a sort of Augustus John, bloke with three wives and a mass of enfants. He's long ago bust up the real community, runs it really as a house agent business, but gets really rather superior people. Cutting it short, this bloke's getting a bit old and lazy, wants an assistant, and picks up our young David. Expatiates to him on the glory of it. Wages and commission—delusive of course. Will meet all these people as equal. Can "write" in his spare time. Bliss, joy of David. Par One ends with Nunc Dimittis.

Part 2 is written by me, with the fire-works. He will meet people just about as cultured as they make 'em, and talk, talk, talk, quite good, even brilliant talk. But nothing but. See the young man coming worshipping, and then gradually disillusioned? (I'm getting tired, can't extend this properly.) Meanwhile, one of the middle-aged wives of the A. John bloke falls in love with him, while he falls for a Georgy-ish but sensible girl his own age. (Must avoid repeating Very Heaven here.) I'm not quite sure of the end. If I give the girl money, it's an easy let-out, and a bit too Ethel M. Dellish. A man who marries a girl with money is buggered up anyhow. My present idea is to have all these amiable rentier talkers assembled in an old fort (like the Vigie) outside an idealised St Tropez. They can look down on the harbour. Submarine there. All are talking with accustomed brilliance. David and the girl in a corner. Hum of planes. Submarine begins frantically to cast off. "More of these beastly manoeuvres," says some one. Planes nearer. "Oh, never mind them," says someone else, "Let's go on talking" . . . Plonk! Crash! They are wiped out by the first bombs of the next war. The torn pages of pseudo-A. John's books go fluttering away in the mistral.

I want this second part to be as amusing and up to snuff as South Wind in its own way.

That's the plan, though I haven't fully developed Part 2.

What do you think? Title: Let's Go On Talking ????? I want Part 2 to show both the charm and the futility of genuine upper class culture. I want to make them as instructed and amusing as anything in Norman or Aldous,[9] but . . . They *do* nothing. Personally I want the bombs at the end—in other words I want to blow up the Norman-Aldous world with the realities you and I know.

Advise.

Always affectionately,
Richard

P.S. I've skimped this second part badly. I ought to have added that there would be a chorus of peasants, fishers and traders, living a purely non-mental, predatory, realistic life, to contrast with the over-refined idealism of the others.

P.P.S. So warm that we bathed yesterday and to-day. Sea as cold as bug, but lovely for a very short dip.

R.

1. *Seven Against Reeves;* "50, 35 and 97" are the numbers of copies sold daily.
2. See *Artifex, Sketches and Ideas,* London, 1935.
3. Not identified.
4. Legal costs in connection with Netta's divorce.
5. In connection with her divorce from RA.
6. RA says his own *Encyclopedia Britannica* was sold by the Patmores; see Letter 74 n. 2.
7. Albatross Continental Library, a John Holroyd-Reese publishing enterprise.
8. In the paragraphs that follow, RA sketches the novel that was to become *Rejected Guest,* London, 1939, although the plot was considerably changed.
9. Norman Douglas and Aldous Huxley.

79. To Eric Warman (SIUC)

20 May 1938   22 Boulevard de Chamblandes,
                                               Pully, Lausanne, Switzerland.

Dear Erik,

Here we are. The weather is lousy, but otherwise O is K. Netta stood the journey very well, although it rained like bug all the way from Avignon to Annecy. I wish to Christ I could just once see Avignon when it wasn't raining. I've been through it umpteen times, and invariably in the rain.

Switzerland. Ha, ha! Palace of the League of Nations, roads like billiard tables, no hooting of cars, trams as smooth as prams, lake, mountains, snow-crests, protestants, neatness, everything twice as dear as in France, the most respectable suburbia in the world, no poor, no beggars, no proletariat apparently. There must be whores, but where? It is a bourgeois utopia, and I should go crackers if I had to live here. The only thing lacking to the place is Bernard Shaw, who ought to be the Swiss mascot, and swim in the lake, eat lettuce in Jaeger underclothes and guide intelligent women to socialism for a modest retaining fee of 30,000 a year. It is the epitome of enlightened unimaginative virtue, the peak quotation of sober righteousness and making money "honestly." This, my dear boy, is a perfection of civic organisation such as England has never dreamed of—no slums, handsome public buildings, fantastically neat clean streets, infinite garden suburbs, well-drilled vineyards, fruit trees in every garden, and real genuine beauty of lakes and mountains, even the picturesque past most carefully preserved. It's quite unbearable. Everything which is not obligatory is forbidden.

I am now through with Doubledays, and shall probably go to Holts as you suggested. I am waiting only to hear from Pinker if they will meet my terms. I'm not bidding them up, you understand, I only want the same agreement I have been getting. There are about eight other American publishers trying to butt in, but my fancy is for Holts; and if they come up to scratch I shall disregard the others.

Now, lissen. Heinemanns are making a real effort about this Uniform edition. The first six pocket vols are manufactured, and I've just passed the final proof of the wrapper. There will be a Crown 8vo edition too, but only 2 volumes at first. (They still have Chatto stock to get rid of.) C. P. Snow's pamphlet is now on the machine, and they should be all set before long.[1] In great confidence, I must tell you that I've staged a reconciliation with the Times and am going to write for the Supplement again. I think they *may* give the Uniform edition a leader.[2] This is just "hopes," so for god's sake don't mention it. But I've been wondering whether you could get in an article somewhere if I had Heinemann send you an advance set of the books and Snow's pamphlet? The first six vols are: All Men, Col's Daughter, Soft Answers, Hero, Voltaire, Very Heaven. In the Crown 8vo, All Men and Women Must Work.[3] I have advised Heinemann against sending out review copies, so if you had an advance set you'd be in a privileged position. Snow's panegyric would give you something to kick off from. If you think you could wangle an article, let me know, and I'll have the books and the pamphlet sent to you as soon as they are available. Can you think of anyone else who should receive a set? I DON'T want to send them to the old gang—Straus, Mac-Carthy, etc, etc. Only to people who are genuinely interested and would like to write about them. Snow's pamphlet is going to have a bibliography, which I think will rather surprise you. It certainly surprised me—I didn't know I'd spoiled so much paper. I think you'll be delighted with the books when you see them. Heinemanns have taken immense trouble and spared no expense, and I think they are the nicest pocket edition on the market.

As you can imagine, the appearance of 'Works of' is rather an event for me, a sort of jubilee of 25 years of writing. Advise me, if you can, of any means of getting the event noticed favourably!

I hope all goes well with you. Let me have your news.

Ever yours,
Richard

1. See C. P. Snow, *Richard Aldington: An Appreciation*, London [1938].

2. See Letter 80 n. 4.

3. The Uniform Edition of the Works of Richard Aldington consisted of sheets from previous editions rebound with new title pages. Only the following were completed: no. 1, *All Men Are Enemies. A Romance*, London [1938]; no. 2, *The Colonel's Daughter, A Novel*, London [1938]; no. 3, *Soft Answers*, London [1938]; no. 4, *Death of a Hero. A Novel*, London [1938]; no. 5, *Voltaire*, London [1938]; and no. 6, *Very Heaven*, London [1938].

80. To Eric Warman (SIUC)

2 July 1938   Astor Hotel
                                                   Princes Square W.2
                                                   [London]

Dear Erik,

What sort of time are you having in Czecho? Good, I hope. They sound rather nice people. I look forward to hearing about your adventures.

Last week the law moved with unprecedented rapidity, and we were married on Saturday.[1] That cleared up many of our immediate difficulties. But there is no infant and no signs of its appearing, although it is already nearly a week late.[2] Probably it has heard of Hitler, and prefers to stay where it is.

I don't know if you saw before you left that J. O'London ran an article of mine with photograph as its leader and had a short puff of the Uniform.[3] The T.L.S. has done much the same thing. Last week they ran a short review of the Uniform, and this week they have a signed article with a photograph. Evidently they don't wish to commit themselves too far.[4] Heinemanns say that Joseph Sell is going to do an article in the Manchester Evening News.[5] They also have hopes of one in the News: Chronicle,[6] but so far as I know nothing has happened yet.

After all I haven't gone to Harpers. At the last moment the Viking weighed in with a 33% better offer, and as I think them one of the best publishers in U.S. I naturally accepted it. Doubledays don't seem to be doing much with Reeves, so it's as well to be changing. I don't like leaving so much work tied up with them, but it can't be helped.

Since you left there has been much ballyhoo about Test matches,[7] more ballyhoo about an M.P. and official secrets, and a doctor is being prosecuted for aborting a girl of 14 who had been raped. The royal standard is still over Buck Pal. So all is well.

When do you get back?

                                                   Ever yours,
                                                   Richard

P.S. Women Must Work has just been banned in Ireland.[8]

1. Netta and RA were married Saturday, 25 June 1938.
2. Their daughter Catherine was born 6 July 1938 in London.
3. See RA, "What Science Means to Me: A New Conception of Man's Place in the Universe," *John O'London's Weekly,* 24 June 1938, p. 1.
4. See RA, "Knowledge and the Novelist," *Times Literary Supplement,* 2 July 1938, p. 448; and "Richard Aldington," *Times Literary Supplement,* 25 June 1938, p. 429.
5. See Joseph Sell [William Haley], "Richard Artifex," *Manchester News,* 6 October 1938, p. 8.

6. Not traced.

7. Championship cricket matches played between Australia and England.

8. See Public Record Office of Ireland, Register Number 986, *Register of Prohibited Publications* (*As On the 31st March, 1940*), p. 70, which shows 10 June 1938 as the "date of prohibition order" for *Women Must Work. A Novel,* London, 1934.

IV

SCREENWRITER-BIOGRAPHER: 1939–1946. LETTERS 81–105

The Aldingtons remained in Le Canadel until February 1939, when they left France for New York City via London. The war that RA saw threatening in 1935 seemed imminent; RA must have felt the time had come to take his new wife and daughter to the United States. English newspapers created quite a scandal about the couple, and RA was avoided by many old friends. In New York, however, Pascal Covici, a partner in the firm that had published RA's first novel, *Death of a Hero*, remained loyal. Covici was now senior editor at the Viking Press, which became RA's American publisher. After living in New York City for six weeks, the Aldingtons spent their summer in Rhode Island; there RA finished his novel *Rejected Guest* and, with Basil Dean, dramatized his *Seven Against Reeves*.

In New York City that autumn, RA had difficulty finding the general literary work that had been available to him in London; he did some lecturing at eastern universities, but this did not pay well. In June 1940 RA returned to Old Lyme, Connecticut, renting a house near the one where he had lived in 1935 with Brigit. That summer he sold serial rights to the *Atlantic Monthly* for his memoirs published in book form in 1941 as *Life for Life's Sake*. At forty-eight RA wrote what he felt then was his farewell to Europe; certainly it was a farewell to the two Europes he had known prior to the world wars. The first installment appeared in the September issue of the *Atlantic*. Now RA was ready for an even more important literary commitment made earlier that year: the editorship of *The Viking Book of Poetry of the English-Speaking World*.

A conversation between Harold Guinzburg, Viking president, and RA generated the idea for the anthology. Once plans were settled on, RA began working in the Columbia University Library near his New York City apartment; at Old Lyme he was near the Yale University Library. That fall the Aldingtons moved to Washington, D.C., since RA felt he needed the resources of the Library of Congress; they stayed from November 1940 to February 1941. When RA's library work on the anthology was completed early in March, the Aldingtons left for Florida. Both RA and his daughter had suffered an attack of influenza, and doctors advised a warmer climate for Catherine's recovery. RA's plans were to stay in Florida until mid-April and then travel to Frieda Lawrence's ranch in New Mexico where he hoped to stay until October.

RA was delighted with his new home at Jamay Beach, Nokomis, Florida, possibly because it reminded him of his beloved Mediterranean coast of France. He stayed at Jamay Beach for about a year, and his letters from there suggest the beauty of the temporary home in America that appealed most to him. The task of correcting proofs for his huge anthology and preparing a bibliography for it delayed a visit to Frieda Lawrence until May, and the Aldingtons came back to Florida in July rather than in October as they had planned. RA explains that the altitudes of the Lawrence ranch made Netta, Catherine, and himself ill, and, although he agreed with DHL about the beauty of the ranch, he disliked the summer storms and the "appalling diseases." Furthermore, he was bored by the society there.

Happy to be back in his peaceful cottage on the Gulf of Mexico, RA was engrossed for a time with the critical reviews of the Viking anthology but in January of 1942 he began to work on a new project: a biography of the Duke of Wellington. This first biography since his 1925 *Voltaire* was one of several books RA suggested to Viking and may have been selected because the time seemed appropriate to recall England's defeat of an earlier European tyrant who had threatened her. *The Duke* (1943) was the first of the important biographies that would constitute RA's major literary work during the next decade. The period between the two wars, the time that RA satirized in his novels was ended; now his vision needed new form.

In July 1942, RA, taking a respite from the Wellington biography and the anti-saboteur beach patrol for which he was acting as "Deputy-Sheriff," made a journey by rail to a Writers' Conference held at the University of Colorado in Boulder. When he returned in August, he decided to move to Hollywood. The remoteness of Jamay Beach, gas rationing, Netta's lack of companionship, and the closing of the school Catherine was to attend all contributed to RA's reluctant decision, but the need to increase his earnings was the final motivation. He had sold Hollywood film rights to *All Men Are Enemies* almost ten years earlier; he had reason to hope for success as a screenwriter, and a lecture tour booked for January and February was in hand. The Aldingtons left Florida for the last time in September traveling by car and stopping in Boulder to see friends RA had made on his July visit.

During RA's three and a half year stay in Hollywood he worked as a free-lance writer for several motion picture companies. None of his film scripts was ever used, but while he did not find the pot of gold he may have been looking for he was fairly successful financially, and, although time for his literary work was short during this period, he did manage to produce a surprising number of books. He finished *The Duke,* begun in Florida and eventually to win the James Tait Black Memorial Prize; he wrote *The Romance of Casanova* on commission for Columbia Pictures, which did not film it although it was published as a novel in New York and later in London; he edited and wrote a fine introduction for *The Portable Oscar Wilde,* using unpublished Wilde manuscripts and letters from UCLA; he provided an introduction for *Great French Romances,* which included his 1925 translation *Dangerous Acquaintances;* and he also completed an anthology of verse in translation (for *The Encyclopedia Britannica*) that was never published. When RA left Hollywood in April 1946 he did so on medical advice that he take a rest; he went to Jamaica, where Netta's mother was building a home, and planned to return to California in a few months. RA wrote in an early letter from Hollywood that he liked the Los Angeles area very much and that he would "never return to Europe." Now, leaving for Jamaica, he writes that Hollywood has become a madhouse where, because he tried to do screen work and write a book at the same time, he nearly repeated the nervous collapse he had suffered during the 1920s.

RA enjoyed what was to be his last look at America when he traveled by car from Hollywood to New Orleans; from there the Aldingtons flew to Jamaica via Mobile, Tampa, Miami, and Cuba, arriving in May. As early as June he gave up the idea of returning to Hollywood and was thinking of a trip to Rio de Janeiro and Buenos Aires, "perhaps returning to France in 1947," but in August 1946 he was in New York and arrived in Paris in September.

81. To H.D. (Yale)

20 July 1939

The Scallop Shell,
Peace Dale, R.I.

Dear Hilda,

I was very pleased to have your letter, especially as I hadn't heard from you for so long. I had a feeling that in some way I had unwittingly offended you. This was the last thing I wanted to do, as you have been so particularly kind and generous.

We came over last February, and spent about six weeks in New York seeing friends. Paul Willert, who runs the Oxford University Press here, was particularly nice to us. He is a great collector of Central European refugees, and passed one of them—a medical student—on to us as a nurse for Catherine. We're now trying to get her family out of the clutches of the Nazis.

In April we came to Rhode Island, and spent a whole month with Leonard Bacon and his family. Leonard was one of our opponents in the Imagist days and still thinks it's all rot. But he's an extremely cultivated and pleasant person and has a perfectly lovely estate here. His mother's family, the Hazards, practically own Peace Dale and indeed seem to run most of the State. They also own multitudes of houses. We spent May, June and part of July in the house of T. P. Hazard at Saunderstown, where by the bye Jim and Mildred Whitall have a house. Their boy is now 15, and crazy about yachting. Now we are in another Hazard house, belonging to Miss Caroline, who is 83 and was once president of Wellesley university. We have it until the end of September, and where we shall go then I've no idea. I'd like to go west, though I love New England.

Last week Netta and I left Catherine with Mrs. Bacon, and went motoring up north of Boston. It is strange but rather lovely country, with ranges of small mountains not unlike parts of the Jura and Alsace, and numbers of glorious lakes. All the forests were cut down for timber in the past, but have now sprung up again in dense almost impenetrable thickets of second-growth trees. Moreover, literally hundreds of thousands of acres of farm land have been abandoned in the past quarter of a century, and that is rapidly reverting to forest too. Economically I suppose it's a tragedy of waste and incompetence, but I rather like the feeling of this great American forest re-establishing its power. Even here in Rhode Island the same thing is going on—hundreds of farms reverting to scrub which in ten years will be forest. Some of the wild creatures are coming back too—deer, foxes, woodchucks, only too vigorous skunks, and multitudes of squirrels, chipmunks and so on. Up on one of those silent Maine lakes, which is almost inaccessible through the fierce growth of young trees on the banks, I heard a loon just before dusk. It's a weird terrifying sound, beginning like an Indian war-whoop and then going off into demoniac laughter. One could easily imagine some primitive genius loci exulting over the defeat of the white man by the wilderness. You really ought to take a look at northern New England—it's a much more impressive "waste land" than Tom Eliot's.

I didn't see Ezra. He arrived in New York, gave out (rather courageously, considering the anti-Fascist feeling here) a number of pro-Fascist interviews and then, as he would say, "vanished into the hinterland" with his buddy, e. e. cummings. I haven't the faintest idea where he is—Idaho maybe. I believe he lectured at Harvard, and rather perplexed the students. But I have seen Slonimski, who is still fascinating and eloquent, but has unfortunately abandoned Greek philosophy for rabbinical theology. A sense of loyalty to his people, I suppose, but quite ridiculous for a man of his gifts. He is Dean of his faculty in some Jewish university. His life is dignified and uncorrupted by the prevalent yahooism. But what a waste!

I sent you my books not so much with the idea of plaguing you to read them, but as a little attempt to show how much I appreciated what you were doing for me. I have a novel, called Rejected Guest, in the press with Heinemann and the Viking Press.[1] Since then I've been working with Basil Dean to make a dramatic version of Seven Against Reeves.[2] He hopes to produce it in the autumn, either in London or New York. It is thoroughly and unashamedly low-brow, designed to make morons laugh. It is a complicated performance—trying to tell a story, present characters, and produce surprises all in words of one syllable. But it's great fun, and I thoroughly enjoy it. Whether it is a success and indeed whether it is ever produced depends entirely on Dean, who is only responsible for the scenario.[3] He may hate my dialogue.

Catherine is a very healthy young woman, with blue eyes and dark hair, and singularly like the photographs of me at her age. She is just beginning to say words and to totter about holding on to her pen, and creeps with incredible energy. She is an amiable infant and very little trouble. I like her very much indeed.

I feel very much ashamed at not having paid you my share of Goddard's fees,[4] but lawyers, doctors and Patmores between them relieved me of all my savings. With all the upsets and events I worked more slowly than usual—in fact that last novel was so much interrupted that I was over a year on it. Delightful rumours that I was "finished" were circulated, and naturally editors took advantage of the position to knock down prices. However, since the announcements of the new novel are out, I've been able to re-establish the status quo and even a bit better. I will start paying that off as soon as ever I can.

Let me have your news some time, and do come to America. It's much nicer than Europe at present. The place is so big that it's easy to avoid the thugs and morons.

With all good wishes from us both,

Richard

1. 1939. Viking Press published first.
2. 1938.
3. Not produced.
4. Expenses arising from H.D.'s and RA's divorce.

82. To Eric Warman (SIUC)

4 October 1939   c/o Viking Press,
                                                       18 East 48th Street,
                                                       New York.

My dear Erik,

You will observe by the date of this that it has taken exactly a month for my letter to get your reply. I hope the mail service will improve. It has been rather harassing not to receive news of friends. If you want to get any news over here quickly remember that half an ounce is carried by the Atlantic Air Mail for 30 cents.

I am concerned over the position you find yourself in, and think you were too precipitate in leaving Aske.[1] I had two letters from Pinker in my last mail, and in the latest he says that he believes there will be something of a boom in books owing to the curtailment of other amusements. He may be right. At all events, after saying first they would postpone my novel, Heinemann (he says) have now decided to go ahead with it. It will be panned to hell, of course, as it is not exactly in tune with current sentiment.[2]

I would strongly advise you to leave Jean at the farm and try to get back with Aske. Articles will plainly be no good as long as the restriction on the size of newspapers lasts. But books are mostly made of esparto grass, and of course don't consume anything like the amount of paper a newspaper does. Ralph[3] may be right about books.

I am sending you a note for Frere—who has changed his name from Frere-Reeves to Frere by deed poll—but I cannot guarantee your reception. The last pre-war letters I had from him were almost dementedly patriotic and full of denunciations of people going to America! Since war I have not had a word from him. So for all I know my name may be dirt. But he can't do more than turn you down, though he can be damned offensive if he wants. You must judge yourself whether it is worth trying, but at best it is a slender hope.

I do sympathize with you deeply in your predicament and only wish you were over here. Conditions are not easy, but there is some chance and, of course, I could have helped you to meet relevant people here. I am working hard to get my foot in somewhere here, but with only moderate success. My novel subscribed only 4000, plus 1200 to "previewers," a small book club of the Viking. It has had excellent reviews, especially in the N.Y. Times,[4] but I don't think the sales have been anything but sluggish. If they don't pick up, the outlook will be dark. I am now in New York, seeing editors, but they are all in a dither and can't make up their minds whether to use all war stuff, some war stuff or none. The only things I have landed are some articles in the Atlantic Monthly, and a trial article for the American Mercury which thinks I might do its monthly literary article.[5] I've done other articles on spec, but nothing has come of them. I'm to see some more editors. I gave a reading of my poems at Wellesley university this week, and go to Harvard on the 19th. But no offer of a university job has come through. There are many efforts being made to get me a Hollywood job, but there also nothing has come through. I may have to do one of the usual grinding lecture tours. It is very tantalising to be on the very edge of several things and yet not be able to make any of them. I feel as fed up with my run of bad luck as you do with yours.

One trouble here is that everything is well paid except intellectual and artistic work which is under paid. For example. You have to pay a servant in N.Y. about five pounds a week, but for a lecture to a great university I get only 20 pounds, and have to pay about 3 pounds travelling expenses, work two or three days to prepare the lecture, and give up the best part of 2 days to travelling to and from the university. Similarly an article of the tripe variety in one of the big magazines pays from 70 to 200 pounds, but in the "good" periodicals only 10 to 20. Topicality dominates everything.

I do hope you get a break somewhere and will be able to make some money.

All the best to you,

Richard

1. Warman left the employment of Aske to take his daughter, Jean, to the safety of the country.

2. See RA, *Rejected Guest. A Novel*, London, 1939.

3. Ralph Pinker, RA's literary agent.

4. See J. S. Southern, "A Novel of Britons between the Wars," *New York Times Book Review*, 24 September 1939, p. 6.

5. See RA, "Norman Douglas and Calabria," *Atlantic Monthly*, June 1939, pp. 757–60, and "For Armistice Day, 1939," November 1939, pp. 684–86. RA did no work for *American Mercury*.

83. To H.D. (Yale)

c/o The Viking Press,
18 East 48th St.,
29 November 1939   New York.

Dear Hilda,

I have delayed answering your last letter because I hoped to be able to send you better news of my situation here. As ever I am something of a misfit—too high-brow for the popular magazines, not sufficiently academic and docile for the universities. Hollywood is respectful but unresponsive. My novel[1] has sold about 8500 and will probably reach the 10,000 [mark], thereby exactly earning the 300 dollars advance. No doubt I could get that for a new novel, but at the moment there seems nothing to be done on those lines, and I don't want to write a novel merely for the sake of getting out another book.

The educational world here is interesting, full of grandiose projects and vague aspirations, but with an intellectual achievement inferior to Europe. Vast sums are expended on sumptuous academic buildings, but the quality of the educators is of no importance, and there are far too many stupid young people trying to secure a diploma. The disinterested love of learning and culture is almost unknown. And there is no common program, merely a "democratic" chaos. Only the sciences seem to escape the dim mediocrity, because they can command almost unlimited funds and the various Boards of control don't know enough to interfere with them. The proposed ideal of giving *everyone* a higher education is not only fantastic in itself, but means that nobody gets a genuine higher education unless he administers it to himself by going to Europe.

However, I continue to give readings and to visit universities. Yesterday I was at a new place, Queens College, N.Y., which provides an entirely free 3 years course to 1600 adolescents of N.Y. city. Two of the men on the English Faculty are great fans of yours. I found loyal readers of yours at Harvard and Princeton also.

I am going to give a reading at Yale and in March I shall spend a week at Wesleyan as "visiting poet." I shall also give a reading to the Library at Philadelphia, which you doubtless know all about. In journalism I continue to write for the Atlantic[2] and the Saturday Review[3] and have sold two articles to Esquire,[4] but otherwise have had no success. It is discouraging, but I keep on.

In spite of all these difficulties, I wouldn't be anywhere else, particularly in Europe. The chaos here is a friendly one, in which there may be a nook of quiet, but the European chaos seems to me hopeless. How can this struggle result in anything but an all around collapse, financial, economic, political, cultural? The war against Hitlerism will probably result in Bolshevising Europe, including England. Suppose at the cost of enormous sacrifices they do clean up Hitler, what are they going to do about Stalin? And Mussolini? And the Japanese? And what earthly reason is there to suppose that peoples and governments will be any wiser, more tolerant and constructive after this war than they were after the last? All this talk about federation of Europe is boloney, and nobody knows that better than the people who are talking about it. An excellent idea on paper, but you'd have to get a new species of European for it to work.

I wonder very much whether you have returned to London. And if so, how life goes on there. I hope all has turned out well.

Recently I met Margaret Widdemer, whom you will remember. She has a sumptuous apartment on Park Avenue, and seems to be quite affluent. I met Ridgeley Torrence there. Strange how superior American poets are to their published works. I have also seen Joe Auslander and his wife, Audry Wurdeman (Pulitzer prize). They are in charge of the Dept. of Poetry at the Library of Congress, which seems an admirable job. Archie MacLeish is head librarian. A nucleus for a nest of singing birds!

All good wishes,
Richard

1. *The Rejected Guest.*
2. See Letter 82 n. 5.
3. See "D. H. Lawrence: Ten Years After," *Saturday Review of Literature*, 24 June 1939, pp. 3–4; and "Somerset Maugham: An Appreciation," *Saturday Review of Literature*, 19 August 1939, pp. 3–4.
4. Possibly "Going Native Nearby," *Esquire*, February 1940, pp. 56, 100; and "Errant Knight of Capri," *Esquire*, December 1941, pp. 74, 230–31.

84. To Eric Warman (SIUC)

13 August 1940   R.F.D. 2
                                                        Old Lyme, Conn.,[1] U.S.

Dear Erik,

Your letter of July 31st just in—about the quickest I've had for many months. I'm glad to hear that you have started about the business of getting Jean over.[2] I will get in touch with the New York Committee at once. Unluckily I don't know the exact name of the address of the Committee and don't find it anywhere in the N.Y. Times. I shall therefore have to write to N.Y. for the address, and then write again to the Committee—or no, perhaps I can do it more quickly by sending the letter to the Viking in my personal one, and asking them to send it over to the right address at once. That will save a couple of days.

As soon as I get the information of what I must do and have complied with the formalities, I will cable you; or arrange for the N.Y. Committee to cable their opposite number in London to inform you. I'll hurry this through as fast as I can, for the raids seem to be getting rather warm and frequent.

I understand your worry about Jean's faults of speech and so on. As she will have to go to school here, they will probably soon disappear, and form into an American model.

I wish you would let me have at once as many practical details as possible, about hours of bed-time and the like. Remember, our knowledge only goes up to two years. She ought to like it here, as the ice cream is excellent and young females much desiderated.

I have no plans for when we leave here or even about leaving here. Much depends on what sort of an autumn we get. The fall is usually lovely, but it can be very cold, and this house unluckily has no central heating. I am working very hard to get my memoirs finished,[3] but the anthology[4] is a huge task, and will mean vicinity to a public library—unless I get the Hollywood job.[5] The only really good libraries in the East are Harvard, Yale, New York and Washington. As Washington is furthest south I might try that for the winter, unless it is too expensive. Owing to the huge expansion in American defense, the capital may be overcrowded with new officials, delegates &c. I must write to friends, and find out. Otherwise, I should be tempted by the coast of Florida.[6]

About a fortnight ago I gave a series of lectures at Columbia University.[7] It would have been all right but for the fact that a heat wave was on, and I had to lecture in temperatures of 95 or more. One afternoon it was 98.6.

The first instalment of my memoirs will be in the September issue of the Atlantic. But as everything here tends to be ahead of time, it will actually be out a week from now on the 20th Aug. Of course, only about a third of the book will appear in these four instalments.[8] But it was a real stroke of luck for me, and solved financial difficulties for some time to come. They pay 1000 dollars for each instalment.

I haven't been able to do anything about your book here, owing to my not knowing the people concerned. I hope Macmillans will take it, and that it will have a good run in England; though the times are the reverse of favourable for book publishing.[9] I can't make up my mind whether to allow Heinemann to go ahead with the two books I'm working on or whether to hold them up until after the war.[10] There is one thing I wish you would do for me if you can—get hold of the Atlantic and tell me if you think the detached moderately humourous tone of my memoirs would be offensive in England now. You could see a copy at the English-speaking union in St James's Square or possibly at the American consulate, where you will have to do a certain amount of waiting about while Jean's papers are being fixed up.

I wish I could give you some hope of speedy and effective aid from this side in the war, but it is difficult to make any forecast. Everything seems to be part of an enormous muddle, which I suppose is what democracy means. Most of the upper classes in the East are strongly pro-British, but the average masses neither know nor care what is happening.

Let me hear from you when you have time.

Ever yours,
Richard

1. See Letter 87.
2. Warman had proposed that the Aldingtons take his daughter, Jean, for the duration of the war, but subsequently decided to keep her in the country in England.
3. See n. 8.
4. See RA, *The Viking Book of Poetry of the English-Speaking World,* New York, 1941.
5. See Letter 93.
6. See Letter 86.
7. See RA, *Ezra Pound and T. S. Eliot. A Lecture,* Hurst, Berkshire, 1954; and RA, *A. E. Housman and W. B. Yeats. Two Lectures,* Hurst, Berkshire, 1955. Cf. Miriam J. Benkovitz, "Richard Aldington and His Postscript," *Columbia Library Columns,* November 1983, pp. 11–22.
8. See RA, "Farewell to Europe . . . ," *Atlantic Monthly,* September–December 1940, pp. 375–96, 509–30, 643–64, 773–96; published with extensive variations in book form as *Life for Life's Sake. A Book of Reminiscences,* New York, 1941.
9. See Letter 76 n. 2.
10. RA's poetry anthology was not published in England until 1947; *Life for Life's Sake* was not published in England until 1965. See nn. 4 and 8.

85. To Henry Slonimsky (SIUC)

23 August 1940   Old Lyme.
Dear Harry,

It was a great pleasure to have your letter. I have been intending to write to you, but the constant drive at these two books[1] has prevented me. As you surmised, it was the heat in New York which kept me from coming to you.

I am very happy to know that your interest in Lawrence continues, and that you will lecture on him. I fear I can tell you nothing about his Jesus and Judas fantasies. Wasn't it Middleton Murry who wanted to play Judas? But there were in Lawrence towards the end strange moods of destructive passion. You will find expressions of it in Pansies. There is one called Attila,[2] which he wrote on Port-Cros, when he was there with me.

I had a pile of new French books, among them a Vie Romancée of Attila. Lawrence read it, and greatly approved of Attila for destroying Roman towns!

You have probably read them, but the books which would throw light on this I think are: Twilight in Italy (A lot of mystical quasi-philosophic stuff); the cancelled preface to Sons and Lovers in the Letters; the Introduction to the Memoirs of M.M.; Kangaroo, particularly the chapter called The Nightmare, the following one called Revenge, Timotheus cries! and L.'s reflections on the Beatitudes; the end of Aaron's Rod; Apocalypse; Pansies; Last Poems.[3] Don't neglect Pansies and Last Poems. Though often so loose in form and careless in expression to be unworthy of the name of poetry, they contain a great deal of L's intimate thought. You should perhaps take into account that L was strongly attracted by animism. He had read Tylor.[4] Cf his poems, Pansies, and Mornings in Mexico.[5]

Lawrence is quite right about the religion of the Italians, i.e. it is sexual, with salvation through paternity. South of Naples you never see either God the Father or an adult Jesus, even on the cross. The pictures are invariably that most ancient of Trinities, Osiris, Isis and Horus, reappearing as Joseph, Mary and the infant Jesus. At the church of St. Januarius (the blood liquifier) in Naples I bought one of those little coloured religious cards. On the back was a prayer to Joseph, beginning: 'O padre putativo di Dio'! Whether he is the titular saint of cuckolds I couldn't discover. In Sicily Mary is the old Mediterranean Magna Dea, and swipes the whole show. Incidentally, I have seen old women kiss their fingers passing a statue of Mary, as people saluted the statues of the gods in antiquity. But also in Sicily there exist shrines of a mysterious San Calogero, evidently Byzantine. It is tempting to speculate whether this "fair old man" might possibly be Zeus.

Serious religion, especially of an abstract and philosophical kind, doesn't interest me; but Mediterranean religion, with its innumerable gods and idols and myths, does. It was a hobby for years. The fascinating thing is the strange tenacity of the Egyptian and Hellenic myths after so many centuries. I think you underestimate the creative religious power of the Egyptians, and I would urge you to dip into Breasted, Budge, Hall, Petrie &c. And I think you find a great deal of interest in Sir Grafton Eliott-Smith's Human History.[6] In my view, the mythology of Christianity represents a triumph of the very ancient Egyptian myths over both Judaism and Roman Hellenism. In this connection the flight into Egypt has symbolical meaning, and the Jesus story closely follows the Osiris story. The three days drama of the Passion was in existence in Egypt in 2000 B.C. Note that the subtlest and most heretical of the Gnostics were

Egyptians or living in Egypt. There is of course an infinite amount of contamination and exchange and blending of beliefs in the Mediterranean. How does Jesus so soon become the stern Kosmokrator of Byzantium? In Rome only a little earlier he was Orpheus.

The early Mediterranean gods were Sun gods, fertility gods, lifegivers, and hence were rather benevolent. They were followed by a pack of War gods, Power gods, Local Patriots—Iaveh, Rome, Athena. Jesus is the first successful benevolent god, for Mithraism had that unpleasant blood sacrifice.

But why do I carry coals to Newcastle? You know all these things infinitely better than I.

I wish I could persuade you to come and have a look at this part of Connecticut. This is an America of which New York is almost the antithesis, the America of powerful forests, rocks, rivers, beautiful but violent, a harsh land that was conquered by indomitable courage and energy. The men who civilised this land had dreadful limitations, but they were magnificent. All this land needs is to be loved. It has been conquered by the iron-willed pioneers and exploited by their successors, but now if it is loved and treated as men treat the soil they love, it will be of great beauty.

I must break off now. I have to go to Middletown to make arrangements about the refugee child we are taking in.[7]

Our love to you both,
Richard

1. *The Viking Book of Poetry* and *Life for Life's Sake.*

2. See D. H. Lawrence, *The Complete Poems*, New York, 1964, p. 497.

3. See D. H. Lawrence, *Last Poems*, London, 1932; *Pansies*, London, 1929; *Apocalypse,* London, 1931; *Aaron's Rod*, London, 1922; *Kangaroo*, London, 1923; "Introduction," in Maurice Magnus, *Memories of the Foreign Legion*, London, 1924; *The Letters of D. H. Lawrence*, ed. Aldous Huxley, London, 1932; *Twilight in Italy*, London, 1916.

4. See Sir Edward Burnett Tylor, *Anthropology: An Introduction to the Study of Man and Civilization*, London, 1881.

5. See Letter 68 n. 11.

6. See Sir Grafton Elliot Smith, *Human History*, New York, 1929.

7. See Letter 84 n. 2.

86. To Eric Warman (SIUC)

11 March 1941   Jamay Beach, Nokomis,
                                                Florida, U.S.

Dear Erik,

Your letter came just as we were leaving Washington. We are delighted with your news, and wish you both every happiness. I don't think

you will have any difficulty with the divorce (except that of legal rob-
bery), even though your case is obviously and entirely just. But I shall
feel happier when you are out of reach of the law sharks. I am very glad
your painful and unhappy situation has had this most pleasant of solu-
tions. Please give our best wishes to the lady.

This place is 15 miles south of Sarasota, which in turn is about 20
miles south of Tampa. We are on a long narrow island, joined to the
mainland by two bridges over a narrow creek, which opens into a large
lagoon. The cottage is about 30 yards from the Gulf of Mexico, and behind it is a sandy stretch of land with palmettos, palms, southern pines,
and mangroves along the edge of the lagoon. The mangrove roots are
covered with oysters, so that they do literally grow on trees. The beach is
covered with tropical shells, and after a storm such as we had two days
ago, it is covered with the oddest assortment of sea creatures and plants,
looking like the contents of Dali's pictures—conchs, sponges which look
like livers and pancreases, bits of coral, sea cucumbers, fan shells, king
crabs. Altogether a curious harvest. Although it is so far south, the temperature is decidedly cool and the water not yet very pleasant.

We drove 1100 miles from Washington, and had some difficulty in
getting out, owing to snow. We went through all the Gone with the
Wind country,[1] and a sorry sight it still is, with vast tracts of abandoned
country, swamps full of dead-looking trees covered with long trailers of
Spanish moss, and the most wretchedly squalid shacks I have ever seen.
Also there is a lot of malaria. But when you leave Georgia for Florida,
you soon reach an area of prosperity, with a predominantly white population, and plantations of oranges, tangerines and grapefruit.

Probably we shall spend some time here, though I should like to go
over to Frieda's New Mexican ranch;[2] but I rather quail from the drive
of 2000 miles each way. The road surfaces are good, but the roads are
often very narrow and crowded with fast-travelling cars. The motor casualties in the U.S.A. are much higher than the casualties from bombing
in England!

I have turned in the MS of my anthology, and the Viking are really
pleased with it. I hope it will be a real success. My memoirs had on the
whole a very good press (including front page with portrait in the Book
supplement of the N.Y. Times) but I don't think it has sold more than
three or four thousand.[3] I feel sure this is not the time to issue them in
England.

What has happened to Ralph Pinker?[4] And what is my position in re-
lation to him, I wonder? Would it be possible for you, as my new agent,
to take over all the agreements he has in his possession? Let me know.
With this I enclose a letter from the Mechanical Copyright Corporation.

I don't imagine there is anything but a trifling sum involved, but you might ring up Stanley Unwin (who is joint holder of the copyright of my poem) and find out what the permission is. The M. C. Protection Corp. enclosed an agreement, which of course I haven't signed.[5]

Under an arrangement with Heinemann they are taking any royalties of mine as a set-off against money advanced; but they were to continue to pay Pinker commission. I see no reason why you shouldn't get this, though in present circumstances I fear it will be small. If the existing stock of my back list books has not been destroyed, there might be some sale for them, if only because other books are less obtainable. I had a biggish debt with Heinemann, though this was reduced by Rejected Guest.

Let me have news of you as soon as possible, and once more our warmest congratulations and good wishes.

Ever yours,
Richard

1. See Margaret Mitchell, *Gone With the Wind*, New York, 1936.
2. Frieda, widow of D. H. Lawrence, now lived on Kiowa Ranch at Taos, New Mexico.
3. See Herbert Gorman, "Memoirs of a Vanished World: Richard Aldington's Reminiscences Have More than Passing Value," *New York Times Book Review*, 12 January 1941, pp. 1, 15.
4. Ralph Pinker had been accused of misusing client's royalties.
5. Gramophone Co. wished to issue a recording of RA's poem "After Two Years"; see *The Complete Poems of Richard Aldington*, London, 1948, p. 44.

87. To H.D. (Yale)

30 April 1941   Jamay.
Dear Hilda,

I was very glad indeed to get your letter and to know that you are surviving the ordeal in apparently good spirits. Evidently some letters have been lost. I did not receive the one you speak of, and two or perhaps three of mine evidently did not get through. I'll send this by air mail.

Here is a summary of our existence. In June last year I signed a contract with the Viking for my reminiscences,[1] an anthology of British-American poets,[2] and a third book yet to be written.[3] In the middle of the month we moved to a place on the Connecticut River, about seven miles from Old Lyme, very beautiful—I love that river. I worked very hard, for the Atlantic bought my memoirs for serialisation on condition the book was done by September, and at the same time I was taking books weekly by the armful from Yale for the anthology. I finished the memoirs in August and at the end of October we spent a week in New

York and then moved on to Washington, where I worked every day at the Library of Congress.

Washington is a really nice town, but of course you must know it. I liked the big boulevards with trees and the very opulent public buildings. When we had time we often drove to Mount Vernon partly for the sake of seeing the old house, but chiefly for the gardens and the magnificent view over the Potomac. I hadn't time to do sight-seeing, since I was working overtime to get the anthology done before America actually gets into the war. In this I succeeded, and turned in the script on the last day of February.

I hope you will like the anthology if it ever gets to you. It was 1250 pages of text, with nearly 1300 poems by over 300 poets from Beowulf to Dylan Thomas (b. 1914)!! I have picked five poems of yours, more than any recent poet except Lawrence. They are Sitalkas, "Never more will the wind" from Hymen, Lethe, Mid-day and Cities. Of course they will be paid for, and the publishers are now sending out the letters for permissions. That is a big job as there are over 250 copyright poems, and on my advice the Viking are writing to the publishers (in this way they can arrange for a number of poets in one letter) and asking the publishers to communicate with the authors. They are paying pretty well so there shouldn't be much trouble.

This paragraph is entirely confidential, and the fact in it must be kept quiet until the public announcement. The Literary Guild of America has bought the anthology for its September or October choice, and the first printing will be 100,000 copies. Unluckily the money return to me is not as good as that large number seems to imply. The cost of producing such a book is tremendous—we estimate our permission fees to copyrighted poets and living poets without copyright whom we are going to pay too, will run to $3500 or more.* And to compete with the Oxford Book we have had to cut the price to $2.50. My share of the Literary Guild will be only $2000, and royalties on the first 50,000 of regular sales will be only about another $5000. I don't despise this, indeed I'm very relieved about it, but $7000 isn't very much on a sale of 100,000. I should say that the book will not be an American giant, but will be printed on a rather expensive thin paper, on the lines of the Nonesuch Blake.

I don't know how to get you a copy of my memoirs and of the anthology when printed. I sent copies of the memoirs to England, and not one apparently has turned up. My theory is that such frivolous freight as books just doesn't get put on board ship, and quite right too. Perhaps Atlantic transport will improve if the Americans really co-operate as they apparently mean to do. Probably even you don't realize how cautiously the President has to move, and what a tremendous barrage of persuasion has to be put up before each step is taken.

We left Washington by car on March 2nd, and came to this island off the west coast of Florida, about 60 miles south of Tampa. It is a most attractive place, with nearly five miles of sand beach and hardly a person ever visible. Yet we have a nice little cottage with all the American gadgets and I have a wooden hut with shelves and a desk to work in. At the end of May we are going to New Mexico to spend the summer with Frieda and her Capitano,[4] and then return here in October—I have taken the cottage for another year from then. Both rent and living are much cheaper here than in the north, and this seems the best temporary solution of our problems, providing I can write here. Later there will be the problem of Catherine's education, and she is bound to pick up a Southern accent.

Catherine enjoys life here very much, running on the sands, bathing and picking up shells, and playing with another little girl. She is well and sunburned and beginning to say "cute" things. Americans are awfully nice to small children, in fact they spoil them. Why so many of the children are horrid is a mystery. Do you remember the small American boy at the Bargello and "sup'm raare"? I'm glad to say Netta is very happy here. We got into rather a stuffy upper-class set in New England (and you know what that means) which made her restive.

Do you ever hear anything of Tom Eliot? I saw Frank Morley in Washington, and he said Tom was Fire Lootenant or an Air Warden—I forget which. Now he will probably write something cheerful. By the bye, among the latest refugees here is André Spire,[5] the French poet we used to know. The Nazis have stolen all his property, but he sounds very cheerful. I ran into two of your old friends (forget their names) when I lectured in Philadelphia in January—they spoke of you with great affection and admiration. I have Norman's address, and mean to write to him. He ought to get out of Portugal,[6] not healthy for him. Robin Douglas wants to get him over here, but I can't see Norman crossing the ocean at any time, least of all now.

I do hope you and Perdita will be all right. I worry about you sometimes. Try to write more often—Air Mail letters seem always to come through. Give my love to George Plank. And if there is anything I can do for you, please let me know.

With all good wishes,
Richard

1. *Life for Life's Sake. A Book Of Reminiscences*, New York, 1941.
2. *The Viking Book of Poetry of the English-Speaking World*, New York, 1941.
3. *The Duke: Being an Account of the Life & Achievements of Arthur Wellesley, 1st Duke of Wellington*, New York, 1943.
* Total cost of producing book about $40,000!

4. Frieda Lawrence and Angelo Ravagli, officer in the Italian army. They were married 31 October 1950.

5. Cf. RA, "André Spire," *English Review,* October 1920, pp. 345–48.

6. Norman Douglas, while on a visit to Vence, had escaped to Lisbon, where he remained at least from late January 1941 until shortly before 12 January 1942, when he arrived in England.

88. To A. S. Frere *(privately held)*

14 June 1941   Kiowa Ranch,
                                                                                     San Cristobal,
                                                                                     New Mexico.

Dearest Frere,

It seems queer to be writing from this address. I am sitting in a tiny hut, about 9 feet square, in which Brett lived in the early days up here. She must have been devoted to Lawrence to put up with it, but it makes a good workshop.

> "The Percy out of Northumberland
> An avow to God made he"—

I swore to myself that the first real letter from here should go to you, but it is a little difficult to order so many mixed impressions. On the route we took, following the Mexican border through Texas, we covered about 2400 miles in a week. It is a thrilling drive, and if the fates are benevolent, we'll make it together one day. I was impressed by the stupendous bridges in Louisiana, built under the Huey Long regime. There is one over the Mississippi and marshes about a mile long rising in a long beautiful curve to about two hundred feet or more. (You may have seen the similar one near Charleston, S.C.). Texas is a grand country, starting with rich prairie land covered with wild flowers and gradually rising to desert with great clumps of mountains. At El Paso we turned north and followed roughly the course of the Rio Grande. Except that a river in a desert is remarkable I'm bound to say that the most picturesque aspect of the Rio Grande is its name, and you and I have seen much finer gorges in Switzerland, Tyrol and the Pyrenees than the Rio Grande canyon between Santa Fe and Taos. Incidentally, the Texas desert is more picturesque than the New Mexican, and both are evidently inferior to Arizona.

Santa Fe, I regret to say, is a fake—a pseudo Spanish colonial and pueblo Indian town rebuilt about 15 years ago for the tourist trade. Trust Americans to exploit anything beautiful or interesting to its destruction. Taos is less phoney, but the hand of the "Art Colony" is heavy upon it— you have the impression that the few Indians, cow-boys and ranchers are paid 50 cents to stick around and give local colour. Mabel Dodge's[1] Tamed West for Phonies and Fairies. The Indian Pueblo is about two miles out—the Brett took us and got ticked off by the Indian chief for not registering and paying 25 cents! The Indians don't ring my bell, though I haven't seen any of the dances yet. I vehemently suspect they are a tourist racket too.

Taos is full of bed bugs. We had them at the hotel and they are up here too.

We arrived Sunday 1st June. 500 yards from Frieda's door my car gave up the ghost and took 5 days to repair. Then the day I got it, the drains went wrong and Catherine developed a temperature; so we spent five miserable days in that mud-hole of a Taos in vile weather—cold and wet. Three days ago, Catherine was given her O.K. by the doctor, we returned here and the weather turned fine. But the ranch is a lousy place in bad weather, and whoever persuaded a T.B. patient[2] to try to live here must have wanted to kill him.

The ranch is about 18 miles from Taos by road, though not much more than 10 in a direct line. A few miles out of Taos the State road becomes a bumpy track, and then on a tree you see a sign: Brett, Harold Hawk, Frieda Lawrence. (Old Uncle Tom Cobley has dropped out.) From there you have about 5 miles of steep, bumpy, narrow mud track through the woods to the ranch. The wild flowers are good. There is a blue lupin and a large reddish flower called Indian brush, which is one of the most beautiful flowers I've ever seen.

As you come up the track you know you are approaching the ranch by one of the Brett's phoenixes[3] stuck on a tree. Frieda and Angie have built a large and comfortable house of logs and adobe (with a large phoenix on the porch) and immediately behind it is the original Lawrence ranch. It is virtually one long room, with an L containing kitchen and bathroom—the latter added (I'm glad to say) because Maria Huxley refused to live without a bath. The chimney and hearth Lawrence built are there and so is the little fireside seat with a rope mat where he sat every evening. On one outside wall is a bison and on one of the porches a horse (very bad) painted by Trinidad, the Indian. As you look from the porch, you have the tall pine which Lorenzo liked so much almost directly in front at about 15 paces. It still has the nail on which he hung things but unluckily the Brett also attached a phoenix and Frieda a memorial light which is smashed and doesn't work. Beyond that is a little English orchard of cherry and quince and apple and vegetable garden, then two alfalfa fields, then two or three rough pasture fields, all surrounded by forest of pines, some superbly tall, and beyond that the Taos plateau, and about 30 miles off the Sangre di Cristo mountains. To the left the mountain slopes up steeply, and from anywhere above the ranch where there is an opening in the trees you have a tremendous vista of plateau and mountains. But the effect is less stupendous than you might imagine. The distances look less than they are, the canyon of the Rio Grande is a mere streak in the monotonous desert, and as the plateau is 7000 feet up, a mountain of 13,000 is only 5000 [*sic*]. But the place is beautiful, wild and unspoiled.

Just above the two cottages and slightly to the west there is a barbed wire enclosure, with tall posts the tops of which Angie has cut into thin diamond points. In this enclosure is the Lawrence chapel,[4] simple and not in bad taste. There is a Brett phoenix on the angle of the roof and two quasi-ecclesiastical windows which the ingenious Angie made out of two old wheels. I haven't been in, but peered in the windows. The interior is divided into two by a sort of chancel rail, and on the end wall is a plain stone inscribed D.H.L. Frieda keeps it decorated with fresh green pine boughs, and it looks rather nice. Rather grotesquely his hat and typewriter are placed just inside the rail and there are one or two pictures. But if you were here I think you'd agree it's all right. After life's fitful fever. . .

At dawn the crested blue jays come screaming out of the woods and there is snow on the distant peaks.

Just outside the enclosure with the symbolical chapel there is a large and flourishing growth of wild raspberries; but whether these also have a symbolical meaning I must leave to your judgment.

Frieda, I am glad to say, is still amazingly her old self, and though well over 60 as full of zest and energy as ever. She was very pleased by your message and evidently thinks a lot of you. "He is zo witty and gay and clev-er." Angie is a little man, a bit like Pino, but without Pino's wit or vices—a bit dull, but very conscientious and industrious. He is always at work on the place, and the craftsman of his nation comes out in amateur pottery about which he is very modest, though it is better than much of the stuff produced by the Taos "artists." The stock of the "ranch" was well summarised by Catherine, who breathlessly informed me: "There's a piggie and a moo-cow and a little calfy and three sorses." Among the sorses is the old original Azul, now very old but vigorous. Frieda said: "I'm going to ride that Azul again this year before he gets too old and I get too old."

Brett is an American citizen but the most British upper-class interfering spinster imaginable. She is head of the Bundles for Britain in Taos (quite without success, as nobody here cares a damn about the war) flies the Stars and Stripes and Union Jack on her station wagon, wears a badge of ditto in her hat and the Aid to Britain badge on her buzzim.

Over the bed in her untidy studio hangs a large Union Jack, and behind it a map of the war area. Netta asked if she had flags to pin on it. "Yes, but I'm not goin' to put 'em in till they start movin' the other way." Hitler, she says, is a scoundrel and in a very bad way. His defeat will begin in August. This splendid optimism is not founded on any rational grounds, but on the prophecies of Nostradamus, for Brett, I am sorry to say, is extremely superstitious. She is also credulous, and the Indians gravely tell her the tale. Anything that an Indian says goes with Brett. Did not Lawrence admire the Indians? She is firmly convinced, for instance, that the mountain behind the ranch is infested by a ferocious she-grizzly with a lame paw, though it is notorious that no grizzlies exist in the U.S. except in Yellowstone National park. But you'd like Brett. She's herself, dresses like a fishwife, gives gratuitous advice to everyone, and ticks Mabel Dodge off as if she were a housemaid.

Mabel I have only seen for a few minutes on the corner of the street when Angie introduced me. She is a mousey little woman, but you feel the domineering American woman at once. America is full of these pinchbeck Lady Macbeths. Spud Johnson[5] is a now aging fairy, running a small art gallery, "The Heptagon," in which Brett naturally is boss. The sign-board displaying the names of the seven otherwise neglected geniuses is headed by Brett's, twice as large as anyone else's. She painted the sign herself.

Frieda of course has quarrelled and then made it up with most of the "colony," including Mabel and Brett. Angie and Frieda have a fantastic story of a "plot" to lure them away, steal Lorenzo's ashes and scatter them to the winds. Mabel's idea. I wouldn't be surprised if it were true. What staggers me is that Lorenzo put up with these freaks (though of course he was safe enough from them up here) and why he was so idiotic as to spend a winter in the perishing cold with nothing to protect him but a repaired cow-shed and a wood fire.

Yesterday I walked along the little watercourse to its point of origin in the Gallina Canyon, about a mile and a half of rather rough going. Lorenzo didn't build this watercourse—he couldn't. It was evidently originally laid out by an irrigation engineer. But the dam and several pipe crossings over gulleys have to be kept in repair and the channel cleared. That is evidently what Lorenzo did, and heavy work indeed for an invalid.

Frieda and Angie are evidently poor. Frieda tells me she gets no dividends on the 12,000 quid she has invested in various British securities. I don't know why, because Brett volunteered the information that she gets hers all right through Lord E.[6] They will probably have to sell this ranch and live at the cottage they have near Taos. They have a gold mine there (honest) which brings in $100 a year. Also there are about 10 of the 170 acres of desert which could be irrigated and run as a small farm. "Anyway there we eat," says Angie, who takes a gloomy view of the duration of the war. It is significant, I think, that all Axis partisans keep clamouring for peace and blackguarding Roosevelt and Churchill as "warmongers." Evidently they are uneasy and need peace. However, it may be merely tactical, an exploitation of the large pacifist and still larger indifferentist public here. How indifferent the mass of the people are is shown by the fact that you never hear the war discussed or even mentioned in a saloon or restaurant or any public place, while if the radio in a public place starts giving war news, ten to one it is switched to another station. They simply don't believe that anything that happens outside the U.S. and principally their own state, can have the slightest effect on them. The Taos paper never mentions the war, and the Albuquerque paper only gives a column of garbled "news." We were in Louisiana when the Bismarck was sunk, but the headline in all the local papers I saw was a silly story about Max Schmeling in Crete. I only found out about the Bismarck from a small inside page story. Of course, it is very different in the big cities and in the East. The New York papers are especially good. For some reason of proprietorship the Saturday Evening Post is anti-English as well as anti-Roosevelt; and this is more important than you'd think. It is read by about 10,000,000 people, most of whom believe in it implicitly.

It is rotten for you to be separated from your children, and from Pat. But I am convinced you were right to send them here and right to see that their mother came with them. They wouldn't have fared well without Pat. She is amazingly plucky and I admire her very much. But she doesn't enjoy it any more than you do.

I must stop now. Catherine insists that I come and see the piggie eat.

Our love to you.

Richard

P.S. This morning I said to Frieda: "There's something wrong with that pig of yours, Frieda. He doesn't guzzle his food & he looks melancholy." Yes," she said, "I don't understand it. We've always had such *gay* pigs."

1. Mabel Dodge Luhan.
2. D. H. Lawrence.
3. Lawrence's symbol.
4. Lawrence was buried in Vence [near Nice] in 1930; his body was disinterred in 1935, cremated, and the ashes were taken to the Lawrence ranch.
5. Willard Johnson.
6. Possibly Lord Esher, Brett's father.

89. To Eric Warman (SIUC)

2 August 1941   Jamay.
Dear Erik,

We returned from New Mexico sooner than was planned. The altitude of the Lawrence ranch, nearly 9000 feet, proved too much for us, and we were all ill. When we weren't ill we felt depressed and grumbled about the weather which as usual was "very exceptional." I think that the trip of more than 2000 miles across the continent was the most interesting, but I shall not attempt to describe it. From the Mississippi basin the whole continent tilts upward to the Rockies, so that almost imperceptibly you rise from sea level to 4000 feet, and the country changes from semitropical richness to open prairies (the great ranches of Texas) and eventually to semi-desert which in late May was an immense coloured lake of beautiful wild flowers with innumerable bright butterflies.

The Lawrence ranch is on the lower slopes of the Lobo mountains, looking across the Taos plateau (which is cut by the canyon of the Rio Grande) to the Sangre de Cristo mountains. Indeed the whole horizon is ringed by mountains, but as they are only about 10,000 to 13,000, and the Taos plateau is at least 7000, they don't look very high. The ranch is high enough to be back in rain, so that most of it consists of magnificent pine forest, though clearings have been made for a little rough pasture and there are two alfalfa fields. Just behind the two cottages is a small enclosure with the Lawrence memorial chapel.[1] The wild flowers are beautiful—blue wild lupins and a kind of Canterbury bell grow in profusion, and there are tall blood-red pentstemons and a stiff vermilion flower called Indian paint-brush.

The place is beautiful enough, but I see why Lawrence went back to Europe and stayed there! The country has appalling diseases—typhoid, rabies, Rocky Mountain fever and the horses had just developed sleeping sickness. Every day there is a thunderstorm, and the "society" of Taos is a weary remnant of the Montparnasse champagne bohemia, still keeping it up to 5 a.m. They bored me very much.

Now we are back on our peaceful Florida beach, gradually subsiding after all this turmoil. The days are hot and sunny with high white clouds which often build up into immense snowy alps towering into the blue sky. There is a continuous cool breeze off the sea, and along the whole edge of the island is a swaying frieze of tall grasses, about five feet high. Apart from the owners we are the only people here, so that three cottages and four cabins are empty. How much I wish you and Peggy[2] could come and occupy one of them and see the palms and the pelicans and all the rest.

Naturally we are again following the news with intense interest. According to their boastful predictions the boches were to have mopped up the comrades by August 10th.[3] It is now the 2nd, and they are still very much where they were two or three weeks ago. So for the first time things begin to look a little bit hopeful. But everybody here is mildly giggling at Halifax. Two or three weeks ago he announced portentously that Germany was about to receive a colossal aerial bombardment, since then the British raids have tapered off to little or nothing. Since Crete and the failure to relieve Tobruk British prestige has fallen to a new low ebb here, and threats and promises of "what we are going to do" are simply laughed at. However, I am glad to say that the American consuls returning from Germany bore witness to the fact that considerable damage was done to the Rhineland and northern ports by the July raids and that hundreds of thousands of people have been evacuated from those places. But to have a really decisive effect aerial bombardment must be continuous and crescendo, and these lulls and taperings off (whatever the explanation) are fatal. I am giving you what people and the newspapers say here—for all I know it may be nonsense.

The first mild squeeze of the war is being felt here as you may know. Every town and village has large receptacles for old aluminum pots and pans; in the Eastern states petrol cannot be bought between 7 p.m. and 7 a.m. (a mere preliminary bit of eye-wash); the cost of living has risen three and a half per cent in a month; cars, refrigerators and electric toasters are to be rationed; and so on. Threats come from Washington that income taxes will be three to five times as high in the coming year. The present rate of exemption is $2500 for a man and wife, plus a deduction of one-tenth of total income when earned, plus $400 for each child. So unless these allowances are lowered, the new taxes will not touch either the workers or the lower middle class.

My work on my anthology is completed except for answering last-minute queries by telegraph. It is a huge affair—over 1300 pages. The Literary Guild have bought a license to print 60,000 copies for their subscribers, and the total first impression will be 100,000. I hope this will annoy a lot of my unfriends. Entre nous, the financial returns will not be so brilliant as this sounds. The Literary Guild only brings me $2000, and the cost of the book is so high that my share is only 7 cents a copy, for the first 30,000 of straight sales. If it goes beyond that (which is improbable) I get 14 cents. It is due September 1st, and I'll let you know what happens. I wrote Evans telling him about all this, and if he answered his letter never arrived.[4] I don't know what I can do about Pinker, who never writes to me; and I am sure what you tell me about him is true. The only thing is to wait until a fitting time arrives for an investigation, when I should like to turn over to you the agency for all my work in England and Europe. But it will be a long time before that is worth a cent to anyone, if it ever is. By the time this mess is over I shall be as old-fashioned as antimacassars.

I was not able to read more than a fraction of your book, as I had to return the MS. What I read seemed to me very good indeed, and I wish I could get hold of the book again. Good luck to the next one.[5]

Wish I could send you a few cartons of cigarettes, but it's not allowed. I imagine the situation will continue tight for a while, and then gradually ease as the huge ship-building programme here begins to show results. But Mr. Hopkins can tell you more about that than I can.

I am so glad to hear that you and Peggy are so happy, and look forward so much to seeing you both. When will that be?

Ever yours,
Richard

1. See Letter 88 n. 4.
2. Identified by Warman as "a close friend."
3. In the Nazi invasion of Russia.
4. Charles Seddon Evans, chairman and managing director of William Heinemann Ltd, RA's principal British publishers at this time.
5. See Eric Warman, *Pattern for Murder*, London, 1942; his next book was not published until ten years later.

90. To Henry Slonimsky (SIUC)

19 October 1941   Jamay.
Dearest Harry,

It begins to look as if I shall not get up to New York after all. Frere has not arrived, and I suppose that his mission was cancelled on account of the latest series of disasters in Russia. I haven't heard from Mrs Frere whether the mission is cancelled or merely postponed; but she is evidently too disappointed to write. She has been separated from her husband for fifteen months now, and she was counting the days and hours until he arrived. An insignificant drop in the present ocean of human suffering, but it makes one want to swear.

Yesterday I picked from my shelves by chance Hazlitt's lectures on the English poets,[1] which I had not looked into for a long time. There are good things in it, but how astonishingly little English poetry was known in his day. Hazlitt was a great man in his way with a passion for poetry, yet he is almost pathetically ignorant of his subject. And the later essays on his great contemporaries are full of prejudice and wrong judgment. He never mentions Shelley, and only brings in Keats for the purpose of attacking the insignificant Gifford. It made me see how much has been done in the last century to make English poetry available—poetry which a professional critic in the 1820's had never even seen can now be bought by anyone for a few cents. Yet Hazlitt lived in a brilliant epoch of poetic genius, and we seem to have little to boast of. I wish I could trundle off in Wells's time machine and see what, if anything, of our epoch will be remembered in 2040. But by then there will probably be no poetry allowed except hymns to Hitler.

I must be naif—some things still shock me. It is reported in the Nation[2] that in his radio broadcast from Rome Ezra Pound has called on the negroes to revolt against "the white Jew Rooseveldt." I find that really horrible in all its implications, a sickening degradation of a human spirit who once meant a good deal to me and to you. I remember that young American when he was first in London, his apparent vitality, his amusing sayings, his intense enthusiasms, his real charm and generosity, his gifts. He seemed so much more alive than his English contemporaries, the Georgians. Was all this a sham? Or can it be that mere rancour, the disappointment of comparative failure, can lead a man to such Judas depths?

Why have we to live in such a ridiculous and savage epoch? What are we going to do about these brutes? I have recollected a piece of dialogue in my novel, Very Heaven, published early in 1937. It runs: "But have you considered the problem? You have certain groups of men, dangerous maniacs if you like, who have succeeded in imposing on large and powerful masses the doctrine of war for war's sake. War is no longer a means to an end, but an end in itself. All national resources must be devoted to that end. Sooner or later the doctrine will be put into practice. Hegel's Gewalt. What are you going to do about it?"

"Discourage it."

"But how? You can adopt the policy of half-hearted force, which will inevitably bring you in, and on an inferior footing—you'll get beaten. Or you can adopt their policy, which means that you become the very thing you wish to resist. Or you can be completely unarmed and passive, which means that you become a province of the aggressor, and that your children are trained up in his doctrine. Take your choice."[3]

That passage was written in the Austrian Tyrol in July or August, 1936. It seems to me that subsequent events have not disproved it.

But I shall depress you.

Affectionately,
Richard

1. See William Hazlitt, *Lectures on the English Poets,* London, 1818.

2. See "In the Wind," *Nation*, 11 October 1941, p. 334.
3. See RA, *Very Heaven*, London, 1937, pp. 356–57.

91. To Leonard Bacon* (Yale)

26 May 1942   Jamay.
Dear Leonard,
   The days slip past, as the Psalmist remarks, and I leave letters unanswered. The fact is, this Wellington book[1] is proving much more of a task than I expected, and in spite of every diligence Masséna is only now recoiling from Torres Vedras. How long it will take me to get to Toulouse I hate to think.[2] It is surprising how long it takes to work out what exactly happened in a battle and how difficult it is to condense the narrative to a few paragraphs. Without Oman[3] I should be lost.
   I have supplemented by reading every personal narrative of the Peninsular War I can get hold of, and by a stroke of luck what Congress hasn't got Yale nearly always has. I hope I may have been of some service to Knollenberg by giving him, at his request, reports on some of the books he hasn't got.
   It is amazing to find in 1808–14 many of the phenomena we deplore or rage against to-day—the unscrupulous enemy (and Boney was *very* unscrupulous, a real preview of Schicklegruber), the fifth columnist, the rash or silly journalist, the slick politician, the wild rushes of public opinion, delays in "war production," inflation, sinkings of merchant marine, &c. &c. The heartening thing to remember is that Boney had 375,000 troops in Spain, Wellington never more than 40,000 English, 30,000 Portuguese and 20,000 Spaniards. Of course, the resistance of the Spanish people & guerillas was all important. In the earlier stages he was as short of cavalry as the boys this time have been short of planes. And he had to conduct his first (unsuccessful) sieges with too few Engineers, because the Duke of York[4] disapproved of them! The more I read the more I perceive that those damned Hanoverians, especially George III, were the curse and misery of England.
   We have had here two months of the most lovely weather I have ever experienced any where—cloudless sunny skies, warm seas and a cool north-west breeze. Our agricultural neighbours complain of lack of rain, and it is a fact there has been very little since November. Finally, the rationing of gas has left the place entirely to the few residents.
   You will be amused to know that I am now a Deputy Sheriff of Sarasota County, with my credentials labelled "Defense Only," so I cannot arrest anyone for parking or brawling. There is a real danger on this coast, as you may have read in Sunday's Times,[5] and we are very short

of man power for patrol. The volunteers are not yet properly organized. Our patrol car is in Connecticut, and there seems no way of getting it down, so we have to do the best we can.

I hope all goes well with you, and wish we could meet sometimes; but this seems more unlikely than ever until the enemy are quelled.

Ever affectionately,
Richard

P.S. In case Philip does not remember, I hope you will let us have news of Martha immediately.[6]

---

*Leonard Bacon (1887–1954), American poet and recipient of the Pulitzer Prize for verse in 1941, was a long-time friend of RA's despite Bacon's disapproval of Imagist poetry. RA's autobiography is dedicated to Bacon and Howard Lowry. Bacon was a professor of English at the University of California early in his career, and a 2d Lieutenant in the U.S. Air Service during World War I. RA was fortunate to have so good a friend during his first year in the United States. As he records in his letters, RA spent many happy days working in a studio Bacon shared with him at Bacon's home, The Acorns, in Peace Dale, Rhode Island. In subsequent years, even though RA had moved elsewhere, Bacon continued to be helpful and give good advice; for instance, to complete the Wellington biography when RA was about to abandon it. (See also the Annotated Index.)

1. See *The Duke, Being an Account of the Life and Achievements of Arthur Wellesley, 1st Duke of Wellington*, New York, 1943.

2. Movements of the French and British and allied armies in the Peninsular War (1810–11). Masséna commanded the French army.

3. See C.W.C. Oman, *A History of the Peninsular War*, Oxford, 1902.

4. George III's son, Frederick Augustus, was a field marshal and commander-in-chief.

5. See George Barrett, "Glow of Cities Still Aids U-Boats," *New York Times*, 24 May 1942, p. 10E.

6. Philip Oliver-Smith was married to Bacon's eldest daughter, Martha, subsequently Martha Bacon Ballinger.

92. To Eric Warman (SIUC)

6 August 1942

c/o Viking Press,
18 East 48th Street,
New York City, N.Y.

Dear Erik,

Your letter was some time in arriving, but may have been waiting some time, since I was away at the grandiosely named Writers Conference of the Rocky Mountains. In point of fact, it is a mild racket which enables a compatriot of ours (Ted Davison) to gather kudos for the University of Colorado—to which end he works very hard; and doubtless some good accrues to the assembled writers. There were no less than 100, all with MSS—a dreary prospect.[1]

But I greatly enjoyed the trip, and even the tiring and over-crowded railway was interesting. The journey took 65 hours each way, so you can imagine it was not without incident. What amazes me more and more in the States are the immense areas uncultivated and apparently uninhabited. Even in old states like Georgia you go for hours through beautiful pine woods with hardly a village or even a house. I suppose it is more inhabited than it seems. Boulder (where the Conference was held) is 5000 feet up on the edge of the Rockies. We were taken on one trip through very beautiful scenery to the old mining town of Central City which is now almost abandoned. Incidentally I went through T. S. Eliot's home town, St. Louis, and am not surprised that he left.[2] Unlike other great American towns, it seemed, from the hurried glimpses I had, both noisy and dirty.

At Boulder I met a representative of Knopf, the publisher, who struck me as very sniffy and standoffish. After a day or two he melted, and admitted that he had been prejudiced against all English by a certain well-known novelist who was sent out to "do propaganda." Judging from what Hoffman told me, this gentleman contrived to offend whole areas, and I was not surprised but relieved to know that no more will be sent.[3]

You will be surprised to know that I have decided to move West, to California, especially since I had intended to stay here in Florida which I like so much. But the rationing of petrol in the East has made it pretty well impossible for us to work in this remote place, and as I have a chance of a job in the movies it seems the sensible thing to go to Hollywood. Netta has not seen anyone to talk to for months, and the school where we intended to send Catherine is closing down. It is necessary to get into a town for the duration, and I certainly prefer the West. We shall try to get permission to go by car, which is so much easier and cheaper for us and more comfortable for Catherine. I am certainly sorry to leave Florida, and hope to come back, especially if I can muscle in on the movies. However, I'm not depending on that, and have a lecture tour booked for Jan–Feb.

If you have any spare time and energy I strongly advise you to study the American periodicals and try to knock off stuff to please them. They are paying fantastic prices—300 pounds for short articles and stories. They want stuff with a contemporary English background, but complain that the English writers just won't take the trouble to understand American prejudices and methods of expression. I admit that I have so far been unsuccessful, but Chambrun is hopeful, and very nearly landed me a plum the other day. I continue to try. Your agent, I feel sure, would be glad to handle any stuff you could send him.

Thank you for the copy of the song and for your great kindness in taking so much trouble about the Pinker episode. I'm not going to guarantee Allen and Unwin against anything, suspecting the whole bunch. What I want to do is hand over to you, and to you only, the handling and control of my literary affairs in England, provided it ever seems worth your while. There is nobody else I trust, and I might as well be robbed by one as by another. I suppose it needs a solicitor to take control, but I'm hanged if I see why I can't give my work to the person I want. There will be quite an accumulation of unpublished books of mine (published here but not in England) when and if the war ends.

It is really monstrous that your case should have been held up all this time, when so simple an affair could have been settled ages ago.[4] Don't try to tell me it isn't a racket because it is. I hope you are not being robbed too outrageously, and also hope that the affair will soon be settled. It makes me furious that years of peoples' lives can be frittered away in these stupid formalisms merely to provide fat fees for legal parasites.

We shall be 3000 miles further away in California, but I still hope you and Peggy will turn up one of these days. I shall keep my eyes open for possible opportunities for you in Hollywood, and will write you about it. I suspect that entry is harder and the standards higher than are admitted by those who haven't been able to get in. It will be interesting to see how it turns out. We expect to start sometime in September, but can't yet determine a date until other things are cleared up.

I'm glad to know that Jean is well and happy, and that she is so successful at school. Catherine is also very well, and can swim and dive with astonishing success in one so young. She is really almost too fearless in the sea, which luckily here is shallow, warm and calm. I groan in spirit at having to leave this beautifully lonely shore, but no doubt it is good for me. As soon as I got to Boulder I realized that it was wrong to keep Netta and Catherine here during their youth.

Netta joins with me in all good wishes to you both.

Ever yours,
Richard

1. This Thirteenth Writers' Conference, sponsored by the University of Colorado at Boulder from 20 July to 7 August, listed RA as a "General Advisor" together with the Director, Edward Davison. RA lectured on "The Artist and Its Habitat," participated in a forum on "The Writer and the War," and took part in a "Poets' Recital."

2. Eliot spent his first seventeen years in St. Louis except for annual vacations to the New England coast.

3. Not identified.

4. Warman was divorcing his wife, Violet.

93. To Eric Warman (SIUC)

30 December 1942   8439 Sunset Boulevard,
                                            Hollywood, California, U.S.

Dear Erik,

Start not! The above address is no phony, but the fact. I dropped into a job (alas, only for a few weeks) with Paramount soon after we arrived here, and as my agent[1] thinks I have a chance as a free lance we tried to find a place about equally distant from the various studios. The Hollywood practice is that most writers are taken on for a specific job for which they are paid so much a week while it lasts. Everything happens with startling suddenness. I was given a book to read and then had an interview with the producer. We discussed it for about an hour while my agent sat silent in a corner, and then the producer suddenly stood up and said: "O.K. Come at nine tomorrow morning. 'Bye." When we got outside I said to my agent (an awfully nice chap, by the bye): "What does this mean?" He said: "You're hired." And so it proved. Two days before I had finished my "treatment" a Board meeting decided not to proceed with the film after all!

I like Hollywood *very* much indeed, and I feel sure you would. To begin with, the climate is perfect—sunny every day but not too hot. We have had one rainy day since Sept. 17th. Los Angeles, Hollywood, Beverly Hills, Pasadena etc, are all one big town of about 3,000,000, but so arranged that everywhere are wide streets, many trees, and enough car parking space. Hollywood is on the slope of a range of hills with wonderful views over Los A., and Sunset Boulevard runs into Beverly Hills at one end and down-town Los A. on the other. Although the war is naturally affecting all the easy side of life, one can see that in normal times it must be very pleasant. Among other things there are quite good second-hand book shops which have good bargains. The other day I got fourteen volumes containing all those rare minor works of Ruskin for $1.40—I never could afford to buy them in England as there were no cheap reprints.

One faint amusement here is observing the stars in their courses. For instance, one day I was lunching in the staff restaurant at Paramount when Veronica Lake and Cecil de Mille sat down at the next table. I am rather a fan of V. Lake, and I think she is even prettier off the screen. Did you see I Married a Witch?[2] The other day I saw a large poster of Don Ameche, with Don Ameche accidentally posed just below it.

I was so delighted by the victory of the 8th Army[3] that I composed instantly a song with the refrain: "Rommel's on the bummel with a hee-haw ho!" It is curious that other letters from England use almost your identical words about the war in Europe being over in 1943. I hope you may be right, but I don't believe it for a moment, and bid you beware of wishful thinking.

I come back—in all seriousness—to the hope that you and Peggy may be able to come here after the war. If I really make good in the movie world, all you will have to bother about is the passport and quota. Unfortunately I haven't yet made good, and don't know if I shall—so it would be absolutely unfair to make now any promise, which I might not be able to keep. I flatter myself that you will agree that my judgments of the pre-war situation and my actions thereupon were not altogether wide of the mark or lacking in common sense. If you agree to that, let me say that I now think you and Peggy and Jean would be happier here than anywhere else I know. I wouldn't say this to most English people, for anything that smacks of the old school tie is anathema here, but I believe you could overcome the prejudice against the English which certainly exists and that you'd have a better life once you could fit into the scheme of things. Believe me, this Pacific coast of America is not only beautiful and unbelievably rich, but many people think it will be one of the great creative centers after the war—and I am inclined to agree. I can't claim to be a hell of a success myself, but I've been unwell until recently, and then I have been too sharp-tongued in defending England against all and sundry! This will make you smile. There is much I could add but will not—all I will say is that I wish I had come here twenty years ago. Whatever happens I shall never return to Europe.[4]

Catherine now goes to a nursery school on the fringe of Beverly Hills, a place frequented by scions of the movie moguls. Boy! does she have a good time. They are pretty strict about discipline, but the school is very well equipped and intelligently run. Many of the classes are held out of doors in the garden, and I sometimes glide slowly past (incognito!) in the car to watch them. It is certainly very pleasant to see children so well occupied. This of course is a private school, but I wish you could see the public schools—Hollywood High School is a very swagger place.

People move about so rapidly. There is a Canadian friend of mine, a professor of history and a Lieutenant in the Royal Canadian Navy, who was with me in Florida in April. He said he might be going to England, and I meant to give him a letter to you. Suddenly he disappeared—and now I get a letter saying that he was in the Dieppe show and is now back in a naval college somewhere in Canada. He saw T. S. Eliot and missed C. P. Snow and you, he says. I wish you had seen him, a very nice fellow and intelligent.[5]

Could you spare me a copy of "Pattern for Murder"? I would like to show it to my agent here, and see if he thinks there would be an opening for you.

It's tough about Vi. I feel she wasn't a bad girl, but she never really appreciated you. It's tough that you have to pay those costs, but what will you? The lawyers must be fee'd. But you have been let off lightly.

What are you planning about Jean? Some time ago I cancelled the affidavits and withdrew the deposit for her entry here, as you said you meant to keep her in England. But they can be renewed when and if you wish.

Ever affectionately,
Richard

1. Alvin George Manuel.
2. Veronica Lake starred in *I Married a Witch* (1942).
3. At El Alamein, where General B. L. Montgomery's British 8th Army inflicted a severe defeat on Field-Marshal Erwin Rommel's German-Italian force in October 1942.
4. The Aldingtons arrived in Paris from Jamaica in late August 1946; see Letters 103 and 104.
5. Not identified.

94. To Leonard Bacon (Yale)

12 June 1943   Hollywood.
Dear Leonard,

It was good news to hear from Martha and then from Mrs Faust that you and Patty[1] may be coming here soon. I hope that you will benefit by the change and by this really delightful climate, and you may be sure that your friends here will be happy indeed to see you.

Oddly enough when this news came I was on the point of sitting down to write to you about my own affairs. Although you may be here before this reaches Rhode Island, I still think I will put the matter to you, in the hope that if it reaches you I may benefit by your advice.

Roughly, the position is: What to do next?

In the four years since we arrived I have published Rejected Guest, Life for Life's Sake, the Viking Book, and have The Duke in the press.[2] All this has been pleasant work, but unluckily with only the American market, it has not covered expenses, and we are now living on money brought with us from Europe. Faust is most kindly trying to work me in to a movie company, but after my experience with Paramount I have very little hope of that. It is a great nuisance that by his procrastination Harold Guinzburg lost me the Book of the Month selection for my anthology by three days. Of course, if The Duke were selected, that would solve everything, and I could look forward to writing some more biographies. But the Viking Press are very dilatory and unbusinesslike, and after having the MS for nearly four months have not even got the book in type, though they profess to think very highly of it and to have great hopes.

Leonard, I simply cannot write for the popular magazines. It is too stupid and degrading.

Novels are out of the question at the moment, at least my kind of novels.

I wish you would turn this over in your mind, and give me the benefit of your advice. Everything else is quite perfect. I am delighted with California and my little family, but here is this infernal difficulty of getting the right work done in a changing peculiar epoch. I think I bet correctly with Wellington—Viking now seem to think so—but you can see how one might easily waste a year's work by doing something for which the cultivated public would feel no interest. At the moment I am writing a short story about Herman Melville and I have written a child's book (which Netta has illustrated) but I don't think either have the slightest chance in this very odd literary situation.[3]

Your advice about the memoirs and about sticking to Wellington[4] was A I at Lloyds, and I would indeed be grateful for advice now.

Excuse the inevitable egotism of this.

> Ever affectionately
> Richard

1. Martha Stronghan Bacon, wife of Leonard Bacon.
2. See RA, *The Duke, Being an Account of the Life and Achievements of Arthur Wellesley, 1st Duke of Wellington,* New York, 1943; *The Viking Book of Poetry of the English-Speaking World,* New York, 1941; *Life for Life's Sake. A Book of Reminiscences,* New York, 1941; and *Rejected Guest: A Novel,* New York, 1939.
3. Neither of these was published.
4. In a letter dated 27 June 1942 (Yale), RA wrote Bacon that he had decided "all work I have put into this Wellington book has been wasted and must be abandoned." Bacon persuaded him to continue.

95. To Eric Warman (SIUC)

31 October 1943   Hollywood.
Dear Erik,

After a period of discouragement about air mail to England, I am going to try again and see how it is working now. Will you make a note of the date when you receive this, and let me know? It is ridiculous only being able to exchange about six letters a year.

You will think I am indeed growing old and foolish when I say that I think you will make a tremendous mistake in leaving the Civil Service if you have a decently reasonable job.[1] It is going to take a very long time to clean up the mess of this war, and I think it a terrible mistake to trust to writing in such an epoch. The 20s were bad enough, but I don't like to think of the late 40s. These luxuriously conducted quarrels have to be paid for, and it is wonderful to see what heroism people can show in giving up the purchase of books.

Your optimism has been justified, but I think only because of Russia. Old Sindbad the Nazi pulled a hell of a boner when he attacked the Reds, and it looks as if the steppes are going to be the graveyard of German arrogance. Sometimes I feel I ought to be sorry for the poor boobs, and then I think, to hell with them, they started all this, nobody else wanted it, so let them be squashed. To-morrow night the U.S. abolishes the dim-out. It has never really been dim, except by comparison with the lavish lighting of pre-war days; but I'm wondering if we shall really see much difference.[2] Electric power is needed for war plants, and I think there won't be very much to spare for splash lighting. However, it's a good omen that the lights go up again if only in theory. I am hoping we may have the outdoor Christmas trees again for Catherine. Hollywood Boulevard has a mile of gigantic Santa Claus, but the lighted Christmas trees which went with them have gone.

No, you hadn't said a word about your work on the United Nations stories book (of which nothing seems to have leaked out here) but I'm very pleased to know that you did so well out of it.[3]

Have you in your Stygian darkness heard a new Western dance-song: "Pistol-packin' Momma, lay that pistol down"? because, boy oh boy, if you ain't heard that, you ain't heard nothing. It's Catherine's favourite tune, and mine too. When it comes over the radio (and it does about every half hour) we drop whatever we're doing and dance to it.

> "Lay that pistol down, baby, lay that pistol down,
> Pistol-packin' Momma, lay that pistol down!"

I would most willingly send you a copy of my book on Wellington, but I don't think the time has arrived for sending such frivolities as books across the ocean in your direction. However, when the rush of Christmas mail to the forces overseas has subsided, I will trot down to Hollywood main post-office and ask them what the situation is now. Some time ago they were refusing packages of an unessential nature. I take it that for spiritual democratic man the essentials are grub, money and weapons, and the inessentials books, art, music.

The book seems to be doing rather well, although as it has only been out for three weeks it is still a little early. I judge by the fact that the Viking Press write promptly and politely and offered a larger advance for another biography, that a number of people after varying periods of neglect have suddenly discovered that we are so nice and must come to see them, that the Hollywood bookshops have increased the display about seven times in numbers, that my agent here sent me a bottle of wine and that the Chicago Daily News has asked me to contribute[4] while the Los Angeles Book Fair will send a car for me if I will attend and make a brief speech.[5] These seem to me symptomatic of a moderate success, but of course nothing very much.

I believe Dali is horribly hard up, though his book has had some success here. I should say his real crime is that he says the time for eccentricity is over and we must now have discipline and austerity. By the way in the University Library I came across a book on the surrealists with a long introduction by Herbert Read. Good heavens, what slush! Such a really slimy mixture of pretentiousness, stupidity and abject toadying to "the latest thing in art."[6] It was positively years since I had looked at anything by that brand of English high-brow, and I must say it was a shock, especially when I reflected that at one time I was pretty much that kind of idiot myself. I suppose you have read Eliot's custard about Kipling. Gosh, what a humbug. I notice he dropped the Kipling swastika.[7]

Probably Dali's "Secret Life of Salvador Dali" has not been published with you, as it is long and has plenty of illustrations. But it is certainly worth seeing. He's certainly cracked, but knows it, and anyway it doesn't matter much in a painter. After all, van Gogh was completely cuckoo and yet did some wonderful things. Dali has the same peculiar impulse to cut bits off himself, an impulse he has hitherto resisted, but of course he's still young.[8]

Catherine is back at school again, and very proud of the fact that she has passed from kindergarten to First Grade. She electrified us by stating: "I can spell now, G-O-D, dog."

With all good wishes,

Ever yours,
Richard

1. Warman was working as a censor.
2. Lights on the east and west coast were put out or shaded to deny German submarines navigational landmarks.
3. See Eric Warman with Maurice Moiseiwitch, *Valour Without Frontier*, London, 1943.

4. See RA, " 'Liberty Is Won for a Nation by Courage Against Fear,' " *Chicago Daily News*, 1 December 1943, p. 14C.

5. RA spoke on Thursday evening, 18 November; see "Library's Book Events Start Tomorrow," *Los Angeles Times*, 14 November 1943, sec. 4, p. 6; cf. "Los Angeles Book Fair a Big Success," *Publisher's Weekly*, 4 December 1943, p. 2094.

6. See *Surrealism*, ed. and intro. Herbert Read, London [1936].

7. See *A Choice of Kipling's Verse Made by T. S. Eliot with an Essay on Rudyard Kipling*, London, 1941. *The Writings in Prose and Verse of Rudyard Kipling*, New York, 1897–1920, has on the cover and title page a small medallion with an elephant's head and a swastika. Swastikas were also used to decorate the inside covers of the Mandalay edition, New York, 1925.

8. On Christmas eve, 1888, van Gogh broke under the strain of working with Gauguin in the "yellow house" at Arles and cut off part of his left ear; see *The Secret Life of Salvador Dali*, New York, 1942.

96. To Leonard Bacon (Yale)

19 December 1943   Hollywood.

Dear Leonard,

That is excellent news—that Philip has been in New York. Odd to think that he has apparently nearly circumnavigated the globe since we saw him here. The Atlantic is now a much better place since they have got so busy they have started sinking whales after getting rid of most of the submarines. But somebody blundered at Bari the other day—that bombing of 17 ships (if really true) hurts.[1]

I look forward to your book very much.[2] The delay in receiving copies must be most irritating to you, but then you'll recollect that the strain on postal and other transport must be terrific.

Thank you for mentioning the Jacobi book on Jung.[3] I shall note it as a work to be read when and if I get any leisure, for as soon as I leave Warner's I must get down to Whistler.[4] I have plans for extending that subject into some lines of enquiry which I hope may entertain The American reader. I fear I shall have to look a long way before I find anyone as favourable a topic as Wellington—of whom everybody has heard and most people knew little or knew what was demonstrably untrue. Byron of course is an attractive subject, and I have thought about him a good deal—I nearly began a biography of him in 1924 as a protest against the very unfair centenary articles and books in England. But so much has been written about him. I feel the bloom is off the grape. Nelson is a wonderful figure, but the British Whigs never hated him as they hated Wellington, and so he is less of a surprise. Incidentally I disapprove strongly of his behavior during the Naples revolution and after.[5]

It was good of you to speak to Cumberlege. The camel of scripture has more chance of negotiating the needle's eye than any book of mine has of getting on the list of the Oxford Press. Besides I'm not particularly anxious to appear in England until after the war.

The life of writing for the movies is a strange one, but I should be very glad if I could succeed. Far from being easy, it is a very difficult and specialized job, and most of those who have succeeded, started young and gradually worked their way to the front. Unfortunately, the superstition of a reputation means that I have to start at the top and succeed at once, or not at all. Wolfgang Reinhardt, with whom I am working during Blanke's illness, is a charming and cultivated man. I hope he's not too highbrow as I have a tendency that way myself. However, I have an elopement, a duel, an earthquake, and a death in the snow, and I am fighting hard for a mad king and a shipwreck. Mr. Reinhardt is against a shipwreck, which I think ought to be very interesting to a public suddenly made aware of the perils of those who go down to the sea in ships. Perhaps he is afraid of the expense. But at the moment I would rather bring off this film than be president of Harvard, and I can't think of anything more genteel and confidential than that![6]

When I get a little more time I must tell you something of what I have learned about the interior of a Hollywood studio.

With our warmest love to you all and the best of good wishes for Christmas.

Ever affectionately,
Richard

1. See Sidney Shalett, "Nazis Sank 17 Ships in Bombing of Bari," *New York Times*, 17 December 1943, p. 1.
2. See Leonard Bacon, *Day of Fire*, London, 1943.
3. See Jolande Jacobi, *Psychology of C. G. Jung*, London [1942].
4. Following the successful biography of Wellington, RA planned a book on Whistler, but did not complete it.
5. Nelson has been criticized for refusing to recognize peace terms reached by Cardinal Ruffo and for not delaying the execution of the rebel Carraciola.
6. See Letter 97.

97. To Eric Warman (SIUC)

12 February 1944   Hollywood.
Dear Erik,

It looks to me as if the person charged with mailing my last letter to you forgot about it for two weeks and then put on five cents instead of thirty.

I forget what stage my news is in. Anyway, the biography of Wellington has been a success, very good reviews and 21,000 copies in print, most of them sold. I just got the news of this when my agent got me a job at Warners trying to find a new story for Max Reinhardt's Miracle[1] with Wolfgang Reinhardt as producer. I have been 9 weeks on the job and yesterday turned in the "treatment," as they call it. Quite a good job, I think, and so does Reinhardt. I'm now standing by to see if the business side will agree to production so that we can start the screen play. It would be in technicolor and cost a coupla million dollars, so I'm none too hopeful.[2] Still, even if I leave here on Monday I shall be able to afford toothpaste this coming year.

The process of making a script in Hollywood is curious. The producer is the important person. He gets an idea or buys the rights in a book or play, and then hires a writer to carry out his notions. Hence the Hollywood belief that the writer is unimportant. But in point of fact, so potent is the written word, so dominating the creative imagination that the writer unconsciously always pulls the script his way. At the end of 9 weeks tussle hardly a shred of Reinhardt is left—all is Aldington. Of course this will probably kill the thing for the screen, but the interesting point is that I did it unintentionally. I tried quite honestly to write what he wanted, and I believe he thinks I've done it—it was quite a shock to re-read and find that in the various re-writings and scratchings out all of his notions had been discarded.

This paragraph is in confidence between us, especially the part about my earnings which I don't want known in England.[3] The minimum wage for a beginner as a Hollywood writer is $125 a week. The highest paid people get about $2500. But you must remember that you have to work at high pressure, and that failure probably loses any future chances, and that most "assignments" only last about 4–16 weeks with long periods of "resting." So only writers on long-term contracts really make big annual incomes. For this job I have been paid $750 a week, from which you must deduct 10% agent's fees, 20% withholding tax, and various other little fees and taxes, which brings the net down to $525. It is impossible from the long hours to do any other work, and indeed the contract forbids it. And even though your screen play is a prodigious hit you don't get another cent.

English writers are not much required and not very successful. For instance both Christopher Isherwood and Keith Winter seem to have failed.[4] In fact the one who has lasted longest is Aldous Huxley, who has just got a screen credit for "Jane Eyre." There is much jealousy of a writer with a really literary reputation, but Huxley has triumphed over it all, which pleases me.[5] I believe the main reasons for the failure of the English writers are that they despise Hollywood and show it, that they think writing for the screen is easy when it's very difficult, and that they won't take the trouble to study the medium—they just want big money. Competition of course is fierce. I suppose that 200 writers are about the employment limit of the industry, and I know there are at least 2000 in Los Angeles County! The only way to avoid disaster is to have some other form of earning a living which can be taken up and dropped at a moment's notice. In other words you have to go on writing books, but be prepared to drop a book at a day's notice, work for several weeks in a frenzy at screen work, and then return to the book.

Which brings me round to your own plans, which I had in mind when telling you my experience. I've been here 18 months, and have worked 13 weeks, earning $9500 gross or about $7000 net. With Hollywood expenses it's not brilliant, and we'd have been in the soup if The Duke hadn't been a success. Now, if this "treatment" of The Miracle is a success with the financial guys at Warners, then I'll stay on; but if it isn't, then I may never get another assignment. So, if you had something certain to fall back on, a commissioned book to work on (say) I'd strongly advise you trying your luck here for six to twelve months. If you made good, swell; if not, you'd have a line of retreat. But of course, as soon as the war is over there will naturally be soldiers clamoring for jobs, and justice will demand that they come first.

Otherwise, I think your agency plan as outlined a sound one, but I would strongly advise building up a connection with America and the Dominions, which are certainly the future markets for commercial writing.

Yes, Chambrun has been handling my periodical stuff recently, but I've sent him very little. The best he did was $300 for a story in Esquire.[6] The place to get in is the Reader's Digest, which pays $1500 up for one of those phony little pieces. I can't write them successfully—wish I could.

Winter is already over here—if winter you can call it. These brilliant sunny February days, with a cold tang in the morning (about 45 Fahrenheit at 9 a.m. rising to 60–70 in the afternoon) are really lovely. From April to December we're apt to be 80–90 which some people find hot. I don't, and there is nearly always a cool night breeze. The six to eight months of practically uninterrupted sunshine are what I like. Again many grumble—but human beings grumble at everything. I'm perfectly content here, and the only other places which attract me are the wilder parts of California and the North-West, the Rockies and Florida. In fact so far as one is master of one's destiny I don't intend to cross the Atlantic again. Of course America isn't perfection, but I've always liked it from the first day I landed, and I like it more now. I wonder very much how you'd feel about it? I believe you'd like it. By the way one Englishman who is a great but unostentatious success in Hollywood is James Hilton—makes pots and everyone likes him.

Always,
Richard

1. Max Reinhardt brought *The Miracle* by Karl Volmoeller to the Century Theatre in New York for ten months from 15 January 1924.
2. Warner Brothers did not use RA's screenplay but released their version of *The Miracle* in 1959; the screenplay is credited to Frank Butler.
3. Because his comparative success might affect his settlement with the Patmores made at the time of Netta's divorce.
4. Winter's many screen credits include *Uncle Harry*, 1945; Isherwood's first screenplay was *Diane*, 1955.
5. Huxley's screen credits include *Pride and Prejudice*, 1940; *Jane Eyre*, 1944; *A Woman's Vengeance*, 1947; and *Prelude to Fame*, 1951.
6. See RA, "They Come Back Different," *Esquire*, December 1943, pp. 64–65, 289–94.

98. To Eric Warman (SIUC)

11 April 1944   Hollywood.

Dear Erik,

This letter-head will tell you that I have got on fairly well.[1] I spent about eight weeks producing a 72-page "treatment" of The Miracle with Reinhardt. There was a "conference" over it with Warner, who liked it very much, and I got permission to write the screen-play. This was followed by a row between me and Reinhardt, who wanted to make changes for the worse in my story—I really think he was jealous of the commendations I got from the "boss." However, I won this, and was supported by authority, and have now done 105 pages of the screen play. Just finished an important section yesterday, and am working out dialogue for the next set of sequences.

Anyway, this is my 18th week here; I think I am good for at least another 8 weeks, perhaps longer; and my agent is optimistic about the future.

I wish to goodness you were at hand to talk over movie possibilities with you. There is much I have learned by trial and error which I think would help you. If you are dealing with Korda you are dealing with the man who pays least to authors. If with MGM, they are the people who pay most. The minimum wage for a screen-writer here is $150 a week, and you ought to get more than that. In submitting stuff for motion picture companies, NEVER submit a screen play or any unpublished novel or story. An "original" for the screen must be in "treatment" form, which is a narrative in the present tense, arranged in scenes and sequences, with scraps of dialogue. Seventy pages is a long one. They prefer about 50. They will also read synopses of 8 to 10 pages.

I understand the Hollywood companies are getting ready to set up studios in England and France as soon as the war is over. In this they are probably over-optimistic, but there will be emissaries over there, and you should try to contact them. I believe the idea is that production will be cheaper in Europe than here.

This Miracle job has indeed been a miracle for us, and made everything easier. It is unlucky that it comes when income tax takes so much, but one has no business to complain. I wish there was some way you could get out here. I sometimes please myself with the idea of piloting you about, and showing you some of the places here. But it would be folly for you to come without funds or the certainty of a job. It is certainly not a cheap place. Ian Dalrymple doesn't sound American. Is he?

I am pleased indeed that you liked Life for Life's Sake, but I am very dubious about publishing it or anything else in England. Let me put it thus: Since I ceased publication in England[2] I have had progressively better sales and better reviews here; and this I attribute largely to the fact that the flow of hostile comment from reviewers there was cut off at the source. Now, I am doing well here, people like me, and like my work. Why, for the sake of a handful of chicken feed should I run the risk of the usual spite and obloquy? I don't believe for a moment they would disarm before Life for Life's Sake. The English who had it to review here only sneered. Now if I could get four or five years work in the studios here I could save enough for us to live on in a very modest way; and then I wouldn't care. But for the time being I shall refuse to publish in England.[3]

Netta is very happy here. She now goes daily to the Otis School of Art, which she says is excellent, with at least one first-class painter on the staff. Her work is certainly improving rapidly. Catherine now has started regular school work, but still likes school so much that she complains about having to take holidays! Three afternoons a week she goes to play at a ranch belonging to Robert Young which is loaned to the school. Two other afternoons she goes to a so-called Girls Club, which takes her on picnics, to the ice and roller skating rinks, and other expeditions. Luckily, the "Club" is allowed just enough gasoline to get them around, and certainly the exercise and companionship are very valuable to her.

By the way, William Faulkner is here at Warners—very Southern, very shy, but pleasant.[4] We also have Tom Job, author of Uncle Harry.[5] And I have just discovered that the Sherriff on the Writers Directory board is Journey's End Sherriff.[6] I must look him up. Or must I? I see some of the stars occasionally—Hedy Lamarr, Bette Davis, Sydney Greenstreet, Peter Lorre, etc.

The Duke goes on selling, about 200 a month. I am very proud of the fact that the U.S. Navy bought 1250 copies recently. It is interesting that the Navy should be reading the life of a soldier.

That seems to be about all the news I have, for spending 8 hours a day on Warners lot concocting melodrama does not conduce to much else. I very much hope they will shoot The Miracle, but it is impossible to tell until they have seen the play.

Next time I'll try to tell you about the comic-fantastic side here, though it is less, far less than rumored.

Ever yours,
Richard

1. RA writes on a Warner Brothers letterhead.

2. RA's last book published in England previous to this date was *Rejected Guest. A Novel*, London, 1939.

3. RA began to publish again in England in 1946.

4. William Faulkner has eleven Hollywood screen credits dating from *The Road to Glory*, 1936.

5. See Thomas Job, *Uncle Harry*, New York, 1942; Job was a screenwriter for Warner Brothers and Twentieth Century–Fox.

6. See R[obert] C[edric] Sherriff, *Journey's End*, New York, 1930; his screen credits include *Goodbye Mr. Chips* (1939) and *That Hamilton Woman* (1941).

99. *To Lawrence Powell* (UCLA)*

9 November 1944   Hollywood.
Dear Powell,

This to say that we spent a very pleasant evening with you, and to thank you for the care and trouble you gave to the exhibition.[1] I sent out all the leaflets to people in Hollywood, but I don't suppose they'll do anything. Every hen is busy with its own tail-feathers, as Lorenzo used to say.

After thinking it over I feel it would be more appropriate not to print or reprint anything of mine. At least so my interior daimon counsels. As long as I can support my family by writing acknowledged trash for the movies I want to cut out all other writing (last week I refused articles to "P.M." and Sat. Rev. of Lit) of any kind. It is very good of you to make the suggestion, but at present my cue is silence.

Now here is a message for Norman.[2] If he looks about by the roadside he will see that since the rain the young fennel shoots are sprouting. By going over these very carefully and gently he is sure to find some caterpillars, either little black ones with a kind of white saddle, or larger and more brilliant ones with black and orange markings and rings of a delicate green-blue. These are different stages of the same insect, a common but beautiful creature, The Common American Swallowtail, Papilio polyxenes (Fabr.) It is very variable within limits, and the variety here in the West is almost certain to be asterius (Cra.) It is quite easy to rear them. Be content with three or four, and keep them in a glass jar with a covering of open muslin or even paper with tiny air holes. Give them fresh shoots of fennel every day and throw out the old with disjecta. (Catherine has two in a large glass tumbler at present.) He should note the date of finding them, make a little sketch of their shape and colours, then note each metamorphosis, either sloughing of skin or complete change to chrysalis, with date, and then look every morning to see if they have changed into butterflies. This usually occurs about 3 weeks after change to chrysalis. He must get used to calling them larva (caterpillar stage), pupa (chrysalis stage) and imago (winged stage). These words like the scientific names were not invented to snoot the public but to insure absolute accuracy. He should be most meticulous in noting date and place, even hour, of finding insects, and watch their habits.

When you come here I'll have my cases of insects, books to show him, and I'll let him have a setting board and pins &c., and try to show him how to begin. It would be well worth your while to spend a few dollars to equip him. Even if he's not a born biologist he'll learn useful habits of observation and accuracy, and have a fascinating life hobby.[3]

Netta is going to ring up your wife and arrange an evening. Meanwhile if you and Norman cared to come in here to me any morning Monday through Friday between 9 and 2 p.m., we could have a serious seance of entomology untroubled by the frivolous and prophane vulgar.

I am still plugging away daily at Homer, and wondering more every day why contemporaries think they are writing or can write poetry.

Yours sincerely,
R.A.

---

*Lawrence Clark Powell (b. 1906) and RA became friends shortly after RA's arrival in Hollywood. Wherever he had lived since his early days in London, he sought out the best libraries available, and Powell was then university librarian and director of the Clark Library at the University of California at Los Angeles. Subsequently, Powell became dean of the Graduate Library School and, finally, professor emeritus at the University of Arizona. An author himself, Powell was able to help RA in many ways including assistance in arranging the publication of Kershaw's bibliography (1950) and RA's *Jane Austen* (1948). In his professional capacity, Powell put his library's resources at RA's disposal, helping him obtain special books and manuscripts.

1. Of RA's books of which the UCLA library had then (and has today) a fine collection.

2. Powell's son; he abandoned butterfly collecting when RA told him he had to kill his specimens with cyanide.

3. RA makes many references in his letters to his hobby of butterfly collecting; images drawn from it also appear often in his poetry and prose: see, for example, "Childhood," in *Complete Poems*, p. 55; and *Very Heaven*, London, 1937, pp. 366–67.

100. To Eric Warman (SIUC)

10 August 1945   Hollywood.

Dear Eric,[1]

Your letter from the remote past of July 21st comes tapping like a message from the Pyramid age. How justified is dear old Wells in his passion for science—for though the released sub-atomic energy is at present only destructive it can be, may be, and even possibly will be used constructively.[2] I agree with your base of despair, especially in view of the cult of the envious, stupid, ignorant, unteachable average man. I wish the world could be taken over by a committee of scientists, intellectuals and organizers, instead of being run by vile newspaper writers and cows who have the only virtue—and what a virtue!—of collecting the votes of the mentally pauperized.

To hell with the Pope, by the way.

But you are right, and your conclusion is that of Voltaire—cultivons notre jardin.[3] It is the only way. Once let yourself be bull-dozed into thinking you are responsible for the world—and that way madness lies. And why not escape? You'd escape from a fire, an earthquake, a sub-atomic bomb, if you could, so why not escape from the poison gas of the average man and his friends? Balls to him. Pah to him. I, like you, think of those nearest first.

By the time this reaches you the whole war will be over. To-day (in case you've forgotten) we've been listening to the rumours of Japanese surrender, which, I imagine are basically true.[4] They'll have to give in. I suppose you won't agree, but I feel the deepest sorrow for Japan and admiration for the heroism and devotion of the Japanese people. All they asked was to be left alone. America, followed by the howling pack of European nations, went and bombarded them and forced them to humiliating concessions—they who had worked out so exquisite and beautiful a civilisation. Then when they attempt to revenge themselves, they are destroyed.[5] It is hard on them. I keep thinking of the Japanese tanka:

"Each time that an extra is circulated

The widows of friends and foes

Have increased in multitude."

Alas! it is now widowers and men made childless who increase, thanks to our gallant airmen.

My Casanova troubles are lightened, but not over. Viking refused (as I hoped), not wishing to be linked with anything so vulgar as a radio company. The book will be published by a new and wealthy firm, Duell, Sloan and Pearce.[6] I lunched with Duell yesterday, struck the bargain, but he was off to Mexico to fuck a young woman, and my agent will continue the negotiations by cable, drawing up the contract soon. Anyway, this secures to me the $10,000 already paid by Columbia, and (I suppose) something from Duell, plus the chance of very much more IF the movie people go on with it. I have my doubts. The point is, Eric, that I loath their guts and they know it, and that makes things difficult. However, other things come along. I have the Encyclopaedia Brittanica anthology which is worth $2500;[7] I have just agreed to do an Oscar Wilde omnibus for Viking with introduction for $1500;[8] I have done an introduction on French novels for the Pilot Press (as I told you) for a miserable 100 quid; and sent a blank verse translation from the Italian to the Phoenix Press at their request.[9] Personally I don't want anything more this year—I'll make about $14,000 and after that you work for the tax dept. not for yourself. If the Columbia people pay the $30,000 to shoot Casanova, I'll have to persuade them to pay it next year, when there may be some tax abatement. However, I'm not too hopeful.[10]

I wish you could be here on a proper quota basis, with a backing of about $5000. It is difficult to muscle in on the rackets, especially for an Englishman, but you could do it, clean up nicely and then retire. Only, you have to turn up with a flourish of strumpets—or trumpets, which ever is most practical. Anyway, some piece of publicity. But you need about two years income behind you so that you can refuse poor offers and hold out. So many people come here hoping to clean up in a few weeks, and are simply starved out. What little success I've had is due to the fact that I have other work, and didn't mind when I had nearly a year without a job. When they found I could hang on, they came back again.

I'm very pleased to know about your success with the book versions of movies.[11] It is a good racket, and unless there is an unforeseen slump here I think you can hold it. I mean, the money, though good in England, is not worth enough translated into dollars to tempt the average Hollywood writer. However, there are multitudes of sharks here, and I haven't and shall not say a word to anyone, in case of stirring up jealousy and competition.

Netta has got her first commission as a portrait painter—only $100, but the victim is delighted and is recommending her to others. Netta has worked hard, and I'm very pleased she has this success.[12] After the war we hope to get a "colored girl" who will take the burden of cooking etc off her. At present the brutes can get fabulous wages, and do nothing for them.

You are getting into the expensive period with Jean, I can see. Apart from her keep, Catherine's clothes cost more than Netta's, and her education $80 a month![13]

Netta says: "Tell Eric I think he's wonderful, because I agree with him."

Ever yours,
Richard

P.S. Do you want me to talk to my agent about coming out here? Send me copies of your books, especially the new movie ones.

1. At Warman's request, RA had begun to spell his friend's name Eric instead of Erik.
2. An atomic bomb was dropped on Hiroshima on 6 August 1945 (Japanese date).
3. RA's version of the final words spoken by the protagonist of Voltaire's *Candide*.
4. A second atomic bomb was dropped on Nagasaki on 9 August (Japanese date); the Japanese initiated surrender negotiations the next day.
5. This view seems to be based more on RA's appreciation of Japanese art and culture than on a clear view of Japanese policies during the early 1940s. This is curious given RA's ability to see clearly what was going on in Europe in the mid-1940s.
6. See RA, *The Romance of Casanova. A Novel*, New York, 1946; see Letter 101.
7. See Letter 105 n.1.
8. See *The Portable Oscar Wilde*, ed. and intro. Richard Aldington, New York, 1946.
9. Not traced.
10. No movie was made.
11. Warman had innovated the highly successful "book-of-the-movie."
12. Not traced.
13. Jean Warman was thirteen; Catherine Aldington, Netta and RA's daughter, was seven.

101. To Eric Warman (SIUC)

25 August 1945   Hollywood.

Dear Eric,

I can't help feeling a bit gloomy that the censorship job is ending. Of course it was super-footling and quite unworthy of you, but England's economic situation seems to me so desperate I feel worried about everyone who hasn't a govt. job. I felt quite sick when Washington announced so abruptly the end of Lend-Lease.[1] Do you know that the adverse trade balance for civilian goods in 1944 was 1000,000,000 pounds? With all overseas investments wiped out, most of the merchant marine at the bottom of the seas, and a perfectly staggering short term debt held abroad— how on earth is England going to buy food? This "nationalisation" is a mere nostrum, won't do anything. Attlee's share the wealth is really a share the poverty.[2] You must now be tasting the full bitterness of victory.

Now with regard to what I can do for you with my work.[3] My affairs in England are in such confusion, owing to the glorious deeds of Pinker, that I have put them into the hands of my young brother, who is a rather successful solicitor in Dover.[4] He now has most of my agreements, and is investigating publishers, and trying to collect royalties due. I'll enclose a letter of introduction to him, and he can tell you what if anything of the old Routledge stuff may be available. Ask him to look up the agreements and see if there is an out-of-print clause returning the books to me, and in any case what Routledge are doing. The books available, so far as I remember, are: Letters of Voltaire, Candide, Four French Comedies of the XVIIIth Century, Fifteen Joys of Marriage, Voyages of Cyrano de Bergerac. The biography of Voltaire was bought by Chattos, who in turn sold it to Heinemann.[5]

I am just negotiating a contract with Duell, Pearce and Sloane, for my "Casanova in Love," a novel written under subsidy for Columbia, of which they may make a picture, but may not. Now I can't offer it to you, because Heinemann would be angry. But they have known that the book is being written for some time and have said nothing. So why don't you write or cable me an offer—you needn't pay an advance, if you pay a good royalty. I will thereupon cable Heinemann, and if they shilly-shally and Elek likes to take the book "blind"—there you are. It is a "popular" book mind you, refused here by Viking as not being "Aldington"—to hell with them. Duell saw it here and jumped at it.

Without strings I can offer you a complete new translation of Boccaccio's Decameron. It was published here by Covici Freide with illustrations by Jean de Bosschère, bought by Doubleday, who have re-issued it cheaply and sell it in thousands.[6] It really is about the best Boccaccio there is. It has never been published in England. The book is long and the only way to do it economically is to get some clever popular artist to illustrate it and sell it as a Christmas gift book. Then when that sale is dead, re-issue it cheaply without illustrations. There are at least two cheap Boccaccios on the market, one an Everyman,[7] but I believe mine is more complete. If you are seriously interested, I can send you a copy of the American edition.

Netta and I have done a child's book which may be published here. The text would have to be altered a bit for England, and Netta wants to re-draw her illustrations. I have mentioned this to Heinemann, but Frere has not so far "bitten," and if he doesn't mention it in his next letter I'll hold it for you.[8]

I have a prose translation of the 12 Months of the Year Sonnets of Folgore da San Gemignano, a poet of the 14th century in Italy. This should be done with the text of Navone en regard. Similar to my 50 Romance Poems.[9] This is a thoroughly highbrow performance, and I may produce it through the University here or one of the fine printing presses. It was issued in a limited edition in 1917 by Bubb of Cleveland, Ohio—never published in England.[10]

Finally, I am translating into blank verse the Pastor Fido of Guarini— another highbrow thing. I sent one scene of it to the Phoenix Press for "Translation," at their request—so you may see it therein.[11]

You'll realise that the novel and child's book are subject to Heinemann not wanting them. I don't believe they will, because Frere keeps up the "no paper" blurp.

I am simply worked off my seat here. On top of the Encyclopaedia anthology, I have just been asked to edit and introduce an omnibus Oscar Wilde (copy by October) and Duell wants the Casanova by Jan 1st. The Viking are paying me $1500 for the Wilde introduction. Yesterday I was pleasantly surprised by a letter from the Encyclopaedia saying they had decided to pay me $1000 more than the amount they originally offered! I think they realised what a terrific job it is. Literally I am working ten hours a day to get these three books done. Since V.E. day[12] it has been one request after another. This happens—the few authors who have the restraint to keep silent throughout a war are the people who are wanted immediately after, when readers are looking for something else.

Yes, I wish you could come here. Rationing and other restrictions are being relaxed already, and I suppose the most gigantic boom followed by the most gigantic slump in history will occur. Perhaps not—some controls are being maintained. But "business" went back into the White House with Truman, and it wouldn't surprise me if a new brand of isolationism went too.

How is Jean? Catherine seems to enjoy music very much—it is taught here more intelligently, I think. It ought to be, as education is frightfully expensive.

Ever yours,
Richard

1. Lend-Lease prevented a large-scale repetition of the war-debt difficulties of World War I, but with victory over Japan in September 1945 it was shut off.

2. Attlee defeated Churchill and the Conservatives largely on the appeal of his program of nationalization.

3. RA considered having Warman and his partner, Paul Elek, act as his literary agents in England.

4. RA's brother was P.A.G. "Tony" Aldington.

5. See *Voltaire*, London, 1925; *Voyages to the Moon and the Sun*, London [1923]; *The Fifteen Joys of Marriage, Ascribed to Antoine De La Sale, c.1388–c.1462*, London [1926]; *French Comedies of the XVIIIth Century*, London [1923]; *Candide and Other Romances*, London [1927]; *Letters of Voltaire and Madame du Deffand*, London, 1927; and *Letters of Voltaire and Frederick the Great*, London, 1927.

6. See *The Decameron of Giovanni Boccaccio*, trans. Richard Aldington, New York, 1930.

7. See *The Decameron of Giovanni Boccaccio*, trans. J. M. Rigg, London, 1930 [Everyman's Library]; and *The Decameron of Giovannia Boccaccio*, trans. John Payne, London [1931].

8. Not published.

9. See *Fifty Romance Lyric Poems*, trans. Richard Aldington, New York, 1928.

10. See Folgore da San Gemignano, *The Garland of Months*, trans. Richard Aldington, Cleveland, Ohio, 1917.

11. *Translation*, London, 1946, contains no translations credited to RA.

12. 8 May 1945, the day of victory in Europe for the Allies in World War II.

102. To Leonard Bacon (Yale)

12 September 1945   Hollywood.
Dear Leonard,

Your letter was very welcome, as your letters always are. I am delighted to know that you have finished the draft of your version of Camões.[1] It is a noble work, and you must have used the midnight hours to get it done.

"I too, my lord, have not been idle" (if you don't know that story, remind me to tell you). I have now completed my Oscar Wilde "Portable" for the Viking. I modestly think it isn't bad: The Decay of Lying, The Critic as Artist, Dorian Gray, Salome, The Importance of Being Earnest, De Profundis; selected poems, prose poems, reviews, epigrams, published letters, 12 unpublished letters I found in the Clark Library; a collection of Wilde anecdotes from about 20 books; and an introduction of 11,000 words.[2]

Meanwhile I have written a little tribute to the martyred land of Italy, which Netta is illustrating,[3] and tomorrow I start on the final text of Casanova with no great enthusiasm but some determination. In the evenings I work on the great anthology, which I suspect I am making so complete there will be enough left over for a second book. I am now clearing up Greece, in the midst of Rome, and pushing into the Dark and Middle Ages of Latin. But when I finish the Casanova, I must take a holiday, though the Ency. want my book in September 1946.

In despair of clearing up the tangle of honest and dishonest publishers, piracies and what-not of my work, I have put all my literary affairs outside U.S. into the hands of my lawyer brother,[4] who tells me he is uncovering all manner of hocus-pocus. Charming epoch, whose only attention to an artist is to tax and to cheat him! However, now that my brother has taken it off me I cease to be irritated, and have indeed devised a reasonable life. As you know, I gave up smoking three years ago; now, after several experiments, I have finally given up drinking, and feel so much better, more energetic and more cheerful—sleep better, work better, play better. As a drink I use these delicious fruit juices (which only America furnishes) with soda water. (It was a little tough while they were rationed!) Then I never read a newspaper or listen to the radio. I try once more to live Im Ganzen, Guten, Schönen, as I did before this misery dropped on us all 6 years ago. The sub-atomic bomb solves it all. Either the knaves and fools must submit to the cardinal disciplines, or they blow themselves and us to nothing. I can do nothing to influence people directly, but may perhaps do something indirectly by reminding them in a small way of other things. In any case culture like charity begins at home. Personally I think you are doing more for the world by translating Camões than by yelling your head off in Times Square. If newspapers and radio newscasts were abolished, people forbidden to travel except after passing a rigorous examination (you and I would set the papers—and how nasty we should be!) universal suffrage abolished, Uncle Joe[5] suffocated in a sewer, and the government of the world entrusted to a joint committee of scientists, we might look for a little peace. As it is vogue la galère.

It is surprising to me that the U.S. (and I presume the minor allies) still want a Navy. What's the use of it, when one subatomic bomb can blow up a whole squadron? But, as we know from personal experience, nothing is so conservative and blank stupid sometimes as the military and naval mind. It may catch up in time, so that Philip would not find a quarter-deck to walk. On the other hand, the Navy gives leisure for writing, a good deal of knowledge of foreign ports (always exactly alike in my experience) and much longer and pleasanter holidays with his family than would be possible in business. I believe peace-time married officers are often given long periods of shore jobs, which enables them to live with their families. On the whole, I think Philip may be extremely sensible about this.

With all good wishes,

Ever yours,
Richard

1. *The Lusiads*, trans. Leonard Bacon, New York, 1950.
2. RA describes the contents of *The Portable Oscar Wilde*, New York, 1946, except that "The Decay of Lying" is not included.

3. See *A Wreath for San Gemignano*, New York, 1945.
4. P.A.G. Aldington.
5. Joseph Stalin.

103. To Eric Warman (SIUC)

8 June 1946   Chatham Hotel,
                                                               Montego Bay,
                                                               Jamaica, B.W.I.

Dear Eric,

It seems a long time since I heard from you, and I daresay you have been wondering why the hell I haven't written. To be brief—the time has been consumed in travelling, in dealing with the stupendous amount of red tape involved in travelling, and in recovering from the nervous symptoms I began to develope in Hollywood.[1]

We had quite a journey across America, by car 2200 miles from H'wood to New Orleans, thence by plane via Mobile and Tampa to Miami, and then to Cuba and Jamaica. It is a great relief to be out of the U.S.—both of us were about at the end of our power of endurance of the raucous bastards. Nevertheless, we enjoyed the car run across California, Arizona, New Mexico, Texas and Louisiana. Between Tucson and Arizona and our starting point we passed hundreds and hundreds of trailers making for California. There were hundreds more parked in Tucson itself, people resting before making the arduous and to some extent still perilous trip across the desert. There is a new rush on—a climate, not a gold rush, by people who have saved enough out of the war earnings to live simply and seemed prepared to live in a trailer to be in the sun. Certainly there is no chance of their getting a flat or house.

Jamaica is rather a disappointment—turns out to be very hot and muggy, malarious, and politically a kind of negro republic flying the Union Jack. The people are mostly lazy, and the big idea is to wangle loans and grants from England. It has the depressing quality of derelict countries—the old sugar estates gone to hell, the coconuts dying of one disease and the bananas of another. The scenery is very beautiful, so are the Mediterranean colours of the sea, and the bathing A 1. But we are constantly scared of malaria for Catherine, and there are too few white people to make any society. There are many half-castes, shrewd business people; and the only tolerable company is that of the few elderly descendants of the last remaining "great" families. We had two old sisters to lunch to-day, who own a place 1700 feet up in the mountains over the most hellish "road" I ever tackled, and I have driven in Portugal and New Mexico! But in their place, Kemshott, you really get a sensation of being out of this century, in a sort of tropical Cranford with an immense and beautiful solitude surrounding it.[2]

We think of spending a month or two or three more here, and then making our way to Rio de Janeiro and Buenos Aires, perhaps returning to France in 1947. A certain amount depends on how Casanova sells, but I think we shall make that trip anyway.[3] We are letting Catherine run wild here after almost two years of continuous school—even her holidays had to be under school auspices. It was staggering to see how in less than a week she changed from an American to a British colonial child—has a rather prissy English accent and goes around in jodhpurs. She has learned to ride a bike and a moke, to swim and dive, and goodness knows what else. I hope it is an experience she will remember with pleasure in later days.

How is Jean getting on? Do let me know, and also tell me about yourself and your own doings. The books of yours you sent did not reach me before leaving Calif, but other books have been forwarded, and I know these will come along in time. I hope they're having a good sale and that you're making plenty of money—as you deserve to make.

I am not working on anything at present—a strange sensation after such a long grind, alternating studio and book work. You may have seen the introduction to the French novels (Pilot Press). There should be more to come in the next couple of years. Let me know if you can't get free copies, and I'll have them sent to you.

How are conditions in England? Still lousy, I gather. The American loan should go through this month. Let me know if it does anything towards loosening the stranglehold of the officials and red tape. I must say the British have done better than the Americans in this island. The place was wide open for U.S. trade, but owing to the strikes the Yanks could deliver very little, and no cars. Last month British ships (apart from Canadians) brought in almost 5000 tons of goods including over 30 cars. If only they could get another 300 in this month, they would skim the cream off the market before the Yanks can get going. By the way, you ought to be getting more sugar and bananas—ships have been sailing with such cargos two and three a week ever since we arrived a month ago. But of course it takes a hell of a lot of bananas to make much impression on 45,000,000 people.

Ever affectionately,
Richard

1. See RA to Eric Warman, 10 April 1946 (SIUC) where RA wrote that he had been "near a nervous collapse owing to intense work," and on "medical advice," was planning

to take a rest. "We are going down to New Orleans to try and get shipping to Jamaica . . . where Netta's mother is building a house."

2. In *Cranford*, London, 1853, Elizabeth Cleghorn Gaskell portrays English village life during the second quarter of the nineteenth century.

3. They did not visit South America.

104. To Lawrence Powell (UCLA)

28 July 1946   Jamaica.

Dear Larry,

We have been wondering very much how you are all progressing, as this is the week when you make your move to Culver City. And then you'll be hitting the trail for Colorado and those glorious mountains. There is something quite terrific about that West and South-West of America which nobody yet has succeeded in getting into words. Lawrence got something of New Mexico into St. Mawr[1] (a silly story)— the descriptive parts, I mean. Nobody else that I know of has got even near the aloof grandeur of the landscape—as distinct from all the poppy-cock about rangers, forty-niners, Indians, buffaloes and all the other pests of the district, including pioneers cannibal or not cannibal![2] I wish Lawrence had seen Utah, Colorado and Arizona—all finer than New Mexico in my opinion.

We have had rather a mixed time here. In the first place we fell into a prolonged heat wave, then we had to be inoculated against typhoid, and still have the threat of malaria—especially with Catherine who cannot be made to take the proper precautions. (For your benefit, Fay,[3] if you and the boys ever get into malaria country—3 grains of quinine every two days, and be in screened apartments from sunset to sunrise, the Anopheles mosquito only operating at those hours.) Then I have been a pest to the family with my neurosis and anxiety—and am only just beginning to pull out of it. I am not a Socialist I discover, and this "government control" of everything and everybody in British territory gives me the willies. Don't be taken in—Socialism isn't justice, it's a dismal tyranny of bureaucrats. We are hopping it, and I'll be damned if I ever get back into British dominion again, if I can help it.

After much discussion and a good deal of mental distress, we have come to a compromise. Netta cannot endure America, and I find it a bit raucous myself; she would like England, but I say to hell with it, damn England; Catherine wants to stay in Jamaica. So we have decided to risk rationing and revolution and return to France, if we can circumvent the immigration officials (upon whom be hell and brimstone) of U.S., England and France! My friend Gribble promises us his furnished studio in Rue Campagne-Première (remember it? just back from the Dome) as long as he is with the Reparations Committee in Belgium. Our real difficulty is with visas and passports, for the British will only give us six months passports and the French apparently only two months visas. O God damn them!

What I have in mind is to do a biography of some 18th century Frenchman, rather on the lines of The Duke, but from the French point of view. At present I rather favour Louis XV who has never been treated humanely by any British or American writer, and who must have been a nice chap to have so many women like him.[4] And I might also do a novel with a French background, while getting on with 90s anthology.[5] (Here I can't do a damned thing, and feel like an exiled criminal.)

Now do you think you could write me a couple of letters of introduction on U.C. Library notepaper? I might never use them, though I probably would, but the point is that I am collecting as many such as possible—Europeans being impressed by them as you know, and they might help with the French authorities. Letter 1, from you as U.C.L.A. Librarian to Director of Bibliothèque Nationale, recommending me to read in 18th century—slight panegyric of R.A., reference to the fact of having translated Cyrano de Bergerac, Laclos, Regnard, Marivaux, Le Sage, etc., biography of Voltaire, volume of Great French Romances in press with Duell, Sloan and Pearce. Letter 2, to your friend the Maire or ex-Maire of Dijon, shorter, more personal, taking for granted he knows who I am. Any other letter to a Frenchman in official position you know. If these were written in French very much to the good, and add your French degree after your name.[6]

Forgive the trouble—I know it's a bore. But we're going to have a tough time crashing the international barriers.

We plan to fly to New York on or about the 3rd September. Now don't trouble to send the letters here (that would cost postage) but send them to me care Duell, Sloane and Pearce, 270 Madison Avenue, New York 16. by ordinary mail, marked TO AWAIT ARRIVAL. Send them, if possible, about the 25th of Aug, but if you'll be away then and have to send earlier, mail them to Charlie Duell personally with a note asking him to hold them for me. You can never trust the postal clerks in those big offices to do what they're told—Duells are still sending half my mail to Sunset Boulevard, with hideous delays in consequence, as Al Manuel's girl secretary is no fire-ball at the job either.

Good God, what an epoch, when one has to plot with this minuteness!

In this hotel there's a north of England merchant who managed to circumvent the British officials and fly here by way of Paris, Eire, New York, after 8 weeks of ceaseless effort. He had to go to Liverpool for the French visa and then fly to London to get his tickets the same day! (All devised to prevent people travelling). I asked him how life is in England. "Ey, lad, it's 'orrible. Can't call ower souls ower own, we can't. Ye can't get nothin' to eat like, and they waon't let you do nothin' you waant t'do. Gooverment Caontrol, they calls it. Lot 'o' bloudie tyranny I ses. Wy, we couldn'ta bin much waorse if th' Gairmens 'ad a got there. I don't 'old with it."

So I opine that either Messieurs Attlee and Bevin will have to pull in their horns or they'll hear from the electorate.

I have a hunch that in spite of all these festering fools we shall meet one of these days in Paris. May it come soon!

Our love to you all,
Richard

P.S. Catherine has got religious here, the first effect of which is that she gravely tells us she is going to paradise and we shall go to the "fiery pit." Charming guys these Xtians.

1. See D. H. Lawrence, *St. Mawr*, New York, 1925.
2. Probably a reference to the Donner-Reed party of emigrants to California who, stranded in the Sierra Nevada in 1846, resorted to cannibalism to survive.
3. Mrs. Lawrence Powell.
4. RA did not carry out this plan.
5. Possibly *Religion of Beauty, Selections from the Aesthetes,* London, 1950.
6. For a description of Powell's years at the University of Dijon, where he earned a doctorate, see "Délicieuse Ville, Mélancolique et Douce: Dijon, 1930–32," *Robinson Jeffers Newsletter,* January 1983.

105. To H. D. (Yale)

26 October 1946   Hotel L'Aiglon,
                                                232 Boulevard Raspail,
                                                Paris (14), France.

Dear Dooley,

I reproach myself for the delay in writing you, but it is only possible to write letters by taking time from other things. As you know, the rationing in these European countries is very inefficient and time-consuming by its minuteness. (The American system was really very good by comparison.) Then I have taken on really more work than a man of my age should do, while extra dollops have fallen on me from the Encyclopaedia Britannica. I think I told you about the Anthology of Poetry of the Western World[1] I am doing for them. Well, I turned in the final script before I left Hollywood, but on arrival here I found a letter saying that they had changed their mind and instead of omitting had decided to include The Bible, Homer, Virgil, Lucretius, Dante, Chaucer, Milton and Goethe!

The Bible, Chaucer, and Milton I could do easily of course, but in a non-English-speaking country it is impossible to find the various translations of the other works, and so many of them are out of print one has to pay fantastic prices and write humble letters to booksellers for them. Most of them haven't yet turned up. Then we have ennuis with our baggage, the French asking enormous Customs duties and vast railway charges, which I have had to have officially investigated—which involved ceremonious calls on Frenchmen, exchange of signed books, including those of a poet-bureaucrat with the appropriate name of Noel Bureau! (What would Freud say?) Then, as if all this is not too much, the Comtesse de Vogüé has asked me to write the article for England in the international tribute to Antoine de Saint-Exupéry.[2] She is a rather tragical figure, doping herself with "scotch" to try to forget him—they were to have been married the day after he was killed,[3] so how can I refuse? And then, as always happens in Paris, we are caught up in social engagements, which are the more "scattering" (as you used so wisely to say) because we lived much to ourselves in Florida and Hollywood. The most amusing person we have met as a new acquaintance is old Senator Hollis, "the only Democratic Senator for New Hampshire, sir, in seventy years!" He quit the U.S. when the Senate refused to ratify Wilson's treaty and has lived here ever since. What is stupendous is that he has made himself a great authority on French wines, and gave us a bottle of Romanée-Conti such as I thought no longer existed.

The enclosed photograph is of Catherine, as you will have guessed. She is a nice little girl, a little given to fussing over trifles, a bit of a perfectionist, but intelligent, warm-hearted and responsive to ethical training. She has improved enormously since we got her away from the pernicious influences of Hollywood and Hollywood children. Some of those movie children were quite ghastly—I have horrid memories of Barbara Queen Young and "Happy" Daniels, which latter by the bye is English and the worst of the lot. Her pop has gone legit,[4] as the Hollywood trade papers say, which means he is acting on Broadway again. At the present moment I can see Catherine from the window scooting up and down the sidewalk with Daphne Craig, the last of Gordon's many infants. I do hope you will be able to see her when you leave Switzerland. But this I beg you not to do precipitately, because it is most important to build up after so long an illness.

Do you want any books from here or England? Just let me have a list, as long as you like, and they shall be sent you. Say whether to Kusnacht or to where.

My eye has just lighted on one of the publications of the Metropolitan Museum which I bought in New York in August. There is really a great development of the U.S. art galleries, particularly the National Gallery in Washington and the Metropolitan—really fine things and beautifully produced little guides and handbooks. The Metropolitan is particularly nice because they have a large set of rooms with a restaurant etc for the little people, where children can be left to turn over art books or play or have a glass of milk under supervision while pop and momma look at the pix. You must admit the Americans are nice about such things. Unfortunately, the country becomes impossible as soon as one passes the mental age of 16.

I have been meaning to ask you but have constantly forgotten— whether you heard the broadcast on the Imagists I wrote for the B.B.C. earlier in the year?[5] It had to be handled rather delicately on account of Ez wasn't so hot with the public, but I got by O.K. Story is H.D. first, the rest also ran. If you didn't hear it I'll mail you the one copy of the script I have. Should you ever want to do anything for the B.B.C. let me know, and I'll try to wangle same. By the way, they refused to notice my Wellington on the air saying superciliously that it is "not original," but they will review my Selected Works of Oscar Wilde.[6] To which I replied that I quite understood—the Selected Works of Oscar Wilde are all originals, while of course they couldn't touch a homosexual like the Duke of Wellington. Methinks I scored.

I do hope you're getting on all right, Dooley. And please do seriously let me know what I can do. I haven't had an answer to the Greek Reader idea,[7] but that is because the U.S. transatlantic air pilots are on strike, so no air mail comes in. But if you think you'll be up to the fatigue of the job, I'm sure they'll want you to do it. Ask Bryher what she thinks.

With love from us all,

Richard

1. Although RA worked intermittently on this project for years and again reported it as finished in late 1959, it was never published.

2. See *Confluences* for 1947, which combined numbers 12–14 to form a book devoted to Saint-Exupéry; RA's article appeared in French translated from English.

3. RA is either exaggerating or ill-informed: when Saint-Exupéry was lost, he had a wife and the comtesse a husband.

4. Barbara was the daughter of the actor Robert Young, and "Happy" was the daughter of Mark Daniels, architect, actor, and author of *Birth of a Nation*, a one-act play.

5. RA is listed as "Scriptwriter" for an Eastern Service (Purple Network) broadcast Saturday, 13 July 1946, entitled "The Imagists." The program, no. 92 in the "Book of Verse" series, opened with H.D.'s "Hermes of the Ways" and closed with her "Garden," both read by Joan Hopkins.

6. *Oscar Wilde. Selected Works*, London, 1946.

7. RA had suggested to Viking Press on H.D.'s behalf a Greek reader as a companion volume to *The Portable Oscar Wilde*, New York, 1946.

V

EXPATRIATE-HERO: 1947–1962. LETTERS 106–154

The Last Years

In 1947 I was staying with Richard Aldington at his villa in the south of France. He had no financial worries at that period, he was pleased with the work he was doing, the cellar never ran dry and, as a matter of principle, the local peasants saw to it that the food rationing regulations imposed by Paris were systematically circumvented. A golden time on the whole—on the whole, because the mornings were shrouded in holy dread while we waited for the arrival of the mail. "*Monsieur Aldington*," the mailman would observe admiringly as he cascaded a few dozen letters on the terrace table, "*vous avez un véritable courrier de ministre.*"

Richard didn't share the *facteur's* innocent pleasure, not by a long chalk. Agitatedly ripping the envelopes open so as to know the worst at once, "Netta," he would ask his wife, "do you remember somebody called so-and-so? . . . I can't make out whether this is a bill or a receipt . . . God Almighty, what am I to say to this moron? . . . Who on earth . . . ? Why on earth . . . ? What on earth . . . ?"

Listening commiseratingly one morning to these lamentations, I came up with a suggestion.

"Would you like me to deal with some of this stuff for you, Richard?"

"My dear fellow, as if I'd dream of landing you with such a hideous chore."

"It wouldn't bother me."

"You mean it?"

"Of course."

"Then, *yes!* I'll be everlastingly grateful. Open everything and answer the pestilential bastards as you think best. Tell the whole bunch to go and bugger themselves would be my advice."

"What about letters marked 'Personal' and 'Confidential'? Do you want me to open them, too?'

"Christ, yes: they're the worst of the lot."

So I opened everything and typed replies which Richard lightheartedly signed, unread.

"If anyone should ever have the mad notion of publishing my letters, Alister, do you know what our old friends the critics are going to say? They'll say, these are the dullest bloody letters we've ever read, except that from 1947 onwards they become sheer masterpieces, witty, stylish, dazzlingly intelligent—the publishing event of the season, the ideal Christmas present."

It's a bitter blow but the critics won't be paying me any of the compliments Richard predicted since the editor of the present selection has been too shrewd to include anything not written by Richard; I'm willing to bet, however, that the first part of his forecast will be thoroughly vindicated. There won't be a single "literary journalist" to notice his generous enthusiasms, his love of life, his capacity for absolute and unquestioning devotion, his readiness, his eagerness to help his fellow writers—F. S. Flint, Remy de Gourmont, T. S. Eliot, André Spire, and yes, most of all, H.D. to whom Richard gave throughout his whole life his admiration, his devotion, his consideration and tenderness.

Why should Richard Aldington provoke such detestation on the part of practically everyone with access to a newspaper, a magazine or a publisher? Mystery! This animosity reached its bedlamite paroxysm with the publication of his *Lawrence of Arabia* when Robert Graves and other of Lawrence's gaping worshippers organized one of the grubbiest little cabals in literary history; but even before then Richard couldn't do a thing right. It's true that his books, especially *Death of a Hero* weren't notably conciliatory; but other writers have produced anticonformist books without being lynched. No doubt Richard's sheer vitality exasperated and exasperates the etiolated reviewers of London and New York; but then how is one to account for the fact that D. H. Lawrence, for example, has been allowed to get away with it? And why should Richard's prodigious scholarship give such offence (one sturdy no-nonsense critic, I remember, rebuked him sharply for quoting Dante) to the same individuals who are awe-struck by the phoney erudition of Ezra Pound?

Whatever the reason, it's a lopsided tribute to Richard, I suppose, that he can still, more than twenty-five years after his death, infuriate literary "schools," journalistic scribblers, newspaper editors, and what is known as the "Establishment" in general.

Alister Kershaw
Maison Sallé
1 August 1987

1947–1962

The Aldingtons lived in Paris, first at a hotel on Boulevard Raspail and then in a studio on the Boulevard Montparnasse, until the summer of the next year. During this time RA reestablished old ties and made arrangements to publish his work in Europe where wartime restrictions were ending. He was obstructed by many of the same problems regular commerce was encountering: paper shortages, blocked currencies, and various government regulations; nevertheless, between September 1947 and February 1948 almost five thousand pounds in royalties accrued to him. In July the Aldingtons had to vacate their Paris studio. They left for St. Clair, Le Lavandou, in the south of France where they were to live until the spring of 1951. RA wrote that he felt as if he "had come home after a long absence."

Freed from Hollywood's pressures and happy because he was again on the French Mediterranean coast, RA's creative spirit renewed itself. Only a few months after he arrived, he was halfway through an "educational book" for Evans Brothers, nearly halfway through another anthology, and had a novel and two more biographies in preparation. He had begun some of this work in Paris or possibly even in Jamaica or Hollywood, but, in any event, in the four years after he returned to France, his publications included *Four English Portraits, The Strange Life of Charles Waterton,* and his important biography, *D. H. Lawrence: Portrait of a Genuis, But.* . . . During these productive years he also edited *Walter Pater* and *The Religion of Beauty: Selections from the Aesthetes,* and he wrote an introduction to the Chawton edition of the works of Jane Austen, and almost a dozen introductions to Penguin editions of D. H. Lawrence's books. His *Complete Poems* was published in 1948.

If 1947 proved important to RA as the beginning of a renaissance in his creativity, it was also important to him in another way. This was the year that Alister Kershaw, a young Australian poet who was attracted to RA's work, first met the man he so admired. RA tried to assist the younger writer to establish himself, and Kershaw repaid this kindness by becoming indispensable to his older friend as secretary and personal representative in literary matters. He also provided a home for RA in his latter years. We need only read a few of the twelve hundred letters RA wrote to Kershaw between 1947 and 1962 to see how capably and faithfully Kershaw served him. One of the introductions RA wrote during these years was to *A Bibliography of the Works of Richard Aldington from 1915 to 1948*, which Alister Kershaw, who was to become RA's literary executor, compiled during the Le Lavandou years.

Sometime during 1950, RA's wife Netta decided to stay permanently in England, although his daughter Catherine remained with him. The Villa Aucassin, St. Clair, became too difficult for RA to manage himself. In the spring of 1951, therefore, he decided to move to a pension, Les Rosiers, in Montpellier where he lived until 1957. Netta and RA continued to correspond, and in later years Netta visited her husband and daughter in France. RA traveled to Italy with his daughter in 1954, but, except for excursions within France, these were the years when the writer who was now in his sixties and often ill—"a quick rap-rap from the boney-handed one, . . . leaving me shaky," he wrote in 1952—had lost some of the wanderlust of his youth. His income was also falling, and he had not only to support himself and his daughter, but also to maintain payments to the Patmores in accordance with the divorce settlement made in 1938. But these problems of old age, ill health, and a difficult financial situation would soon be augmented by a fight for literary survival because of the two controversial biographies, *Pinorman* and *Lawrence of Arabia*.

RA's biography of D. H. Lawrence had aroused some criticism when it was published in 1950 because, although he greatly admired Lawrence and championed him early and late, in his biography RA portrays him as a fallible human being as well as a great artist. Some of Lawrence's friends and critics found that typical RA approach objectionable. *Pinorman* angered many in literary circles because RA made public Norman Douglas's penchant for boys and his pretentiousness in a rather nasty portrait. He also criticized Douglas for his stance in the Maurice Magnus affair, and questioned the literary merit of some of Douglas's writing. Everyone regarded the book as an attack on Norman Douglas except RA.

While publication of *Pinorman* occasioned some savage sniping by a few of Douglas's friends, *Lawrence of Arabia* brought a barrage of adverse reaction from critics, press, the reading public, and RA's anathema, the "Lawrence Bureau." RA began his T. E. Lawrence biography at the suggestion of Alister Kershaw, for whom Lawrence was a boyhood hero; in his introduction RA tells that he expected to be writing about a genuine hero, but as he went forward he realized more and more that the TEL legend was mostly of Lawrence's own making. Today most historians agree that RA's version of Lawrence's life was generally correct, but, even so, legends do not die easily. In 1955, although RA documented his biography carefully and his publisher's lawyers made sure that he could support his statements before Collins would publish his book, the rain of abuse that fell on RA was catastrophic and led to great financial loss for him when publishers would not reprint his titles, retail outlets banned them, and a hero-worshipping public refused to buy his books. Forty years of work were washed away in a flood of persecution.

The T. E. Lawrence biography took an inordinate amount of RA's time and energy during these years. Existing correspondence with friends who helped him in his research verifies his caution, and once the book appeared he still spent much time and effort defending it. Nevertheless, RA found time for other literary work. George Sims, who operated the Peacocks Press, printed limited editions of critical lectures on Pound and Eliot and on Housman and Yeats that RA had given at Columbia University during his time in the United States. He also wrote two other biographies: one was of the French poet Mistral and won the 1959 Prix de Gratitude Mistraliene (a rare honor for a non-French author); the other was of Robert Louis Stevenson. *Frauds* may have been suggested by the TEL biography. RA also wrote a number of introductions in French and English to a group of books of photographs; this assignment was arranged for him by his good friend Eric Warman. Some additional introductions to Penguin editions of D. H. Lawrence's books also date from these years.

Even with this continued literary work and the many titles in print before 1955, RA was in serious financial trouble after *Lawrence of Arabia* came out. The book was very successful, but RA had had a large advance, and the subsequent royalties were being paid into a trust fund for his daughter Catherine. Therefore, when various publishers previously loyal to him did not reprint his books because of the hostility provoked in the press and among the reading public by the T. E. Lawrence biography, RA, who had supported himself by his pen for more than forty years, found himself almost completely without income. He was also late in his payments to the Patmores, who were clamoring for money in view of his apparent financial success with the TEL biography. He was forced to borrow two hundred pounds from Eric Warman to avoid a writ and bad publicity that might affect sales of the Lawrence book. All this was quickly apparent to Alister Kershaw when he came to visit his friend during the Easter holidays of 1957; he made plans at once to buy a small house in the Loire Valley where RA and his daughter could live rent free.

During the final five years of his life RA enjoyed better times than the prospect early in 1957 seemed to promise. He wrote in September 1956: "I should have realised that one can't afford to write the truth without a private income," but his literary fortunes did improve as the uproar about the *Lawrence of Arabia* book died down. Reprintings of the TEL book did not benefit him directly, but some of his other works were brought back into print in various countries, including even England. RA's health remained a problem; he returned an advance on a Balzac biography that he had begun because his doctor decided that the work would be too much for him. Nevertheless, he felt the need to keep busy with other literary work. He completed a work on D. H. Lawrence for a German publisher and translated, with Delano Ames, the *Larousse Encyclopedia of Mythology*. He wrote a foreword to the third volume of Edward Nehls's *D. H. Lawrence: A Composite Biography* to which he also contributed in a recording session with others who had known Lawrence. He wrote introductions in English and French for three more books of photographs and an introduction to the fine D. H. Lawrence critical biography by his good friend and French author F.-J. Temple. The *Larousse* and all the introductions to the books of photographs were arranged for him by Eric Warman, to whom he had appealed for help in obtaining writing commissions.

This sort of loyalty from his old friends helped to make RA's last years comparatively happy ones. Alister Kershaw's help was considerable, and in 1958 RA notes that a group of his friends contributed to a fund for him—he particularly mentioned the Duttons in Australia. During these last years Bryher, who had first written to him about his poetry when he was a soldier in World War I and who had been a longtime friend of his first wife, H.D., made substantial gifts to RA and his daughter.

This financial help enabled him to travel more than he had during the difficult Montpellier years. He was able to spend time at Aix-en-Provence, near the Mediterranean coast he delighted in and his daughter's school, and away from the Berry's colder winters. In 1959 he visited Zurich for a medical checkup; Catherine joined him there, and they saw H.D. and probably Bryher. In December 1960 RA was in Rome with Catherine, and in the spring of 1961, on a final visit to the country that was so influential in his life and art, he spent almost two months in Venice.

RA's last journey must surely have been one of his happiest. In the midst of all the gloom of his literary misfortunes following the T. E. Lawrence biography, one bright spot was the steady and increasing demand for his work outside England, especially in translation for Eastern European readers, and most of all in the Soviet Union. The letters of his last years grumble about royalty payments not made because of blocked currencies or for other reasons, but quite often he is surprised by the amount of a payment that does come through, especially from the Soviet Union where RA was astonished by his popularity. When the Soviet Writers' Union invited him to celebrate his sixty-fifth birthday in Moscow in 1957, he had refused because of his poor health at the time, but when, in February 1962, he and Catherine received a similar invitation to spend three weeks in Russia as the Union's guests, RA agreed to celebrate his seventieth (and Catha's twenty-fourth) birthday there.

RA's work had been published in the Soviet Union since *Death of a Hero,* and many of his novels and other books had been printed there, both in Russian and in English. An edition of 225,000 copies of *All Men Are Enemies* quickly sold out. Ironically, Soviet scholars ranked RA considerably higher among twentieth-century British writers than did his own countrymen. That RA should be so honored just before his death was happy and fortunate. His letters and diary entries that tell of his visit make heart-warming reading.

Sadness as well as happiness marked RA's last years. A great sadness of old age is the regular and inevitable loss of contemporaries; RA reveals the grief he felt when dear friends such as Roy Campbell, whom he admired above all poets of his day, and Carl Fallas, with whom he had marched off to World War I, were lost to him only three months before his own death. A heavier blow was the death of H.D.; when she died in 1961, RA noted poignantly (and erroneously) that her cremation had taken place on the anniversary of their wedding. The letters to H.D. from their separation by World War I until her death are second in number only to those to Alister Kershaw and cover the longest span of time. The years between their visit to Paris in 1912 and the end of the Great War were "the good time," but they were friends for most of their lives.

RA returned home from the Soviet Union via Paris in mid-July; he died on the 27th in the little house he usually referred to as "Chez Alister Kershaw." The hamlet of Maison Sallé where RA lived for five years when not traveling or in the Midi is just over a vineyard-covered hill from Sury-en-Vaux. From the hill you can see the sharp rise on which stands the fortress town of Sancerre that gives the wine of the district its name. Maison Sallé is a peaceful, quiet place across the Loire from where the main road goes through Cosne. After more than a quarter of a century, the farmers there remember RA as a friend and neighbor whom they had learned to love and whom they held in awe (even though they had never read any of his books) in that curious way Europeans regard their artists and intellectuals. RA's books still line the walls of almost every room of this house in which he spent his last years and give a feeling of his presence there. They are also an oddity: all these books, mostly in English, tucked away in a French hamlet in the Loire Valley. The wanderer from the South Foreland is buried in a small, walled grave-yard, and even that solidly English "Richard Aldington" seems strangely lost on a simple marble slab among the more elaborate stones engraved with Gallic names.

106. To H.D. (Yale)

18 January 1947   162 Boulevard Montparnasse,[1]
                                                  Paris, France.

Dear Dooley,

It has troubled me that I have been unable to write, but twice in the past six weeks I have gone down with particularly vicious attacks of in-fluenza. Apart from the fact that I have to take care this doesn't reach my lungs, one is left so depressed by it, that the arrears of things to be done appear quite mountainous. At such times the ignoble self-slaughter of Europe during the past decade becomes an intolerable thought, the more so since they pride themselves on their heroism while trying to jump on any available political bandwaggon. The collapse of Greece after Chaeronea[2] seems less awful—though indeed "from what a height of bliss" they fell!

But here I am playing the elegant Jeremiah like another Matt Arnold, when it is now my principle that one should try not to say or write any-thing that is not at least consolatory if not positively and vulgarly cheer-ful. I entertained myself during my forced stay in bed with some lovely Japanese colour prints (Toyokuni, Hiroshige, Kuniyoshi) which I was lucky enough to pick up cheap here owing to current prejudices, and with some books on Japan I picked up in the corners of Hollywood bookshops. Then I have been reading a good deal of Goethe (in transla-tion) to set off against your German romantics. Goethe was a great per-son and a real consolation in these days. I have several volumes of his prose but cannot get hold of the Italian Journey and Sojourn in Rome,[3] either in French or English. It is a wonderful comment on our culture that I had to ask Heinemann to advertise to get these volumes of Goethe, that when they came they turned out to be the old Bohn books sixty to a hundred years old, and that most of them were still uncut! Here I could find none at all, though I did get a bilingual text of the Divan.[4] Such is the practical attitude towards the father of modern culture.

These Goethe researches are caused by a Selected Pater[5] which I have undertaken as a companion book to the Wilde. These modern "Select-eds" are proving very popular and are based on certain principles. The authors chosen are mainly prose writers; the length of the book is about 300,000 words; every item chosen must be complete in itself; there must be a lively, informative and unpedantic preface. The Viking Press have been very successful with these in U.S., and (in confidence) Heinemann are now thinking of running a whole series in England under my editorship. The tone of the introduction is very important, for while it must be scholarly it must be unaffected and quite free from the horrible taint of highbrow exhibitionism, and at the same time free from the fawning and playing down of the Everyman[6] type of writer. If Frere and I decide to go on with this project,[7] I do hope we shall be able to find somebody you would care to select and arrange.

It is perhaps foolish to be giving so much thought to such things when I am menaced by a recall to Hollywood at any moment. Needless to say, I don't want to go, but the terms of the offer are so good that if it really becomes official (and nobody knows better than I how easily contracts there fall through at the last moment) I can scarcely refuse, at any rate for six months.[8] I don't look forward to travelling in a world where transport is still monopolised by V.I.P.s and other government parasites or to six months in the ergastulum of the "writers' building," but then Europe is neither so cheerful nor so prosperous that one can neglect such an opportunity. Perhaps my doubts will be all settled by the offer not coming after all! Such is often enough the Hollywood way.

I hope Perdita is going along happily in the U.S. No doubt it is easier to adjust to that milieu at her age. For my part I feel that the intense immigration of scum and dregs from mitteleuropa in the last century was quite fatal. The native original white Americans are now a minority crushed by the descendants of these creatures, the true "awful Americans" of whom we used to complain. But they're in the saddle now, and their hatred of England, the English, is the measure of their hatred of the English-descended Americans. I think much of this incessant propaganda against the "backward South" is due to the fact that it is now the most English part of the country.

For all these years I have managed to keep on friendly terms with our old friend Harry Slonimsky, but alas, he has a bigotedly Zionist wife, and so relations are strained. So everywhere relations are poisoned by these political hatreds.

Catherine is going on pretty well at the Sévigné, is picking up French, and making one or two friends. This is being a difficult time for her—the change within one year of Hollywood, Jamaica and Paris must have been a great strain. Her present best friend (for these "best friends" are liable to sudden and capricious revolutions) is Daphne, the last of the numerous Gordon Craig progeny distributed so liberally. He is 75, but still chipper, and still harping on his daughter, i.e. the "art" of the theatre. It sounds humbug to me, but then I am not a theatre-goer and unable to understand these refined improvements.

I hope you are going on well and finding occupation in Lausanne? I shall not let so long a time pass in silence.

With love to you
Richard

1. The Aldingtons had moved to this address about 16 December 1946.
2. Site of defeat of Athenians and Boetians by Philip of Macedon in 338 B.C.
3. *Italienische Reise* (1816–29).
4. *Westöstliche Divan* (1819).
5. *Walter Pater, Selected Works*, London, 1948.
6. Series published by J. M. Dent and Sons Ltd.
7. They did not.
8. RA did not go to Hollywood again.

107. To H.D. (Yale)

2 May 1947   Montparnasse.
Dear Dooley,

How do you like my beautiful American type paper? I have to be very parsimonious with it because I don't think I can get any more, and the stuff here is so frightful I can't use it for writing to America.

I am a little troubled that you have not yet received the letter of notification from the solicitor together with the list of May's books. Solicitors are such awful fools and knaves in England that one can't trust them to do anything—no French notary or American attorney for that matter would have sent out so crassly ignorant a list.[1] If you don't hear from them soon, will you let me know, and I'll ask them about it. They did not deign to acknowledge my letter. If you are collecting early Imagist stuff there is quite a bit in May's library, chiefly you and Ezra and one or two of my bits of things. Yours are the most important.

I am very glad you settled the Frobenius mystery,[2] for I should hate to think old Ez was really nuts. Do see to it that Miss Jordan[3] keeps on removing "all traces of direction" from your letters to Ez. It is an amazing thing to have to say to a free-born American, but that darned F.B.I. got such a hold during the war and is so suspicious about everyone that they would be after you. I told you, I think, how two of the brutes suddenly descended on me in Los Angeles and questioned me—trying to find out if I listened to Ez's broadcasts, when I saw him, how we corresponded etc. It reminded me much of the persecution of Lorenzo in

England during our little war. What brutes all these people are, and how they do loathe the artist and the free man and woman!

Many things are going pretty well with me, in spite of the fact that I am having to fork out money to those Patmores over the divorce. However, yesterday I had a letter from Prague to say that ten thousand copies of a reprint of All Men Are Enemies sold out on publication day—cheque enclosed for 262,265 francs! To-day a note that Finland has paid an advance of $200 for Casanova,[4] and a request for Czech rights of the Colonel's Daughter,[5] and Slovak rights of All Men.[6] I didn't know Slovak rights were separate, but apparently they are, as the man refers to the Czech translation.

I am working on two reprints for England which young Wingate is doing under license from Heinemann as they haven't paper. One is a new edition of Fifty Romance Poems[7] (the one Bruce Rogers designed so beautifully for U.S.) and the other a Complete Poems.[8] The latter aren't really as bad as I thought they were, though the only really successful one is A Dream in the Luxembourg which is in its sixth impression.

It is miserable weather here to-day—cold and rainy, and they call it May! I do hope it doesn't go south and spoil your pleasure in Lugano. I have never stopped there, but on the two or three occasions I have seen it from the train I have thought it looked most beautiful. I was in Capri as late as 1937, and alas, all our walk along to the Migliara had been dug up (destroying the lovely wild flowers) in Musso's battaglia del grano—wretched little patches of parched wheat and oats not ten inches high, worth nothing. All that beauty destroyed to—not even to make a Roman holiday, but to gratify a Milanese yahoo.

Do you read newspapers? I am cutting down as much as possible, and wondering whether one should not stop. It seems to me my happiest days with you were when we never read a newspaper and thought of Greek and Italian and art. Talking of which, they are devilish slow in putting the Louvre back into shape. I go sometimes to see our Lady of Melos and the Greek and Roman things, especially those bronze copies of the Greek. There are two or three beautiful Antinous, at which nobody looks. It is nice to have all these things to oneself. But there are few pictures yet—the Leonardos, Mantegnas, and so on, just a sprinkling, a kind of anthology of the non-French schools. The French are at the Petit Palais.

Are you writing or publishing anything? Have you got a Collected Poems[9] in print, because somebody has stolen my copy, and I can't get hold of another here. The English bookshops here are putrid—all tosh for Tommy Atkins and G.I. Joe and the wandering bureaucrats.

Your fish-hawk makes me think of the marvellous white-headed eagle who used to come and sit on the parallel bars just outside the cottage in Florida. A most dignified and glorious bird.

Love
Richard

1. May Sinclair, who had died late in 1946, had bequeathed to Ezra Pound, H.D., and RA £50 each, one or two specified books (Aristotle's *Poetics* and Euripides in Greek to H.D. and Rabelais and Aeschylus to RA), and a choice from her library. To facilitate his choice, Sinclair's solicitors had sent RA a list, which had numerous errors in spelling. See RA to H.D., 18 April 1947 (Yale).
2. RA had confused Johannes Froben (1460–1527), the German printer of Basel, and Leo Frobenius (1873–1938), whose work Ezra Pound had urged H.D. to read. See RA to H.D., 18 April 1947 (Yale); H.D., *End to Torment*, New York, 1979, pp. 27–28.
3. Viola Jordan.
4. 1948.
5. No Czech translation has been traced.
6. Not traced.
7. *Fifty Romance Lyric Poems*, New York, 1928; Wingate's reprint appeared in 1948.
8. 1948.
9. H.D., *Collected Poems*, New York, 1925 and 1940.

108. To Lawrence Powell (UCLA)

7 August 1947

Villa Aucassin,
St. Clair
Le Lavandou, Var,
France.

Dear Larry,

It was very good to have your warm-hearted letter and to know that you are well. Netta and Catha were very pleased to hear from Fay. We are relieved to know that the new house has turned out so pleasantly—will you try to give me a notion just where it is when you next write? You are between "the village" and Culver City, aren't you? Yes, the hibiscus and bougainvillea and red-flowering eucalyptus—how beautiful. The Disposer of events has settled your lives in a pleasant place—under blue skies and between flowers and books. I would add "wine," but I know you have a permanent front seat on the waggon.

Our address will show that we have come back home to the Mediterranean. This is the California of Europe—not a doubt about it. The mountains back of this village are not unlike the Santa Monica hills, but higher. I look out from my window over the green and gold of mimosas to the blue ocean under a cloudless sky. There are little vineyards and cypresses, peach and almond trees, two or three palms (not up to California standards), cork trees, pines, canes, and lovely sandy beaches between wooded headlands. You must come and see it when you are in Europe, and we shall try to give you a bouillabaisse de Marseille.

We flew from Paris to Marignane (the air port of Marseille) on July 30th, and luxuriously drove by hired car, and wonderful lunch on the old port at Marseille (which is intact—the part the Germans blew up is further on) and then got here in the evening. I have this villa until December, and move to another then which I hope will be permanent. This place belongs to an Englishman with the ridiculous name of Sir Hildebrand Harmsworth, a brother of Lord Rothermere. It is nicely fixed, but the local people stole nearly everything in the way of linen, cutlery, glass, china, etc after the American troops went forward. Practically every unoccupied house was looted before the French authorities could get control. A few miles from here is a monument to the landing of the U.S. 3rd Division, but except for Toulon and St Tropez, everything has been repaired and you wouldn't know there had been a battle.

My anthology[1] is due out this fall in London, and I will have a copy sent you, as it differs in some respects from the Viking. Heinemann have been very decent about it. They have paid outright for a first edition of 20,000 copies, and under the British tax laws this enables me to receive the money free of income tax, which is 45% in England plus super-tax. Then on later editions they will pay 10% royalty. I have heard nothing from New York about the Encyclopaedia anthology,[2] or at least have had letters from Brockway but no proofs, though I turned in the script before leaving L.A.

I have finished my Selected Pater (not as good as the Wilde) and have done an Introduction to a new collected edition of Jane Austen. All Men Are Enemies is to be reprinted in England soon, and I am still wearily negotiating for the Complete Poems and Colonel's Daughter.[3] The paper situation is worse in England, and this socialist government seems to have bankrupted the country with some kindly assistance from Washington. I am supposed to be doing an educational book, and would like to get on to a novel.

We have Mr Frere (the chairman of Heinemann) and his wife and children staying with us, which naturally puts a lot of work on Netta. She will be writing when they leave at the end of the month.

Our love to you all,
Richard

P.S. Yes, we did get the Daphnis imprint[4] after a long delay—a charming piece of work, I thought.

1. *Poetry of the English-Speaking World*, London, 1947.
2. See Letter 105 n. 1, and *passim*.

3. See *All Men Are Enemies*, London, 1948, and *The Complete Poems of Richard Aldington*, London, 1948; *The Colonel's Daughter* was not reprinted at this time.
4. A privately printed keepsake (fifty copies) of an excerpt from George Thornley's seventeenth-century translation of Longus's *Daphnis and Chloë*. When Professor Powell titled this "Winter Pastorale," RA said, "Stop being pretentious and leave off the French *e*."

109. To Lawrence Powell (UCLA)

3 March 1948   Le Lavandou.
Dear Larry,

I am so glad Kershaw got in touch with you, for at any rate it brings you a bit nearer. I have been meaning to write, but have an immense amount of writing to do as well as infinite "business" mail about copyrights and translations. Luckily, Kershaw is most competent, and helps enormously with typing and mail—otherwise I should go nuts! We have about 70 active translations in about a dozen languages to watch, and I have infinite negotiations about the re-issue of my books in England and recovering (which I've just done) all my pre-1939 U.S. copyrights which Doubleday sold down the river during the war.

Are there any firms starting up in the West? New York seems in a very Philistine mood, and though I am tied up to Duells for books now just completed or in progress, I've been wondering if any new Western publisher might be interested in republishing any of my novels or the Complete Poems which have now just gone to press in England. Let me know.

Your suggestion that Kershaw might publish the American edition of his Bibliography[1] in California put that idea in my head. Or rather revived it, for I had suggested it to Al Manuel, but he is still hypnotised by New York. My idea is all to break out of the ruts and away from the commercial publishers in a new hopeful post-war epoch. It would be fun if we could start up something in California—native and international writers—and razberries to New York and London.

I have strongly advised Kershaw to accept your suggestion of publishing the Bibliography in Calif. He left yesterday for a few days vacation in Marseille, but when he comes back I'll have him write you and get in touch with your friend.[2] I know Kershaw will make a good job of this, and anyway I'll be here to overlook it. The one thing that worries him about California publication is that there are so many books, so many different editions and so many translations that the Bibliography must be rather bulky; and he wonders if your friend realises how big it must be? The American Bibliography is complicated enough, going back to 1914, but the British and foreign are terrific! Will you ask your friend about this? We would give him book rights in the U.S. and U.S. occupied territories, Canada, and a free market outside England and British Empire.

He could therefore probably count on Library sales in Latin America and such European countries as have any dollars.

Kershaw has sent to U.C.L.A. some of the earlier translations and will send a copy of each new one as it comes in. I believe a copy of the German Casanova is wrapped up and addressed to you in his office downstairs. He will see the others come along, as he is very keen on having U.C.L.A. the repository of my works—it being a good deal nearer to Australia[3] than London is!

Are you and Fay planning a trip to Europe this year? Even with the new rate of exchange living and hotels are still pretty expensive in terms of dollars, because stuff still has to be bought on the black market and the scarcities seem to be eternal. Things are improving slowly, and would improve much faster but for the continual and senseless political strife. Bread is still rationed, so are meat, butter, cheese, oil, bacon, rice, spaghetti, margarine, jam, chocolate, sugar etc. Most of these things are not obtainable even with ration coupons, and the black market prices are terrific. Before butter disappeared entirely it was two dollars a pound! I had to pay a hundred dollars in December for a ton of small logs and kindling.

On the other hand, the hotels and restaurants are working hard to smarten up, and they can get things which the ordinary citizen can't. We read in the newspaper about all that America is supposed to be sending, but all I can say is that none of it ever reaches us or anyone we know. Fresh eggs are 25 francs *each* and oranges 130 francs the kilo. Ordinary people are not allowed to buy any flour, and the shops have just been forbidden to sell cakes and pies.

Netta joins me in love to you both, and Catha sends her love to the boys. She now talks French beautifully.

Ever yours
Richard.

1. See Alister Kershaw, *A Bibliography of the Works of Richard Aldington from 1915 to 1948*, intro. Richard Aldington, Burlingame, California, 1950; also published in London, 1950.
2. William P. Wrenden.
3. Kershaw's homeland.

110. To H.D. (Yale)

11 March 1948   Le Lavandou.
Dear Dooley,

I am in the midst of writing the introduction to "English Aesthetes, Ruskin to Rachel Annand Taylor"[1] and completing the selections. Going through the hundreds of books of the period I have collected here I found a duplicate of old Ruskin's Queen of the Air,[2] which I am sending you under another cover. It is badly printed, but if you can stand that I think you might find it interesting.

The Earthly Paradise[3] is quite charming, I think. I bought a copy in Hollywood in early 1946, and re-read it there and in Jamaica—odd places for that very localised English stuff. I have found of late years that I get an added enjoyment if I read poetry, pen in hand, and note any lines and passages I like by copying them at once into a note-book. Thus I have quite a number of little bits from the E.P., and without having fully decided, intend to include them among a series of such extracts from the poets of 1870–1900 in the Aesthetes anthology.

The Morris prose is a damned nuisance. I can't get anything that satisfies me, but I'll go on trying until the date-line for sending in my script.

My secretary calls me the Human Book of the Month Club—in November, the French Casanova;[4] in December, the Anthology in England;[5] in January, the Swedish Casanova;[6] in February, the German[7] and in March, the Spanish Casanova,[8] with a whole spate of other translations due this year. In England I have in the press: Introduction to Collected edition of Jane Austen;[9] Selected Works of Walter Pater (uniform with Wilde);[10] Four English Portraits,[11] George IV, Disraeli, Waterton, Dickens; a reprint of All Men Are Enemies;[12] a reprint of Fifty Romance Poems;[13] Complete Poems of R.A.;[14] and possibly a reprint of Death of a Hero.[15] I suppose they'll hold up the English Aesthetes[16] until next year.

The German edition of Casanova was issued in Zurich, and printed I see at Rapperswill. Did you ever go to Rapperswill? It has, or had, a wonderful German fairy-tale castle on a hill covered with grape vines. You could go in and sit in a baronial hall with walls twelve feet thick and drink cool white wine out of tall-stemmed glasses. It's on the main motor road to Liechtenstein, which is how I discovered it. Another Swiss showplace I like was that baroque Einsedeln. Could you not in the spring make a little tour of some of those places? They must be still quite intact, and give one a much better feeling of the old romantic Germany than Germany itself. Not far from you, over the first pass beyond Lac Leman is Gsteig, which you must know. I simply loved that old inn—the Bear, isn't it?—where they had nothing for lunch but schinken mit eier, but where all the flowery meadows seem crystalline.

It is suddenly full spring here—many wild scented iris and freesia and orchis and wild lavender in bloom. Wonderful on top of the mountain (as we call it, but it is only about 1500 feet) from which you can see across the Esterel to the French Alps. It is just a far off distant line of snow peaks, but I don't think Mont Blanc is visible. It must be hidden by nearer French-Italian mountains. I must say I think the Alps knock the Rockies for a loop, don't you? I was never so disappointed in my life as by Pike's Peak, which I imagined another Rigi or Dent du Midi. Colorado Springs, just under Pike's Peak, was a hell of a place when I was there in 1942—full of America's swankiest champagne Bohemia, who had fled there from Hollywood, Florida, and Fifth Avenue to escape the Japanese and German bombings! Fact. I never saw such a pack of craven loons.

I hear dismal mutterings about "complete financial collapse of England" in June. I suppose the situation is pretty desperate, but I knew that in 1946, long before Mr Attlee and his bright lads awoke to the fact. Perhaps the dire prophecyings are only bread-line talk to get a better hand-out from Uncle Sam, and what is known as "preparation" for a devaluation of the pound. It is pegged at 4 dollars and 18 Swiss francs, but on the free or "black" market, the pound remains persistently at about 10 Swiss francs and 2 dollars. The legal exchange on the U.S. dollar here suddenly shot from 120 to 305 francs! The pound, I believe has dropped from 860 to 750.

I'm so happy to think that you are working tranquilly on Topsy[17] and Ned[18] and all of them. Don't tell me Top was in love with Guggum?[19] Liz *is* Guggum, isn't she? I was delighted by finding the other day that D.G.R.[20] dismissed some man from his list of acquaintances "for irreverential remarks about Guggum"! Marvellous.

With Love,
Richard.

P.S. Two parcels have come through from you—all our thanks.
P.P.S. Why does Janie Morris suddenly disappear from Mackail's "William Morris"[21] and Georgie B-J's "Memorial"?[22] Was there some scandal to be hushed up or what? Or is it that they just get bored with her as a character?

1. *The Religion of Beauty. Selections from the Aesthetes,* London, 1950.
2. London, 1869.
3. By William Morris, 1868–70.
4. *The Romance of Casanova,* New York, 1946; the French translation, printed in Belgium, appeared in 1947.
5. *Poetry of the English-Speaking World,* London, 1947.
6. 1947.
7. 1948; printed in Switzerland.
8. 1947.
9. 1948. RA's introduction appeared in the first volume of the six-volume "Chawton Edition."
10. 1948.
11. *Four English Portraits 1801–51,* London, 1948.

12. 1948.
13. 1948.
14. London, 1948.
15. The next reprint appeared in 1968.
16. See n. 1.
17. William Morris.
18. Sir Edward Burne-Jones.
19. Elizabeth Siddal Rossetti.
20. Dante Gabriel Rossetti.
21. 1899.
22. *Memorial of Edward Burne-Jones,* London, 1904.

111. To H.D. (Yale)

16 June 1948   Le Lavandou.
Dear Dooley,

Under another cover I sent you this morning a copy of H. C. Beeching's Anthology, A Paradise of English Poetry.[1] I liked the book very much, and asked my English book-buyer if he could find another copy for you. And the excellent man has done so. Beeching's taste is limited, but within those limits admirable I think, and he makes discoveries. He is good with Browne of Tavistock, for instance, and I like his Donne selections. His is better on the 17th century than I am. The book is nicely printed, don't you think?

I have still not quite recovered from the disturbance of that unnecessary journey to Paris. That club of English I described was so repulsive to me; and then it is so distressing to find what mean malicious whining nationalists the English have become in their loss of empire—as if it were not a good thing to lose, and they could now possess their souls![2] The philistinism of America is one thing and the philistinism of England another. Which is worse? The English I think. The Americans are plain brutal barbarians, but the English deliberately want to sully and destroy.

A letter from Rachel Annand![3] The wonderful book-buyer (William Dibben) tracked her down, went to tea and took her a letter from me, to which she has replied. Most excitingly she says she has just finished a big book on the Renaissance in France.[4] Of course the vile publishers are hesitating, wondering if they have enough paper!!! Liars. All her books are out of print of course.

I think she was pleased that I like her work and apologised for not having recognised her quality sooner. Of course she finds "post-war London dreary." I wish to goodness I were rich enough to get her out and send her to live wherever she wants—Italy or France. When I think of the wealthy fools wasting money, of the money poured out for parasites and sycophants of these vile governments, and think of a sensitive artist like that imprisoned. . . . Think of her learning, which has never received the least recognition, and the "honorary" degrees lavished on people like Eliot and Jack Priestley and Morgan Forster!! She says:

"You have an enchanting address. Somebody once said I was unable to write a book without mentioning Antinous and Aucassin; and perhaps it was true. I have a passion for that prince of Beaucaire who described the way to hell so invitingly."[5]

Here is something you must *not* mention. Frere is planning—plotting is better perhaps—to re-issue Lorenzo in the fall of '49. But only miserable Penguins—a million copies, made up of 100,000 copies of each of ten titles.[6] He wants me to write a life to come out at the same time.[7] Of course it would mean several thousand pounds to me from England and America, but I hesitate and feel inclined to refuse. I don't like this proletarianising of literature, nor the insolence of keeping L. out of print as long as it suits Heinemann's book, and then throwing him to the wolves when they see a chance of picking up some money—squeezing the orange dry—only to discard L. for good and all. What about Frieda? "I don't give a damn about Frieda," says Frere. Only too plain he doesn't. I don't know what to do about it. When I offered in the first place to do the life, my idea was to provoke a reprint of the familiar "little red books" of the Secker type. I never thought of Penguins, for until recently Frere and that type of publisher spat at Alan Lane.

Kershaw—my admirable secretary—is in London, and just when I need him. There are two sets of proofs due this month; royalties from Milan, Prague and London held up by "exchange controls" (curse them); the Albatross edition of "Rejected Guest" is due out to-morrow, needing correspondence and sending of copies to translators; my arrangements in America are in a mess, and need constant letters. Meanwhile, I am trying to write this biography of Waterton.[8] And so on and so on. I hope to goodness the girl doesn't marry him—Kershaw[9]—for I shall never find anyone half or a tenth as efficient and devoted. What says Racine? Vénus toute entière a sa proie attachée!

This is a very whining letter, of which I ought to be ashamed. I am. If I had time I'd tear it up and write another. I must *not* let these exterior things be so shattering—"the aim of culture is not rebellion but peace."

No chocs yet.

With love,
Richard

P.S. I have been reading Fred Manning's "Eidola."[10] His war poems are strangely akin to mine, sometimes on identical themes. His are very much better of course. I am glad to have re-discovered them.

1. The "new edition" published by Rivington in 1897.
2. RA met Frere in Paris on Friday, June 4, and returned to Le Lavandou before June 10.
3. Rachel Annand Taylor.
4. Not published.
5. Aucassin, hero of the late thirteenth-century legend *Aucassin and Nicolette.* He was depicted as the son of Count Garin of Beaucaire.
6. RA wrote introductions to thirteen reprints of D. H. Lawrence's works published in 1950 and 1953. All but the first two, *Mornings in Mexico* and *The White Peacock,* were issued as Penguins. In addition RA compiled *Selected Letters of D. H. Lawrence* (Aldous Huxley wrote the introduction); this was also a Penguin Book.
7. *D. H. Lawrence: An Appreciation,* published as a Penguin Book in 1950.
8. *The Strange Life of Charles Waterton,* London, 1949.
9. She did.
10. 1917.

112. To H.D. (Yale)

18 February 1949   Le Lavandou.
Dear Dooley,

By the same mail as your letter came a card from Campbell to say he had just received a proof of his Times letter![1] So, unless that is a trick, it should be out tomorrow. The situation may develop.

I think you are quite right about Walter.[2] Don't you remember his telling us that he had been born in Germany, and though duly registered at U.S. Consulate with Murican eagles all over the document, the fact that the place was German and his name part German caused difficulties? But artistic collaboration is no sin in contemporary France, which is busy tracking down the numerous gangsters who were officially decorated for murdering innocent people under pretence of "liberation." That Liberation business was at least 50% humbug.

Curious you should mention Fred.[3] I also saw a good deal of him in the twenties, particularly after Galton died. But unluckily Fred became such a dipso, it became very painful to know him. My friend Kershaw is at this moment writing a note on Manning,[4] and I have one, perhaps two of Fred's poems in my Religion of Beauty.[5] That great work will be going to press soon, having been held up for months owing to the great difficulties of tracking down some of the copyright holders. Poets who died about 1900 and are still copyright and whose publishers vanished 30 or 40 years ago. We have had to turn out the British Museum, Somerset House and god knows what, and Alister has even had an office at Heinemann to help. By the way I do *not* include you, because you are too young and belong to the future. Both Fred and Banabhard[6] looked back, and belonged to the past. Ezra was a puzzle, but I think he belongs to the new rather than the old in spite of his innumerable imitations.

I still hear from Banabhard, who writes amusingly, and is altogether extraordinary at 75.

Flint published In the Net of the Stars,[7] Cadences,[8] and a third book with Monro, title of which I forget.[9] He will be remembered because of his association with us, but he had no real energy, no staying power. I understand he was "dispersed" to Manchester with part of the Ministry of Labour during the panic days, and is now probably retired. I think he is still alive. I wrote him from Florida twice in '41, but had no reply. André Spire knew of him, but I lost touch with *him*.

Your legal name must appear on the book[10] as copyright holder, but as I've had no sub for U.S. clippings since 1930 I shan't get your reviews. I look forward very much to seeing the book.

Of course I remember the Greggs. What a very unfortunate occurrence.[11] Were they on their way back to U.S.? Otherwise, it wasn't very smart to choose a naval port as a place of residence.

Apropos your Yale shelf, I heard the other day that they bought Crosby Gaige's collection of my books, including the MS of "Voltaire."[12] I wish this had gone to California, to be all together. Crosby also had all my presentation copies from Amy.[13] But I know he collected you too, and he may have had a complete set of your books as he was a great admirer.

I am sending you a duplicate from my books. It is Frederick Myers's The Renewal of Youth, which I think has some fine passages, particularly in the two long poems, The Passing of Youth and the Renewal of Youth.[14] It is a battered copy, but a rare book as it was never reprinted. Myers will be a familiar name to you from his long association with the Psychical Research Society. I think him rather a good poet—at any rate he thought and experienced before he wrote, which is something. There is a very good essay on Vergil in his Essays, Classical.[15]

How are the mighty fallen—I got a genuine first edition of Atalanta in Calydon[16] recently for sixpence! Thirty years ago you couldn't have got it for six pounds, and in thirty years time it'll certainly be worth more than that. How stupid these fashions are. As a Romantic-Hellenic poem in dramatic form Atalanta has not even a rival in English. To neglect or despise it is simply stupid.

There is a great improvement in material conditions here. The franc seems to be really stabilised at last; industrial production is higher than pre-war; last harvest was good, another good one seems probable, and the winter has been mild; wholesale food prices are tumbling, and rationing is almost gone. We have unrationed meat, bacon, eggs, all canned goods, practically everything that is still tied so tight in England. And all this has happened within less than a year of getting rid of the dead hand of communist-socialism! There are still traces of it, but it seems scotched for the moment. When will England realise that its "restrictions" and "scarcities" are not due to the war but to the Socialists?

By the way, my last batch of books contained the two vol edition of *The Well at the World's End*,[17] which completes my set of Morris's prose romances and of Morris apart from his socialist stuff which doesn't interest me. I found this among his poems recently, under title Pomona:[18]

> "I am the ancient Apple-Queen,
> As once I was so am I now.
> For evermore a hope unseen
> Betwixt the blossom and the bough.
> Ah, where's the river's hidden Gold!
> And where the windy grave of Troy?
> Yet come I as I came of old,
> From out the heart of Summer's joy."

How beautiful that is! It haunts me. I do wish I'd had it in my anthology.

With love from us all
Richard

1. See Roy Campbell, "Mr. Aldington's Poems," *Times Literary Supplement*, 26 February 1949, p. 139; a letter protesting the review "Mr. Aldington's Collected Verse," *Times Literary Supplement*, 5 February 1949, p. 90. On 11 February 1949, RA sent H.D. a copy of a letter received "a couple of days ago" from Campbell enclosing the letter intended for the *TLS* (Yale); it differs in length and detail from the published version. RA had predicted that it would not be published.

2. Lowenfels.

3. Frederic Manning.

4. Alister Kershaw confirms that he did write an article on Manning; it was never published, but Kershaw's effort encouraged RA to write one himself, which appeared in *Australian Letters*.

5. See *The Religion of Beauty. Selections from the Aesthetes*, intro. Richard Aldington, London, 1950, p. 348, for two poems by Manning, "Kore" and "Still Life."

6. Rachel Annand Taylor.

7. F. S. Flint, *In the Net of the Stars*, London, 1909.

8. F. S. Flint, *Cadences*, London, 1915.

9. Possibly *Otherworld*, London, 1920.

10. See perhaps, H.D., *By Avon River*, New York, 1949.

11. Frances Gregg (Mrs. Louis) Wilkinson and her mother were killed in the bombing of Plymouth. See Letter 13 n. 1.

12. RA, *Voltaire*, London, 1925.

13. Amy Lowell.

14. Frederick Myers, "The Passing of Youth" and "The Renewal of Youth," in *The Renewal of Youth and Other Poems*, London, 1882, pp. 123–39 and 202–32.

15. Frederick Myers, *Essays Classical and Modern*, London, 1921, pp. 106–76.

16. Algernon Charles Swinburne, *Atalanta in Calydon*, London, 1865.

17. London, 1896.

18. In *Poems By The Way*, first published by Morris's Kelmscott Press, Hammersmith, in 1891.

113. To Lawrence Powell (UCLA)

10 March 1949   Le Lavandou.

Dear Larry,

Don't bother to send any material to Kershaw. So far as I can learn the British publisher has the script at the printer already, and intends to publish in May.[1] I was to receive copy of a circular they are sending out, but it hasn't come, and as I don't know the publisher's address I can't send him a list of people for the circular. For the moment I am out of touch with Kershaw, who left London last week to stay with Scottish relatives in Berwickshire. On Sunday it rained here, but northern Europe seems to have had a heavy snowfall, and probably Kershaw is snowed up. This whole bibliography has been a mess so far. I hope they get it straight now.

Thanks for having Dahlstrom send the Jane Austen.[2] I hope he put them in small packets.

It will give you some idea of currency troubles in Europe. A firm in Bonn, Germany are translating my Pater with introduction.[3] Of course, Pater is in the public domain, and I said I'd sell them my rights in the introduction etc. for 50,000 french francs (about $200). Well, they applied four months ago for permission to transfer that small sum, were told it would come through in 2/3 weeks. Nothing has come! Meanwhile, as Luce knows all the big boys, *he* has been allowed to take out $57,000 for Life and Time! There's an awful lot of jiggery-pokery going on over here, Larry, and the folks are getting bitter about it.

Thank you very much for sending the copy of Le Gallienne[4] (which I needed) with the Blunt bookplate. It is very kind, and I'll let you know as soon as it arrives.

This Life of Lawrence[5] is the hardest book I've ever undertaken. He chops and changes and contradicts himself so often, and the people who wrote about him make so many mistakes in facts and dates that it all drives me nuts. Now, when you remember what a tough time the Lawrences had during the war of 1914–1918, and what a godsend of relief the Armistice must have been, you would suppose Frieda would remember at least where they were on that day, wouldn't you? Heck no. She remembers the wrong place! But for the check of the Letters I'd give it up in despair.

We still haven't got those D.H.L. reprints[6] finally signed up. The latest is that they have to apply to Frieda, formally through her literary agents for her approval! Frieda has been writing me and Frere that she does approve, highly. Why not accept that? No, they must waste more time. Then, I have pointed out to them that The Man Who Died[7] in an edition of 100,000 at about 25 cents will almost certainly cause ructions in the British Bible belt, which is just as bad as the American, and proportionately more influential on account of the Bishops sitting in the House of Lords. Well, the publishers evidently hadn't read the book, now have read it, are scared from Montezuma to Tripoli, but can't make up their minds what to substitute. I fought like a hep-cat to make them put in Studies in Classic American Literature,[8] but they wouldn't. I've just been re-reading that chapter on Moby Dick[9]—it really is great.

Thank you for the nice things you say about All Men Are Enemies. When one is getting almost daily bashings from reviewers, such things are a great comfort.

Affectionately,
Richard

P.S. I enclose a letter from Sir Stanley[10] which you might like to keep as a souvenir of his visit, which you made so pleasant to them both.

1. The British edition of Kershaw's bibliography was published in London in 1950; see Letter 109 n. 1.
2. RA's introduction to the "Chawton Edition" of Jane Austen (see Letter 110 n. 9) was published separately in Pasadena, California, in 1948.
3. See Letter 106 n. 5.
4. Possibly Richard Le Gallienne, *The Romantic '90's*, London, 1925.
5. See RA, *D. H. Lawrence: Portrait of a Genius, But. . .* , New York, 1950.
6. See Letter 111 n. 6.
7. See D. H. Lawrence, *The Man Who Died*, London, 1935; the novel was first titled *The Escaped Cock*.
8. See D. H. Lawrence, *Studies in Classic American Literature*, London, 1923; but in a letter to Amy Lowell, 9 June 1919 (Harvard), RA expressed dislike of this work, calling it "dreadful stuff."
9. See "Herman Melville's 'Moby Dick,' " chapter 11.
10. RA had written Powell a letter of introduction to Sir Stanley Unwin, who visited Los Angeles en route to New Zealand (24 December 1948 [UCLA]).

114. To Leonard Bacon (Yale)

19 December 1949   Le Lavandou
Dear Leonard,

This is to wish all good things in 1950 to you and yours, above all the success of your Camões[1] and Marny's novel.[2] Let us hope that for all the 1950s will be less dismal than the 1940s.

Christmas has now become such a department store racket that it should only be kept up for children. Catha decided quite on her own that she would not have a tree and presents this year (of course, the little wretch knew she'd have to get some!) but chose a week at Monte Carlo. I hasten to add that this does not imply a precocious vice for roulette and baccarat, but more respectable motives. She is full of natural history at the moment, and pines to see the Monte Carlo aquarium, the oceanographic museum and the regional museum. She has also heard that there is an ice-skating rink—though I fear that with the modern spirit for having everything out of season the rink only functions in summer. We shall see.

On the 2nd of January Netta leaves us for a few weeks to visit her mother in Jamaica, whom she has not seen since she left Jamaica in 1946.[3] Owing to the hideous complications of foreign exchange and "control," Netta has to go to London, stand in a queue for hours for kind permission to be on board a plane which merely lands and re-fuels in New York. She apparently isn't allowed even 50 cents to buy a hot dog and a copy of the Times at the air-port. She then has to fly to Bermuda, change to some Latin-American plane and arrives in Kingston between 1 a.m. and 3 a.m. in a country where everybody after dark carries a gun for protection against the martyred negro proletariat! The British have only one untorpedoed ship making the Bristol–West Indies trip, and apparently no direct planes. What a mess! Long before it's cleared up, there'll be another war.

No other news, except that after a year's drought we've at last had rains, so that we get unrationed electricity again. France has made a wonderful come back, and in many ways we are almost back to pre-war, except for the terrific high prices! Shops are full of all sorts of things hardly anyone can afford to buy. In fact we've gone direct from scarcity to over-production without any intermediate period!

Ever affectionately,
Richard

1. See Letter 102 n. 1.
2. See Martha Sherman Bacon, *A Star Called Wormwood*, London 1950.
3. Netta decided to live permanently in England after this visit to her mother. See Letter 116.

115. To *Lawrence Powell (UCLA)*

8 January 1950   Le Lavandou.
Dear Larry,

I have been swamped for weeks under Lawrence proofs. You can imagine the task—nine of DHL's books with Introductions. British and

American proofs of my biography (135,000 words) AND the Index. In the midst of it I got pretty bad grippe and a touch of bronchitis, and had to go on working in bed until my fanny was as sore as the proverbial bear's head! Well, it's all done, except for Etruscan Places,[1] which should be here to-morrow. But so far as England is concerned everything is held up owing to the election. The Constitution is different from U.S. They MUST have an election in July 1950, but they MAY spring it at any time before if it suits them politically! You can imagine how that helps business.

I am modestly hopeful about the biography but of course you can never tell. Both Duells and Heinemanns[2] are greatly taken by it, and go so far as to call it (to me not in ads!) one of the best literary biographies in English. Certainly it is a good story which should interest people.

What I fear is that it may have the same fate as the Waterton,[3] which has had TOO MANY GOOD REVIEWS! That sounds crazy, but what has happened is that they have made long feature articles (like the Time one)[4] telling people so much about what's in the book that the sales so far have been disappointing. In England, the R.C.s got after it and boycotted it, and of course there were the usually spiteful reviews of personal enemies. But the real damage has been done by the feature article reviews. Nobody's paying 3 bucks for stories he can get for 15 cents along with a lot more.

Which is rather ironical—a woman killed with kindness so to speak!

Netta is held up indefinitely in London on her way to her mother in Jamaica by a pretty piece of red tape. Although she is a British citizen the U.S. Consul in London won't give her a visa because she is domiciled in France and ought to have gone to the U.S. Consul in Marseille. All the visa is needed for is to change at La Guardia Field from the London–New York plane to the New York–Bermuda plane! She won't even leave the airport. She has lost her place on the plane, has had to pay ten dollars for a cable to Marseille, and of course has hotel expenses in London.

I am without my secretary, and it looks as if I shall lose him, for he is probably getting married this month. A pity. As to that bibliography,[5] the man Jacobs must be either a crook or a moron. It was supposed to have gone to the binders two months ago. I believe Wrenden saw him in London. I never met him, and I think Kershaw made a frightful mistake in giving him the book. It looks as if the guy hasn't even money to pay his printing and binding bills!

Seems I have nothing but bad luck all round. Just heard that my lawyer brother who is supposed to look after my affairs in England has forgotten to pay some income tax which is going to cost me about 6000 dollars I haven't got. I knew nothing about it, any more than I did about that non-payment of tax in U.S. for my movie sale in 1933.[6] What is one to do? You can't do any more than pay experts and lawyers to help you.

I have a Slovak translation[7] here for your U.C.L.A. collection. It would have gone off sooner but for Kershaw's absence and the fact that I have been so busy with proofs.

I wonder what you'll make of Europe. Fortunately the exchange will be very much in your favour.

All good wishes for 1950,

Ever yours,
Richard

1. See D. H. Lawrence, *Etruscan Places*, London, 1932.
2. RA's New York and London publishers for the Lawrence biography.
3. RA, *The Strange Life of Charles Waterton, 1782–1865*, London, 1948.
4. See "Birds of Bigotry," *Time*, 12 December 1949, pp. 104–8.
5. See Letter 113 n. 1.
6. *All Men Are Enemies* was filmed in Hollywood in 1934 by Fox.
7. Not traced.

116. To A. S. Frere (privately held)

1 March 1950   Le Lavandou.

Dearest Frere,

I think the only thing to do is to send you Netta's extraordinary letter from Jamaica,[1] which is all I have heard from there. She went away cheerfully, leaving many clothes and all her drawings etc; wrote one very affectionate letter from London, then after hearing of this income tax demand a brief and flurried letter saying she thought she would get a job. I wrote her at once to Jamaica suggesting she think again, and got this one in the eye just a little while back. You see she says nasty things about Alister as well—the only two real friends I have are cows according to her. (How women hate a man to have friends!) Apparently she rowed with Alister, told him he was "a brutalised labourer" (!), and paid no attention to Patsy's[2] messages and invitations. I, of course, knew nothing about all this; and when you've read her letter you'll know as much of the situation as I do. Something happened in London, but what? The Douglas[3] referred to is nobody—the brother of Netta's girl friend, Jean,[4] with whom she was brought up, and a pansy anyway. Note that the parcel weekly she asks for would have to be paid in dollars, and alone would cost as much as her living here.

I have written Tony[5] asking him to send you privately—not to the office—the relevant documents in this income tax business. Of course, the

Ps[6] have a very cute London solicitor who has been amusing himself by cutting up the little provincial solicitor, and having a lark at my expense. Those bastards always resent us—look how they love to get a publisher into court on some utterly phoney "obscenity" charge or to take it out of an author in the divorce court. If you have a really good solicitor who can talk turkey to them, all may be well. But from what Tony says, I suspect they have found some ambiguous clause in a Finance Act and are perfectly willing to go to law over it, of course with the connivance of the Inland Revenue. The fact that it is insane to pay income tax twice over, especially after paying the iniquitous rate of 45% on every pound, has nothing to do with law.

Reverting to Netta's letter, you may wonder why you have to come into it at all. Because, in trying to cheer her up in London over this situation I had quoted from you.

The whole situation is a bewilderment to me. And apropos Netta's demands for things from here, I have a feeling that artist's materials may still be on the banned list of imports—certainly the pencils I got her from America. And may there not be duty on the sketches? I don't know what to declare them at, and a declaration too much at variance with the Customs estimate would, I believe, make them liable to confiscation and her to a fine. And who is going to struggle through the Customs with a huge Algerian coloured blanket-rug and that reproduction of Matisse?

Why do I bother you with these things, when you have a hundred other things to bother about?

There was something else I meant to say but it has gone clean out of my memory. Anyway, you'll see that any chance of getting down to work is out of the question until these things are settled. I was hoping the income tax thing was over, and indeed wrote Netta twice to Jamaica saying it was, but she never answered. Evidently didn't believe it.

Your idea of telling Pollinger to shut Frieda up is excellent. Don't forget. What she wants is some uncritical panegyric of him as a Great Religious and World Leader which would bugger up his book sales for years. But if she were to repudiate this book[7] publicly it could be harmful in the hands of enemies.

With love,
Richard

1. Not with this letter; see Letter 114 n. 3.
2. Patricia Wright, who became Kershaw's wife.
3. Not identified.
4. Not identified.
5. RA's brother, P.A.G. Aldington.

6. The Patmores.

7. *D. H. Lawrence: Portrait of a Genius, But . . .* , which Frieda Lawrence was criticizing.

117. To Leonard Bacon (Yale)

16 May 1950   Le Lavandou.
Dear Leonard,

Your news is indeed saddening. I feel we ought each to sit upon his own dunghill, potsherd in hand, and send for Eliphaz the Temanite, Bildad the Shuhite and Zophar the Naamathite.[1] If the ensuing dialogues turned out as well as the original it might be worth while from a literary point of view!

I do hope you will not think me intrusive if I venture to suggest that you and Patty are sacrificing more than you should by keeping that poor patient in your own home. Nothing is gained thereby except daily and hourly affliction for your dear selves, and the patient is happier in the calm routine of a well-run clinic, especially as a doctor is always at hand. While we are all members one of another, I do not think such sacrifice is justifiable. Forgive me, if this sounds intrusive, for it is not meant so.

The deaths of friends are hard to take. Only a few months ago I lost my dear Charles Prentice, who was quite literally harried to his doom by the selfishness and neurotic restlessness of his wife. Was Blake in Florence? Did he not read Greek with you there? I seem to remember you speaking of him with affection and admiration in those days. I am sorry to hear about Benét. I knew him so slightly—a few days in Paris. We lunched, I think, in a restaurant looking over the ruins of whatever Roman buildings the learned have now decided form the Cluny museum. Well, these things are not otherwise but thus, as a once famous and now forgotten poet remarked.

I am greatly interested in your novel,[2] and hope you will persevere. Setting aside all questions of natural aptitude and endowment, I believe all the talk about the art and craft of fiction à la Henry James, Flaubert, Joseph Conrad is bunk. The essential is to be interesting and readable, and that is achieved by living the book, not by outside plotting and planning. Readability is a gift. Dickens had it, Meredith hadn't. Dumas père had it, Stendhal hadn't. But to me a novel isn't a novel unless the author *makes* me read it. No author can make me read a detective story! I have read Conan Doyle—as a task.

If I can get hold of a copy of your Lusiads[3] I am going to present it to Roy Campbell in the hope that he may in turn present it to the British public. Campbell is a South African, and therefore more aware of the great Camões than the average Britisher who imagines Cabot and Drake did all the discovery. One of Campbell's books of poems is called Adamastor.[4] He is a huge big fellow, very famous in Spain and the Midi as a bull fighter! He is a bigoted Roman Catholic and has amused himself by cuffing the heads of communist poets, like Spender & MacNeice or those who played that way for safety by cuffing their ears in a light and genial fashion. I imagine that a really virile work like the Lusiads will be thoroughly known to him, and that he will welcome a good translation, all the more since he has no axes to grind. He speaks Provençal (a rare accomplishment) and Spanish is a second language, since his wife is a Spaniard.[5] Hence of course the regrettable religious mania. However, when he is out of her view, he isn't so religious as all that. He is the only man I know who fought through both wars and the Spanish war (on Franco's side of course) for fun. His piece on the B.B.C. fellow travellers who from the rear wrote "war" poems has always delighted me:

> "Oh, well may he weep for the soldier;
> Who weeps at a guinea a tear." etc.[6]

What have I done to the Saturday Review, and—more important— why have they lost their ethics? I have a book on D. H. Lawrence due out this week in America, after a really terrific reception in England. Well, first the SRL gives it for review to Harry T. Moore,[7] a somewhat brash academic go-getter, who himself has a book on Lawrence in the press and was in agonies of frustration and annoyance that I had forestalled him. Well, that's all right. One must take what's coming, though the action was hardly friendly. But what do you say to the fact that they released this unfavourable review "far in advance of the general release date"? I quote my publisher, who goes on: "We have their apologies but no real explanation." One first result is that Time which was going to feature the book is holding its review up indefinitely. They wanted to be out first; and of course not having seen the notice I don't know what has been said against the book. A dirty business, but I long ago decided that literary journalists are dirty. Now don't write and tell me it was all a mistake, because I shan't believe you. I have had that done to me before, and it is one of the most damaging foul blows an author can receive—a supposedly authoritative attack circulating uncontradicted for weeks before any other voice is heard. By that time the rumour is usually too established to be checked.

I don't allow myself to be worried by public affairs, for where there is no power there is no responsibility. It is natural that Americans should be a little panicky. After all, the national and educational mythology presents England and monarchy as the enemy, and suddenly you are confronted with an utterly ruthless colossus[8] who makes Machiavelli look a saint and Torquemada a philanthropist! Perhaps America doesn't worry enough!

Ever affectionately
Richard

1. Friends of Job who met to mourn with him; see Job 2:13.
2. Leonard Bacon published no novels after this date.
3. See Letter 102 n. 1.
4. London, 1930.
5. Mary Campbell was English, not Spanish.
6. See "The Volunteer's Reply to the Poet," in *The Collected Poems of Roy Campbell,* London, 1949, pp. 286–87, lines 49–50.
7. See "D. H. Lawrence," *Saturday Review of Literature,* 29 April 1950, p. 20.
8. The U.S.S.R.

118. To Leonard Bacon (Yale)

19 January 1951   Le Lavandou.
Dear Leonard,

Your most kind letter about the poems[1] amazed as much as it pleased me! It is charming of you to write so kindly, but I am sure you allowed your critical judgment to be swayed by your affection. My impulse to send you the book arose from the feeling that at least it deserved one reader not animated by hostile prejudice. The book did not have one favourable review in England, and some were animated by a real hatred which is hard to explain. And after forty years of publishing I am now pachydermatous to the bites of these mosquitoes of the press. My offence is satirising T. S. Eliot and Ezra Pound,[2] who are now the gods of literary England, and also in having for many years "sold" well enough to be able to live free.

But though I naturally don't subscribe to these (as I think) unfair depreciations, I think you are too kind. The first poems have a historical interest. The first three are the first "Imagist" or modern free verse poems ever published, as the files of Poetry will show.[3] They appeared a month before H.D., in I think Nov 1912, and were followed by Pound's changing his style! They were three years ahead of Eliot's first publication, which was Prufrock in 1915.[4] (See also files of Poetry.) When I went to the war Eliot took over my job as literary editor of the Egoist (which was publishing the new poetry in England) and (I think unintentionally) the credit for what I had done. I was the first ever to print a poem by Marianne Moore, for instance.[5] And so forth. Of course one of my crimes is that I thought and think D. H. Lawrence a real writer, a real contributor to human experience (for all his faults) while Pound and Eliot are simply professeurs manqués and hence appeal to the academic mind.

The rest of my poems never reach anything like the quality of Lawrence. The Luxembourg[6] is the best, but its importance to me is that writing it showed me I could tell a story and hence write a novel—which I thought I couldn't do. I thought I couldn't do dialogue. You will find hardly any dialogue in the early parts of Death of a Hero. It was only as I went along that I found I could write dialogue. But I was so pressed for time and money that I couldn't afford to re-write the book and cut out all the silly divagations, but had to sell it as was.[7] In fact it was only in the 1930s that I was able to live without worry and to give a reasonable time to a book. Since the 1939 war I've again been driven, and never able to work without overworking.

Well, I accepted the fact that I am not a poet as long ago as 1938.[8] Anything in the line I have written since I have immediately destroyed; and if it were possible by a thought to destroy all the rest, every copy, I would do so instantly. I bitterly regret having given myself away as I did, and I can say with sober truthfulness that the publication of those not very harmful pages has brought me little but insult and bitterness. In the early days they were called crazy and futurist, then almost immediately after, out-of-date and mere bravura! Honestly, yours is the only generous letter I ever had and I know that comes from your warm heart and not from your real judgment.

On top of this Korea trouble here we have a bad winter and an influenza epidemic! It is cold even here on the Riviera, and I am servantless, as my "regular" is laid up and no substitute available. I am in terror of Catha getting it, but the doctor assures me that it is not very dangerous to children, but to the old chiefly. This at last seems to indicate some common sense in the Disposers of Events! I think one of the differences I felt in returning from America is not that America is "a young country" (which is nonsense) but that the population is in the majority young, whereas here it is old. There are too many old people in Western Europe. So many of the children in France, even of devoted parents, still show the effects of the years of war privation. May America never know it! 1861–65 was enough suffering for any people, without the modern horrors.

Ever affectionately,
Richard

1. See RA, *The Complete Poems of Richard Aldington*, London, 1948.

2. In *Stepping Heavenward, A Record*, Florence, 1931, and in "Nobody's Baby," in *Soft Answers*, London, 1932.

3. See "Choricos," pp. 39–41, and "To a Greek Marble," p. 42, *Poetry: A Magazine of Verse*, November 1912; "Argyria" appeared on p. 134 of January 1914, *Poetry*.

4. See T. S. Eliot, "The Love Song of J. Alfred Prufrock," *Poetry: A Magazine of Verse*, June 1915, pp. 130–35.

5. See Marianne Moore, "To a Man Working His Way Through a Crowd" and "To the Soul of 'Progress,' " *Egoist*, 1 April 1915, p. 62.

6. See RA, "A Dream in the Luxembourg," in *The Complete Poems of Richard Aldington*, pp. 243–74; see Letter 51 n. 3, and *passim*.

7. Elsewhere RA says he did rewrite; see Letter 48 n. 9.

8. RA's last long poem, *The Crystal World*, was published in 1937.

119. To H.D. (Yale)

31 August 1951
Villa les Rosiers,
Ancien chemin de Castelnau,
Montpellier,
Hérault, France.

Dear Dooley,

Your letter comes just at a break between bouts of over-work, and I reply at once. A young Australian[1] (friend of my "secretary" now in Paris) came and last night took Catha and me to the best restaurant here, and gave us soles done in some wondrous sauce with mushrooms and prawns and cheese and a marvellous Chablis-Moutonne; then partridge from the Cevennes with a Hospices de Beaune, and Roquefort sheep's-milk cheese. These luxury French meals are a marvel—one doesn't eat much in bulk but all is delicious and Lucullan, and the wine so delicate there is no oppression!

I am so glad you have had Perdita et famille and will again. But why not try Rome in October? It is so lovely then, the heat's over, the vendemmia coming in, the wine carts, the Campagna refreshed by the first rains, and tourists rapidly departing. I loved so much the Octobers of 1922, 24, 26 I spent there—came to feel that the autumn in and about Rome is better than the spring. The castelli, alas, have been badly damaged, but ROMA is intact. If ever I can wrest the leisure and devises from the bitter world I am going once more to Rome—those Vatican marbles, and the Papa-Giulia, and all the churches, & palaces. I think hooting of motor horns is still forbidden, so the town is not nerve-racking like the places in the Midi. Think of it. You can buy uva di Calabria again! Remember them.

I hear quite often from Ezra—letters addressed (I think) by Dorothy.[2] He wants me to write a "Life" of Ford. But biography is such hard work, such day-in, day-out drudgery of verification and "fact-searching" that I shrink from another, having still months of L. of Arabia before me.[3] Ezra does not sound unhappy, but I think letters to and from him may be read as he is very cautious. I think you are right about the "disciples" at hand—that Laughlin of New Directions is one, sees him weekly I think. But Dorothy, yes, yes, poor Dorothy, I had thought of all that. She was so pretty in her English way, and such a martyr. In Rapallo—about 1929— she seemed to be crazy with exasperation at E.—hated that curious hum-groan he used to utter while writing.

Washington I liked well, but was not there in summer. Surely E's hospital will be air-conditioned? It is D. who will suffer from the heat if she is in a small apartment. That summer heat in the East and South must be endured to be credited—and the heat of the Mojave, California, Arizona and New Mexican deserts. I don't think there is anything like it in Europe, unless perhaps in parts of Spain. They say Ecija is "the frying pan of Europe"—I was there in April so didn't frizzle. In Florida in summer on the sea-edge life was just possible, but a mile inland one expired under the humid heat. I liked it. But for the war I might be there yet, though I've found so much of interest in Provence and Languedoc that I'm glad I came.

So far as I can discover the "mystery" about the death of Lawrence of Arabia was 99% the creation of the newspapers. True, one of the witnesses at the inquest talked vaguely of a large grey foreign car, but I dare say that was newspaper-suggested—I vaguely remember the stories myself. The truth is he was a very reckless rider, and had a super-powerful bike which would do 112 miles an hour. There is evidence of several accidents before in which he escaped by a miracle, and he said himself that his scorching "would end in a tragedy one day." There is also the fact that he was utterly at a loose end when discharged, and so especially reckless. I don't think he cared whether he lived or not.

As to Ezra again—of course it is most dreary that he should be imprisoned like this, but how would he live in this age of inflation if he were released? There would have to be a subscription, I suppose, and all that. I feel sure USA would be glad to be free of his cost, but both sides are tangled in the web of legal procedure. I think an indictment for treason (if that is what he was indicted for) can't be dropped—there must be a trial or such an impediment as insanity. Obviously it suited American vanity to declare he was mad rather than to admit that he had deliberately gone over from "democracy" to fascism. They just can't release him without causing a fearful uproar, especially as he has come out so insultingly as an anti-Semite. I may be all wrong about this, but this is how I see it. His letters don't sound unhappy, but, as I say, they may be subject to scrutiny. I hadn't heard that he may not be seen alone, but it is very probable. On the one hand regulations to prevent passage of means of escape; on the other the fact that if he is a paranoiac there is always the chance of a sudden murderous attack, as supposedly happened in the case of Tasso.[4]

Did you know that Wyndham Lewis has gone blind?[5] It is a great misfortune for him. I suppose the Freudians would say that he has come to hate the world so much he doesn't want to see it any more; but the oculist says it is some inner growth which has destroyed the optic nerve.

I must back to work.

With best love,
Richard

1. William Denison Deasey.

2. Dorothy Shakespear Pound, who was attending to numerous needs of Ezra, her husband, incarcerated in St. Elizabeth's Hospital, Washington, D.C., after being charged with treason for his Rome Radio broadcasts to American troops and subsequently declared insane.

3. RA, *Lawrence of Arabia. A Biographical Enquiry*, London, 1955. Cf. RA to H.D., 9 August 1951 (Yale): "When I don't write the only reason is that I am so tired with work that I've no energy for anything but reading and little motor excursions to the many fascinating places near here. This book is the hardest nut I ever had to crack—a life of Colonel Lawrence. You'll think enough has been done on him! So do I. But much is left to say about that mysterious creature. I have done about 70,000 words, still have about 40,000 to do—then start in and re-write! Then type out copies for publishers!"

4. During the last twenty years of his life, Tasso developed an acute egotism accompanied by a persecution mania, which manifested itself in episodes such as his throwing a knife at a servant he suspected of spying on him.

5. See Wyndham Lewis, "The Sea-Mists of the Winter," *The Listener*, 10 May 1951, p. 765, where Lewis described his condition.

120. *To Pascal Covici** (Texas)

22 September 1951   Montpellier.

Dear Pat,

Thank you very much for the Henry James, which has greatly interested me. I think Mr Zabel has done a real service by this book,[1] both to the public and to James's true reputation—the latter in contradistinction to all coterie reputation and flimsy "revivals." Apart from The American, Roderick Hudson, Portrait of a Lady, I have always been rather repelled by his fiction.[2] I have for instance a complete Yellow Book to which H.J. was a frequent contributor, and though the stories are not disfigured by his later mannerisms I can't get enthusiastic about them.[3] His book on Hawthorne I like very much,[4] though I often find myself entirely disagreeing with him about other authors—being myself for example a bit of a Whitmaniac.

It is the last part of the book from p 490 on which introduces a very attractive James, and this is chosen and presented with much skill. Most people never live in the world, because they are too conceited to experience it. Mechanical pleasures, passively undergone without any mental or physical effort, have made it impossible for them to realise that nothing worth experiencing can be achieved without preparation and effort. In his genuine and continued enrichment of his own life by learning to fit into other modes of being James is—unconsciously perhaps?—in the great tradition of Goethe. He—James—is the very imposing uncle of Logan Pearsall Smith. These essays on—evocations of—Boston and London, Paris and Rome, and so forth, are wonderfully well done.[5] They put him with the best of the 19th century worshippers of the genius loci. And the journals are first rate.[6] But was he really a great artist in fiction? Was he a creative writer on the really high level? I can't see him as anywhere near Melville and Hawthorne.

"A professional author" says Mr. Zabel. Why, certainly, if that means James gave up his time to writing, but he was no more "professional" than Swinburne or the Goncourts, having that perilous privilege of the unearned income which cuts off from common humanity and lifts the hard discipline of making art accessible. Turgeniev's scorn for Zola— James's scorn for H. G. Wells. Class feeling aside, isn't there more of living tissue in Nana than in Smoke and all the rest, in Kipps than in all these over-elaborated salon pieces?[7] It seems to me that James mistook the disinfectant negations of subsidised puritanism for high distinction; just as he mistook his fumblings for something to say (having nothing more really to say) for an arduous straining after les nuances and le mot propre.

But who am I to make these utterances? I really know nothing about him. I think of Lamb House, bombed out, with the piano that had been his lying out in the rain, the mobilisation of all men and women being so ruthless in the England of 1941 that nobody could be spared to save it.[8]

I wonder how he compares with Meredith? But why compare? Things—writings and people and arts—are sufficient in themselves. I see so little point in continuing the Oxford fussing about literary Hierarchy—as if writers were a set of Anglican prelates, with Deans senior to Prebendaries, and Milton-Ebor and Shakespeare-Cantuar on their archepiscopal thrones. Hence of course the British insistence that all "true genius" is really eminently respectable, not to say church-going. Pauvre Leléan![9]

Ever yours,
Richard

*Pascal ("Pat") Covici (1888–1964), a Romanian-born publisher, began his career in Chicago where he published RA's *The Love of Myrrhine and Konallis, and Other Prose Poems* in 1926. Later Covici became associated with Donald Friede in the New York publishing house of Covici, Friede, Inc., that published RA's *Love and the Luxembourg* (the American title for *A Dream in the Luxembourg*) in 1930 following the U.S. edition of the highly successful *Death of a Hero, A Novel* (1929). Eventually Covici was associated with Viking Press, which also published some of RA's later work. RA and Pat Covici remained constant friends and correspondents, as letters dating from 1924 to just before RA's death attest. (See also the Annotated Index.)

1. Morton Zabel, *The Portable Henry James*, New York, 1951.

2. Henry James, *The Portrait of a Lady*, Boston, 1881; *Roderick Hudson*, Boston, 1876; and *The American*, Boston, 1877.

3. Henry James, "The Death of the Lion," *Yellow Book*, April 1884, pp. 7–52; "The Coxon Fund," *Yellow Book*, July 1884, pp. 290–360; "The Next Time," *Yellow Book*, July 1895, pp. 11–59; and "She and He: Recent Documents," *Yellow Book*, January 1897, pp. 15–38.

4. Henry James, *Hawthorne*, London, 1879.

5. See, for instance, Henry James, *Portraits of Places*, London, 1883; *The American Scene*, London, 1907.

6. See *The Notebooks of Henry James*, ed. and intro. F. O. Matthiessen and Kenneth B. Murdock, New York, 1947.

7. See H. G. Wells, *Kipps*, London, 1905; I. V. Turgenev, *Smoke*, London, 1867; and Emile Zola, *Nana*, Paris, 1880.

8. For many years, RA's family lived in Rye, Sussex, where historic Lamb House, which James purchased in 1898, was located.

9. Epithet applied to Paul Verlaine who although a "true genius" was certainly not "respectable." In a letter to F. S. Flint, RA writes: "And Verlaine, ce pauvre Lèlian" (8 February 1915 [Texas]).

121. To A. S. Frere *(privately held)*

1 October 1952   Montpellier.

Dearest Frere,

What a go-getter is Harry T. Moore! I suppose he fears that I may retaliate on his book in kind.[1] Apropos, there was a venomous attempt to depreciate Portrait of a G. over the Canadian B.C., possibly from the same source.[2] I think there can be little doubt that Mr Moore intends to push himself into the position of Greatest Living Authority on DHL, and as he is largely phoney I think he'll succeed, if only by analogy with his ex-compatriot the Saint of Russell Square.[3] Malapropos, you know that Mary Campbell (Roy's impedimentum or baggage) is a pestilential gossip. When she was at Aucassin, to pull her leg, I told her that TSE is a German Jew from St Louis. "Well!" says she wide-eyed, "I *never* heard that before." And I could hear the news ringing down the corridors of Chelsea and Kensington. As a matter of fact, the joke may not be so wide of the truth as it looks. Ever been to St Louis?

Frieda[4] is so tiresome with these yanks. They have only to flatter her and tell her *she* was the real genius, and she gives them L's pictures and MSS. (Talking of which, from the catalogues of MSS I've seen it looks as if Pino[5] boned those two MS books of Last Poems,[6] and that they've been lost in the mess. Perhaps Carletto[7] still has them hidden somewhere. They belong to Frieda.) I suppose Moore has some money, for I think he bought up everything in the way of papers he could find—the proofs of Sons and Lovers with some notes said to be by Jessie,[8] and anything that Ada[9] had, plus those Russell-Lawrence letters he edited, a fine help to L's reputation! Robbing grave furniture.

Am I right in thinking that after March 1955 anyone can publish Lorenzo on payment to Frieda of 10%? If so, it might be worth your while to make a complete Letters. Moore may have been able to buy L's early letters to Jessie, and there must be more or less love letters to Helen Corke. Aldous's[10] edition lacks the letters to Frieda, to Brewsters and to Mabel,[11] as well as to Ada and her friend. His placing of undated letters is not always right, and there are fearful boners in Frieda's and Ada's dating. Brewster, on the other hand, has only one, and that doubtful. I don't suppose Aldous wants to take up the task, and I most certainly don't, though I'll willingly give any editor notes on the proper dating. If Moore has got the Corke and Chambers letters, he could hold it up; so probably you'd have to make him editor. But would it be worth the expense? There would probably be very nearly half the present edition to add.

Frieda obviously has some early versions of published poems (and in one or two cases I personally think these better than the definit[iv]e texts) but does anybody want a variorum edition of L's poems? Such things are so academic and boring. Possibly Moore got hold of some early note-books of L's from Ada. But what a pity if these have to be dragged out. Far too much of L's rejected or immature work has been reprinted. Why drag up that silly Xmas story?[12] Other stuff could have been spared. I am pretty sure that Secker advised L. not to publish The Virgin and the Gipsy,[13] and it would have been well to suppress it along with Love Among the Haystacks,[14] A Modern Lover,[15] and other semi-failures. I often wonder why so good a publisher as Secker issued those two Psychoanalysis books.[16] There are good passages, but on the whole they do L's reputation no good. (I suppose Moore would want to include in a new Letters those mere scraps of notes to Mabel— "send up a bag of flour and half a side of bacon by Trinidad" and all those little lady C. notes to Pino!) I tremble to think what will happen if in 1955 you are no longer able to control the copyrights. Well, we've done our best, and it's not our fault if the world which persecuted him when alive cashes in on him and vulgarises him when dead. Shelley survived, but you'll admit Mary was several intellectual and moral pegs above Frieda—turned down Trelawney and Hogg. I believe Frieda would have married all Lorenzo's friends from Aldous onwards if she could.

Apropos, I have ploughed through that Devils book of Aldous's,[17] and the devil of a book it is. Ape & Essence[18] was hard to take, but this is in some ways worse—the nasty obsessions of a nasty fellow, a scatologist and a sadist out of Stekel. There are some passages in the book made me want to vomit, and the description of Urbain Grandier's burning is vilely sadistic.[19] So this is what comes of finding God among Los Angeles Hindoos! Well, he's lost one very faithful reader, and for good. I'm through with him.

Catha and I went to the International Wine Fair yesterday, though there was very little wine on show. All industrial stuff and side-shows. I took her into the Algerian Café, where they were playing that squawk and tom-tom "music" of theirs and droning away in yah-illah-wallah style. Suddenly a high yaller in pink satin drops her tambourine and executes a too-too realistic danse de ventre! I explained hastily that it is a ritual dance left by the Carthaginians, but I guess I wasn't believed.

Much love.
Richard

1. See Harry T. Moore, *The Life and Works of D. H. Lawrence*, New York, 1951.
2. Not traced.
3. T. S. Eliot.
4. Lawrence.
5. Orioli.
6. See D. H. Lawrence, *Last Poems*, ed. Richard Aldington and Giuseppe Orioli, Florence, 1932.
7. Carletto Zanotti.
8. Jessie Chambers.
9. Ada Lawrence (Mrs. W. E. Clarke).
10. Aldous Huxley.
11. Mabel Dodge Luhan.
12. Not identified.
13. D. H. Lawrence, *The Virgin and the Gipsy*, London, 1930.
14. D. H. Lawrence, *Love Among the Haystacks*, London, 1930.
15. D. H. Lawrence, *A Modern Lover*, London, 1934.
16. D. H. Lawrence, *Psychoanalysis and the Unconscious*, London, 1921; and *Fantasia of the Unconscious*, London, 1922.
17. Aldous Huxley, *The Devils of Loudun*, New York, 1952.
18. Aldous Huxley, *Ape and Essence*, New York, 1949.
19. See *The Devils of Loudun*, chapter 8.

122. To Alan Bird* (NYPL)[1]

4 February 1953   Montpellier

Dear Bird,

On the contrary, I think this discovery of Montague Robert Junner's birth certificate important.[2] We had searched everywhere and failed to find it because we looked under *Lawrence!* The identification of the two Montague Roberts—Chapman and Lawrence—is not so difficult. First we have the fact that in the will of Caroline Chapman[3] (d. 1911) a sum of about 20,000 was bequeathed to Thomas Robert Chapman and one of the trustees was Charles Athill Stanuell, who was also an executor and trustee under the Will of Thomas Robert Lawrence. Second, the Will of Thomas Robert Lawrence gives the name of his eldest son as Montague Robert—surely impossible as a coincidence, especially since in TEL by his friends M. Robert Lawrence says he was born 2 yrs and 8 months before TEL. 2.8 before Aug. 1888 brings us to *December 1885! Another* coincidence, m'lud and gentlemen of the Jury? I think you've found it. But I think Jix and Holyroyd-Reece should also get photostats of the original declarations of birth of the 4 daughters of TRTC and his wife, and of William George and "Frank" (Qu Francis?) Lawrence killed in 1915.[4] These should give plenty of signatures and show the similarity of his methods in true and false declarations. Note he cannot abandon the petty snobbery of "gentleman" even when safety counselled its danger. Note also that we have in this certificate a third family name for Sarah— in this case Lawrence or Laurence (spelling immaterial) which is also suggestive. I think that document on top of the others plus the signatures cooks the Lawrence goose no matter how hostile the Court might be.[5] You can have one or two coincidence—you can't have a score.

Odd fact—although "Will" and "Frank" were both killed in 1915, the Will of 1917 includes Will as a beneficiary!

The will was witnessed by Ernest Barker of New College, who conceivably might have been an old friend and have been the recommender to the Union Library—but was he a Fellow in 1897?[6] Not worth looking up.

It is most kind of you to be reading my script, especially since it is so mangled by write-ins. I much want to hear if you think I have been unfair to TE anywhere and if you think any of the little jokes misplaced. I felt that a subject so arid entitled the author to a grin or two, but there has been criticism of both these points. It is suggested I under-rate TEL as archaeologist, but how can one rate an archaeologist whose sole contribute to the science is $2\frac{1}{2}$ chapters in the Wilderness of Zin, those chiefly topographical? The lazy little bastard (literally!) never troubled to write any paper on Carchemish.[7] True, there are his gifts to the Ashmolean, but are they claimed as his discoveries? The only other evidence is Woolley's rather damaging recollections. As a soldier he has been grotesquely over-rated, and I think I have listed any action he really did take, but much of his time was spent with his theatrical costumier in Cairo dressing for the part. And I think I've leaned back to praise his writing. Certainly I think 7 Ps[8] immensely over-praised, for it is strained, insincere and rhetorical throughout; and in my opinion The Mint[9] is dull. I heard lately that an American publisher has refused it as unlikely to sell! I'm sure it won't, even in England. It irritated me by beginning with a palpable lie. He represents himself as starved for 6 months, having lived on meals cadged by hanging outside Clubs, so much so that the M.O. notices his emaciation. Also his boot has split at the welt. Up to within a few weeks before enlistment he had been receiving 1200 a year from the Col. Office, had received at least 4000 under his father's will, owned a 200-guineas motor bike, and expensive gold wrist watch, and at least 1000 books, plus 200 a year from All Souls! If such a person had starved for 6 months he is either a liar or a bloody idiot who ought to have been incarcerated.

Your letter cheered me immensely—and the chef is back in the front line again!

Adieu,
Richard

*Alan Bird, distinguished educator, writer, and lecturer on literature and art, first wrote RA in 1949 to express his pleasure at RA's translation of Gérard de Nerval's *Aurelia*. By late 1950, Bird had matriculated as a graduate student at Wadham College, Oxford University, and RA was working on his TEL biography. RA asked Bird to provide him with material about Oxford and to investigate the details of Lawrence's parentage. By the time Bird left Oxford, he was so involved in RA's work that he was supplying books, giving suggestions, and verifying facts. *Lawrence of Arabia*, to an important extent, depended on Dr. Bird's advice and assistance.

1. This letter was published in *A Passionate Prodigality: Letters to Alan Bird from Richard Aldington*, ed. Miriam J. Benkovitz, New York, 1975.

2. As possible proof of Lawrence's illegitimacy.

3. Lawrence's presumed aunt.

4. Younger brothers of T. E. Lawrence.

5. See chapter 1 of *Lawrence of Arabia* where RA presents his proof of TEL's illegitimacy by showing that Thomas Robert Tighe Chapman, who had four daughters by his wife, changed his name to Thomas Robert Lawrence and had five sons (of whom TEL was the second) by Sarah Junner.

6. He was not, becoming a Fellow (Classical) of Merton College in 1898; see the Annotated Index.

7. Where TEL went in 1910 on an Oxford scholarship to explore Hittite civilization as an assistant to D. G. Hogarth.

8. *The Seven Pillars of Wisdom*, London, 1922.
9. *The Mint* . . . , London, 1955.

123. To H.D. (Yale)

2 September 1953   Montpellier
Dear Dooley,

Well, letter communication with la Suisse now seems normal, though along with yours of the 29th I got one of the 9th![1] You certainly sound ever so much better, and if you are strong enough to make them without fatigue those excursions sound excellent. Is there a Tiergarten at Zürich? It is most healing (to me at any rate) to go and get into rapport with the animals, particularly the big ones like elephants and bison. The Los Angeles zoo had three bison—pop, mom and the kid (as the keeper explained) and pop sure was as big as a house and very calm.

Poor old Ez.[2] We must try to cheer him. Doing a life sentence in that noisy bug-house can't be very lively. This is what comes of "back-seat driving" in the motor-car of life! By which I mean that government, banking, economics, even music and painting are primarily practical activities, out of which certain practices grew up which were eventually recorded as theories. Without the slightest practical experience of any of them (except lying on his bed in Paris blowing a bassoon) old Ez starts laying down the law as to what ought to be done, and ends up by bellowing ridiculous insults at Jews, Winston, Franklin D. and so forth (about whom he knew nothing) over the Italian radio—with these unlucky results.[3] I don't know whether he really understands Chinese and Confucius in the know-all-Dick manner he asserts. Arthur Waley told me a European needs ten years under a teacher to learn the Chinese characters, and then there are innumerable pit-falls and chances of misunderstanding. Didn't Amy try her virgin hand at Japanese?[4]

I wonder if the saga of my Colonel Lawrence book[5] to date will amuse you and perhaps wring a word of condolence?

(1) The script was finished and sent in April 1952, with the warning that since the book contained unpublished matter which could be sold to newspapers the typing had better be done confidentially. Instead of being done by the typists in Collins's office, as I meant, it was done in her spare time by the private secretary of one of the partners—and three months were wasted in consequence.

(2) This gentleman had private views on the transliteration of Arabic place names—he altered about six tenths and left a chaos, which took me days to correct.

(3) Instead of 3 copies as I repeatedly asked the girl made 2, which caused much delay later on.

(4) An officious ignorant in Collins's office wrote a memorandum pointing out certain errors in my script. It had to be sent back here, and two weeks of my time were consumed in writing another memorandum to show that the errors were not mine but the reader's. Profound apologies. Meanwhile we were getting towards the end of 1952.

(5) Before selling Collins the book, while writing it, and again when sending it in, I specifically said that I could not guarantee them against libel, nor could I promise to get permission for quotes. They quite understood, that was all right, they would deal with it.

(6) After some further weeks Collins wrote in injured tones to say that his solicitors found libellous matter in the script. As if that was news to *me*, who had been telling him so for months.

(6) Everybody then (except me) then took long Xmas holidays.

(7) The solicitors turned out a long and piffling memorandum—which showed complete ignorance of the facts—and I spent weary days pointing out these facts to them. They then turned in another memorandum of alleged libels, without giving me the slightest hint of how to get round them! I had to ask a friend[6] to take the script to London and sit with Collins and the lawyer at a table and work out each problem.

(8) The lawyers (about Feb.) then discovered that some of the most important evidence was (as I had told them all along) from unpublished but copyright letters. I had to have the script back again, take all these important quotes and re-write them in my own words as my opinions, but giving the source in general terms.[7]

(9) Collins then announced the book was going to his printing works in Scotland, when someone in the office discovered they had "forgotten" to get permission for the other quotes.

(10) This was finally accomplished in July 1953, when Collins wrote he could not send the book to press until 4th Aug., as all the hands at his printing works were taking their annual holiday.

(11) On the 5th Aug. the strikes started here.

(12) On the 31th Aug. I received a letter from Collins printing works to say they had sent off 42 half-galleys some days back and were now sending 60 more. Neither of these packets has reached me, and it is clear that they did not pay any attention to my repeated requests that the proofs should be sent in packets open at the ends, registered and customs declared. Oh no, they knew best, and sent them out as usual, which means (and how bitterly I know it) that they will lie in the French Customs for 4–8 weeks. And of course I miss another publishing season.

Meanwhile of course the American edition is also held up as publication must be simultaneous.

And the weirdest part of the whole thing is that Collins and Knopf[8] between them have paid or are paying advances amounting to 10,000 pounds, and by their self-created delays are losing money, i.e. the interest on the advances!

The lord knows when it will be out, and though I have my Heinemann contract for Pinorman,[9] it must wait until the other book is out of the way.

I assure you all this is true, and this is how the biggest and most successful London publisher gets along when faced with a book out of the ordinary run.

With love,
Richard

1. On 5 August a general strike had begun in France.
2. Ezra Pound had been confined at St. Elizabeth's in Washington, D.C.
3. Pound's radio broadcasts were considered treasonous and resulted in his arrest by the U.S. Army in Italy.
4. Possibly RA is thinking of *Fir-Flower Tablets* (Amy Lowell with Florence Ayscough, translations of ancient Chinese poetry), New York, 1921.
5. *Lawrence of Arabia. A Biographical Enquiry,* London, 1955.
6. Alister Kershaw.
7. The estate of T. E. Lawrence held the copyright and the executor, A. W. Lawrence, would not permit direct quotation. Stanley Weintraub wrote 30 April 1991: "My problem in doing *Private Shaw and Public Shaw,* which RA hoped might confirm some of the allegations he had picked up but couldn't prove, was that I had Arnold Lawrence sitting on me. Permission to quote was dependent entirely on him and he had the last word on what I could or couldn't use" (letter to Norman T. Gates).
8. The American edition was published by Henry Regnery, Chicago, 1955, after the arrangement with Knopf did not materialize.
9. *Pinorman. Personal Recollections of Norman Douglas, Pino Orioli, and Charles Prentice,* London, 1954, was published before the American and English editions of *Lawrence of Arabia.*

124. To Netta Aldington* (British Library)

17 September 1953   Montpellier.
Dearest Netta,

I am 24 hours later than I need have been in despatching Pinorman,[1] partly from the indolence which shrinks from the bore of wrapping, addressing, registering &c., and partly because I hate the mean insolent faces of these P.T.T.[2] creatures who have done France so much harm by these precipitate strikes, undertaken and fought to a finish before the Government had time to announce its programme in full. To be sure there is no reason why the PTT and the rest should have more public spirit than all the other self-interested groups. They could hardly have less.

Anyway, it—the script—comes today by registered post, Customs-declared, as papiers d'affaires. Frere not only has his copy, but has signed the agreement, paid the advance, and submitted his blurb. I suppose he will announce this autumn.

I don't think there is anything to be done about the Scandinavian market, where my publishers are Bonnier, Hasselbach, Fritzes Bokförlags, Wahlström & Widstrand, and Suuri Rakkaus Tammi (Finland). They have done most of the novels but NOT Wellington[3] and DHL,[4] the latter of which was taken by Bonnier who cried off because of the Corean war. Something might be done with them but not until AFTER the TEL is published. The TEL itself may have to go to firms who are friends of Holroyd-Reece[5] (you know why) but the Pinorman is wide open. I doubt however that it would move the virtuous Scandinavs.

The galley proofs of TEL are corrected and back in London, but now comes another snag. Knopf are cutting up rough about the Lowell Thomas section, which undoubtedly is a merciless exposure though just and carefully documented throughout. There is a battle going on in Collins office either today or tomorrow and Alister is flying over to deal his swashing blow on my behalf. The point is that L.T. and the Knopfs are N.Y. buddies, and even if they accept reluctantly to stand by my text the danger is that in the sneak American fashion they will alter it and trust that I can't do anything about it. Collins has told them we will not consent to any alterations unless insisted on by a New York attorney approved by us. Knopf, you understood, bought the book firm and can't get out of the bargain, but it is better to come to some understanding on this point than to have the book issued by a hostile publisher. The alterations insisted on by the English lawyers must run to 10,000 words, so we must yield something to America. I am suggesting that the authorship be acknowledged as : TEL by R.A., Joynson Hicks, A.K.,[6] W. Collins and the NY attorney—I shall ask for Morrie Ernst.

A fellow called Politzer, Collins's promotion and publicity, came down here for a day last week. Like many Englishmen he is clean and hardworking and that's about all; yet I liked him. I groused about the alterations forced on me, and he replied: Don't worry, there's more than enough left to start the biggest controversy of years. I told him I would not engage in it myself, but that if they (Collins) wish to make any reply I will gladly furnish them with ammunition. I am absolutely confident. I have lived with the evidence of this damned man for three years, and I am confident I know more of his life and cheats than his own mother and brother. Almost every paragraph in the book has its little number corresponding to a like number giving book and even page from which the information is derived in a List of Sources which fills 22 galleys.

I don't know when Frere wants to publish, but I have asked him. Collins now says regretfully "February," and it may be later unless this damned Thomas business can be settled at once.

Rothermere has read or is reading the script. Politzer thought it was a mistake to send it to him—the book is not for the D.M.[7] But he (P.) says most confidently it can and will be serialised. There is a crack at Northcliffe and others at yellow journalism in the book which would put the Rother off. So much personality! Where and what is truth?

Catha very well after her many days on the sands at Palavas. I had meant to take her off for two weeks at this end of September, and lo! comes this damned Knopf business and the proofs. So much money is still tied up with the TEL that I can decide nothing until that is all settled.

Love from us both,
Richard

P.S. Clothes and French conventions! She has just set out for a lemonade apéritif with her friends, Place de la Comédie, and it is essential that she wears kid gloves! Luckily the avarice of French parents forbids silk stockings as yet. The autumn trousseau. . . . That black and white check cotton with yellow trimmings I bought her for Pâques has undone me. Though not a model, it was three weeks ahead, and at Lavandou she scored a succès de snobisme. Back here she found several of her friends wearing it. Now, Dior is hardly good enough, and I am told anecdotes of her friends, such as e.g. their mothers pay 22,000 for one tweed coat and skirt. "Let them" say I, "I won't." Sète has good things cheaper than here, but no! it is not "à la mode." Useless to say all these things are factory copies.

---

*Netta Aldington (1911–77), born McCulloch, was RA's second wife; she had previously been married to Michael Patmore, son of Brigit Patmore. RA traveled in Italy with Netta in 1937; later lived in France, not returning to England until 1938 where they were married that June. Their daughter, Catherine, was born shortly afterwards. The scandal caused by RA's desertion of Brigit for her son's wife made things socially uncomfortable for RA in both England and the United States for a while; the terms of the legal agreement made with Brigit and Michael Patmore to obtain Netta's divorce were to haunt RA the rest of his life. Netta was an artist: she illustrated RA's translation *A Wreath for San Gemignano* and painted in watercolors. RA's long poem, *The Crystal World*, was dedicated to Netta as *A Dream in the Luxembourg* had been dedicated to Brigit. From 1950 until her death Netta lived in England, while RA and their daughter, Catherine, continued to live in France. (See also the Annotated Index.)

1. London, 1954.
2. Poste-Télégraphe-Téléphone, the logo of the French post-office network.

3. *The Duke: Being an Account of the Life & Achievements of Arthur Wellesley, 1st Duke of Wellington*, New York, 1943.

4. *D. H. Lawrence: Portrait of a Genius, But . . .* , New York, 1950.

5. RA may refer to a plan to set up (through Holroyd-Reece) a company in Liechtenstein in order to avoid British taxes.

6. Alister Kershaw.

7. *Daily Mail.*

125. To A. S. Frere (privately held)

15 October 1953   Montpellier.

Dearest Frere,

When your letter came I was just putting in this sheet to send a bit of news I thought would give you a laff. The drongo[1] was due to leave Mutual Security yesterday 14th. On the 12th, with their concurrence, he got a temporary job on Eunesco! He had suggested coming down here, and I had proposed meeting him by car at Tours. The latest is that he can't fix any date, but will come down "later." It wouldn't surprise me if he got in there, although with high-bruffs to deal with he naturally had much tougher sledding than with former "executives" and bureaucrats.

Your news about the negotiations over TEL is gratefully received though not wholly reassuring. I think Putnams are rather small to handle it, and if they start fussing about L. Thomas another month may be wasted. I think the "reaction" that TEL is not well known in USA is not unfounded, though they all make it before they read the book and partly as a piece of buyer's depreciation. But it is a fact that *all* English "figures" have been played down in US for over a decade, with the exception of WSC[2] who anyway passes as one of our boys on Mom's side. The Colonel's snob tactics which worked so marvellously in England weren't so successful in US (of which he knew nothing) and I'd say that Lowell Thomas who has persistently beaten the big drum is now far better known there. That is why I must have a yank publisher who will let me take his scalp. Thomas and not TEL will be the news and the fight in US. They will accept anything against Englishmen, but I dared to show up a "leading CBS commentator" as a fraud and a fool. Collins and Jix[3] have toned down the original a good bit. A pity, for I think it had some laffs—on our side!

I shall be much relieved when a US contract is signed, partly because time runs short, partly because I had based my "budget" on the MFH's[4] repeated assurance that receipt of the 15,000 was "assured" and "certain" by August. Then I got that visit and the letter I sent you! Pum. However, other things came in, and I can hold on without dipping into few remaining dollars.

By the way, I feel very glad I took up that Norman-Lorenzo business[5] (about which I had felt hesitant) for lately from private letters I see that old Doug's venom has been doing its work and there is a new anti-Lawrence movement on those lines. I do hope what I say will spike that. I think N. comes out pretty badly, and not just on the point that he completely gives away the fact that he did himself more venomously exactly what he accused L. of doing—i.e. caricaturing people vilely for personal motives. (There is always or nearly always a weird impersonality and that not wholly unkind titter in Lorenzo's stuff.) But the thing that got me was Norman's treachery. Now I am *sure* that in 1926–8 both L. and Frieda believed that reconciliation in Pino's shop was sincere. And in 1930 Pino thought so. It wasn't. It was done just to keep in touch, to find fresh opportunities for getting at L. such as the sneer at the frontispiece to Venus in the Kitchen. The stuff he wrote into Pino's custard is about the most venomous of all,[6] and probably I am the one person still alive able to answer it. I do wish it were possible to get L's introduction to M.M. back into print.[7] Do you realise it has been out of print for about 25 years, while that fatuous and pretentious pamphlet of Norman's has been freely circulating?[8] As to Norman's preposterous insinuation that L. caused Magnus's death. . . . I would ask you or any decent man this: If, after years of near starvation, you and your wife had 171 pounds in hand, and an American pansy wanted by the police, a man whom you knew only through Douglas and who had already begged off you, came and asked you for 35–40 of your hard-earned pounds so he could go to Alexandria (!) would you give it? God, I wouldn't. And what did Norman do? At the time he didn't give his dear friend a bean, but cashed in on his death by taking money from a personal enemy of L's[9] as hire for his pamphlet! I still believe people have enough decency to be revolted by that hypocrisy and cynicism.

Enough! I rave and bore you.

Well, we've had four days of rain here, and by now have the feeling that there never was or will be anything else, though at this very moment I see a gleam of sun. Floods said to be in the low lands between here and Béziers. I had thought of nipping off for a few days as I haven't been out of the area this year, but the rain spoils it all; and I must be on hand for page proofs and that accursed yank business.

Mom. I pray you consider Mom. It is a yank female who starts this flurry in B. Guiana;[10] it is a yank female (Mrs Luce) who starts this unnecessary and most unwise business over Trieste;[11] a yank female is to tell us all about inside Russia.[12] Their mixture of arrogance, ignorance and completely self-satisfied will to power is capable of starting another war. They know *nothing* and think they know everything—and those fat-arsed, Gillette-shaved, arrow-collared, homogenised senatorial shits are babies in nappies to their frightful female will. Mom's the word. Many thanks for writing. Someday I R.I.P.

Much love,

Richard

P.S. You don't say if your people were able to contact the MFH's about *date*. My latest from St James's[13] is that Feb 1st is "absolutely firm." But they said and repeated that about the Knopf contract. You had perhaps better try to make sure.

1. Alister Kershaw.
2. Winston Churchill.
3. Joynson-Hicks & Co., solicitors.
4. MFH refers to William Collins, who was a "Master of Foxhounds."
5. The quarrel about Maurice Magnus between Norman Douglas and D. H. Lawrence, in which RA took Lawrence's side in *Pinorman*.
6. In *Pinorman*, RA accuses Douglas of rewriting Pino's memoirs to distort Pino's true feelings toward D. H. Lawrence. Of the frontispiece that Lawrence drew for *Venus in the Kitchen, or Love's Cookery Book by Pilaff Bey*, [G. Orioli], ed. Norman Douglas, intro. Graham Greene, London, 1952, Douglas, writing in the preface as "Pilaff Bey," makes fun of "this picture of a fat naked woman pushing a loaf into an oven."
7. See Maurice Magnus, *Memoirs of The Foreign Legion*, intro. D. H. Lawrence, London, 1924.
8. See Norman Douglas, *D. H. Lawrence and Maurice Magnus: A Plea for Better Manners*, and Letter 127 n. 6.
9. Not identified by RA except as "wealthy person who had a grudge against Lawrence" (*Pinorman*, p. 179).
10. The British Colonial Office accused U.S. born Janet Rosenberg and her husband of leading a Communist inspired plot to subvert the government of British Guiana. See "Wide Guiana Strike Called by Leftist," *New York Times*, 12 October 1953, p. 1.
11. As ambassador to Italy in 1953, Clare Boothe Luce helped lay the diplomatic groundwork for a conference that resolved the status of Trieste, a dispute that threatened war between Yugoslavia and Italy.
12. Not identified.
13. William Collins Publishing, whose address at this time was 16 St. James Place.

126. To Netta Aldington (British Library)

Palm Sunday 1954[1]   Montpellier.
Dear Netta,
    Pinorman will be out on the 15th (Thursday). A set of proofs was sent Frieda, and I enclose a copy of the marvellous letter she wrote.[2] That instant response to writing that "brings alive" was always her greatest gift. There is no harm in your showing the letter, but don't let it out of your hands. If it is quoted in the press, Heinemann must give it out, and I don't want it garbled by one of those London journalist shits.

Frere also came through wonderfully. He had to go to Italy and Germany, and when Kingswood took no notice of my request to see and pass the jacket, I put it down to what happens when the boss is away. Nenni! It was a planned surprise—a design which brings back my pre-war Altarmira bull,[3] with the C.L.S.[4] and PINORMAN in a diagonal between them. Delissous. After all, Frieda and Frere know the truth and life of it all, and you had a last glimpse. Like Frieda, though, I wonder what "ordinary people" will think? Not much, I should guess, they can't.

The Lawrence book should be out in May, though Hart, Storrs, Winterton etc. are doing their damnedest to get it stopped or delayed. I don't altogether trust Collins, who have too many personal friends in the other camp. But everything is in type, last-minute corrections and references included, illustration blocks made and proofs passed by me. If they go to press after Easter, they can make a date in May easily, as it won't be necessary to bind all the first 30,000 before issuing.

Tomorrow we leave for A Daou for the holidays, and it is cold and pouring with rain! Lavandou will be dismal if it continues. Catha is spending the day with her "set" in the house of one of her friends at Palavas. They are to have a picnic lunch on their own (to which Catha extravagantly proffered a whole chicken!) and the parents give them goûter and dinner and will drive the girls back to Montpellier. I learned with displeasure that there are Parisiennes among the guests. I hope she won't lose too much of her freshness and naturalness in contact with silly town girls.

Her latest feat—in the French diction class she went to the platform de the mistress and declaimed a poem. The mistress said condescendingly the delivery wasn't bad, but it was clear Catha hadn't been able to rise to the level of the author's thought and had misrepresented it. Whereupon she and her friend Françoise[5] go into gales of girlish laughter. Sternly asked why, she had to confess she had written the poem. After class the mistress said to her privately: "Alors, Mademoiselle, il paraît que vous avez tous les talents, pour le sport et pour la poésie." "Mais je n'ai pas le don de réussir à l'école." "Ah! pour ça, il faut travailler." She just got over half marks on her term, but didn't get her tableau d'honneur, and as usual could do better if she tried.

Love from us both,
Richard

P.S. A man in Berkshire[6] is to bring out a limited "press" edition of 350 copies at 27/6 of one of the lectures I gave at Columbia in 1939.[7] I have signed up with Frere to do a book on Mistral, Provence and Languedoc;[8] and though the contract hasn't yet come through I am also doing them a big book about English poetry.[9] So I shall be kept busy—and what a relief to get away from "Colonel" Lawrence and his filthy world! What a set they are, from Churchill downwards.

1. 11 April 1954.
2. See Frieda Lawrence to RA, 29 March 1954 (SIUC): "Of course I swallowed 'Pinorman' like a raw oyster. You made it all alive again. You give this wonderful bit of living, unique, never to be repeated."
3. Part of the cave art in the caverns of Altamira, Spain, which RA visited in 1933.
4. A nonexistent literary society to which A. S. Frere, Thomas McGreevy, Norman Douglas, Pino Orioli, Charles Prentice, Brigit Patmore, RA, and others were supposed to belong. See also Letters 57, 65, and *passim*.
5. Françoise Battisty.
6. George F. Sims at Peacocks Press.
7. *Ezra Pound and T. S. Eliot. A Lecture*, Hurst, Berkshire, 1954.
8. *Introduction to Mistral*, London, 1956.
9. RA's works include no such book.

127. To Eric Warman (SIUC)

8th May 1954   Montpellier.
My dear Eric,

Many thanks indeed for your nice letter which is much appreciated. The English certainly are a strange people, infected with a murk of snobbish hypocrisy. "In England every artist wants to be a bourgeois"— or in rare cases (such as Norman's) when he doesn't, his friends undertake to make him one posthumously.[1] Le Bourgeois Malgré Lui. Norman's set of hangers-on have been busy as beelets building up a fictitious and factitious figure of him as their "adorable Uncle Norman" who was "a perfect dear."[2] Reminds me of when Firbank was going to Hayti and wrote a p.c. ending: "and they say the president is a *perfect dear.*"[3]

Norman made no effort to conceal his habits and tastes, and I'm damned if I see why the public should be imposed on. Why should we go on having Victorian wax dummies foisted on us as biographies? And you might make a note to remind those ladies who find the book "regrettable" that they have lived through book after book exposing the frailties of a really great writer like Lawrence—usually with malicious intent, and often highly exaggerated—without finding them "regrettable."[4] Not being a bourgeois I admire a great artist more than a great bugger, who claimed to be a "gentleman." Discuss the same unto them.

Of course, when you wrote you hadn't read chapter 7, which I think is an even greater "regret" than the sod part.[5] That crowd thought they had really got Lawrence down with that cock-and-bull Magnus story.[6] They forgot me!

Your query about the previous disposition to boys and rejecting of "vice" is delightful, and might be pushed back into metaphysics— Predestination versus Freewill. But don't overlook the fact—I think it is a fact—that there is such a thing as an "acquired taste"—i.e. the overcoming of a natural repugnance or indifference out of snobbery or curiosity or sheer perversity, and the experiment repeated quells the repugnance and becomes a habit? Norman's awful truffles are a case in point. He had got so tired of really nice food that he had to have queer over-spiced dishes—ditto in sex. I would illustrate this by a story I heard as a student among a group of young barristers from the Temple. You know that when cases are held in camera the Court is much less pompous and sadistic than when the brute public is present. One young barrister mentioned that at a County Assize he had been present when a red-cheeked rustic was indicted for carnal knowledge of a sow. When the indictment was read the Judge leaned forward and in quite a fatherly way said: "Now, my boy, tell us—whatever induced you to commit such a disgusting offence?" "Well, zur," said the boy cheerfully, "Oi be that lusty Oi can vuck anything." I daresay that was the case with Norman.

There will be a bigger row when the Lawrence of Arabia book comes out. His friends have been moving heaven and earth to get it suppressed, but they haven't succeeded. Collins will publish, and without alteration. They may include Churchill's letter (a piteous giveaway) and my answer, which shows him up.[7] As an author and publisher you will understand the causes of delay—first the necessity for complete *legal* proof and not merely historical or literary proof (which took time, and is only just complete) because we have to meet libel at every turning; and second the difficulty of getting all the contracts synchronized, involving as they do at present publication in Gt Britain, France and USA in book form, and serialisation in G.B., U.S.A., Australia (two states), Canada, France and Germany, with others in the offing. Alister assures me that the final difficulties will be smoothed out this coming week, the documents sent for my signature and the publication date announced when they return to London. The book is all set and ready to print. I hope we can make June. It depends on the lawyers, damn them. I suspect— though I have no evidence—that all this delaying and letting people think the book was suppressed (which I know was not ever contemplated) may have been a shrewd publicity device. But don't tell anyone that! I am weary of the subject after 3–4 years, but I think you'll find it a facinating psychological problem. And I look forward to hearing your views.

It is a curious thing about the London reviewers—they are always against an independent writer in his life-time and try to cash in after his death. Lawrence and Norman could do nothing right while they lived. Neither can I. If they try to cash in on me posthumously, you write to the Times and tell 'em I said they're all shits! Make a note of it.

I am glad indeed to know that you prosper, and that you continue to write as well. It is good to keep such interests. You know I have always wished you well.

I hope Jean is happy in her new life, but of course happiness is subjective and relative. "How to be happy though married," and you know the Scotch poem about the maid envying the wife's home and the wife envying the maid's freedom! Catha romps along the same primrose path, but is much devoted to sports, and—horresco referens—is now actually working for an exam. I must have her medically examined as well.

At the moment I am at work on two new books, both involving a lot of work, and one really a bit beyond me. Never mind, I'll do my best, and learn from the literary eunuchs of the Press that I'm gaga. I have to confess I find that I work much more on the easier of the two books, which will be finished first by a long chalk.[8]

Affectionately
Richard

P.S. I enclose a copy of Frieda Lawrence's letter about Pinorman which you may like to see.[9]

1. The quotation that RA applies to Norman Douglas is attributed to Oscar Wilde; see RA, *The Portable Oscar Wilde*, New York, 1946, p. 682.

2. In response to RA's *Pinorman*, London, 1954.

3. See Miriam J. Benkovitz, *Ronald Firbank. A Biography*, New York, 1969, p. 225 n. 6: "To my knowledge there is no evidence of any kind that Firbank went to Haiti."

4. RA refers especially to Nancy Cunard who defended Douglas against RA's *Pinorman*.

5. In *Pinorman*, pp. 145–63, and *passim*, RA criticizes Douglas's literary accomplishments.

6. D. H. Lawrence tried to recover money he had lent to Maurice Magnus by publishing Magnus's *Memoirs of the Foreign Legion* (1924). Lawrence's introduction led to a quarrel with Douglas, who responded by writing *D. H. Lawrence and Maurice Magnus* (1924). Lawrence replied two years later. For RA's version of the Magnus-Douglas-Lawrence conflict, see *Life for Life's Sake*, pp. 375–76; *D. H. Lawrence: Portrait of a Genius, But . . .*, pp. 217–29; and *Pinorman*, pp. 171–204.

7. RA quotes from Churchill's letter; however, Collins did not publish "without alteration."

8. See RA, *Frauds*, London, 1957, and *Introduction to Mistral*, London, 1956.

9. See Letter 126 n. 2.

128. To Netta Aldington (British Library)

12 May 1954   [Montpellier]

Dearest Netta,

In the greatest confidence—you must not speak of it. The delay with the TEL has had nothing do to with Churchill and Hart.[1] It was over a very complicated set of agreements turning the property into a Trust for the little one, tax-free—a lawyer's masterpiece. The whole delay has revolved round a lawyer's squabble. In the event of the Inland Revenue deciding to carry the thing to the Lords, who should be liable for Tax, Collins, or the Trust? My lawyer—who drew all these complex documents—claims there is 99.9% certainty that the tax can't be enforced. Collins's lawyer disagrees. I have just been on the phone to Alister, and have authorised a settlement. It could have been made 3 weeks ago but for the need of lawyers to make money!

Even when Collins re-announce, do not let this be known. They don't want to advertise the fact that they have just made such a contract—and you can see why. Nobody else will know but Alister and myself. The re-announcement and publication of the book will disperse the Lawrence Bureau[2] lies, and they will or should be useful publicity.

Pinorman is doing very well indeed. The hangers-on of course are furious. The funniest, I think, is MacKenzie.[3] He can't realise that the fine-old-Scottish gentlemen pose is gone for ever, deader than coffin nails.

Frieda has written a wonderful letter to Nancy,[4] pulling her back hair down. I sent it to Frere and not direct to Time and Tide. I think he'll send it on. It's good publicity.

Hot here, all of a sudden.

Love
Richard

1. That is, their efforts to prevent publication of the book about T. E. Lawrence.
2. Those attempting to keep intact the legend of T. E. Lawrence.
3. See the *Spectator,* 30 April 1954, p. 518.
4. See Nancy Cunard, " 'Bonbons' of Gall," *Time and Tide,* 17 April 1954, p. 517, where she denied the truth of RA's characterization of Norman Douglas in *Pinorman.* For Frieda Lawrence's defense of RA, see her reply to Cunard in "Letters to the Editor," *Time and Tide,* 29 May 1954, p. 724. Nancy Cunard wrote a rebuttal; cf. *Time and Tide,* 5 June 1954, pp. 752, 754.

129. To Alan Bird (NYPL)[1]

21 February 1955   Montpellier

My Dear Bird,

This habit of quoting from memory should be checked!

What I said: "The book" (i.e. The Mint) "will never be publicly issued intact, and, even if it were, would probably disappoint most readers except those determined to worship everything 'T.E.' did."[2]

S'mit y' ludship, ludship's remarks unfounded, and client's prophetic remarks fully justified by event. The book has not been *publicly* issued intact, but only sub rosa for a few hundred smut-hounds, and even then I wonder if the Queen Alexandra bit is in.[3]

The English press is incredible. The Telegraph published a Cape sneer against me because Lawrence wrote a blurb for Custot's Sturly which I translated (I had "probably" never heard of it). Now, Lawrence failed to translate Sturly, and so did some other unknown person, because they didn't know how to get the technical French words. Bruce Richmond wrote me Lawrence had failed, would I do it? I did it and successfully since Custot invited me to stay with him at Monaco and work there at the Oceanographic centre.[4] How characteristic of the Bureau. They sneer at the man who could and successfully did do the job at which the great Lawrence failed! You can't learn French by scattering sovereigns off a camel.

I saw Sheppard snubbed by an undergraduate. In his affected pansy way Sheppard said that "the highest achievement of humanity was to write Greek verse." Slight pause, and an undergraduate remarked artlessly: "Greek verse? I always thought it was a recreation of country parsons!"

Eric Kennington is to be slapped down by a letter from a friend who had read the Shaw-Shaw letter, which Kennington hasn't.[5]

There is to be quite a do over here soon—45 minutes on Radio France (even including 5 from the insignificant author) and more articles.[6]

And there were extracts in Illustrated from Lawrence's C.O. at Uxbridge.[7] How sickening journalism is! The full letter from Squadron-Commander Breese was an admirable picture of the disgust of a regular officer for the abnormal creature wished on him. L. was constantly "on the mat" at Uxbridge as "consistently dirty," "insubordinate," "refusal to obey order re kit," "persistently late on parade." His Flight-Commander and Segt reported he was bone lazy! Such a pity it was not given entire; but journalism is an accursed thing. It has to flatter the mental laziness of the lowest, and has no integrity.

More later. Weather not so bad here, but I've had bronchitis again.

Ever yours
Richard Aldington

1. This letter was published in *A Passionate Prodigality: Letters to Alan Bird from Richard Aldington*, ed. Miriam J. Benkovitz, New York, 1975.

2. RA refers to an earlier evaluation of the literary merit of TEL's *The Mint*. . . .

3. In the passage RA refers to, T. E. Lawrence describes Queen Alexandra (wife of Edward VII) in her old age. RA had seen *The Mint* in 1951 but had promised not to quote or paraphrase from it. He did not, therefore, mention this passage (which *was* included when *The Mint* was published in 1955) in his TEL biography.

4. See Letter 130. Custot was at the Oceanographic Center at Monaco founded by Jacques Cousteau.

5. The "friend" was Rob Lyle, whose letter appeared in *London Magazine,* June 1955, pp. 75–81.

6. RA did not participate in this program; Alister Kershaw spoke for him.

7. G. F. Breese, "The Storm over Lawrence," *Illustrated London News,* 26 February 1955, pp. 6, 9.

130. To Eric Warman (SIUC)

23 February 1955   Montpellier.

My dear Eric,

Yesterday I got a shock on learning that Collins refused my solicitor brother the 200 for the Patmores. Now, I had been told that 18,000 copies cleared the advance, and that 29,000 had been sold. Even allowing for half of the balance as export or "sale and return" that still left me a credit of about £1200. Collins stand on the fact that the book is now owned by a Trust, and though I repeatedly asked him Allie as Trustee apparently did not give his authority on account of this illness. Of course there is another point which Collins did not admit, and that is they want to hold my cash as possible income tax, in case the Inland Revenue refuse to accept the Trust deed.[1]

Well, I wrote Alister express, enclosing a letter for him to send on to you in case he approved, and I now realise that to-day is Shrove Tuesday—hence no mails delivered in Paris. And more delay.

Would you consent to advance the 200 to my brother (P.A.G. Aldington, 25 Castle St, Dover) against my promissory note, the money to be paid as soon as Collins is cleared up, or, failing them, by Mrs. Colin out of money she is receiving for me. In addition to articles, she is very hopeful of an American sale with advance of the book I have arranged with Frere. And damn it! Frere is somewhere between New York and Melbourne, and while accepting the book wrote that he would draw the contract on his return—in April!

If you can help me out of this I shall indeed be grateful, for publication of a Writ would be fatal now.[2] Perhaps that's what Collins want—gives them a chance to withdraw the book.

We have got a big show coming off here early next month. Radio France are giving up 45 minutes to the book (instead of 5 minutes as first planned) and even the insignificant author is to be allowed a word or two. That is on the 7th. On the 5th Noir et Blanc will have a full-page illustrated article, and Allie is to arrange with Miroir de l'Histoire for an article on the efforts to stop the book before publication.[3] He knows it far better than I, as he dealt with it, and has the correspondence. He and Delarue hope this can be put out in England, but I don't know how. I'll ask Mrs. Colin.

The BBC have excelled themselves. They now propose I should debate the book with Hart—for Canada! Not bloody likely. In the first place, it is an insult after they have denied me England. In the second place I should be a fool to debate. I stand by the book, which none of the attacks has touched. In the 120 or more reviews I've seen only about 15% even mention the facts I prove, and not a single one speaks of those unpublished letters in the Brit Mus! Yet the interpretation of L's tortured psychology and the motives—stated by himself!—for entering the RAF are contained in those letters and only in those letters![4]

There is a flaming attack on me, calling me a liar, in some Dublin paper because I mentioned (without reference to source) that TEL asked Shaw to write on Casement—interesting from the sexual psychology point of view. Well, the topic comes up more than once in those same letters, and the fact is confirmed by Blanche Patch in that book (p 82) of hers on GBS![5] What can one do against such a mixture of bad faith and ignorance and refusal to correct printed and insulting falsehoods?

Did you see Peterborough printed Cape's sneering reference[6] to Sturly[7] with the patronising remark that I probably never knew Lawrence wrote the feeble blurb, which, by the way, he tried to excuse on the old trick that it was a "parody." I printed the facts of that Sturly business in Life for Life's Sake, 1941.[8] (So much for not knowing about it!) What happened was that I reviewed the original for the TLS. Later, Bruce Richmond wrote me that Lawrence and another unnamed person had both failed to translate the book—would I do it. Now, Lawrence's difficulty and everybody's was that you couldn't translate the book without the names of all the sea creatures, and they aren't in any French-English dictionary. I saw how to do it. I got French and English textbooks, found the scientific Latin name in the French book and then looked it up in the English. When there wasn't an English word I gave the scientific name. It was even too successful for the French author, Custot, jumped to the conclusion that I was a scientist and invited me to come and work at the Monte Carlo aquarium! But how typical all this is of the Lawrence Bureau. The whole episode is distorted to the glory of the man who failed, and to sneer at the man who could and did do the job successfully!

I just don't get it. What's the matter with the British? Haven't they got over the 1940 jitters yet? Hitler's dead and gone, and they won't have a Gauleiter for some time. He'll have an American accent.

Try to help me if you can, Eric, for I really am solvent, and I have written urgently to the solicitor insisting that the American offer be accepted at once. A large advance is agreeable, but with a good firm a sound royalty is what matters.

Ever,

Richard

Did you see Time? Now I'm "crabbed and dull." What next. But Time has been one of the Colonel's cheer-leaders. I remember they used him as an example of the real hero to bash down some phoney like Gibson the dam-buster.[9]

1. To provide for his daughter, Catherine, and to protect the royalties from *Lawrence of Arabia. A Biographical Enquiry* from current taxes and the claims of the Patmores, RA had set up a trust deed with Alister Kershaw as trustee. See Letter 128.

2. The Patmores were attempting to collect payment due them under the terms of the divorce agreement. Warman lent RA the money.

3. F. J. Temple confirms that Radio France gave the forty-five minute program. Articles in *Noir et Blanc* and *Le Miroir de l'Histoire* were not traced.

4. T. E. Lawrence's letters to Mr. and Mrs. George Bernard Shaw. Most reviews tended to attack RA for revealing T. E. Lawrence's bastardy during his mother's lifetime and for being transparently hostile to Lawrence—they were not able to refute RA's "facts."

5. Blanche Patch, *Thirty Years with G.B.S.*, London, 1951, p. 82.

6. See "Peterborough," "London Day by Day: A Blurb—For Mr. Aldington," *Daily Telegraph*, 10 February 1955, p. 6.

7. See Pierre Custot, *Sturly*, trans. Richard Aldington, London, 1924.

8. Pp. 267–68.

9. Wing Commander Guy Penrose Gibson led the attack on the Muhne and Eder dams in World War II. See "Autopsy of a Hero," *Time*, 14 February 1955, p. 29.

131. To Eric Warman (SIUC)

18 September 1955   Montpellier.

My dear Eric,

I am grateful to you—among greater services—for sending me the Catalogue.[1] This is the true author's memento mori, the Egyptian mummy at the feast of the Muses: Let us eat and drink, for tomorrow we are remaindered. What a graveyard of innocents we have here! What Rachels weeping for their lost children who will not be comforted! The consolation of Jarry does not apply here. You know the Story? Alfred Jarry, who used to go about Paris on a bike with bare feet and long hair (because he could not afford shoes or a barber) sometimes sat at the window of his squalid garret shooting dried peas at passers-by, and once nearly hit a baby in a pram, whose mother showed signs of disquiet. "Calm yourself, dear Madam," cried Jarry with exquisite politeness, "If the child dies, *I* will make you others." What the lady said is not recorded.

What a casualty list! Sir Richard Burton (alas!), Marte Bibesco (ha, ha) and Eddie Marsh (hee, hee). Wilfred Blunt, by God, and that book on Abd el Kader[2] is a good one, and should almost be news with all this fracas in N. Africa.[3] Ought I to know Frank Bowen? Alas that England's Wooden Walls are remaindered, and a thick red line of Wooden Heads substituted in our defense. Burke of Limehouse, who used to be held up to me as an inimitable model of literary glory by your colleagues at 40 Museum St![4] Erskine Caldwell, whose opulence I surveyed (I trust without envy) at Hollywood—he expressed his unlimited contempt for the Evening Standard which could afford to pay only 400 pounds for four short articles—2000 dollars transferred at once, when I was refused and rightly 10/6 for a poem. Anne-Marie Callimachi, whose portrait you have read without knowing it in the pages of Seven Against Reeves.[5] And an intro by Sachie Sitwell.[6] Tuttest of tuts. I always thought John Clare a bore, and when doubled by Grigson. . . . Did you ever read Grigson's intro to the Oxford Bacon's Essays? Just for a moment, remember what Bacon was and is—Lord Chancellor of England, a great philosopher, a pre-scientist, a prose writer of the highest rank—and Mr. G.G. very condescendingly but not unkindly pats him on the head after severely rapping his knuckles! O God, O Montreal.[7] I like the blurb on Somerset de Chair, who, unlike the great Lawrence, was severely wounded in the Near East. You will find I quote him to the effect that TELawrence was known in the Near East, but not until AFTER the war through films, books, radio, and propaganda. Sorry that book failed.[8] The bluffing of the Irakians by that little force was a masterpiece of daring. Morrie Ernst! Ha, ha. He claims I owe him 250 dollars which I don't. Nuts to him. Falcon Press Classics. You should see D. Patmore's "Pater" which is almost entirely dug out of mine. The sincerest form, of course, but when it comes to selling letters and a picture stolen from me. . . . British Bats.[9] Eric, I believe I once had a fan letter from Brian Vesey-Fitzgerald. Now lies he there, and none so poor to do him reverence. Sorry about Fuseli who had ability. Gielgud—Early Stages of what? Vine Street? Charles Graves. Honest Robert.[10] Metternich, translated by Dorothy Todd.[11] At one time she edited the London Vogue. She stood me some good lunches. Is she in London? I wish I could help her.

Those Norfolk books of Williamson and Lilias give me the pip.[12] Now Henry[13] read somewhere (in the 20s) that England was under-nourished through eating white bread, which is true, owing to the idiocy of city dwellers who insist on dead white bread which must therefore be milled until the nutriment and vitamins are cast out to the swine. (Literally) Henry works up a fantastic idea that England has loaned its immense (and non-existent) money to "backward" countries (!) who have repaid by selling us this pestiferous bread—which is solely the result of popular stupidity and mill-owners' rapacity. So Henry decides to save England by growing grain in Norfolk. Of course loses his money. But growing grain in England isn't the point. English or foreign, it's the milling that matters. Anyone with any sense buys standard bread. You know it as well as I do. It is even worse in USA. There the wheat is so ruthlessly milled, and the millings of course made into pig-food, that yanks have to eat pork and bacon in order to get the vitamin B 1, which should be in the bread.

My affairs are straightening. The American ed. is due out surely in Oct, and ditto German.[14] Collins owe me about £2000, and they are trying to evade payment on a very flimsy trick. I have a lawyer after them. Mrs C. and I together muffed a 3000 dollar contract from Reinharts, but we'll get another. Frere is blowing hard on his fingers after reading my Mistral book, which I think and prophesy will be in your catalogue 6 months after publication if it is ever published.[15] Yet it's a nice book. But I'm on the Frauds[16] (which I think will give Frere apoplexy) and have signed for another biog.

They say crime doesn't pay. Well, it pays a damn sight better than honesty and hard work, I give you my word. I think I must train Catha to be a Marseille gangster's moll. Then she'll live in luxury and wear the stolen jewels of the Aga Cunt. You know, Oscar said that the difference between the French and the British is, that in France every bourgeois wants to be an artist, and in England every artist wants to be a bourgeois. Profound and perfectly valid at his time. Nowadays, the difference has shifted—the French know their number is up, and the British don't.

> When the Russian tanks come rolling down the Strand
> They'll be met by Eisenhower's Irish band,
>   Und der Kanzler's staff will say
>   As the Churchill trombones play:
> "Wie gut it is our Yankosachsenland."

Heil Stalin!

Ever

Richard

1. Not traced, but apparently a list of remaindered books that inspired RA's commentary on the "casualty list."
2. Wilfred Jasper Blunt, *Desert Hawk*, London, 1947.

3. During the summer of 1955 the French government changed its Moroccan policy to support Mohammed ben Yussef and Moroccan independence.

4. 40 Museum Street was the address of Allen and Unwin Ltd, one of RA's early publishers; see [Thomas] Burke of Eltham, *Limehouse Nights*, London, 1917; see Frank Charles Bowen, *Men of the Wooden Walls*, London, 1952.

5. RA, *Seven Against Reeves. A Comedy-Farce*, London, 1938.

6. Not traced.

7. RA quotes Samuel Butler, "Psalm of Montreal," in *The Shrewsbury Edition of the Works of Samuel Butler*, vol. 20, pp. 392–93; *Essays by Francis Bacon*, intro. Geoffrey Grigson, London [1940]; and *Poems of John Clare's Madness*, ed. and intro. Geoffrey Grigson, London [1949].

8. RA quotes Somerset de Chair, *The Golden Carpet*, London, 1943, in *Lawrence of Arabia. A Biographical Enquiry*, p. 280.

9. RA, *Walter Pater. Selected Works*, London, 1948; Derek Patmore, *Walter Pater. Selected Writings*, London, 1949. See Letter 74 n. 2.

10. Robert Graves, *Lawrence and the Arabs*, London, 1927; Sir Arthur John Gielgud, *Early Stages*, London, 1939, rev. 1953.

11. Constantin de Greenwald, *Metternich*, trans. Dorothy Todd, London, 1953. See Letter 41 n. 5.

12. Henry Williamson, *The Story of a Norfolk Farm*, London, 1941; Lilias Rider Haggard, *Norfolk Life*, with footnotes by Henry Williamson, London, 1943.

13. Williamson.

14. RA, *Lawrence of Arabia. A Biographical Enquiry*.

15. RA, *Introduction to Mistral*, London, 1956.

16. See RA, *Frauds*, London, 1957.

132. To Alison Palmer* (Temple)

13 November 1955   Montpellier.

Dear Mrs. Palmer,

Many thanks for your letter and for all the information you so kindly collected for me.

You evidently missed the big window displays of my Lawrence in London, of which I have photographs somewhere. I think that these and the immense newspaper gabble aroused the cupidity of the booksellers and they expected immense sales. In fact Collins "subscribed" about 18,000, and by the end of June they were over 31,000. This of course includes sales out of England, but I can hardly think that a failure, when you think that 5000 copies are still almost a best-seller!

It is strange that you do not seem to have heard that it was published in USA by Regnery of Chicago on the 26th Sept. Collins had already sold about 3000 copies there, but in spite of that Regnery subscribed 3500. There have of course been the usual abusive reviews supplied by the British Information Agency, but I hear there have been some impartial ones, especially in the Atlantic Monthly.[1] But I have not seen this, and it may have been suppressed by British government influence, as the big articles in "Time" in USA and "Paris Match" in France were stopped at the last minute.

An individual cannot fight a government, but of course if I were not right they would not have to use all these dirty tricks. However it is small comfort to know that I shall be vindicated 20 years after I am dead!

Yes "Murder in France"[2] is by the Alister Kershaw of the bibliography.[3] It is very strange. He is the gentlest and kindest of persons, yet has this singular interest in murder. It is almost the only thing we can't agree about. To me murder is either a terrific tragedy like "Orestes" or "Macbeth" or it is something so squalid and repulsive I don't want to hear about it. I can't bear murder for murder's sake, the modern "public's" insistence on a corpse in every tale with a sort of cross-word puzzle and man-hunt to follow. Life is for living, not for death.

I sometimes wonder (not too conceitedly, I hope!) whether some of the disproportionate hatred my harmless writings arouse may not have some basis in this death-worship, since I am an unrepentant life-worshipper. I have a faint memory of that Malcolm Ross broadcast[4] and of wonder at its destructive hate of me. Why it should be crime to publish the only more or less authentic life of D. H. Lawrence[5] I don't know. But perhaps Mr Ross or some friend of his was preparing one. There has been one lately by a Mr Harry T. Moore,[6] which has a great many mistakes in it, or so Mrs Lawrence tells me, and I suppose she knew her husband's life![7] There was, I remember, some correspondence about it in The Listener,[8] when it was proved that my account of the raid on Lawrence's picture show was the only accurate one, and Mr. Moore's was wrong.[9] But, dear me, how trifling these things are!

Mr. Sims is publishing two more of my lectures on poets.[10] I hope he can prod his dawdling English printer into activity so that the book can appear before Xmas, for my Mistral book[11] is already with Heinemann's printers. I have had another battle to get that book published. The publisher's rule to-day is the one which Saroyan ironically described long ago in his definition of a best-seller: "to write a letter to ordinary people telling them what they know already." Simply because Mistral is unknown seems to the modern publisher a reason for allowing him to remain so. Yet he was a great poet and a fine man, but above all one who brought poetry to the people, who fought to save the culture of the people from the attacks of industrialists and bureaucrats, and whose memory is revered by the 11,000,000 who still speak the langue d'oc. The people of the langue d'oc are a minority race, occupying here much the same place as the French do in Canada. Of course if I had written some sentimental trash about a Provençal Maria Chapdelaine,[12] all would be well. But I have tried to advance Mistral, not myself. And that is a mistake.

My daughter is longing for the snow to come down in the Pyrenees and Cevennes so that she can go ski-ing. I hope it doesn't come as far down as Montpellier, for with my bronchitis I can't go out, and that is very tedious.

If you come to France next summer I do hope you will try to come this way, that is, if I survive the winter.

I am doing a series of radio "interviews" on English and American poets in French every other Tuesday.[13] My daughter, who is now bilingual, is much distressed by my British accent!

With all good wishes,

Yours sincerely,
Richard Aldington

---

*Alison McKennon Palmer (b. 1895), a former English subject who immigrated to Canada in 1928, began correspondence with RA in late 1954 at the suggestion of George Sims whose Peacocks Press she visited. Sims had been to see RA, bought books and manuscripts from him, and published his *Ezra Pound and T. S. Eliot*. As with Eric Warman, RA's exchange of letters with Palmer began when she wrote expressing admiration for his work. When Warman wrote in 1933, however, RA was at the peak of his literary success, without financial problems, and enjoying traveling and living in southern France with Brigit Patmore. When Mrs. Palmer's first letter reached him in 1954, Netta was no longer living with him, his career was beginning to falter, and money problems were becoming severe. His letters to her are particularly useful in clarifying some of the complications surrounding the publication of his *Lawrence of Arabia*, and in detailing RA's own feelings about T. E. Lawrence.

1. Cf. B. H. Liddell Hart, "T. E. Lawrence: Man or Myth," *Atlantic Monthly*, November 1955, pp. 70–71, 74, 76.

2. 1955.

3. *A Bibliography of the Works of Richard Aldington from 1915 to 1948*.

4. Not traced. A review of *Lawrence of Arabia* by Sir Ronald Storrs was broadcast on "Third Programme" of the BBC on 30 January 1955.

5. *D. H. Lawrence: Portrait of a Genius, But. . . .*

6. *The Intelligent Heart: The Story of D. H. Lawrence*, New York, 1954.

7. But see Letter 113 where RA disparages Frieda's memory of events in her life with Lawrence.

8. Cf. "Letters to the Editor," " 'Son and Lover,' " P. Coutts Trotter, 19 May 1955, p. 898; Hardiman Scott, 26 May 1955, p. 942; Richard Aldington, 2 June 1955, p. 985; P. Coutts Trotter, 16 June 1955, p. 1079.

9. RA, *D. H. Lawrence: Portrait of a Genius, But . . .* , pp. 341–42; cf. Moore, *Intelligent Heart*, pp. 408–9, 418–19, and *passim*.

10. *A. E. Housman and W. B. Yeats, Two Lectures*, Hurst, Berkshire, 1955.

11. *Introduction to Mistral*, London, 1956.

12. Louis Hemon, *Maria Chapdelain*, Paris, 1921.

13. RA was interviewed by F.-J. Temple for Radio-Montpellier, France, during fourteen monthly sessions of fifteen minutes each from October 1955 to December 1956. Subjects touched on included RA's childhood, his first poems, Imagism, Italy, the *Egoist*, W. S. Blunt, Yeats, Roy Campbell, Joyce's *Ulysses*, Pound, London during the 1914 war, F. S. Flint, World War I, D. H. Lawrence, Norman Douglas and Maurice Magnus, Pino Orioli, and *Death of a Hero*. The series, titled "Entretiens Inachevés (Unfinished Interviews)," was interrupted for the Christmas holidays and not resumed in 1957 because RA left Montpellier for Sury-en-Vaux. He was in poor health and "too tired to use up his energy for a few other interviews."

133. To Eric Warman (SIUC)

15 August 1956   Montpellier.

My dear Eric,

I have been trying to write to you ever since Catha got back, and have been constantly interrupted. My most grateful thanks to you for your kindness to her during the London visit. She evidently enjoyed going out with you very much, and the joy of that made up for her boredom with and dislike of the smoky pubs to which she was taken. It was most kind of you.

So Jean is married. Give her my love and all good wishes.

I have worked myself very hard trying to deal with the situation created by the Lawrence fans. Frere is at last recovering from his panic, although all along he has seen the documents which prove my case— talking of which, an article in the N.Y. Nation by C. P. Snow says that although the "Establishment" rallied against me to a man *publicly,* they now admit *in private* that I am at least 85% right.[1] This strikes me as characteristic of the English gent and his "honour," which he has just dropped once more in the mud, Suez side down.[2]

Anyway, the new edition of the Anthology is due out on the 17th Sept.; the Mistral in Oct; and the Frauds in Feb. I have completed the RLS for Evans, but have not yet heard from them nor had the money which was due on the 1st!

The great trouble is that the yanks won't commit themselves until these books are out in England, and so the delay has cut me out there. Further, Collins have completely diddled the simple-minded solicitor supposed to be "acting" for me. They present him with plainly absurd figures, cutting me down from at least 1000 to 150. He refuses to accept. They refuse to yield. So I get nothing!

Catha says you will be down here in September. I shall be delighted to have you, and hope you will spare enough time for us to see some of the environs of this place. Bring your camera, for I think I can show some interesting sites. Last week-end we had my old friend Sir Alec Randall, who was delighted with the Camargue and the Saintes Maries. Unluckily he had with him a Canadian,[3] whose view of life was bounded by Time and TV, which gummed everything.

Mrs Colin has gone to Frankfurt (Germany) I believe but if you can do it without bother I'd be very grateful if you would bring me from her office an immense script—the Supplementary Anthology of English poetry, of which I have no copy.[4] It is a work which would be grabbed if there were any real interest in poetry, but under the reign of reviewers' culture, publishers regard it with horror. The book contains hundreds of poems they and their boys have never heard of. And scarcely a sod.

Will you let me know the approx date of your arrival and stay? I want to keep the period clear. Every year in Sept Catha and I drive to Pyrenees and have terrific lunch with my old friend Gustave Cohen. If you are here at the date he settles this year I'll arrange for you to be included. You will enjoy it. Gustave is a wonderful friend, and as he lunches with me each spring, we have a gastronomic contest. In April I blew him to Chateauneuf-du-Pape (we'll go there together) and that raised the standard again, especially as the wine happened to be excellent. You should see a real French hero—he has been a cripple since 1915 when he was wounded by a hand grenade in the Argonne. Folly of these wars!

I suppose you are sharpening bayonets, while the world laughs at Sir A. Eden and his piffling military threats? Haven't the Brits yet learned that satellite states don't make war without the permission of their masters, and that HMV[5] in Washington says sternly: "Can the rough stuff, Tony." Pou-ah! What a pack of phonies. America and Russia will arrange their own compromise, and Eden will make a speech and lose the canal.[6]

Well, let us look on the bright side. I shall live for your visit.

All thanks and good wishes, dear Eric,

from

Richard

P.S. Of course I forget the most important! Catha says she thinks you would take on the chore of being my executor. It would be a tremendous relief to me if you would. There will be nothing but copyrights, royalties due, scripts which can be sold, and so forth. I think my Letters might make a posthumous book but as literary executor you must have full powers of suppression and selection.[7] As I am domiciled in France I think a special form of will is required.

1. See C. P. Snow, "The Irregular Right: Britain Without Rebels," *Nation*, 24 March 1956, pp. 238–39.
2. The last British forces left the Suez Canal Zone in June 1956.

3. Not identified.
4. Not published.
5. Cf. advertising slogan of the Victor Talking Machine Company: "His master's voice."
6. In November 1956, French and British forces invaded the canal zone following its seizure by the Egyptian government; they withdrew at the demand of the United Nations.
7. On RA's death, Alister Kershaw was named his literary executor. See Letter 147.

134. To Alison Palmer (Temple)

18 June 1957   Montpellier.
Dear Mrs. Palmer,

I don't know how to thank you for the unexpected and generous gift of Roy Campbell's script.[1] His death[2] was a shock and a grief to me, the more so since in the past year I have lost other old friends[3]—though scarcely one so dear—and my health seems to get worse rather than better.

There are strange aspects of this review. Perhaps the strangest is that I have never seen it before, and did not know of its existence! For many years I gave up subscribing for press cuttings, and nobody troubled to send me this magnificent tribute which would have cheered me. It is all the more valuable since it was written before I ever met Roy.

He was a great poet and such a fine man, quite alien to the town and public house intellectuals and semi-communists of London. His father was a doctor and Natal Senator.[4] Roy was a magnificent man, six feet two, tremendously strong, a great hunter and fisherman, who was at Oxford but served aboard ship in the fo'csle, was soldier, professional fisherman in Provence, twice won the water-jousts at Martigues, was a celebrated razeteur (snatching the cockade from the horns of bulls), a picador, and finally a farmer in Portugal. He ran away at 16 to join the Army in World War I, and was sent home to his parents. He fought through the Spanish war on Franco's side. At 37 he volunteered for the war against Hitler and served in the Royal Welsh Fusiliers, the South Wales Borderers, the 12th East African Deception Unit and the King's African Rifles. He was severely wounded and contracted recurrent malaria, and returned to England (he had volunteered for the Imperial Army) on a hospital ship. Although only 55 at his death he had been so crippled for the past 18 months by his wounds and was in such pain that in a way this sudden death was a release. He had always prayed for sudden death, and he had just returned from Holy Week in Seville. As he was a devout Catholic that is significant. Many Masses have been said for him in many parts of the world. He was so warm-hearted and cheerful, with fearful prejudices, which seem to go with men of genius. It was a great honour for me to know him, and I am quite overwhelmed to know that he praised my poems so highly.

Thank you also for the very fine new stamps, which are very well designed. I am so glad that Canada and the other great Dominions are breaking away from the old servitude of no stamps but the royal family! Theoretically I am a monarchist, but I sometimes feel indignant at the contempt with which all writers and artists are treated by Buckingham palace, while it so sedulously cultivates racing touts and bookmakers and weedy youths in busbies. But this is treason, so hush!

I am in a bad state, physically and nervously and financially, but hope on. Good friends[5] have come to my aid, for I am so weak that a daily walk of 1500 yards exhausts; and I am to be moved to a cottage near Sancerre (Cher) where I can live rent free and try to live by growing vegetables and raising chickens &c. My daughter will go to work in Paris.[6]

I have finished the last proofs of Stevenson, and must now get down to a convict's task of a book on Balzac—a terrible chore! I think I can't start until after the move. It is really disgraceful the way authors are robbed nowadays. In June, I at last received accounts of my Italian sales for 1956. For sales of nearly 25,000 I get less than 300 dollars, with a deduction of 16% Italian income tax. Why should I pay Italian income tax? My agent tells me Poland is reprinting 10,000 Death of a Hero, and for that I may get 100 dollars and they'll owe me the rest! The London Times last week carried a Tass despatch saying that Russia is going to issue or reissue more Western authors—the first three names are Somerset Maugham, Priestly and Aldington! No doubt it is an honour, but that won't buy my daughter a pair of shoes! My Boccaccio at last is to be issued in England, with a generous advance of 215 dollars less 42 1/2% income tax and 10% commission to my agent! That translation is 400,000 words and took me a year's hard work during which time I also wrote some tripe called Death of a Hero. As for the USA, I am still boycotted there (Lowell Thomas and TELawrence) while they pour out money to anyone who backs their H-bomb and petrol policy . . . !

Thank you indeed for the Roy Campbell script. Do you know what they have put on his grave?

> "From the lone shieling in the misty island
> Oceans divide us and the waste of seas,
> But still the blood is strong, the heart is Highland,
> And I in dreams behold the Hebrides."

They were his favorite lines of all poetry, and come from the Canadian Boat Song.[7]

Yours sincerely
Richard Aldington

P.S. When Roy came out of hospital and was demobilised in 1945 still racked with malaria, a grateful England could find no job for him by which he could support himself and his beautiful wife and daughters but that of washing dishes in a restaurant! He told me so himself. And when Desmond MacCarthy got him a job at the BBC as a producer, Roy thought he was to be a commissionaire, and reported for duty wearing his war medals!

1. Campbell's review of RA's *Complete Poems*, London, 1948. The script bears the title "A Happy Pagan." In a letter to Lawrence Durrell, 24 June 1957, published in *Literary Lifelines* [1981], p. 24, RA refers to this manuscript as "a review of my *Complete Poems* by the old Roy himself and in his hand, which seemingly appeared in *Poetry*, Chicago (Ill.) circa 1948," but this review appeared not in *Poetry: A Magazine of Verse* but in the *Poetry Review*, April–May 1949, pp. 115–19, with the title "Richard Aldington, Happy Pagan" and was reprinted in *Richard Aldington: An Intimate Portrait*, ed. Alister Kershaw and Frédéric-Jacques Temple, Carbondale, Ill., 1965, pp. 4–11.
2. On 24 April 1957 in an automobile accident.
3. In 1956, George Gribble and Frieda Lawrence died and in early 1957 Wyndham Lewis and Bruce Rogers.
4. Major Samuel George Campbell, C.M.G., F.R.C.S., a doctor of Durban, South Africa.
5. Sheila and Alister Kershaw.
6. Catherine remained in Montpellier.
7. Anonymous.

135. To Eric Warman (SIUC)

25 June 1957   Montpellier.
My dear Eric,
   Many thanks for your letter. I have sent on the form to Mondadori, who will now forget to send the money until I remind him next month. And the month after.[1]
   The situation of my sort of author is rapidly becoming impossible between the caprices of public taste and the financial exigencies of publishers. Little is left to the author but the abuse of reviewers and the delightful pleasure of seeing his name in print.
   I see no "vista" unless I can go native in Alister's cottage garden, and raise vegetables and eggs while Catha works in Paris.
   Our friend the King of Poland[2] has sent me the first part of his "My Private War Against England."[3] Apparently during the period Sept '39– June '40 (when he was took up by the p'lice) he went about heiling Hitler, wrote insulting letters to people in power, tried to drop in on his old pal George VI at Buck Pal for a chat about Poland, ignored the blackout, gave a party on Hitler's birthday where the Horst-Wessel[4] was sung, and then complains of the atrocious behaviour of the government for sending coppers to arrest him. He and the queen of Poland (otherwise described as Odile) determined to defend the integrity of the royal garret to the last, which they did with a meat-axe and a whirling spray filled

with pepper. If the unfortunate British hadn't lost all sense of fun and humour in their frantic self-importance this work might have a considerable success as unconscious humour. Oh, I forgot to say that when arrested the Queen was wearing no knickers, and seems to have had an altercation about it later with a policewoman. Altogether, it has cheered me up a lot. People are such dreary bores as a rule that I am almost exhilarated by these narratives of splendidly absurd crankery. I don't recollect to have read a modern book so completely aloof from base reality. However, I can't get even Alister to agree with me about the old King, whom I have honoured with a poem which I beg you will not communicate to him:

> There was an old King of Po-land,
> Whose costume though gaudy was grand,
> The unfortunate thing
> For this otherwise king
> Was the lack of all subjects and land.

Here we await the verdict on the Bac exams, and look forward to our haven in Sury-en-Vaux.

Catha sends love.

Always,
Richard

P.S. I forgot to say that while all this was going on the old king and his dame were receiving a subsistence allowance from British public funds! In any other country he'd have been shot. What is the point of anti-Semitism? Surely it's all balls?

1. Alberto Mondadori, director of Mondadori Publishing House, Milan, Italy, who issued translations of a number of RA's works.
2. Geoffrey Wladislas Vaile Potocki, Count de Montalk.
3. Not published.
4. A Nazi patriotic song.

136. To Eric Warman (SIUC)

29 January 1958

Chez Alister Kershaw,
Maison Sallé,
Sury en Vaux,
Cher, France

My dear Eric,

What you tell me of your play[1] and the experts suddenly reminded me of what I used to hear from a playwright friend of mine many years ago.

In addition to what you were told—and practically in those words—he would say: "Always keep in mind the amateur market—three to five guineas a performance." In order to attain this steady income, for apparently there may be hundreds of performances a year all over the country, the writer must keep his dialogue "speakable for amateurs" (no long words, I suppose), keep the subject "presentable to decent people" and limit his cast to six or eight at the outside. In addition there should be only one change of scene in the three acts. I don't think my friend ever made any money, but he was evidently on the right lines.

I've been glancing through—it is too boring to read—"James Joyce's World,"[2] and discover that his daughter Lucia was worse than I realised at the time. She was nuts in fact. So was Roy Campbell's daughter Tessa, and though she recovered, both girls (i.e. Roy's daughters) made unhappy marriages, with crooks! And the daughter of my old friend George Gribble also went nuts and tried to stab him! This would leave the door open for us to worry, but I think the fatal combination for a girl is a literary father and a Roman Catholic mother—which happened in all these cases. The schizophrenia is set up by the utter impossibility of reconciling the father's way of life with the mother's.

Now that the burden of the full-length book is lifted and I am able to rest, I am recovering more rapidly than I ever hoped. My arm seems almost well again, and the complete quiet and peace of this place are most healing. I wish you could manage to drop in. I go to bed early, get up late, have only two meals a day, do my shopping and cooking, read, walk a little, drive to Sancerre to post letters and get the view, write as little as possible but a certain amount. Of course I should be most grateful for any work you can give me or get for me. I can do short things fairly quickly. Recently I did a review (about 1,200) for an Australian paper,[3] and an article (3000) for the N.Y. Saturday Review.[4] For these I received about 88,000 francs. Now they took about 6 days, and a full-length biog takes about a year of frightful work and brings about 550,000 francs less the 42 and a half % British tax in full. I am willing to pay a fair amount, but not to be mulcted in that vindictive way, and nuts to the Hellfare State. I am very pleased that I now have a review of about 800 words to do for USA—book not yet arrived—but it should not take more than 2–3 days and will earn me about 16,000 francs at minimum.[5] Surely, surely if I can get such work—articles, reviews, introductions—it is much better than killing myself with books which are not wanted and which give the highbrows another opportunity to be insulting. The RLS book sold about 2500 to Xmas, and another 500 were bound up in January. About half the advance earned! Pah!

Wonderful how literary history is written. You may have heard of a little pre-1914 paper called the Egoist which ran Joyce's Portrait as a serial, and of which I was literary editor until I went to the wars, and then TS Eliot got my job.[6] Well, of course Pound and Eliot gave Patricia Hutchins the dope for her Joyce book, and I find that what I did for the paper is entirely credited to them, mainly to Pound. Now I discovered and published the first poems of Marianne Moore;[7] André Spire was a friend of Frank Flint's and mine, and through the Egoist Press I published some of Spire's war poems at my own expense;[8] and I found and translated some of Lautréamont.[9] All of this is credited to Pound! Not that it matters—who cares? But they are so anxious for their backstairs renown they grab at anything.

The same female is now composing a work called Ezra Pound's Kensington,[10] to which of course I am expected to contribute glowing tributes to the Maitre, who is giving the author "all information and assistance." But when Nehls asked Pound's information and assistance for Nehls's big book on DHLawrence,[11] Ezra replied that "I never read criticism and biographical tosh." Only when they are about him, one surmises! His one communication to Nehls was to the effect that Ezra's friend Ford Hueffer "discovered" and put over DHL. Now, it is true that Jessie Chambers sent some of DHL's early poems and stories to the English Review, and Hueffer rather hesitatingly published them,[12] and got DHL's first novel published with Heinemann.[13] That was something and, as you know, I acknowledged it;[14] but the Pound-Hueffer team were marked "absent" when the Rainbow was prosecuted in 1915, and were never thereafter heard of in DHL's defense, until after his death.

I wonder if "the literary life" need be so petty? Inevitable perhaps, since it interests only about one per cent of even the most literate nations.

Ever yours,
Richard

1. Not published or produced; this was a stage adaptation of *Relative to Murder.*

2. Patricia Hutchins, *James Joyce's World,* London, 1957.

3. Not traced.

4. See RA, "The Gullibility of the British," *Saturday Review,* 18 January 1958, pp. 11–12, 61–62.

5. See RA, "Lorenzo in Chaos," a review on *The Selected Letters of D. H. Lawrence,* ed. and intro. Diane Trilling, *Saturday Review,* 1 March 1958, p. 17.

6. James Joyce, *A Portrait of the Artist as a Young Man,* London, 1916, was serialized in the *Egoist,* 2 February 1914 to 1 September 1915. RA was assistant editor of the *Egoist* from 1 January 1914 to June 1917.

7. See Marianne Moore, "To a Man Working His Way Through a Crowd" and "To the Soul of 'Progress,' " *Egoist,* 1 April 1915, p. 62; see also Norman T. Gates, "Richard Aldington and Marianne Moore," *Marianne Moore Newsletter,* Spring 1977, pp. 16–19.

8. See André Spire, *Poèms*, London, 1916.

9. See Comte de Lautréamont, "The Songs of Maldoror," trans. Richard Aldington, *Egoist*, 1 October 1914, pp. 370–74; 15 October 1914, pp. 385–86; 2 November 1914, pp. 409–410; 16 November 1914, pp. 423–24.

10. Patricia Hutchins, *Ezra Pound's Kensington*, Chicago [1965].

11. Edward Nehls, *D. H. Lawrence: A Composite Biography*, Madison, Wisconsin, 1959.

12. D. H. Lawrence, "A Still Afternoon," *English Review*, November 1909, pp. 561–65; and "Goose Fair," *English Review*, February 1910, pp. 399–408.

13. D. H. Lawrence, *The White Peacock*, London, 1911.

14. See RA, *D. H. Lawrence: Portrait of a Genius, But . . .* , pp. 67–73.

137. To Eric Warman (SIUC)

21 August 1958   Sury.

My dear Eric,

Owing to les vacances exactly eight days passed before I got a reply from Barclays. I enclose herewith the extract or copy of my account, and also a letter in which they speak of the tax business. I shall now have to see the Maire, but as he is usually out trimming his vines for this year or drinking the produce of past years, I shall have to make an appointment. If he can do nothing I will send a registered letter to the Insêcteur des contributions directes at Bourges—to whom I wrote at least six weeks ago. (I like very much my misprint of Insêcteur for Inspecteur).[1]

I don't know how to thank you for your continued help over this affair, and feel I am imposing on your kindness. If I could learn from Mr Lucas[2] what it is the I.R. want it would help. Obviously the French will not sign an English document, and I can't show any tax receipt until I am assessed and pay.

Catha is here, very depressed about something. She hasn't confided in me, so I don't know.

Weather very bad over here, but Alister writes it has been sunny in Paris. According to the wine-growers here the vintage in this region will be even poorer than last year.

Did Alister tell you that friends subscribed to help me out? His friends, the Duttons sent 750 sterling from Adelaide, and French friends also came through. I can live here rent-free, and when alone I easily get by on less than a pound a day. So that I have been able to rest, and feel ever so much better. Of course, it has been very cheering to have Catha and the Ks.[3] here. I only wish I didn't feel so worried about Catha.

Did you ever meet Tom McGreevy? Long ago in my opulent days I put him up when he was broke. Now he is director of the National Gallery of Ireland, and after years of silence wrote to urge me to let him repay— he must have heard the situation—sending 25 quid from time to time. I told him he owes me nothing, that the little I did was from esteem and affection, but that at this time an occasional 25 would be a real help. Such things restore one's belief in human kindness.

All good wishes as always,
Richard

1. To save him money, Warman tried to arrange for RA's income tax obligation to be transferred from England to France.
2. The chartered accountant employed by the publishing companies with which Warman was associated.
3. Kershaws.

138. To Stanley Weintraub* (privately held)

5 November 1958   Sury
Dear Mr. Weintraub,

Your letter has been forwarded to me from London. I think an impartial and scholarly investigation of the relationship between TEL and the Shaws would be most interesting and valuable.[1]

So far as I know, the "Shaw"-Shaw letters[2] are still in the Museum and still available to readers. In fact, since the actual material letters are now the property of the nation, they could only be withdrawn by a special order of the Home Secretary, and *he* would be under fire in the Commons if he tried it! But I suppose the Director of the Library might put it among "reserved books and MSS," though he could not refuse it to a bona fide scholar, especially if you came armed with a Guggenheim scholarship and a recommendation from the cultural attaché at the US Embassy. As a matter of fact, I don't think you'd have any trouble, except that I am told the "Shaw"-Shaw letters are much in demand at the B.M., so you might have to wait.

The legal position, as detailed to me by the attorney who advised on the book, is that the letters cannot be quoted verbatim (I had to paraphrase every quote) without permission of the B.M. and the TELawrence Trustees—who wouldn't give it. BUT, as they are public property, you may read them, give the information as your own view or surmise, and then refer to the Letters with a number, as I did.[3]

I do not think you would get any help from Lawrence's family and friends, unless you promise to support the hero legend, and to ignore all the evidence I collected.

You will find a good deal of information about Lawrence's relations with the Shaws, and the work they did in re-writing Seven Pillars, in Blanche Patch's "30 Years with G.B.S." (Gollancz, 1951). Unfortunately,

TEL destroyed most of Charlotte's letters to him, but I know there are some. GBS said she told L. things about herself she had never told him! In the end, however, she was disillusioned, for Hesketh Pearson in his life of GBS[4] relates that Shaw said he asked Charlotte one day why they never say anything now (early '30s) of Lawrence, and she replied, "Oh, he's such an infernal liar!" Shaw had told him that long before in an unpublished letter to TEL which was quoted in the Manchester Guardian—I have the clipping somewhere.

One of the "Shaw"-Shaw letters cannot be alluded to, as it is extremely libellous about his friends David Garnett and Robert Graves. Another is rather uncomplimentary to Churchill, and there are jeers at Liddell Hart. But a great many of them are concerned with his reading and records of music she sent him.

I think your greatest difficulty would be, as I said above, that unless you approach them as an avowed worshipper at the hero's shrine, you will get no help from the family and "friends."

If you make use of (as you must) "T. E. Lawrence by his Friends" ed. A. W. Lawrence (Cape 1937) you must be careful to use the first edition only. Since the publication of my book, the "Friends" has been re-issued in an expurgated edition.

Have you the "Four Square" paperback edition of my book, issued in 1957, with misprints and slips corrected, and the addition of three first-hand testimonies—from the Australian Major-General Rankin who saw L. in Damascus, from a Foreign Office official Mr. T. F. Breen on the interview with George V, and from Squadron-Commander Breese, RNAF, who was L.'s commanding officer when he was a recruit in the RAF? If you haven't a copy and would like it, I shall be very glad to send it to you.[5]

Yours sincerely,
Richard Aldington

*Stanley Weintraub (b. 1929), as this first of fifteen letters RA wrote him over the next four years indicates, originally addressed RA because of his interest in the relationship between T. E. Lawrence and the Shaws. The result of his research was his study *Private Shaw and Public Shaw* published after RA's death. Because of the severe attacks on his *Lawrence of Arabia*, RA was most anxious to have an impartial, scholarly review of the intricate relationship between the Shaws and T. E. Lawrence. Dr. Weintraub, who was then beginning his distinguished career and would become an authority on Shaw, never met RA. (See also the Annotated Index.)

1. Professor Weintraub was beginning the research that would result in his *Private Shaw and Public Shaw*, New York, 1963.

2. The correspondence between T. E. Lawrence and Mrs. George Bernard (Charlotte Payne-Townshend) Shaw.

3. See, for example, n. 17 to part 1, chapter 2, of *Lawrence of Arabia: A Biographical Enquiry.*

4. *G.B.S.: A Full-Length Portrait*, London, 1942.

5. RA sent this material to Weintraub. The Four Square Book edition *Lawrence of Arabia* ("With added material") was published in London in 1957.

139. To Geoffrey Potocki* (SIUC)

12 March 1959   Sury.

My dear Count,

Many thanks for your interesting letter. I hope the press—what name are you giving it? The Melissa Press?—will soon be at work and that it will make you an income. With your gifts as a writer, your experience and your contacts, this ought not to be difficult. I think personally that a periodical is a mistake from a financial point of view. You can't compete with the commercial "press" which has a complete stranglehold on distribution, and the best-edited periodical gets out of date. The best things, in my opinion, are small books or pamphlets which will remain valuable, and so have a continuing sale. But you know all this better than I.

Half the funds advanced have already come in, and I hope for more soon.[1]

I did not make quite clear the Robert Cecil Convention.[2] With true sneakiness it was put through for the alleged purpose of suppressing "the traffic in obscene books" between the Continent and England. This unquestionably went on, but equally important to these ruffians was to suppress independent writers like Joyce and Lawrence, who by living and publishing abroad were able to defy them. I never knew why they were so violent against DHL—accusing him of military espionage[3] when his ignorance of all things military was ludicrous to any soldier. Anyway, they were. Orioli's offence was in sending out Lady C.[4] Then he was a friend of Douglas, whose Limericks annoyed them.[5] The Gian Gastone was discovered by Douglas and wasn't worth publishing, but it contained "obscene details" about G.G.'s private life, and that was why Douglas made Pino[6] have it translated and published.[7] The Home Office saw their chance, and launched a prosecution under the Convention. Luckily the Italian Court was on Pino's side, and his counsel pleaded that the translation was exact and of a book freely circulating in Italy. How could Pino be said to have broken Italian law? It was up to the Brits to protect themselves if they didn't like it. Judge concurred, but prosecution asked for a comparison of texts, and two professors were named as referees. Now, like an idiot, Douglas had amused himself when drunk by interpolating "words" and phrases which weren't in the original, which of course might have been fatal. Luckily at the second hearing the profs reported that apart from a few phrases the pamphlet was very accurately translated (Acton knew Italian very well) and the case was dismissed. But that Convention still stands, and you must remember that there is now a Catholic govt in power here.[8]

As a British subject permanently domiciled in France you are perfectly entitled to hold accounts in dollars and Swiss francs. Your visa constitutes an "act of emigration" so far as the British are concerned, and you revisit British territory merely as a tourist. If you re-established domicile, you would of course become liable.

Wyndham Lewis was unquestionably at the front, where he served as bombardier in a Field Battery. But he may have been a war artist in later days.[9] I certainly did not intend Upjohn[10] for him, still less for Augustus John whom I never met. You must guess again.

My father and grandfather had a signet ring showing a bend between three billets (I know not what colours or metals as it was engraved in gold), crest a talbot passant-guardant and motto Semper eadem. I never inquired of the Heralds[11] if this is authentic. I rather think not, since the identical shield (without crest or motto) is one of those on the tomb of Sir Richard Alington in the Record Office. I suspect some ancestor of mine lifted it. Alington and Aldington are quite different families. Did not Sir Thomas Wyatt live at Alington castle?[12] Curiously enough my brother found and sent me our father's commission as an officer in the Buffs during the Boer War,[13] where he is officially described as "gentleman." It was issued within ten days of King Edward's accession, and bears his signature but Queen Victoria's seal. My brother as a lawyer thinks this highly scandalous. But they couldn't have the new seals ready waiting for the old lady to croak (suppose she had heard of it!) and equally obviously the royal seals of England cannot be engraved in a day or two. The Great Seal has to be done before the minor ones.

I was never officially gassed, but I was gassed! By which I mean I had it, though not so badly that I couldn't carry on. By chance in early '17 I was on the receiving end of a great German experiment in gas shelling— it comes into Hero somewhere.[14] They put over (so Intelligence told us) somewhere about 30,000 gas shells that night on a small area of which our billets were the center. The officers stopped, drinking, up the line, and I had to bring the company through the barrage, see them billeted, hand over casualties and alert MD and stretcher-bearers, and then go back to fetch the drunken officers! The gas was phosgene, not chlorine. I also got a good bit of tear-gas on and about Hill 70, and even a whiff or two of mustard later on. But of course it is impossible to say that my bronchitis is a result of the gas.

You mention Lowenfels. It is a strange fact that I have known two American poets fairly well—Pound and Lowenfels, one of whom was imprisoned by the yank govt as a fascist and the other as a communist![15]

Apropos tracing origins by speech. Sayce, the Oxford orientalist, was a Welshman, and related that he met at lunch a famous German philologist who said he could usually place a Briton by his speech. "Where am I from?" asked Sayce. "I may be able to tell you later." The talk went on, and suddenly the German interrupted: "You're a Welshman." "How did you know that?" "You said 'truths' and not 'trewths' as the non-Welsh do." Sayce admits he had never noticed it before.

Affectionately yours,
Richard Aldington

---

*Among the two to three hundred recipients of RA's letters, none surely was more unusual than Count Geoffrey Wladislas Vaile Potocki de Montalk (b. 1903), with whom RA corresponded during his last decade. Pretender to the throne of Poland, itinerant printer and publisher, irreconcilable warrior against society's restrictions, Potocki appealed to the rebel and the Rabelaisian in RA. (See also the Annotated Index.)

1. RA had solicited money from his friends and contributed himself to help Potocki buy a printing press.

2. An international convention for suppression of the circulation of and traffic in obscene publications.

3. In October 1917 D. H. Lawrence was forced by military order to leave Cornwall on suspicion of spying for the Germans.

4. Orioli published and filled mail orders for Lawrence's *Lady Chatterley's Lover,* Florence, 1928.

5. See Norman Douglas, *Some Limericks . . .* , [Florence], 1928.

6. Orioli.

7. *Vita di Gio. Gastone I Settimo ed ultimo Granduca della R. Casa de'Medici, con la lista dei provvisionati di Camera, dal volgo detti i Ruspanti, 1886,* trans. Harold Acton, intro. Norman Douglas, Florence, 1930.

8. The Union pour la Nouvelle République (U.N.R.), a right-wing party led by Michel Debré, won 188 seats in the National Assembly in November 1958.

9. Lewis enlisted in the Royal Artillery in 1915; in 1917, with Augustus John, he became a war artist attached to Canadian Corps Headquarters.

10. Upjohn, a character in *Death of a Hero,* New York, 1929, is generally considered a satiric portrayal of Ezra Pound.

11. Heralds' College, a royal corporation in England.

12. Sir Thomas Wyatt's father bought Allington Castle near Maidenstone, Kent, in about 1493.

13. See Letter 140.

14. See *Death of a Hero,* pp. 327–30.

15. For the Pound story, see E. Fuller Torrey, "The Protection of Ezra Pound," *Psychology Today,* November 1981, pp. 57–62, 64–66. Lowenfels was imprisoned during the McCarthy era.

140. To Geoffrey Potocki (SIUC)

1 April 1959   Sury.
My dear Count,

Slips between cups and lips. . . . The man who was to bring the balance of the press money from England at Easter had to cancel his trip. After some drums and tramplings I have arranged for it to be collected and brought to France by the English wife of a friend of mine who is visiting her home this month, and has promised to bring the money in on her "quota." Until I get it I don't know how much it is; but I'll send as soon as possible.

What an absurd state of affairs where we cannot own or transmit our own money.

I know nothing about the Fortune Press[1] except that I've heard its name. I have never seen any book of theirs.

I am surprised you don't know Francis Carco. His reputation has gone now, but he was a sort of pre-Cocteauish Paris character circa 1914–30. His full name was Carcopino, and he was brother to the Carcopino, now in the Académie, at one time Minister (of Education?) to Pétain. K. Mansfield took him off to slow music, and at the same time took a backhanded swipe at Middleton Murry. I'm afraid she was a bit of a whore. But warum nicht?

Did you know that Ezra Pound "translated" that charming Charles d'Orléans rondeau, and began "God who mad'st her well regard her." This sort of thing is handed around "with bated breath" for admiration. But your friend is wrong too. It is "bon" and not "bonne"; and the meaning is "God! how good it is to see her." I consulted the Sorbonne on this before issuing my own version in Fifty Romance Lyric Poems.[2]

Curious about the penis mightier than the sword. About 1925 my mother bought a hotel at St Margarets Bay which was built circa 1890. One of the rooms, intended as library and writing room, had stained glass windows. And I noticed that the "artist" had in error made the tag THE PENIS MIGHTIER THAN THE SWORD, on a would-be heraldic design!

Your programme of printing sounds good, and I am more than ever annoyed by this delay in transmitting. I am trying to raise more, but my main, indeed sole helper has been sent on a mission to Rome, and won't be back for at least 3 weeks.[3] You are right to concentrate on unpublished work to start with. The Duke of Bedford's letters[4] should indeed cause a sensation. As you have the present duke's permission to publish, all is well. Would you be able to manage a one-page reproduction in facsimile with the Duke's handwriting? This is to shut up the otherwise inevitable squeal that they are "not authentic."

Apropos that I have been reading the Casement Diaries, recently issued in Paris.[5] The Irish-American assertion that they are "forged" is untenable. There was not time to produce them in the interval between his arrest and trial, and they are far too detailed to be invented. That Casement was a really filthy bugger is not to be doubted. Curious what buggers the Irish are—Wilde, Casement, T. E. Lawrence—and such exhibitionists.

I haven't seen my grandfather's seal ring for thirty years—I gave it to my brother. I think the bend is engrailed, now you mention it, but there were certainly only three billets. From hazy memory I should say the field was argent and the bend sable, the billets gules; but I am far from sure, at this distance of time. I think an Alington-Aldington marriage improbable, the Alingtons being Kentish gentry and the Aldingtons Worchestershire yeomanry. However, my brother lately discovered our father's commission as an officer in the East Kent Regiment (the Buffs, 3rd Foot) during the Boer War. This describes him as "Gentleman," which as it is signed by Edward VII is I suppose sufficient warrant. The commission was granted in the first days of King Edward's reign and the seal is still Queen Victoria's. According to my brother this makes the whole document invalid.

Affectionately,

Richard Aldington

P.S. According to Sydney Bulletin of 18th and 25th Feb just in, the economic situation in N.Z. is disturbing, owing to the usual "democratic" abuses—continual increase of trade union wages and hence rise in cost of living and of production, decline of exports, rigid govt "control" of imports with consequent rise of prices of imported goods, constant decline of savings accounts.

1. Reginald Ashley Caton (1897–1971) founded a small publishing firm called the Fortune Press, which he ran single-handed from 1924 to 1969.

2. The line in d'Orléans "Chanson" is "Dieu, qu'il fait bon regarder / La gracieuse, bonne et belle!" which RA renders "God! good it is to see her, so gracious / Good and fair." See RA, *Fifty Romance Lyric Poems*, New York, 1928, pp. 84–85.

3. Alister Kershaw had been sent to Rome by UNESCO.

4. Not listed among the publications of the Melissa Press.

5. Sir Roger Casement, *The Black Diaries*, Paris, 1959.

141. To Geoffrey Potocki (SIUC)

8 March 1960   Sury.

Dear Geoffrey,

It occurred to me that the Queen's Majesty might create HIM Viscount Mellors and HER Duchess of Chatterley, with Oliver Messel as lady-in-waiting. The funeral baked meats will do duty at the wedding, and of course there will be a command performance of the Merry Wives of Battenberg.[1]

Yes, prince Charles was created Prince of Wales about two years ago. I have never understood why the Heir Apparent is born Duke of Rothsay, but must be created Prince of Wales.

I can't answer your query about the judges and the ribbons of Orders, but I'll ask my lawyer brother.[2] I should have supposed that like all servants of the Crown they would always wear the insignia of honours at Levees and Drawing Rooms.

According to my bibliographer there was an American edition of Balls, privately printed, and so far as I recollect pirated, for I never saw a copy, and never knew it existed until the Library of Congress reported it.[3]

The payment from Moscow is not due to any cleverness on my part, for I did nothing but answer civilly one or two letters from Sojuz Pisatelej,[4] as *they* transcribe it. On my 65th birthday I received two long official telegrams of congratulation from Moscow—the more remarkable since nobody else took the slightest notice—even my daughter forgot. The payment was quite spontaneous and unexpected. They transliterate my name as Oldington—not that I give a damn. The 3rd volume of the new Russian History of English Literature has a good deal about me, running to 40 pages or so.[5] It was translated for me by a White Russian in Paris, but it was so boring I couldn't read it, and I seem to have lost it. Have "just" found it! There is also the translation of Mrs Zhantieva's introduction to the English edition they did of Hero.[6] Yesterday I received a letter in Russian which I have sent to Paris. It seems, as far as I could judge, merely to be an official statement that they have published this large edition of All Men,[7] and that they intend to issue a new translation of Hero about Dec 1960 or early in 1961.[8] All this I knew some time back from the letters of Mr Urnov, who also sent me two copies of the All Men in Russian, from which I got the printing number of 225,000.

My own view is that, as you say, they perfectly well know I am not a Left-wing writer, but I think they dislike parlor pinks much more than Tories. Further, I believe that neither the Writers nor the public is so "sold" on communist art as the Party wants. The stuff published in their review Soviet Literature is more boring than Sunday School fiction. The only readable books they get come from abroad. The Writers Union[9] gets me past the Comrades by passing me off as a chief critic of bourgeoise decadence, who may some day be converted to the one true faith. All Men is a most uncompromising plea for individualism and individual liberty, and I hope I don't flatter myself when I see its immense success in Russia as indicating they too would like to be free. Also, there is in the book a lot about the charm of country England, Paris, Rome, an imaginary Mediterranean island, and so forth. The Russian aristocracy used to be great travellers, and I think the new "aristocracy" of bureaucrats, officials, party members etc would like to travel also. Note the large cortège coming here with Mr. K.[10]

All this would be more interesting to us both if I had had the Bank's notice of those 5,800,000 francs![11] Alas, only silence.

Don't you think that perhaps some of the otherwise unaccountable poetic genius of England may come from the "submerged Celts"? Apropos which, somewhere or other I have a very ridiculous German book about me written by a young Nazi who, in accordance with their psychological theories, explained me as a "Typus C," given to hallucinations, and therefore a submerged Celt.[12] As I am such a Teutonic English "typus" that I am always addressed first in German in Italy, I feel the young man was rather off the target. More interesting is the fact that Shelley's mother was descended from the younger brother of Sir Philip Sidney. What is the evidence for the story of Shelley being knocked down in Lyon? I have White's two-vol Life, which is a monument of careful scholarship and completeness, and he says nothing about it. Neither do Shelley's Letters nor Claire's Journal.[13] Some mistake here perhaps?

I am pleased with the two cuttings about you,[14] and should have liked to keep them to show. But in my disorder of papers such things are easily lost, so I return them now to avoid that misfortune. I feel sure the Melissa Press is a good idea, and that if you keep quietly on producing your own work and perhaps one or two friends, you will gradually be acknowledged.

Catha's left-wing mama is my second wife, née McCulloch. She does dreadful commercial things in London, and now boasts of having been elected a member of the "Market Research Society," whatever that may be—some scheme for robbing the public I warrant you. Did you note that in early Jan "sixteen famous American economists" predicted that 1960 would be the greatest "boom" year America ever had? Well, last Thursday Wall Street stocks and shares lost five "billion" dollars in a day, and as you can see from even the French newspapers (the most ignorant of economics in any language I know) the Bourses of the world are reeling under the blow. It is serious because in their desperation the American capitalists will always start a war to clear up their financial difficulties, and they are so ignorant they don't realise either the destructive power of nuclear fission weapons or the advance which Russia now has on them. If the USSR can shoot a missile to the moon it can shoot deadly rockets to any part of the world.[15] There will have to be peace, but it will be a Slav and not a Yankosachen peace.

Ever affectionately
Richard

1. Before marriage to Princess Margaret, Anthony Armstrong-Jones was made earl of Snowdon; in 1917 the English members of the house of Battenberg renounced their German title. RA satirizes the events by allusions to Lawrence's *Lady Chatterley's Lover* and Shakespeare's *Merry Wives of Windsor;* Oliver Messel, British designer and artist, received decorations for Royal Command Performances in 1950 and 1954.
2. P.A.G. ("Tony") Aldington.
3. RA, *Balls and Another Book for Suppression,* London, 1930; *Balls,* Westport, Connecticut, 1932; Potocki's Melissa Press reprinted this in 1962.
4. The Writers' Union.
5. See *Istoriia angliiskoi literatury,* vol. 3, ed. I. I. Asisimov, A. E. Elistratora, D. G. Zhantieva, and Iu. M. Kondrat'ev, Moskva, 1958, chapter 14, pp. 608–22.
6. See Diliara Zhantieva's preface to (Predisloviye) *Death of a Hero,* Moscow, 1958, pp. 3–16.
7. See RA, *All Men Are Enemies. A Novel,* Moscow, 1959.
8. See RA, *Death of a Hero,* Moscow, 1961.
9. The Soviet Writers' Union was intended to represent and defend interests of authors and to ensure their ideological and political conformity.
10. In May 1960 Khrushchev took part in the unsuccessful Paris "summit" meeting.
11. Royalties from the Russian publishers.
12. See Erich Wellner, *Das Dichterische Schaffen Richard Aldingtons,* Würzburg, 1939.
13. The *Journals of Claire Clairmont,* Cambridge, Mass., 1963, were published after RA's death but earlier were widely quoted in works on Shelley; *The Letters of Percy Bysshe Shelley,* coll. and ed. Roger Ingpen, London, 1909; Newman I. White, *Shelley,* New York, 1940.
14. Not traced.
15. Lunik, launched 12 September 1959, was the first spacecraft to land on the moon.

142. To Harry T. Moore* (SIUC)

5 May 1960   Sury.
Dear Harry,

I'd hate to think that fat Fordie had been so goddam mean as to put in an unfavourable official report on the civisme of Lorenzo and Frieda.[1] If he did, what a bastard. Of course, he needed the whitewash himself—he looked as much a Hun as Hindenburg[2]—and, it is true, that pre-war he was friends with the Minister of Education, C.F.G. Masterman. (My belief is that Masterman was dropped from the Cabinet when the coalition was formed in 1915.)[3] I was Ford's secretary while he was writing or dictating that anti-German book, When Blood Is Their Argument, and

I'm pretty sure Masterman got him the job from the Foreign office. I got so fed up with Ford I quit, and Alec Randall took over, finished the second book (I had begun with F.) and got the job at the F.O. I should have had. What a mercy—Alex became an ambassador and a K.C.M.G.![4]

I read Ford's tale about going to Greatham,[5] and disbelieved it before you debunked it so completely. He is a fearful liar. I wonder if you went down with someone from the U.S. Embassy whether Scotland Yard might not now let you know who denounced DHL. Thesigner and Squire boasted—bastards—about acting as common informers over the pictures.[6] I still incline to think that the association with Russell must have been reported.[7] That No Conscription Fellowship (?) was linked up with E. D. Morel and the Revolutionary Committee for Democratic Control—democratic here meaning "extreme socialist."[8] I doubt if DHL knew it. Certainly Morel and all that 1917 Club lot (which included such odd persons as Ramsey MacDonald and Douglas Goldring) would have revolted him if he had met them. I knew Goldring fairly well, and he was Left enough to be called a fellow-traveller. He bolted to Ireland to dodge the draft. Notice how he wanted DHL for his Peoples Theatre, or whatever he called it.[9] My own belief is that L. was so completely self-centered that he didn't realize what these other people were up to.

Has any unpublished letter turned up confirming the L-F row on the quay at N.Y. in 1923? I think in any case that Catherine Carswell's evidence holds good.[10] It is true she is careless and makes libellous statements about Murry and other enemies, but remember she saw Frieda almost immediately after Frieda landed in London; and it wouldn't be Frieda if she hadn't blabbed everything. That used to madden him. Another thing she never would learn was to refrain from speaking of Weekley as "Ernst, my husband"! She was still doing it in 1928, and of course it infuriated Lawrence. She even went so far at Port Cros[11] as to give us in L's presence an extremely frank and realistic account of her wedding-night with Weekley. Well, well. Those were the days.

You are certainly overworked, and I do hope you can get everything cleared before you leave. The introduction to the enlarged Letters may be difficult, simply from the difficulty of condensing so much new information about so complex a character.[12]

Thanks for your note on Kay Boyle for whom I have always fanned.

Don't bother to take time to answer this. I'll look for you on the 13th of July—just wire me from Paris. I think you can make reservation for Cosne-Sur-Loire (there is another Cosne) from Am. Expr. in London, and that should be time enough. Don't let the A.E. clerk shirk his job and tell you reservation isn't necessary. The crush on trains at that period is terrible. Last week-end included the European Labour Day, and my daughter couldn't get a seat on the Friday night train.

Keep yer pecker up!

All good wishes,

Richard

What a ghastly photo of H.D. Grove should be plunged in boiling oil. She was very beautiful as a young woman, and the book is about H.D. at 30, not H.D. at 70.[13]

Nice letter from Sternberg, saying the copies of Mistral are on the way to my agent in London.[14]

Nude Erections (as Ezra calls them) are re-issuing the pocketbook of my translation of Laclos.[15] The fools dropped the introduction which contains the only authentic and documented biographical essay on Laclos in English. But the highbrow legend is that I am merely a translator. Much I care, purring this morning over a *very* nice check from Moscow for royalties on that 225,000 edition of All Men.[16]

---

*Harry T. Moore (1908–81), was professor of English and a research professor at Southern Illinois University. Among his best known works are *The Intelligent Heart: The Story of D. H. Lawrence* (1954) and *The Collected Letters of D. H. Lawrence* (1962). A few weeks before his death, Moore and Ian MacNiven's edition of the correspondence between Lawrence Durrell and RA appeared under the title *Literary Lifelines*. Moore met RA in 1958 in connection with Moore's interest in D. H. Lawrence and especially the *Collected Letters* that Moore was editing. Their extensive correspondence (fifty-seven letters) continued until Aldington's death. A remembrance of their friendship was published in *Richard Aldington: An Intimate Portrait* (1965). Moore was instrumental in obtaining the extensive Aldington collection of books and manuscripts that is described in my "Richard Aldington Collection at Morris Library," *ICarbS*, Summer–Fall 1976. Moore also helped to make possible the publication by Southern Illinois Press of RA's *Introduction to Mistral* (1960), and *Soft Answers* (1965); *An Intimate Portrait* was also published by SIU Press. (See also the Annotated Index.)

1. Some of Lawrence's friends believed that Ford in 1915 had written a bad report about the Lawrences, which was in the files throughout the war.

2. Ford's father came from Germany to England in 1869.

3. Asquith announced the Coalition government 26 May 1915; Masterman remained with the government as director of Wellington House (propaganda department), 1914–18.

4. Knight Commander of the Order of St. Michael and St. George facetiously translated by Britons as "Kindly Call Me God."

5. Greatham, Pulborough, Sussex, the cottage lent to the Lawrences by Viola Meynell in 1915.

6. On 5 July 1929 the police seized thirteen of Lawrence's paintings from the Warren Gallery in London.

7. Russell took an active part in the No Conscription fellowship. He was fined and sentenced to prison for his pacifist views.

8. The Union of Democratic Control was set up by remnants of those who had opposed entry into the way; their aim was to prevent a repetition of the diplomatic errors or crimes

that, in their opinion, caused the war. E. D. Morel was secretary and Ramsey MacDonald was the outstanding politician of the group, which RA refers to as "that 1917 Club lot."

9. In 1919, just before he left England, Lawrence was corresponding with Goldring about the proposed production of his play, *Touch and Go*.

10. Frieda Lawrence sailed from New York for England 18 August 1923. Lawrence accompanied her to the ship where she appealed to him to stay aboard and go with her then rather than later as he had planned to do. Lawrence refused and they had what Catherine Carswell called "perhaps the very worst" quarrel of their lives.

11. Where the Lawrences visited RA. See Letters 46 and 47.

12. *The Collected Letters of D. H. Lawrence*, ed. Harry T. Moore, London, 1962.

13. *Bid Me to Live*, New York, 1960.

14. *Introduction to Mistral*, Carbondale, Ill., 1960.

15. Choderlos de Laclos, *Dangerous Acquaintances (Les Liaisons dangereuses)*, trans. Richard Aldington, first published London [1924].

16. *All Men Are Enemies*. See Letter 141.

143. To Tony Aldington* (SIUC)

30 May 1960   Sury.

My dear Tony,

What next? Did you not know that I had the misery of being old Ford's secretary, and had to take down in longhand the whole of that tedious Good Soldier,[1] drawled and snuffled through his adenoids as he slopped around the room in carpet slippers? I also happened to know the dame[2] who caused the "passion as strong as death," whose "visceral intensity" lasted about six months, until our fat friend picked up someone else—an Australian called Stella,[3] I think. My secretarial duties included the job of taking the frantically jealous Violet Hunt for walks in Kensington Gardens, while she went over and over and over the symptoms and troubles of this fiery Lothario's passion, varied with such coy remarks as: "It was here that I used to meet Andrew Lang by permission of his wife." Meanwhile, at nights Lothario would play and sing, adenoids permitting, what he claimed was his own setting of Heine's Lehn deine wang auf meine wang.[4] The nobility of Edward Ashburnham's[5] character made a poor impression on me, since there is every indication that Ford considered it a life-like portrait of himself—a view which I didn't share. It struck me as being as unfounded as the Hero's descent from a Sussex family of fabulous antiquity, when I knew that Ford's pop was a boche named Franz Hüffer who came to England to write an article about Wagner.[6] Pre-August 1914 Ford himself used to mutter pretentiously: "When I was Einjahrige in the Bonn Hussaren" which abruptly changed to the old Sussex family in August, 14, when he was hastily naturalised English through the influence of C.F.G. Masterman, M.P. After the war, in which Ford was a second loot in the Welsh—sent down the line by old General Hunter-Bunter of the 8th Corps (in which I too served)[7] who saw poor old Ford sitting lugubriously on the fire-step looking the picture of misery, and gave the order: "Send that feller down the line at once—he's depressin' the troops"—after this heroic service (from which FMH modestly extracted 4 war novels)[8] Douglas Goldring met him in Paris in a little group of American hangers-on, and to his bliss heard Ford snuffle out the opening of some braggart anecdote in the old familiar style: "When I was a Major in the Grenadier Guards."

What do you want me to say to your deluded mate in Kansas? Write it out, I'll copy and sign. But don't ask me to read or praise sincerely his silly crap.

Love to you all,
Richard

The assertion that this tripe was originally the Saddest Story, changed to The Good Soldier by an unworthy publisher[9] is just one more of Ford's innumerable bunk-hos. It was called The Good Soldier from the start.[10]

*Letters to his younger brother P.A.G. Aldington (1910–80), who followed their father in the profession of law, are mostly about family and legal matters. During his last years, RA was worried about the future of his daughter Catherine, the monies due the Patmores following the 1938 legal agreement, and his own tax situation. About all these he corresponded with Tony, his brother and legal advisor—he also wrote, with his usual candor, about the cost of his own funeral. (See also the Annotated Index.)

1. Ford Madox Ford, *The Good Soldier*, London, 1915.
2. Not identified.
3. Stella Bowen, to whom Ford dedicated *The Good Soldier*, New York, 1927 edition.
4. See Heinrich Heine, "Lehn' Deine Wang' An Meine Wang'," in *Poems of Heinrich Heine*, trans. Louis Untermeyer, New York, 1957, p. 41.
5. The title character of *The Good Soldier*, whom critics do not consider a self-portrait by Ford.
6. Franz Carl Christoph Johannes Hüffer who became Francis Hueffer.
7. Lieutenant-General Sir Aylmer G. Hunter-Weston commanded the 8th Corps of the B.E.F.; RA's unit, the Pioneers, was a part of the 8th Corps.
8. Ford Madox Ford, *Some Do Not*, London, 1924; *No More Parades*, London, 1925; *A Man Could Stand Up*, London, 1926; and *Last Post*, London, 1928.
9. See Ford's "Dedicatory Letter," in *The Good Soldier*, New York, 1927, pp. xx–xxi.
10. RA is wrong here; he should have remembered that Ford's novel was called *The Saddest Story* when early chapters appeared in the first issue of *Blast*, which RA reviewed in the *Egoist*, 15 July 1914.

144. To Alison Palmer (Temple)

7 November 1960   Sury.

Dear Mrs Palmer,

Your kind letter of the 25th Oct. reached me at Aix-en-Provence, where (and in the Camargue) I spent three weeks with my daughter. She is now regularly attending lectures at the University—though some for-malities of registration have yet to be accomplished. Bureaucracy gone mad! There are so many students at Aix that for the time being she has a room in a small hotel, kept by one of the modern Provençal poets and his wife,[1] who have promised her one of the flats in a house which they are converting. This is promised by the builder for the 15th Nov, but we all know what the modern "working man" is with his loafing, his exi-gencies, and his lack of honour and any pride in his work. So she'll be lucky to get in by Xmas, I expect. Still, it is satisfactory, and I hope to go back before so long. Unluckily, living in a hotel for two of us, and eating at restaurants, is very expensive (for us) even out of season.

I forwarded the DHL Catalogue[2] to a friend in Paris[3] who is a DHL admirer, and hope to show it to others on the Continent. It was most kind of you to send it. The Lady C. verdict[4] now leaves the book vindi-cated in most places except Scotland, Canada, Australia, and N. Zealand. It is being re-issued in French and German, and is constantly in print in Italian and several other languages.

The verdict is important, not because Lady C. is by any means the best of DHL's work, for it is open to objections, but because the art-hating puritanical British public and their representatives chose to make it a test case. To their amazement they have been defeated; Lawrence has been justified as a great writer (which the anti–Lady C. people always de-nied), and it is a useful precedent for the freedom of other writers. As a matter of fact, the fuss is really artificial, and founded almost entirely on the three or four so-called "obscene" words;[5] for much more ardent love-scenes in other books have escaped, simply because the words are not used. Are they so important? Lately, but while the book was still on trial, I had a visit from a very cultivated Englishwoman and her husband.[6] She said that she thought the prosecution hypocritical, since the book contains little that most adult women have not done and had said to them in different terms. She thought it absurd that a married woman already at her second or third lover not know or pretend not to know the meaning of the word "cunt." I said that I thought that partic-ular scene might be a memory of DHL with his German wife,[7] who would have known the German equivalent but not the English,[8] since Weekley was a terrible puritan and most fussy philologist! My own feel-ing is that some of the scenes—intimate—fringe the ridiculous, as when he sticks flowers in her pubic hair!

We still continue to have rain in France, even in the Midi, though there were some brilliantly sunny days. You may judge of the violence of the storms and floodings by this. The Saintes Maries de la Mer (near which my daughter has her Mas) is close to the mouth of the Petit Rhône. One can see along the sands for a couple of miles at least, and as far as we could see they were littered with uprooted trees, brought down by the flooding Durance and Rhône, and then thrown up on the beach by the violent gales blowing off the Mediterranean. People were out with saws and axes cutting them up to dry for fire-wood.

I drove back by Route 7, up the Rhône valley, which has been terribly desecrated by the industrialists since the setting up of the huge hydro-electrical plant near Donzère and Montdragon. Where, even 10 years ago, were age-old villages, and olive-groves, vineyards, cypresses, are now factories, dreadful prison-pens 14 stories high for machine-slaves, gas stations, snack bars, hideous new shops, and quantities of billboards which are forbidden by French law, but the plutocrats are able to defy the law. One of the worst culprits is the government-owned Renault motor-car firm!

I stopped on the way back at Macon, which used to be such a pleasant old town. Part of it is left, but the whole place is spoiled by new factories and tenements and an imported industrial population quite alien to the real inhabitants. Fortunately the hotel is still good. I had a comfortable room, a light but very well-cooked dinner, and a ½ bottle of Moulin à Vent, which grows near Macon. But they would not hesitate to scrap even a great vineyard like that for some hideous factory producing unnecessary articles which have to be got rid of by high-pressure salesmanship and advertising. None of the real vintage French wines ever advertises. There is no need, the supply is limited, and demand always exceeds supply.

I am glad to say that I am still getting better after the depressive years, and feel more active. Now that I am here alone I am able to keep to a rigorous diet, and though wine is not forbidden I am taking my annual month of complete abstinence. I have a horror of its becoming a habit and getting the better of me, which is why I gave up smoking 20 years ago.

Let us hope the winter may not be as severe as seems likely, either in Europe or America.

With all good wishes,

Yours sincerely,
Richard Aldington

1. Not identified.

2. *D.H. Lawrence after Thirty Years (1930–1960)*, catalogue edited by Vivian de Sola Pinto, of an exhibition at the University of Nottingham, 17 June–30 July 1960.

3. Probably Alister Kershaw.

4. On 16 August 1960, Sir Alan Lane, managing director of Penguin Books, issued an authorized, unexpurgated *Lady Chatterley's Lover* in twelve copies. These were handed at

once to the police. The question of the book's obscenity became a test case of England's new law in respect to obscenity, effective the previous year. On 2 November, after six days of testimony, the court declared the book not obscene, and on 10 November 1960 Lane was allowed to release the book to the public.

5. RA is wrong here because the "fuss" was based on much more than three or four obscene words. RA, before the novel appeared, tried to persuade Lawrence to cut one of the love scenes that he thought added nothing to the novel and could hurt Lawrence's reputation.

6. Not identified.

7. Frieda, daughter of Baron Friedrich von Richthofen.

8. Since the German equivalent is *Kunte,* this is unlikely.

145. To Tony Aldington (SIUC)

3 October 1961
Hotel de Sévigné,
Rue des Bernadines,
Aix-en-Provence,
B. du R., France.

My dear Tony,

H.D. died on Weds 27 Sept. Since you don't mention it in your letter of the 28th I infer that you missed the obituaries. As you know, she had been seriously ill since June, and the outcome was only a matter of sooner or later. She was at the Spital Roten Kreuz in Zürich, being visited by friends of course. When Catha and I were in Zürich on the 12th–14th, C. was allowed to see her, but the MD thought it might upset her to see me. On Tuesday the 26th, just a week ago, she received from USA a copy of her latest book of poetry,[1] and seemed interested and pleased. Next day the nurse went down to get her evening meal, and on her return found Hilda unconscious. She was given oxygen, but it was too late. Yesterday, Monday 2nd Oct, her body was cremated. It is to be flown to USA and placed by the side of her parents in Bethlehem Pa. Later, a memorial service will be held in USA.

Although I had been prepared for it, the news is rather a shock. And then she had been extremely kind to Catha and me.

I left the Saintes[2] a day ahead of schedule. The summer broke with a fierce gale off the Mediterranean. The Brise hotel is on the beach, the window-frames and mosquito screens had been warped by the intense heat, so that the wind squawked and howled through my room all night—not to mention the sea. I spent Saturday night in the quiet of Maussane after an excellent lunch with Catha, who returned to her place in the Saintes, and picked me up on Sunday en route to Aix. Arrived here to find the news as detailed above.

Regatta or rather regata is given as of Venetian origin in the Dizionario Scolastico, which is supposed to be accurate. It gives foreign origin of other words, e.g. abate from Latin abbas and Syriac abba. I daresay the O.E.D. would confirm.[3]

How long is it since you had any accounts from Heinemann? They are usually due every six months, three months after the 31st Dec. and 30th June. This might be the moment to ask for them to date—oleaginously of course. We can then find out if they claim the Luxmb[4] is still in print, and you might check on this by ordering a copy through a local bookseller. If it is out of print, we can invoke the clause. If not, I must get around it. I hold USA rights and world market, so if CAP[5] wants to include LXMB I'll tell him he can't have Brit rights. Bloody Stanley Unwin has a lien on many of the earlier poems, but has always been reasonable. Incidentally, in my last accounts was the staggering sum of 3/4 from the Trustees and Guardians of Shakespeare's Birthplace, Stratford-on-Avon, for the use of poem At a Gate by the Way.[6] 3/4 for a poem of 50 lines seems a bit mean even from old Bill. Still more encouraging—some "educational firm" asked Mrs. C.[7] for anthology rights in 3 of my poems, plus 500 records of the book at 5/0 each. They offered 1/2d a minute for the record! The real contempt for poetry in G.B. is thus illustrated. If you win a football pool gamble you are rewarded up to 120,000 quid. By their deeds ye shall know them.

I heard from Molly[8] from Oviedo. She seems to have liked her visit, but for some reason disliked travelling by plane. I suppose she went BOAC, which is held by experts to be about the worst air-line in existence. I'm all for Alitalia and Air France myself.

I think it best to wait to see what CAP has in mind, though I think he wants to co-operate. My own idea is to issue an American Selected Poems (with or without Lxmb) and try to get the right to sell the book in the ex-Empire but without issuing a British edition. Idea is to get sales without exposure to the London reviewers, and without the Ps.[9] getting after the book. CAP tentatively suggests lunch here (Aix) on the 17th, and I'll let you know what happens.

Catha does not start her course at the Faculty here until later in the month, and she thought she might as well be in Saintes until she has to be here.[10] I expect the children are now sighing heavily as they shoulder the white man's burden of school. It is largely a superstition but indispensable.

Both French and Italian papers say the vintage this year is among the greatest (in quality) of the century, but deficient in quantity. This is some compensation for the incredible imbecilities of public life in these times.

Love to you all,
Richard

1. H.D., *Helen in Egypt*, New York, 1961.
2. Les Saintes Maries de la Mer, where Catherine Aldington would one day have a summer home.
3. It does.
4. RA, *A Dream in the Luxembourg*, London, 1930.
5. Charles A. Pearce of the American publishing firm of Duell, Sloan & Pearce. See Letter 147.
6. See RA, *The Complete Poems of Richard Aldington*, London, 1948, pp. 163–64. How the poem was used was not traced.
7. Rosica Colin, RA's London literary agent.
8. RA's sister Margery Lyon Gilbert.
9. The Patmores.
10. Catherine Aldington matriculated at Aix University 15 October 1960.

146. To Alison Palmer (Temple)

16 October 1961   Aix-en-Provence.
Dear Mrs. Palmer,

You will see I am now in the Midi, in a students' hotel, but in a quiet room looking over a courtyard with trees and shrubs and vines ("creepers" as the English call them) beginning to turn red. My daughter has a room in an old house over near the Musée Granet and convenient for the University. The course starts next Monday, but until then she is in the Camargue, with the horses and bulls and flamingos and innumerable water-fowl, not to mention the cowboys. I hope to be here for some time, so please write here until further notice.

I have had rather a tiring six or seven weeks. On the 4th Sept. at Sury I had the visit of relatives of mine whom I had never seen.[1] They were most pleasant and adaptable but three extra people in a tiny cottage were rather a strain. On the 11th Catherine arrived and we started off together for Zürich by car to see H.D. (my first wife from whom I was divorced in 1936)[2] who was in the Roten Kreuz Spital. At the last moment the two specialists thought I should not see her, and Catherine, who was allowed in for a few minutes, reported "Hilda looks very sick." As there was nothing we could do we returned to Sury (for books etc.) and I returned with C. to the Camargue which was very hot and where I picked up a rather bad attack of gastric 'flu. On arrival here I was still further depressed to find telegrams and letters saying that H.D. had died. It was more of a shock and grief than I had expected, and I have been going quietly and refusing invitations. Tomorrow, however, I must see an American publisher[3] for lunch—after years they are beginning to come round again!—and an old friend has just telephoned from Cap Ferrat asking me to dine with him, and I mustn't offend him.[4] I could wish they were not on the same day, as such meetings are now very tiring.

Thank you for sending me the Folio folder. They ought to do well with the Laclos, which never had a proper run partly because of bad presentation by the original publisher, partly because the public was not ready for it.[5] They are using my original introduction (foolishly omitted by the Americans) revised and cut a little by me, with information essential to anyone who wishes really to understand the book, its genesis, its milieu, and its small part as a herald of the first French Revolution. The smart alec critics have always dismissed it as "French obscenity," and I see the Folio blurb-writer snickers at it as "essentially Gallic" in the British way. In fact it was a century ahead of its time, and is a cold if virulent analysis of characters who use their sex for hatred and destruction instead of for love and creation, and of their victims. I hope the illustrations will not be too bad. These contemporary "editors" who write the blurbs and advertisements for publishers are equally distinguished by ignorance, carelessness and conceit. Boccaccio, it is true, was a predecessor (with Petrarch) of the Renaissance, but he is a late mediaeval writer. And Folio I am told (for I haven't yet seen the book) illustrated the Decameron[6] with reproductions of paintings from the late Quattrocentro and Cinquecento—rather as if one illustrated Shakespeare from van Dyke, Rubens and Lely or even Watteau. Then the blurb-writer for the Elek pocket-book[7] called Boccaccio "sophisticated," a meaningless word anyhow, and Boccaccio was eminently natural, with the frank acceptance of life before the Reformation made people self-conscious and hypocritical. I tremble to think of what the blurb-writer may do in America for that book. I am now trying to insert in reprint agreements a clause saying all publicity and blurbs must be submitted to me, but of course they'll simply confront me with faits accomplis, and plead "lack of time." These publishers to-day are ignorant men selling print and paper by "business" methods, knowing and caring little about literature and its values. They doubtless think of Boccaccio as an old-fashioned Henry Miller.

The same applies to Nutting, who is merely "selling" the romantic Foreign Office propaganda about TEL, without any real research.[8] And without integrity. He over-did it in that S. Times sneer at me, for of course that letter to Mrs GBS exists,[9] and it is shameful to write about TEL without having taken note of that essential file of letters.[10] I didn't see the S.T. or the letter of reply,[11] but I heard about it from Dr. Stanley Weintraub of Philadelphia who is completing a thesis on Shaw-Lawrence and their relations,[12] and happened to be in England. He also wrote a letter to the S.T. saying he had just been re-reading the original, defending me and denouncing Nutting, but of course they didn't publish his letter. But the squalid little episode has had one small result Nutting didn't foresee. My friend Kershaw went down to Smith's Paris shop to get a copy of the paperback of my TEL book, and was told they were awaiting fresh copies from England—in the previous week they had sold over 50. What I fear is that pressure (with money compensation) will be forced on Four Square Co.[13] to cease reprinting the book. American publishers won't even read it, though the English paperback is now approaching 40,000. I should have thought England had more than enough real heroes without having to use underhand official methods to support the reputation of a false one. Of course it is linked up with the propaganda of the English and international pederasts, an underground but very powerful clique. The English stage is dominated by them, as Lord Hailsham has openly stated more than once. Rattigan is of the fraternity, but they made a mistake in thinking they could impose his "Ross" on Paris.[14] There was an enormous amount of pre-publicity (obviously paid) but there were some very outspoken reviews, and the thing has only kept going through the popularity of Fresnay the actor. The theatre has had to put on matinees of French classics, and I am told "Ross" may be off very soon. Still, nothing would surprise me less than to hear that Four Square have dropped the book, which then will be out of print.

We had storms here after a hot September, but are back in almost summer weather. I expect the nights are getting cold in Canada, but you will still have that superb autumn colour of the trees.

Yours sincerely,
Richard Aldington

1. Not identified.
2. H.D. and RA were divorced in 1938 not 1936.
3. Charles A. Pearce; cf. Letter 147.
4. Eric Warman; cf. Letter 147.
5. George Routledge and Sons Ltd, London, and E. P. Dutton and Co., New York. See Folio Books's issue of Choderlos de Laclos, *Les Liaisons dangereuses*, trans. Richard Aldington, with wood engravings by Raymond Hawthorn, Westminster, 1962.
6. See Giovanni Boccaccio, *The Decameron*, trans. Richard Aldington with aquatints by John Buckland Wright, 2 vols., Westminster, 1954–55.
7. 1957.
8. Cf. Anthony Nutting, *Lawrence of Arabia*, London, 1961.
9. See the *Sunday Times*, 15 October 1961, where Nutting insinuated that RA, in his book on T. E. Lawrence, had concocted a letter from Lawrence to Bernard Shaw. The letter in question, written from Clouds Hill, 26 March 1924, recounted Lawrence's rape by the Turkish Bey at Deraa: "For fear of being hurt, or rather to earn five minutes respite from a pain which drove me mad [a flogging], I gave away the only possession we are born into the world with—our bodily integrity. It's an unforgivable matter, an irrecoverable position."
10. At the British Library.

11. K. J. Fielding, "Lawrence's Confessions,"*Sunday Times*, 17 September 1961. Elsewhere RA attributed the letter to Liddell Hart under a pseudonym (cf. RA to Alan Bird, 5 February 1962, in *A Passionate Prodigality*, ed. Miriam J. Benkovitz, New York, 1976, Letter 147).

12. Cf. *Private Shaw and Public Shaw*, New York, 1963. Professor Weintraub was not from "Philadelphia" but from Pennsylvania State University, University Park, Pa., and *Private Shaw and Public Shaw* was not his "thesis."

13. Publisher, in 1961, of one paperback edition of RA's book on T. E. Lawrence.

14. See Letter 147 n. 11.

147. To Tony Aldington (SIUC)

20 October 1961   Aix-en-Provence.

My dear Tony,

Owing to the negligence of the people at the Saintes some of my letters went astray, and I've only just received yours of the 29th Sept about Lee[1] and his ill-considered longevity. I'll write to him, and attribute the delay to travelling, which indeed is the fact.

Among the delayed letters was one from Mrs Colin containing the agreement for the American (hardback, illustrated) reprint of my Cyrano. This means at least three weeks delay in getting the advance, unnecessary annoyance to publisher, and possibly much greater delay in appearing—all because of a lazy bastard who couldn't bother to forward letters as he promised.

Cap Pearce and spouse duly turned up for lunch on the 17th. His firm has just been bought up by some gigantic and super-wealthy printing works in Chicago (Ill) and he is very bitter about it.[2] However, he plots revenge by slipping in a few authors he really wants to publish but who will not make money and probably lose it, on the specious grounds of "prestige." He had the 1934 Doubleday edition of Collected[3] in his office and it was read by his female secretary. Asked what she liked she replied (how strange!) "Luxembourg." I told him the position, but he seems not to care about British rights. We more or less agreed on doing a Selected Poems, and the Luxm. plus others to be selected by them.[4] If they have an introduction I have suggested Professor Henri Peyre of Yale, who has a big reputation there, is more or less a fan of mine, and with one review[5] started the sale of my "Mistral." Pearce may want to re-issue other things of mine, but he shied away from the Prince of Mecca,[6] though I showed him the enclosed letter (please return sometime) from Dr Weintraub, who in spite of his name is a distinguished scholar and is as you see preparing a book about GBS and TEL which won't please the Lawrence Bureau.[7] Incidentally in another letter Weintraub told me the Bodleian wouldn't let him see the TEL material there, saying that AWL[8] has asked that it is not shown! What Weintraub is trying to establish (among other things) is how far G. and Charlotte Shaw[9] re-wrote 7 Pills of Wiz.[10] The Bastard himself says they left not a paragraph untouched, but he's such a liar. Typically he turned that snub into a "triumph" by adding "bracing to be judged by their high standards." If he had genius it was certainly for self-advertisement, including his hypocritical pretences at modesty and retirement. Apropos, here Rattigan's Rot is a flop and is coming off[11]—its successor is already announced in Paris.

Anyway, Pearce was friendly, and may be of use in getting books back into print. His firm issued Portrait of a Genius, But . . . [12] and it was the paperback of that (now in the press) which doubtless recalled me to his mind. Apart from the Folio Society production of Dangerous Acquaintances[13] (announced for Feb) I have nothing in England, though I was offered yet another book on DHL and a book plus records of a TV interview with Durrell.[14] I didn't wholly reject at first, but I think I shall. Better keep quiet in England until Mrs P.[15] is hanged or otherwise disposed of. The yanks are less prejudiced, much more numerous, and have much more money than the Brits. What we must work for is to get the few remaining copyrights (particularly Luxm and DHL) away from Heinies, and later the Waterton and 4 English Portraits from Evans Bros.[16] (I don't want the Stevenson[17]—it stinks.) And then wait for post-Patmore. If Penguin came through with an offer I might accept on the basis of an outright payment, so that even if the P's got a lien on those royalties too they'd again find they have nowt but the cost of serving the writ here—26 quid to the bad for them. But, in spite of Alister's strong hint, nothing has come through from Penguins.[18] But, Alister writes that the flurry in the S. Times meant that Smiths in Paris sold over 50 copies of Prince of Mecca (in the Four Square paperback) in less than a week, were out of stock, and re-ordered. But is that Four Square edition still in print? Will you ask your bookseller for me?

While I am on this I want to make some additions to my Will due to meditation on the death of H.D. and the difficulties I hear from her executor about probate. I hope you won't have difficulties. Anyway, my financial prospects have improved since that will was made, and Catha's subsidy has been prolonged, so I don't have that worry.[19] There will be money in Barclays, Cannes, to pay for cremation. Is it necessary to stipulate this in the Will, or is enough that you and Alister should know this? Then:

(1) From funds at Barclays I want you to have at once 100 pounds sterling and Alister 1500 new francs, for immediate expenses.

(2) I want to authorise you, if you wish, to terminate the agent agreements with Colin and Elmo, with Alister doing the agenting. In any case,

as much of the work will fall on him, I want him to have 10% on post-humous advances and royalties.

(3) At Sury there are lots of letters to me which are saleable to yank Universities and also a number of my MSS, ditto. I want to authorise you both to sell them for Catha when you think proper.[20]

(4) My own letters. . . . The international copyright will belong to the Estate, though the actual paper and ink belong to the recipients. From time to time I am asked by "scholars" to allow extracts from my letters or the whole letters to be published. Obviously you will ask fees. In the unlikely event of a book of the letters, Alister is to do the necessary editing and annotating (a ghastly chore) and to have the right of censoring—though I recommend "published and be damned to everybody" as the slogan.[21]

(5) I want Catha to have any of my books if she wants, and to let Alister have the remainder. (Not worth the cost of moving them from Sury.) BUT I want a souvenir book to go to each of the following: Yourself, Daphne, your children, Patty, Tim, Jennifer, Molly, with regrets that the Estate of a lit'ry gent doesn't run to more.[22]

The Codicil will be longer than the Will. Does this matter? I thought I'd get it witnessed by the Consular guys in Marseille, which might help in getting it probed more easily. It must be probed in England if possible, for under French law Netta[23] can claim half, with all sorts of gammon. Perhaps you had better add a souvenir book for her.

Impossible to say if there will be much or any posthumous dough, but the enclosed H.D. obit will show that the "school" is getting recognition at last in USA. Some of the translations are now well-established and will earn something. If the Poems are back in print, as they very likely may be, and the DHL in a paperback, they may be followed by others of the biogs and eventually one or more of the novels—Hero is still in print in English, Russian, Czech, Italian. There are translations in 14 different languages. Alister knows about them, and indeed when he was my sec he negotiated many of them, so can deal with them. Incidentally, the Russ sent me no money for those Short Stories, and have not yet issued the new translation of Hero which is to take the place of the old one, now withdrawn.[24] But they still may.

Our old friend Eric Warman drove over to see me from Cap Ferrat where he has Frere's villa (!) at the miserable rental of 50 quid a week. Eric now very prosperous, and stood me a handsome dinner at the Vendôme here, with a Chablis and Mission Haut Brion of infinite merit.

Molly sent me a card and a catalogue of religious art from Oviedo, but I haven't heard since she returned. Hubert Aldington is still on the prowl. Why does he call himself a "MICE" on his letter-head? Is he a rat-catcher?[25]

Catha due here on Monday, for her Psychology stunts at the University.

Love to all from both,
Richard

1. Not identified.
2. In 1961 Duell, Sloan, & Pearce was acquired by Meredith Publishing Company.
3. RA, *The Poems of Richard Aldington*, Garden City, New York, 1934.
4. None of these publication plans was consummated.
5. See Henri Peyre, "Introduction to Provençal," *New York Times*, 24 July 1960, sec. 7, p. 5.
6. *Lawrence of Arabia. A Biographical Enquiry.*
7. Stanley Weintraub, *Private Shaw and Public Shaw*, New York, 1963.
8. Arnold Walter Lawrence.
9. G. B. Shaw and his wife.
10. T. E. Lawrence, *The Seven Pillars of Wisdom*, London, 1926. See Letter 149 n. 12.
11. Terence Rattigan, *Ross*, London, 1960; RA refers to T. E. Lawrence as the "Bastard."
12. RA, *D. H. Lawrence: Portrait of a Genius, But . . .* , New York, 1961.
13. See Letter 146 n. 5.
14. Not issued.
15. Brigit Patmore.
16. Evans Brothers Ltd held the copyrights on *The Strange Life of Charles Waterton, 1782–1865*, London, 1949, and *Four English Portraits, 1801–1851*, London, 1948; William Heinemann Ltd held the copyrights on *A Dream in the Luxembourg* and *D. H. Lawrence: Portrait of a Genius, But. . . .*
17. *Portrait of a Rebel, The Life and Work of Robert Louis Stevenson*, London, 1957.
18. See Letter 111 n. 6.
19. Bryher was paying for Catherine's college education. See Letter 151 n. 3; on 6 November 1959 RA wrote Alison Palmer (Temple) about "a very handsome 3-year subsidy."
20. Most of these were acquired by Southern Illinois University at Carbondale. See Norman T. Gates, "The Richard Aldington Collection at Morris Library," *ICarbS*, Summer–Fall 1976, pp. 61–68.
21. See Letter 133 n. 7.
22. "Daphne" was the wife of Tony Aldington; "Patty" is RA's sister, Patricia Aldington; "Tim" is Tony Aldington's son by his first wife; "Jennifer" is Tony's daughter; and "Molly" is RA's sister, Margery Lyon Gilbert.
23. RA's wife, who was living in England.
24. RA, *Farewell to Memories* [in Russian], ed. with foreword by M. Urnov, Moscow, 1961.
25. Hubert Aldington was the cousin of RA's father; MICE on his letterhead stood for "Member of the Institute of Civil Engineers."

148. To Alison Palmer (Temple)

25 November 1961   Aix-en-Provence.

Dear Mrs. Palmer,

Thank you very much for sending so promptly the letter about "Lawrence's Confession."[1] The tone of the letter is more insolent to me than I had inferred from the reference to it made by Dr. Weintraub of Pennsylvania in his personal letter to me about it. K. J. Fielding is evidently one of the now dwindling Lawrence hero-worshippers, but it is significant that this is the first public reference made by any of them to those letters in the British Museum. They were read for the first time by one of my reference-hunters,[2] and I was the first to draw attention to them and to quote them as evidence—for what they are worth.

Fielding says my reference is "sketchy." I merely gave the exact press-mark of the letters as catalogued by the MSS Dept. of the British Museum![3] I did not give the date of the letter and did not give its exact words in the printed version, though they appeared in my original script.

Here is what happened. Publishers are a very close corporation, and get underground tips from one another. While my book was under scrutiny by Collins and—contrary to all custom and decency—freely communicated to such enemies as Storrs, Liddell Hart, etc.,[4] Collins learned that Jonathan Cape and the Lawrence Trust intended to refuse me permission to make *any* quotations from TEL's published or unpublished writings. That would have killed the book. BUT Collins had paid me 5000 pounds for it,[5] and meant to get that back, no matter what happened to me. AND the law says that a writer of a biography may, without permission, "make reasonable quotations." To get this legally straight they took the book to Messrs Joynson Hicks, a most ridiculous and damaging choice since I had attacked the first "Jix" (Lord Brentford) for his bigoted persecution when Home Secretary of my friend, D. H. Lawrence.[6] (What an imbroglio!) Consequently, my book contains *some* quotations from TEL, but many (including ALL from the Shaw-Shaw letters) were paraphrased by J. Hicks and given as my opinion, but with references which any honest person could verify. I was not allowed to give either the words or the date of the Clouds Hill letter about Deraa[7]—I could only give the general reference to the whole collection. If Nutting had read those letters he couldn't have missed the passage; but it was easier and more convenient for his purpose to suggest that I had invented it.

Now, the whole squalid episode rests solely on T.E.L.'s own dubious testimony. (That "Lawrence wanted the truth" is one of the biggest lies yet printed in this one-sided battle.) The only evidence in favour of it, which I loyally quoted, is that the RAF doctors found scars on TEL's back, the cause of which he refused to divulge. They *may* have been inflicted at Deraa, but in view of L's particularly queer sexual habits might have been acquired elsewhere. We shall never know.[8]

Did Lawrence in fact enter Deraa with an Arab boy in disguise on reconnaissance? There was no valid military reason, since Deraa was not particularly important (though a minor junction) and anyway on our military maps. General Barrow took it in ten minutes in 1918. But L. may have made the adventure in sheer Irish fecklessness. But, consider, he was blue-eyed, clean-shaven, and spoke Arabic imperfectly; and even youngish Arab males are bearded and dark-eyed and speak their language. The Bey, who is said to have seen him pass and to have kidnapped him for his unnatural lust, *may* have thought L. was one of the Circassian boys doomed by the Turks to these horrible purposes. But suppose the beastly episode did occur, what then? How does it reflect glory on the hero, and how did it contribute to the winning of the war? Certainly, owing to Allenby's successful offensive, the Hashemite irregulars got into Deraa first, and there created a shambles of pillage and massacre and torture of prisoners, as described by General Sir George Barrow, whose division arrived and at once occupied the place, and stopped the outrages—much to Lawrence's anger and disgust. He sadistically enjoyed the horrors. The Turkish troops in Deraa were second-line garrison troops (not much better than gendarmerie) and surrendered at once. Where in all this is the heroism, where the decisive contribution to complete victory in the world war? Read General Barrow's account in his "Fire of Life."[9]

If you get the New York Times Book Review, would you send me their review of Nutting's book—supposing it is ever published. I know privately that it is unfavourable to Nutting, so the review may appear very late or be suppressed.[10]

To turn to pleasanter themes—I hear that the Crowell-Collier paperback of my book of the real Lawrence—D.H.[11]—was published in New York about the 15th of this month. It should be in Canada by now. Although Heinemanns insolently claimed Canadian rights, a flaw in their agreement gave them to me, for which I received—don't faint—the astronomic sum of 100 dollars, less 10% agent's fees. But it is something to have that book back in print, since the Americans have been trying to corner DHL for themselves, ignoring the fact that from 1950, when my book was published, dates the definitive revival and triumph of DHL. You must remember that official England has always backed T. E. "Lawrence," the liar, against D. H. Lawrence, who for all his faults was a literary genius.

I shall return the cutting later, but want to make a copy for my records.

Yours sincerely,
Richard Aldington

1. See Letter 146 n. 11.

2. Denison Deasey.

3. RA gave press marks for letters from T. E. Shaw (Lawrence) to Charlotte E. (Mrs. George Bernard) Shaw and for her letters to Shaw.

4. It was common practice then, as now, to circulate a manuscript to supposed "experts" for evaluation.

5. The advance Collins paid was £4,500.

6. That is, the Right Honourable William Joynson-Hicks, home secretary when the manuscripts of *Pansies*, 1929, and introduction to *The Paintings of D. H. Lawrence*, 1929, were seized, and when thirteen of Lawrence's paintings were removed from the exhibition held at the Warren Galleries in the summer of 1929 and the exhibition was closed. For RA's attack, see *D. H. Lawrence: Portrait of a Genius, But . . .* , pp. 340–42. The member of the firm involved in the T. E. Lawrence "imbroglio" was Lancelot William Joynson-Hicks.

7. T. E. Shaw to Charlotte Shaw, 26 March 1924, in which Lawrence's flogging-rape by the Turkish Bey at Deraa was recounted. See Letter 146 n. 9.

8. Lawrence's taste for having himself whipped was subsequently revealed (with proof) by Phillip Knightley and Colin Simpson, who published the facts in *The Secret Lives of Lawrence of Arabia*, New York, 1970, pp. 191, 220–22, 227–28, and 253.

9. London, 1942.

10. See Stanley Weintraub's review of Anthony Nutting, *Lawrence of Arabia: The Man and the Motive*, New York, 1961, in the *New York Times Book Review*, 31 December 1961, p. 4.

11. *D. H. Lawrence: Portrait of a Genius, But. . . .*

149. To Alison Palmer (Temple)

8 February 1962   Aix-en-Provence.
Dear Mrs. Palmer,

The airmail parcel with the Goldoni[1] was delivered here yesterday, 7th! I can't read the date-stamp because the postal clerk stuck the airmail number exactly over it; but I feel sure that you would have posted the book on the same day as your letter of the 24th. It is simply a scandal that airmail from Montréal to France should take a fortnight. The delay can only be partly due to the one day postal strike—it must be mainly caused by the Customs, who opened the packet, and probably kept it kicking about for a week. I assume that it would come through Orly, and it is notorious that the Customs men there are virulent communists, and do all they can to disrupt "bourgeois" traffic.

All my thanks to you for sending. I re-posted the book at once by air to New York, but fear that owing to the Comrades it may arrive too late. Perhaps not. The translation did not seem to be so bad as I thought it was, but if by chance it is re-issued I must go over it carefully.[2]

I was disappointed by the Arthur Symons introduction, which seemed to me discursive and sometimes rather pointlessly erudite. But, poor man, he never really recovered from a dreadful experience in Italy in pre-

1914. He disappeared, and was found raving mad, almost naked and starving, jeered at and stoned by a vile mob. He was taken to an asylum.[3] Now, there was a law in Italy that an insane person can not be removed unless certified as recovered—and what chance was there for a sensitive Englishman in an institution for Italian pauper lunatics? Luckily England was still the Great Power, the ambassador personally intervened, and got him transferred to England where he got well enough to be allowed out under family supervision. This story was told me by Edward Hutton (the English expert on Italy) who worked hard to get S. out. My first indication that Symons's mind had been permanently damaged came circa 1919 when in the English Review he published some translations of Baudelaire's Poèmes en Prose.[4] I thought they were odd, compared with the original, and found them full of blunders and incompetences. Now, Symons knew French perfectly (in his early days) and made excellent versions. I put this to Hutton, who thereupon told me the story.

There is no news from N.Y. of the possible reprint of L. of Arabia,[5] so I suppose that has failed. My agent might at least have told me what happened, but catch an American spending 11 cents on a letter which won't bring in business.

I hear from Southern Illinois that the first copies of the Durrell book are coming from the binders, so it should be released some time this month.[6] Dr Sternberg airmailed a copy to Durrell (who characteristically didn't notice it was airmailed!) so I may see it before my own copy arrives. They have included a rather silly and splurging piece by Henry Miller[7]—merely to have his name. Well, let us hope the book may help Durrell's reputation a little. He is too much pleased by the easy publicity of TV shows, interviews, silly articles for magazines, and doesn't realise that a permanent reputation is made by the scholars, not by the journalists.

You saw the Meinertzhagen diary-review of L. of Arabia,[8] didn't you? Well, I have sent a copy to the editor of the Times Litt. asking him to forward it to the reviewer of Nutting's book.[9] Nothing will happen, but it will show them both that I know they are deliberately hiding the truth. I sent another copy to my old friend Sir Charles Snow, who did make some faint effort at defence, but of course hasn't and won't do anything effective. Finally, I sent a copy to the London publisher,[10] who admitted that he had never heard of it. If he can't add it to the book, he could at least print it off as a throwaway, and put it in every copy that goes out, while bringing it to the attention of the booksellers. But he won't do that—no money in it. In the long run truth always prevails—but only when it is too late, and people have ceased to care.

Have you read Meinertzhagen's book? Unintentionally he gives a striking picture of British incompetence, intrigue and folly in the Mid East.

And have you read Three Persons by the Canadian soldier-journalist, Sir Andrew Macphail?[11] He wrote long before the real evidence was available, but saw through TEL's pretentions as a soldier. Macphail exaggerates L's status as a writer, but of course it wasn't then known that G.B.S. re-wrote the book.[12] Macphail also has a truly majestic diatribe against Sir Henry Wilson and his intrigues. From this it appears that in 1914 the only general who gave correct strategic advice was Kitchener, who was called "a coward" for his pains!

I see you have again had cold weather. We had about a week of chilly mistral, then two or three glorious days of mild sunshine, now rather muggy cloud.

Yours sincerely,

Richard Aldington

Before re-posting the Goldoni, I wrote in it: "Property of Mrs Alison Palmer" with your address, in the faint hope of getting it back to you, but I expect it will be stolen by somebody as "a reading copy."

1. Carlo Goldoni, *The Good-Humoured Ladies. A Comedy,* trans. Richard Aldington, London, 1922.

2. Not reissued.

3. For Symons's account see his *Confessions,* New York, 1930.

4. See "Charles Baudelaire," *English Review,* January 1918, pp. 49–55.

5. Henry Regnery, Chicago, did not reissue the American edition (1955).

6. *The World of Lawrence Durrell,* ed. Harry T. Moore, Urbana, Ill., 1962.

7. See Henry Miller, "The Durrell of *The Black Book* Days," in *The World of Lawrence Durrell,* pp. 95–99.

8. See Richard Meinertzhagen, *Middle East Diary,* London, 1959, under the date 20 November 1955: "Richard Aldington has just published a book exploding the Lawrence Myth. It is a venomous book but true."

9. Reviews in the *Times Literary Supplement* were anonymous.

10. William A. R. Collins whose firm published the English edition of RA's *Lawrence of Arabia* (1955).

11. 1925.

12. Bernard Shaw did not rewrite Lawrence's *Seven Pillars of Wisdom,* 1922. Both Shaw and Mrs. Shaw, however, helped with the book. Shaw advised on punctuation and badly needed deletions; Mrs. Shaw read proof.

150. To Alison Palmer (Temple)

14 June 1962   Sury.

Dear Mrs. Palmer,

I am sending back by air-mail "Imprimé" under separate cover the copy of A Tourist's Rome[1] with fuller corrections. In fact, all the names of various marbles and other lovely stones should be in italics, but it would be pedantic to insist. Page 8—it is just San Stefano. The absurd Sancti Stefani Rotondi is due to my laziness in relying on a check with Baedeker (who is now full of errors) instead of some more serious authority. San Stefano Rotondo is in another part of Rome. The "now burned" was due to the fact that the newspapers announced total destruction by fire of the Cancelleria. When I returned to Rome I found that this (like most newspaper information) is false. The interior was destroyed, but has been restored, and the stone façade looked intact to me. I hope you are not startled by my qualified defence of Nero.[2] It is true there are dreadful things in his private life, but though extravagant he was apparently not a bad ruler. At any rate some salutary laws (especially in the matter of fire-fighting!) date from his reign, and if he didn't draft them himself he didn't prevent the administration from decreeing them.

It is now settled that Catherine and I fly to Moscow on the 22nd, and I am planning to return to Paris on the 10th July and to get back here on the 12th.[3] Of course it is very flattering to be asked to go to Russia as a guest of the Writers Union, but it will be a strain, and I shall be glad to get back.

Yours sincerely,
Richard Aldington

1. Draguignan, France, 1957
2. Pp. 22, 24.
3. In a letter dated 9 February 1962 (SIUC), The Soviet Writers' Union had invited RA and his daughter to visit the Soviet Union for three weeks.

151. To Winifred Bryher* (Yale)

13 July 1962   Sury.
Dear Bryher,

We returned from Moscow on Tuesday. We were very well received and treated most hospitably. Most luckily I went as a teetotaller and thus avoided their rather excessive potations. Catha did not get to see the school as promised because the rendezvous was cancelled at the last moment.[1] Great developments are taking place there. Modern Moscow is vast and almost a model modern town with wide avenues and tall apartment houses. I think I sent you a card of the new University and enclose another which shows one of the new skyscraper blocks of flats. Leningrad is more interesting to us since it still contains so many fine buildings of the Imperial epoch. Their "cultural" achievements are truly admirable since they have no magazine trash; and newspapers are small, while the cinemas and TV apparently have no trash either, though end-less propaganda. Books are very cheap and circulated very widely in-deed. The music is good and records are very cheap and would be cheaper but for the fact that the exchange has been artificially set at one ruble to the dollar. Even so 90 cents for a large and 70 for a small record are very cheap. I had to give interviews to Moscow papers including Pravda (which has a circulation of 7 millions) and I had to go on the Moscow radio and the Leningrad TV—so many people wanted to hear and see me. I knew that my books are read in USSR but I didn't know how widely, and certainly didn't know that I am revered and loved there. Heaven knows why! The interviews were most scrupulously accurate, and there was no journalistic trickery. I am far more favourably im-pressed than I expected, but of course we saw only what they let us see, and our "contacts" were mainly with authors and artists and publishers, though readers who came to see me were just plain "workers." One woman (elderly) made a 12-hr rail journey just to spend ten minutes in our company.[2] I will try to tell you more later and to answer any ques-tions if I can.

Among my letters here I found the enclosed debit note from my bank. I should not have mentioned it except that I think you should know that your bank made this mistake. I feel it is rather a serious blunder and that you will wish to reprove them. I don't see how the mistake could have been made by Barclays in Paris and feel it must have been the Swiss Bank.[3]

Mrs Fallas writes most gratefully, but no doubt she has written to you.[4]

Thank you so very much for your re-assurance about Catha.[5] She went straight back to the Midi to start work for these Sept Exams. I am get-ting her a correspondence course.

Many thanks indeed for the copy of your book which will interest me greatly.[6] I have not had a moment to look at it and indeed this is the first letter I have been able to write since returning to Sury. I shall write again soon.

All thanks to you as always and kindest thoughts

Richard

*Winifred Bryher (1894–1983) was the legally adopted name of Annie Winifred Ellerman, daughter of the wealthy and powerful Sir John Ellerman who helped RA get established with the *Times* and other outlets for his writing following World War I. Bryher wrote RA because of her interest in Imagist poetry; in France at the time, he suggested she write H.D. for further information, and later Bryher met H.D. in Cornwall—they remained intimate friends until H.D.'s death. Bryher was married twice: first to Robert McAlmon and then to Kenneth Macpherson. She supported the avant-garde film journal, *Close-Up*, and wrote historical novels. Bryher, immensely wealthy, not only was an "other mother" to H.D.'s daughter, Perdita, but also helped RA's daughter, Catherine, and RA himself. It was Bryher, too, who telegraphed RA from Montreux, "Hilda died sleep yesterday." (See also the Annotated Index.)

1. Knowing of her studies in child psychology, their Russian hosts had promised Catherine a visit to a school for exceptional children.

2. Ludmila Pauchinskaja; see Norman T. Gates, "Richard Aldington in Russia," *Texas Quarterly*, Summer 1978, pp. 35–57.

3. Bryher was helping RA financially at this time.

4. RA had written Bryher that the widow of Carl Fallas was in poor financial circumstances.

5. See Letter 147 n. 19.

6. Bryher, *The Heart to Artemis*, New York, 1962.

152. To Mikhail Urnov* (privately held)

15 July 1962   Sury.

Dear Mikhail Urnov,

Well! here I am once more writing to you from my book-lined workroom in Sury looking over the green pastures and vineyards to the Loire which is, however, hidden by the low hills and woodlands.

As you saw, we were both delighted by our stay in USSR and only regretted having to leave. We should like to thank Mrs Urnov especially for the sumptuous repast she put before us and for her kindness in entertaining us. I have her water-colour sketch beside me and shall try to get it framed later on. Please also remember me to Mitya and to your younger son.[1] How did the motion-picture come out? And have you replayed that very amusing tape-recording?[2]

Yesterday was the 14th July (anniversary of the taking of the Bastille and the Fête Nationale) and to-day is Sunday. So for two days the post-office has been closed and I haven't been able to send off any letters or books. For you I have made a small packet of the C. P. Snow pamphlet and the Penguin edition of Seven Against Reeves; and to this I have added an old pamphlet on D. H. Lawrence which Mitya may like to have.[3] I had forgotten what Snow said and was pleasantly surprised to find that he praises Women Must Work very highly. Perhaps Mr Vladikin would be interested to know about this if you could show it to him.[4] Also I find Snow likes Seven Against Reeves more than I thought. I think you will get one or two laughs from the sketch of Mr Willoughby Houghton the would-be fascist revolutionary.[5]

This seems a very poor selection to send and I must try to send something better when London condescends to let me have the books I've asked for.

I am sending copies of Women Must Work and Seven Against Reeves direct to Mr Vladikin but I fear one is only a proof copy and the other a paperback Continental reprint.[6]

I wish I could have been of more use to you over the Thomas Hardy book, which has special difficulties.[7] You must remember that although the Industrial Revolution started in England over 200 years ago, it was for a long time limited to areas of the coal-fields in the Midlands and the Lancashire country and the south of Scotland. Hardy's Wessex was quite untouched and remained almost the country England of Shakespeare until the first world war. W. H. Hudson's books, particularly A Shepherd's Life and Nature in Downland,[8] will give you many particulars of Hardy's England as it was at the end of the 19th century. W. S. Maugham's Cakes and Ale[9] contains in the form of a novel a lot of information about Hardy's real life (not the life imagined for him by writers who wanted to make him "respectable") which Maugham has since denied but only because there was such a row about it that he got frightened for his popularity. But it is an amusing book and true. Another point is that Hardy particularly in his Poems[10] was obsessed by the Victorian gloom about death. But the Poems deserve careful study because they are perhaps the most successful of the realistic poems which came when the great Romantic movement of Scott, Byron, Shelley and Keats had been exhausted by two generations of imitators. Hardy and Whitman had considerable influence on D. H. Lawrence who is one of the most important English poets of this century.

I can't begin to tell you how much we enjoyed our visit and what new interests it has given me. I do my Russian lesson every day but fear I am very slow and stupid about it. The gramophone records which Oksana[11] helped me to get are very good indeed. They occupy me very happily. And then I have the beautiful illustrated books to look over as well as the post-card photographs of Moscow and Leningrad and the reproductions of paintings. I am sending you a view of part of the Seine in Paris. Please excuse the poor colour-reproduction. To your extreme left as you look at the card you will see one of the pavilions of the Louvre and more to the right the two square towers of Notre Dame. The Institut de France is almost invisible behind trees and other buildings, but the dome to the right (behind the modern buildings) is the Panthéon. The building with columns just opposite the right-hand end of the first bridge is the Palais Bourbon where the French deputies meet.

With all good wishes

Yours sincerely
Richard Aldington

*Mikhail V. Urnov (b. 1909) was one of a small group of Russian scholars whose early appreciation of RA's work helped to elevate him to a high place among English authors whose work has been published in the U.S.S.R. Professor Urnov was also a member of the Writers' Union, the group that invited RA to celebrate his seventieth birthday in Moscow. In his diary of the Russian trip that RA made with Catherine, he tells of a jolly evening spent at the Urnovs' home. He may have gone to Moscow tongue-in-cheek, but the letters written after he returned make clear how much RA was moved by the reception the Russians gave him, and how right and fortunate it was that he accepted this second invitation from the Writers' Union. (See also the Annotated Index.)

1. Dmitry and Alexander Urnov.

2. See Mikhail Urnov in *Richard Aldington: An Intimate Portrait*, Carbondale, Ill., 1965, p. 149.

3. RA, *D. H. Lawrence. An Indiscretion*, Seattle, 1927; RA, *Seven Against Reeves. A Comedy-Farce*, London, 1938; C. P. Snow, *Richard Aldington: An Appreciation*, London, [1938].

4. Gregori Vladkin, Russian publisher who had recently reprinted *All Men Are Enemies. A Romance* and *Death of a Hero. A Novel*, announced he had commissioned a translation of *Women Must Work. A Novel*, London, 1934.

5. See chapter 4 of *Seven Against Reeves. A Comedy-Farce*.

6. Albatross Continental Library, a John Holroyd-Reese publishing enterprise.

7. Mikhail Urnov, *Thomas Hardy*, Moscow, 1966.

8. W. H. Hudson, *Nature in Downland*, London, 1900; and *A Shepherd's Life*, London, 1910.

9. New York, 1930.

10. *The Poetical Works of Thomas Hardy*, London, 1920–24.

11. Oksana S. Krugerskaya, RA's interpreter during his visit to Russia; see Letter 151 n. 2.

153. To Winifred Bryher (Yale)

21 July 1962   Sury.

Dear Bryher,

Many thanks for your letter of the 18th. I think you are very wise to postpone the Greenland voyage until next year. No use going all that way to be storm-bound as in Cornwall!

Thank you so much for the help to Mrs Fallas, who does really need it. I have again asked her to state what her situation is. Before I left in June she indicated that she *hoped* for help from the Journalists and R. Literary Funds; but I wonder if anything goes to widows.

I have heard nothing further from Barclays about the NF 1,930, but letters are very slow in France. I shall let you know at once.

There would be much to say about Russia, but one wants to avoid being a travel-bore or posing as an authority on a mere 3-weeks sponsored tour! You will see from the enclosed "address" that they can lay on flattery when they want to. This "address" was read at the birthday feast and received with great applause, signed at table by 17 of the writers present, and then presented to me bound in blue leather with my name and age on a silver plaque.[1] Yet I had much evidence to show that most of what the address says is true, strange as it will sound to Anglo-Saxons who have been taught otherwise. From several different sources (including Samsonov, head of Academy of Sciences Publishing House) I learned that the three most popular English novelists there are Dickens, H. G. Wells, and Aldington (in that order), closely followed by Maugham and Priestley. They are interested, but less, in Joyce and D. H. Lawrence, but greatly dislike Virginia Woolf and Tom Eliot whom they consider false talents. To my grief they are very doubtful about Larry Durrell, but may come around. I tried to find out what it was in my novels is liked by what we should call "working class readers" there, and they agreed that first it was the sincerity and profundity of the emotions, then the vividness of the writing, and then that I so much dislike "philistines"! So there it is.

Believe me, it is not just propaganda books which are so widely distributed, though of course the propaganda is intense. But I saw and handled new editions of Tolstoy, Turgeniev, Pushkin, Dostoevsky, now in course of publication in printings running into hundreds of thousands, as well as many translations of foreign books. The Library of Foreign Literature in Moscow still has as directrice the woman who founded it 30 years ago.[2] It started from scratch and now has about three million books, and the State is building it a vast new library. There seems to be no gutter-press or strip-tease and libel journalism, though of course the limitation of their press is grotesque. The only Western papers available to the public are D. Worker, Humanité, and the Italian and German equivalents. (In sending off signed copies of my own books to people who entertained us I have been careful to use as inner wrapping the two inner pages of the Times, which they will certainly read, and perhaps learn what real news is!) Opera, Ballet, and Theatre are open to everybody, and always thronged, so far as I could see; so too are the museum-palaces and galleries. The Ballet and very numerous folk dancers are rapturously received with many encores. I was encouraged to see that a silly propaganda ballet (which abused the skill of the dancers and orchestra) was very coolly received on its first performance in the new Kremlin theatre. Even our very communist guide had to admit the thing was bad.

Religion is tolerated but not State-supported. The cross still stands on the column outside the Winter Palace, and from the balcony of his datcha, the novelist Konstantin Fedin pointed out to me the (handsome-looking) datcha of the Patriarch or Metropolitan of Moscow. Consumer goods are just coming along in some quantity and the big GUM department store, the outdoor people's markets, and the "Magazines" are thronged with buyers and "window-shoppers." Clothes and food seemed dear, but such things as books and records are very cheap—records are excellent in quality and not one fifth of the cost in the West. Everyone has television—it is of course a great weapon of propaganda. The most wretched wooden huts in the country all have TV, in most cases from 4 to 8 aerials—from which we may infer a family to a room. Everything or nearly everything seems devoted to heavy industry and the towns, particularly Moscow, which is being embellished (in modern style) as lavishly as the emperors embellished Petersburg. Lenin and Peter the Great are the two official heroes, because each broke with the past and "modernised" Russia. Marx has his statue but is never mentioned, and Stalin exists only in Stalingrad. The government believes that the old régime was overthrown because it neglected the people, used harsh police methods, persecuted writers and painters, and irritated the factory workers. So the people are daily told that they "own" everything, the police are the most amiable and gentlest I've seen, writers are protected, paid, but severely controlled, and the factory workers watched. The factory workers are spied on in a most ingenious way. Every factory has its Writers Club, and the workers, particularly the young, are encouraged to write and to submit their writings to a committee of the local Writers Union for publication. Very few are published, but you can see that young and unsuspicious writers would instantly reveal any causes of discontent and any kind of rebelliousness. Similarly, all but the most favoured writers have to spend at least a month a year in a Writers "Home" which is a kind of dull club, where their behaviour and talk will be closely watched by the director and their rivals.

Their famous "Pioneers" are an imitation of Boy Scouts and Girl Guides. The children are delightful—one sang us Polly, put the kettle on—but it is all early "conditioning." There are many war widows, but I saw no mutilated ex-soldier, except for the most amusing writer, Polevoi, who lost an eye at Stalingrad. It is painful to see women employed in sweeping streets, and in the hard work of repairing railway tracks. The landscape we saw was melancholy even in summer, though a little cheered by beautiful silver birches and wild flowers, particularly yellow iris and wild water-lilies. From the main road the country seemed poorly cultivated, the pastures and gardens weedy, the villages dull, the country people apathetic. The river Oka looked melancholy in spite of the Sunday anglers, and Tula—said to have been a fashionable resort in pre-revolution days—looked shabby and dreary. All side roads looked neglected to me. To visit Fedin and on another occasion Kataev (both highly favoured authors) in their datchas, not 30 miles from Moscow, we had to crawl over a preposterously bad road, full of bumps and huge holes. If that is the case on the road leading to a favoured suburb, what must the real country roads be?

Everybody we met was most friendly, most kind, very warm-hearted, and of course flattering—but I'm sure we were both glad to get back to Paris, and to change our luxurious hotel suites for small rooms in a small hotel!

With all best wishes,
Richard

1. The "address" by Pavel Chuvikov, director of the Publishing House of Foreign Literature, is reprinted in "Richard Aldington in Russia," *Texas Quarterly*, Summer 1978, pp. 35–57.
2. Margarita I. Rudomino.

154. To Eric Warman (SIUC)

25 July 1962[1]   Sury.
My dear Eric,

Nice to be in touch with you again after the hiatus, which seemed longer than it was because I didn't have letters forwarded. The only contact with you war-mongering Occidentals was the various birthday telegrams.

Are you coming to France this year? If so, do try to stop off here and have a look at some of the Russian photos and presents. As Catha's birthday was on the 6th (mine the 8th) we shared presents and photos, but I have the electric samovar and Russian tea, including some of the 1962 crop from Georgia, so if you come in time I can make you some Russian tea. I have also a tea-glass in a silver holder. By the way, records are both good and cheap in Russia, and we each brought back some, wishing we could bring more. Records which in France cost from 20 to 30 new francs, there cost 3 to 5! Propaganda? Well, tell me what is propagandized by Pergolesi's Stabat Mater, Vivaldi's concertos, Albinoni and Beethoven? I got Borodin's complete opera, Prince Igor, for about 16 new francs—four large long-playing records.

I haven't formed any autumn and winter projects, though I have played with the idea of Venice and then Aix-en-P. But the journey to Venice is a bore—the direct air-flight is only summer. And Aix is rather noisy. Anyway at the moment I stay here as I am only halfway through a script for the USA.[2] It is more advantageous to sell to USA first, as they can pay money, instead of the chicken-feed the British publishers think is money. Why don't you try your novel over there?[3] They are much more enterprising, and very little affected by our shabby-genteel university know-alls and pedigree literary lap-dogs of journalistic criticism. Of course, they have their own brands of hangers-on, and one needs to take ever more stringent criminal precautions with their publishers than with those of the dear home land.

It turned out that the alarm about Alister's little boy, Sylvain, was entirely false.[4] A children's specialist in Paris gave the child a long examination, reported he is robust and the scare of TB complete nonsense, and moreover he gives every indication of exceptional intelligence. He certainly has a lofty brow and most capacious noddle, as well as being very handsome. He looked very well indeed after a month down here.

Ever yours,
Richard

1. On the morning of Saturday, 27 July 1962, after getting his mail, RA collapsed on the doorstep of his home. His neighbors, Maxim and Suzanne Gueneau, helped him into the house, where he died that day.

2. This work was not completed.

3. Eric Warman, *These Same Men*, London, 1966.

4. Sylvain was erroneously diagnosed as having tuberculosis.

Annotated Index

The Index, limited to names of persons and titles of literary works, including periodicals, refers to the letters and their notes by letter number and tries to give information about everyone mentioned in the letters who could be traced. Persons whose names appear only in the notes are listed without biography. Periodicals named only in the notes are omitted. **Boldface numbers** indicate letters written to the recipient after whose name they appear.

Age d'Or, L' (Cunard), 59

Alaric (ca. 370–410), king of the Visigoths, 64

Albinoni, Tommaso (1671–1750), Italian composer chiefly remembered for his instrumental music, 154

Alcestis (Euripides, trans. RA), 52, 53, 58

Aldington, Albert Edward (1865?–1921), father of RA; practiced law in Dover, 15, 140

Aldington, Catherine (b. 1938), only child of RA and his second wife Netta. Educated at the Universities of Montpellier and Aix-en-Provence, she married Jacques Guillaume in January 1963. The mother of twin girls, Catherine works as a psychologist in Marseilles. 77, 80–81, 87–88, 92–93, 95, 98–101, 103–6, 108–9, 114, 118–19, 121, 124, 126–28, 130–35, 137, 141–47, 150–52, 154

Aldington, Daphne, 147

Aldington, Hubert (fl. 1961), cousin of RA's father; a civil engineer, 147

Aldington, Jennifer, 147

Aldington, Jessie May (1874?–1953), mother of RA and author of five novels and two books of poetry, all published between 1905 and 1917, 15

Aldington, Margery May (Margery Lyon Gilbert) (1898–1985), RA's sister. A poet herself, Mrs. Gilbert lived for many years in India with her husband. 145, 147

Aldington, Netta (born McCulloch) (1911–77), RA's second wife; previously married to Michael Patmore, son of Brigit Patmore. An artist, she illustrated RA's *A Wreath for San Gemignano*, designed the dust jacket for the English edition of *The Romance of Casanova. A Novel,* and did watercolors. *The Crystal World* was dedicated to Netta just as *Love and the Luxembourg* had been dedicated to Brigit Patmore. From 1950 until her death Netta lived in England, while RA and their daughter, Catherine, continued to live in France. 47, 72–81, 87–88, 92, 94, 97–102, 104, 108–9, 114–16, **124, 126, 128,** 132, 141, 147

Aldington, Patricia Joan Le Gros (b. 1908), RA's younger sister, a librarian who lives in Rye, 147

Aldington, Paul Anthony Glynne (1910–80), younger brother of RA; like their father a solicitor in Dover, 55, 101–2, 116, 130, 140, 141, **143, 145, 147**

Aldington, Perdita (Mrs. John Schaffner) (b. 1919), daughter of H.D. She now resides in the United States. 49, 77, 87, 106, 119, 151

Aldington, Tim, 147

Alexandra (1844–1925), queen consort of Edward VII of England, 129

Alington, Sir Richard (d. 1599), a descendant of Alington of Swinhope, whose arms are "sable, a bend engrailed between six billets argent" and whose crest is "a talbot passant ermine, a crescent for difference argent." Sir Richard is also mentioned in *Life for Life's Sake* (p. 147), where RA tells of discovering his tomb on a visit with Bruce Richmond to see the Torrigiani tomb. 139, 140

Allenby, Edmund Henry Hynman, first viscount (1861–1936), British field marshal; commander of the British forces in Egypt in World War I, 148

All Men Are Enemies (RA), 63–67, 79, 107–8, 110, 113, 115, 141–42, 152

Almanac des lettres et arts (Paris, 1917), 14

Ameche, Don (b. 1908), American leading man in motion pictures, who returned to Broadway in the 1960s and became popular on TV as a circus ringmaster. Some of his early 1940 films were *Four Sons* (1940), *That Night in Rio* (1941), and *Heaven Can Wait* (1943). 93

American, The (James), 120

American Mercury, The (New York, 1924–50), 82

American Scene, The (James), 120

Amyot, Jacques (1513–93), French bishop and classical scholar famous for his *Vies des hommes illustres*, a translation of Plutarch's *Lives*, which was translated into English by Sir Thomas North. Shakespeare used North's translation as a source of material for his Roman plays. 35

Anacreon (ca. 570–480 B.C.), Greek poet, especially of love poems and drinking songs, some of whose work RA translated, 16, 25

"Anacreontics" (RA), 25

Anderson, Margaret C. (1892?–1973), founded and edited the *Little Review*, which specialized in experimental writing and published Joyce's *Ulysses* serially. Ezra Pound was her foreign editor from 1917 to 21. 6

"André Spire" (RA), 87

Andronikoff, Natalie, 8

Angel at the Loom (Green and Strange), 1

Anglo-French Review, The (London, Paris; 1919–20), 25

"Another of de Gourmont's War Sketches" (de Gourmont), 6

Anthropology: An Introduction to the Study of Man and Civilization (Tylor), 85

Antinous (d. 130), beautiful Bithynian boy greatly loved by the Emperor Hadrian, 107, 111

"Any Georgian (In Memoriam E.M.)" (RA), 30

Ape and Essence (Huxley), 121

Apocalypse (D. H. Lawrence), 59, 61–62, 68, 85

"Approach to M. Marcel Proust, The" (RA), 31

"A Propos du 'Style' de Flaubert" (Proust), 31

Arabella (the nickname of Dorothy Yorke) (1891–1971), born in Reading, Pa., but spent much of her life in Paris and London. John Cournos was in love with her, but she became RA's mistress in 1917 and lived with him in London, Padworth, and Paris until 1928. D. H. Lawrence painted her portrait (Yale), and characterized her as Josephine Ford in *Aaron's Rod* (1922). She is an important character in H.D.'s autobiographical novel *Bid Me to Live* (1960), where she appears as "Bella Carter." She felt that H.D. had characterized her unfairly as a "brainless sexpot." See "John Cournos and H.D." by Alfred Satterthwaite, *Twentieth Century Literature*, December 1976, pp. 394–410. 11, 17–18, 20, 22–24, 39, 47–48

Aragon, Louis (1897–1982), French poet, novelist, and journalist who, with André Breton, launched surrealism. He illustrated his ideas with his first poetry and a novel *Le paysan de Paris* (1926). Aragon's *Le traité du style* (1928) spoke for the iconoclasm of his generation. Aragon was Nancy

Cunard's lover for several years. Within two years after she discarded him, he visited Russia and thereafter devoted his energies almost entirely to socialist realism and journalism, becoming a leading figure in the French Communist party. When Nancy Cunard saw Aragon in France in the late 1950s, she thought him a "typical bureaucrat." 47, 49

"Argyria" (RA), 118

Aristotle (384–322 B.C.), Greek philosopher, 107

Arlen, Michael (Dikran Kouyoumdjian) (1895–1956), foreign-born British writer whose novels, short stories, and plays reflected the hedonism of the "gay" 1920s. *These Charming People, The Green Hat,* and *May Fair* are representative. 58, 64–65, 71

Armstrong-Jones, Anthony, earl of Snowdon, 141

Arnold, Matthew (1822–88), English poet and critic, 106

Art and Letters (London, 1917–20), edited by Frank Rutter with Charles Gimmel and H. Gilman, July–October 1917, and by Osbert Sitwell, Summer 1919–Spring 1920, 31

Artifex, Sketches and Ideas (RA), 78

Art of Being Ruled, The (Lewis), 40

"The Art of Poetry" (Eliot), 31

"The Art of Poetry" (RA), 31

Aske, Stephen, 82

Asisimov, I. I., 141

Asquith, Herbert Henry, first earl of Oxford and Asquith, 142

"At a Gate by the Way" (RA), 145

Atalanta in Calydon (Swinbourne), 112

At All Costs (RA), 54

Athenaeum (London, 1828–1921), 27–28, 31

Atlantic Monthly, The (Boston, est. 1857), 82–84, 87, 132

Attila (406?–53), king of the Huns, 64, 85

"Attila" (D. H. Lawrence), 85

Attlee, Clement Richard (1883–1967), British statesman, prime minister from 1945 to 1951. A member of the Independent Labour Party since 1908, he served as prime minister for a longer continuous period than any other man since Asquith. His government was notable for social legislation, including national health insurance, extensive nationalization, and granting independence to India. 101, 104, 110

Aucassin and Nicolette (anon.), 111

Augustine, Saint (354–430), church father, bishop of Hippo from 396 to 430, 20

Aurelia (Nerval), 52, 122

Auslander, Joseph (1897–1965), American novelist and consultant in English poetry. His publications include *Sunrise Trumpets* (1924), *Cyclop's Eye* (1926), *No Traveller Returns* (1935), *More than Bread* (1936), and *Riders at the Gate* (1938). Auslander joined the staff of the Library of Congress in 1937. 83

Auslander, Mrs. Joseph. *See* Wurdeman, Audrey May.

Ausonius, Decimus Magnus (ca. 310–ca. 393), Latin poet and rhetorician remarkable chiefly for his preoccupation with the provincial scene in Gaul.

His longest poem, *Mosella,* has flashes of an almost Wordsworthian sensitivity to nature. 9–10

Austen, Jane (1775–1817), English novelist, 108, 110

Autobiography (Cournos), 11

"Autopsy of a Hero" (anon.), 130

Ayscough, Florence J., 25, 123

Bacon, Francis, Baron Verulam, Viscount St. Albans (1561–1626), English essayist, philosopher, and statesman, 131

Bacon, Leonard (1887–1954), American poet, recipient of the Pulitzer Prize for verse in 1941, and longtime friend of RA, 81, **91, 94, 96, 114, 117–18**

Bacon, Martha Sherman. *See* Ballinger, Martha Bacon.

Bacon, Mrs. Leonard (Martha Strongham) (1891–1967) of Berkeley, California, 81, 94, 117

Baedeker, Karl, (1801–59), founder of Baedeker, a German publishing house that issues a famous series of guidebooks, 34, 150

Bairnsfather, Bruce (1888–1959), English cartoonist whose "Old Bill" and his colleagues helped the British muddle through World War I, 13

Balfour, Arthur James, first earl of Balfour (1848–1930), British statesman who held a key position in the Conservative party after 1880 for nearly fifty years, and was prime minister from 1902 to 1905. In May 1915 Balfour succeeded Winston Churchill as first lord of the admiralty; in 1916 he accepted the foreign office in Lloyd George's new government. His decision in favor of Zionist aspirations was embodied in the Balfour Declaration of November 1917. In 1919 he was elected chancellor of Cambridge University. 37

Ballinger, Martha Bacon (born Martha Sherman Bacon) (1917–81), writer who taught at Rhode Island College, eldest daughter of Leonard Bacon. Her first husband was Philip Oliver-Smith, whom she married in 1940. 91, 94, 114

Balls, (RA), 141

Balls and Another Book for Suppression (RA), 141

Balzac, Honoré de (1799–1850), French novelist who was one of the greatest fiction writers of all time, 71, 134

Barfield, Owen (b. 1898), English solicitor, visiting professor, and writer whose works include *Poetic Diction: A Study in Meaning* (1926) and *Romanticism Comes of Age* (1944), 38

Barker, Ernest (1874–1960), English historian, political scientist, and writer who was a fellow of three Oxford colleges between 1898 and 1920 and professor at Cambridge after 1927, 122

Barney, Natalie (1876–1972), wealthy American poet and novelist who lived in America much of her adult life. She was called "L'Amazone" by Remy de Gourmont owing to her skill as a horsewoman, and it was to her that he wrote *Lettres à l'Amazone.* She was hostess at her home at 20 rue Jacob, Paris, to international society, artists of every kind, and lesbians. Her liaison with the painter Romaine Brookes was particularly well known, but she was associated as well with Liane de Pougy, Renée Vivien, Dolly Wilde, and others. Her works include *Poems & Poèmes* (1920), *Nouvelles Pensées de l'Amazone* (1939), and an autobiography. 47, 49

Between St. Denis and St. George (Ford), 5

Bevan, Aneurin (1897–1960), British political leader, 104

Bibesco, Marthe-Lucile (1890–1973), French novelist, biographer, and travel-book writer born in Romania. Her first book, *Les huit paradis* (1907), was published when she was eighteen. 131

Bible, The, 105

Bibliography of the Works of Richard Aldington from 1915 to 1948 (Kershaw), 99, 109, 132

Bid Me to Live (H.D.), 142

Bird, Alan (fl. twentieth cent.), **122, 129,** 146

Bird, William (1888–1963), an American publisher who lived in Paris. In 1921, he started Three Mountains Press as a hobby and there published books by Ezra Pound, Ford Madox Ford, and Ernest Hemingway. Bird also produced the Contact Editions, a series sponsored by Robert McAlmon with money from McAlmon's father-in-law, Sir John Ellerman. In 1928 Nancy Cunard bought Bird's press and with it set up her Hours Press. 49

"Birds of Bigotry" (anon.), 115

Birrell, Augustine (1850–1933), British statesman and man of letters who was chief secretary for Ireland at the time of the 1916 Easter rebellion. His publications in the 1880s, *Obiter Dicta,* and *Charlotte Brontë,* made him a notable figure in literary circles. 37

Birth of a Nation (Daniels), 105

Black Diaries, The (Casement), 140

Blake, Robert (fl. twentieth cent.), Harvard professor of linguistics, a lifelong friend of Leonard Bacon, 117

Blake, William (1757–1827), English artist and poet, 87

Blanke, 96

Blast: Review Of The Great English Vortex (London, 1914–15), edited by Wyndham Lewis, 4, 48

"The Blood of the Young Men" (RA), 16

Blunt, Wilfred (Jasper Walter) (b. 1901), English art teacher, curator, biographer, and writer. Some of his books are *Desert Hawk* (1947), *Tulipomania* (1950), *A Persian Spring* (1957), and *The Golden Road to Samarkand* (1973). 131

Blunt, Wilfred Scawen (1840–1922), English poet and anti-imperialist. RA, Yeats, Pound, and other poets visited him on his seventieth birthday. 113, 132

Boccaccio, Giovanni (1313–75), Italian writer best known for *The Decameron.* RA's 1930 translation of this great work of European literature was long considered one of the best. 101, 146

Bodenheim, Maxwell (1893–1954), American poet and Greenwich Village bohemian who was a protégé of Amy Lowell, 32

" 'Bonbons' of Gall" (Cunard), 128

Bookman (London, 1891–1934), 48

"The Bookshop at Grenay" (RA), 25

"Books in the Line" (RA), 25

Brigitte, ou la Belle au Bois Dormant (Jouhandeau), 49

Brockway, [?], 108

Brooke, Rupert (1887–1915), English poet who died in World War I and whose work appeared in the early *Georgian Poetry* anthologies, 16

Brown, Edmund R. (1888–?), president of Four Seas Company, 1909–30, Boston publisher who issued RA's early books of poetry in the United States; editor of *Poetry Journal*, 1910–30, 25, 29, 31

Browne, William (1591–ca. 1643), of Tavistock, English lyric poet who wrote *The Shepherd's Pipe*, other pastoral poems, and *The Inner Temple Masque*, 111

Bryher, Winifred (1894–1983), legally adopted name of Annie Winifred Ellerman, daughter of Sir John Ellerman, who helped RA become established in London literary circles after World War I. She was twice married, first to Robert McAlmon, and then to Kenneth Macpherson, and wrote historical novels under the name Bryher. She and H.D. met in Cornwall in 1918 and became lifelong friends. Bryher was not only an "other mother" to H.D.'s daughter Perdita, whom she formally adopted, but also helped Catherine, RA's daughter, and RA himself in his last years. It was she who telegraphed RA from Montreux, "Hilda died sleep yesterday." 18, 21, 24–25, 29, 31, 47, 49, 56, 65, 77, 105, 147, **151, 153**

Bubb, Jr., the Rev. Charles Clinch (1876–1936), graduate of Kenyon College (B.A. 1899, M.A. 1902), Keble College, Oxford (M.A. 1903), Bexley Theological Seminary (Hon. D.D. 1924); rector, Grace Church, Cleveland, Ohio, 1906–20; rector, St. Paul's Church, Fremont, Ohio, 1920–36. Bubb ran a private press in Cleveland where, among his other publications, he hand-set and printed five tiny booklets of RA's poetry and translations. Bubb, a noted scholar and printer in the Cleveland area (Shorter of the *Sphere* visited him in 1919), whose 9,000-volume collection of books was one of the finest in Ohio, first wrote RA in 1916; their relationship ended, RA wrote years later, when "Rev. Bubb got mad with me about something he thought disrespectful to Jesus." 14, 16, 101

Budge, Sir Ernest Alfred Wallis (1857–1934), English orientalist who wrote extensively on the ancient Egyptians, 85

Buffoon, The (Wilkinson), 13

Bureau, Noel (fl. 1940s), minor French poet, 105

Burke, Thomas, of Eltham (1886–1945), English writer of fiction and essays who created the character Quong Lee, Chinatown philosopher, in *Limehouse Nights* (1917). With this book and others he popularized the Limehouse district of London. Burke has more than fifty books listed under his name in the British Library *Catalogue*. 131

Burne-Jones, Sir Edward (1833–98), English painter and decorator, an eminent exponent of Pre-Raphaelitism, with its inspiration in the Middle Ages. Burne-Jones's designs for stained glass were produced by William Morris's craftsmen. 110

Burne-Jones, Lady Georgia (fl. nineteenth cent.), wife of Sir Edward Burne-Jones, 110

Burnett, I.A.K., 9

Burns, Robert (1759–96), Scottish poet, 42

Carco, Francis (pseud. of François Carcopino) (1886–1958), French poet who was a member of the group known as the *fantaisistes*. Author of *Au Vent Crispé du Matin*, his work was introduced to British poets by F. S. Flint in 1914. 140

Carcopino, Jerome (1881–1970), French politician and historian who served in Pétain's government and took part in the resistance. He published monographs on Greek and Roman history and was elected to the French Academy in 1955. 140

Carr, Henry, 26

Carraciola, 96

Carrying-off Persephone (Claudianus, trans. Randall), 9

Carswell, Catherine Roxburgh (1879–1946), British writer who began with novels, *Open the Door* (1920) and *The Camomile* (1922), and turned to biography with her *Life of Robert Burns* (1930) and *The Savage Pilgrimage: A Narrative of D. H. Lawrence* (1932). She is probably best remembered for her close association with D. H. Lawrence. 142

Casals, Pablo (1876–1973), Spanish musician, considered one of the greatest cellists of all time, 58

Casement, Roger David (1864–1916), Irish patriot who was in the British consular service until 1912. Captured while attempting to support the 1916 Rebellion by landing arms from a German submarine, he was hanged in London. Diaries by Casement containing detailed descriptions of homosexual practices were circulated privately at the time of his trial and may have discouraged efforts to reprieve him; these were made public in 1959. 130, 140

Catholic Anthology (ed. Pound), 6

Caton, Reginald Ashley, 140

Cavalcanti, Guido (ca. 1255–1300), outstanding member of a group of Italian poets often referred to as the "poets of the *dolce stil novo*." Ezra Pound translated some of his lyrics in *Guido Cavalcanti: Rime* (1931) and in earlier periodical publications. 44

Chamberlayne, William (1619–89), English poet and physician who fought for the Royalists in the Civil War. He is remembered mainly for his heroic verse romance *Pharonnida* (1659). 35

Chambers, Jesse (1887–1944), English teacher and writer whose tormented relationship with D. H. Lawrence became one of the themes of Lawrence's *Sons and Lovers*, 121, 136

Chambrun, Jacques, 92, 97

"Chanson" (d'Orléans), 140

Chapbook (A Monthly Miscellany), The (London, 1919–25), edited by Harold Monro, 1, 9, 31, 33–34, 38

Chapman, Caroline Margaret (d. 1911), the sister of Thomas Robert Lawrence, father of T. E. Lawrence, 122

Chapman, Sir Thomas Robert Tigue (1846–1919), left his wife and four daughters to live with Sarah Maden. Shortly before 1885, he changed his name to Thomas Robert Lawrence. His second of five sons by Sarah was T. E. Lawrence. 122

Colbert, Jean Baptiste (1619–83), French statesman and minister of finance to Louis XIV, who left the monarchy stronger, the nation better equipped, and public administration more orderly than they had ever been, 52

Colin, Rosica (d. 1983), RA's literary agent beginning in 1954. The agency bearing her name still represents RA's estate. 130–31, 133, 145, 147

Collected Letters of D. H. Lawrence, The (ed. Harry T. Moore), 142

Collected Poems (H.D.), 107

Collected Poems (RA), 45, 63

Collected Poems of D. H. Lawrence, 68

Collected Poems of Roy Campbell, The, 117

Collins, William Alexander Roy (1900–1976), English publisher of RA's *Lawrence of Arabia*, 124–25, 149

Colonel's Daughter, The (RA), 57–60, 63–64, 79, 107–8

Compleat Angler, The (Walton), 55

Complete Poems of D. H. Lawrence, The (ed. Pinto and Roberts), 85

Complete Poems of Richard Aldington, The, 13, 86, 99, 107–10, 118, 134, 145

Complete Works of Shelley, The [Vols. 8–10, *Letters*] (ed. Ingpen), 141

Confessions (Symons), 149

Confucius (ca. 551–ca. 479 B.C.), Chinese philosopher and teacher, 123

Conrad, Joseph (1857–1924), English novelist and short-story writer, born in Poland, 117

"A Contemporary of the Future" (Scott), 32

"Corasmin and the Parrots" (Lawrence), 68

Corke, Helen (b. 1880), early friend of D. H. Lawrence and his circle, 121

Coterie (Oxford, 1919–20), edited by Chaman Lall, May 1919–Autumn 1920, and by Russell Green for the issue of Winter 1920–21, 30–31

Cournos, John (1881–1966), Russian-born naturalized American novelist, journalist, translator, and autobiographer. An early friend of RA, he lived in the same house in Mecklenburgh Square, London. During World War I, he served with a British mission in Russia. His novel *Miranda Masters* is based on his own and on RA's circle of friends. 4, 8–9, 11, 17, 18, 44

Cousine Bette, La (Balzac), 71

Cousteau, Jacques, 129

Covici, Pascal (1888–1964), Romanian-born publisher who began his career in Chicago; later associated with Donald Friede in a New York publishing house bearing their names. When this firm failed, Covici joined Viking Press where he worked closely with Steinbeck, Marianne Moore, Arthur Miller, and Saul Bellow. Bellow said: "He loved writers and he lived for literature." 44–45, 120

Coward, Noel (1899–1973), English playwright, actor, and composer whose sparkling treatment of the social mores of the post–World War I period produced successful plays such as *Private Lives* (1930) and *Blithe Spirit* (1941), 60, 72

"The Coxon Fund" (James), 120

Craig, Daphne (b. 1938?), daughter of Edward Gordon Craig, 105–6

Craig, Edward Gordon (1872–1966), son of the actress Ellen Terry, influential English scene designer and producer, 105–6

Hours Press in Paris and later in Reanville. Hours Press published work by contemporary authors, including RA's *Hark the Herald* (1928), *The Eaten Heart* (1929), and *Last Straws* (1930). 47–49, 51–52, 54, 56, 59, 127–28

Cunard, Victor (fl. twentieth cent.), cousin of Nancy Cunard. He coauthored the play *Golden Arrow* (1935) with Sylvia Thompson and contributed "Norman Douglas: 1868–1952" to *Grand Man* (1954). 47

"Current Literature: Georgian Poetry (1918–1919)" (Waugh), 32

Custot, Pierre (1880–?), French author of *Traits galants et aventures du sieur Pierre Defleurville* (1912), *Chichinette et Cia* (1914), and *Sturly* (1923, trans. RA), 129–30

Dahlstrom, Grant (1902–80), leading American painter and designer for more than fifty years; owned the Castle Press in Pasadena, 113

Daily Express (London, 1900–1955), 31, 64

Daily Mail (London, est. 1886), 64, 124

Daily News (London, 1846–1912), became *Daily News and Leader* in 1912, 10

Daily Telegraph (London, 1855–1937), merged with *Morning Post* to form *Daily Telegraph and Morning Post* in 1937, 32, 129

Daily Worker (Chicago, New York; est. 1927), also published in London from 1930 to 1966, 153

"Daisy" (RA), 3

Dali, Salvador (1904–89), Spanish painter, sculptor, and illustrator who has been called the *enfant terrible* of Surrealism, 86, 95

Dalrymple, Ian (b. 1903), born in South Africa but educated in England. He began his distinguished career as film editor, screenplay writer, and director in London in 1928. 98

"Dancers: Palace Music Hall" (RA), 3

Dangerous Acquaintances (Les Liaisons dangereuses) (de Laclos, trans. RA), 63, 142, 146–47

Daniel, Arnaut (fl. ca. 1180–1210), troubador attached to the court of Richard Coeur de Lion and imitated by Ezra Pound in his *Lustra*, 44

Daniels, "Happy," 105

Daniels, Mark, 105

Dante (Dante Alighieri) (1265–1321), Italian poet, 16, 105

Daphnis and Chloë (Longus), 108

Darwin, Charles Robert (1809–82), English naturalist whose *Origin of Species* (1859) is recognized as one of the most influential works of the nineteenth century, 71

Davis, Bette (1908–89), inimitably intense American dramatic actress; a box-office queen for ten years from 1937, she later played eccentric roles. Some of her film releases during the early 1940s were *The Letter* (1940), *The Little Foxes* (1941), and *Mr. Skeffington* (1943). 98

Davison, Edward (1898–1970), Scottish-born poet, editor, teacher, and lecturer who became an American citizen in 1940. He served in the British navy in World War I, and later shared a London apartment with his friend J. B. Priestley. Davison came to the United States in 1926, was a Guggenheim

Eliot, T. S. (Thomas Stearns) (1888–65), American-born poet and critic, who became a British subject in 1927. One of the leading figures of the Modern period, he received the Order of Merit and the Nobel prize for literature in 1948. Eliot and RA began a long and not always friendly relationship in 1917. RA satirized Eliot in *Stepping Heavenward. A Record* (1931). Although he disliked Eliot's poetry, some critics thought RA's *A Fool i' the Forest* (1924) was influenced by Eliot's *The Waste Land* (1922). 26, 27–28, 30–31, 33–39, 41, 44–45, 48, 51, 57, 59, 67, 81, 87, 92–93, 95, 111, 118, 121, 136, 149, 153

Eliot, Vivian, 27

Elistratora, A. E., 141

Elizabeth and Her German Garden (Annette), 60

Ellerman, Hannah Glover, 29

Ellerman, Sir John Reeves (1862–1933), British shipowner and financier, father of Bryher (Winifred Ellerman). Ellerman helped RA to resume his literary career following World War I by recommending him to the editors of the *Times* and *Sphere*, in both of which Sir John had financial interests. RA satirizes, in *A Fool i' the Forest* (1924), a character who could be based on Ellerman. 29, 31, 77, 151

Ellerman, Winifred. *See* Bryher, Winifred.

Ellis, Mrs. Havelock (born Edith Mary Oldham Lees) (1861–1916), English novelist, short-story writer, playwright, and lecturer who was the wife of the English man of letters and writer on social, individual, and sexual psychology whose work strongly influenced modern ideas about sex. Mrs. Ellis went to the United States in 1914–15 twice on lecture tours; her novel *Heaven's Jester* appeared in the *Little Review* in 1914. 6

Elmo, Ann, 147

"Eloi, Eloi, Lama Sabachthani?" (Lawrence), 6

Encyclopaedia Britannica, 78

"Encyclopaedia Britannica Anthology" (ed. RA), 100–102, 105, 108

End to Torment (H.D.), 107

Endymion (Keats), 35

Engels, Friedrich (1820–95), German social philosopher and businessman, the closest collaborator of Karl Marx, 71

"An Englishman in Paris" (RA), 48

English Review, The (London, 1908–37), 25, 29, 31–32, 136, 149

Ernst, Morris L. (1888–1976), American lawyer who specialized in censorship cases and represented American and British writers and their organizations, including the Dramatists' Guild and Authors' League. Ernst wrote books dealing with his profession; he was RA's lawyer for a time when RA was in the United States. 124, 131

"Errant Knight of Capri" (RA), 83

Escaped Cock, The (D. H. Lawrence), 113

Esher, Viscount, 88

Esquire (Chicago, est. 1933), 83, 97

Essays (Bacon), 131

Essays Classical and Modern (Myers), 112

Essays in Biography (Dobrée), 40
"Eternal Verities" (Potter), 65
Etruscan Places (Lawrence), 115
"Eumenides" (RA), 31
Euripides (ca. 480–406 B.C.), Greek tragic poet and playwright; RA translated
    his *Alcestis* in 1930, 10, 15–16, 53, 107
Evans, Charles Seddon (1883–1944), chairman and managing director of
    William Heinemann Ltd, one of RA's principal British publishers, 73, 89
Evening News (London, est. 1881), 67
Evening Standard (London, est. 1827), 15, 64, 131
Exile and Other Poems (RA), 31
Ezra Pound and T. S. Eliot. A Lecture (RA), 84, 126, 132
Ezra Pound's Kensington (Hutchins), 136

Fabre-Luce, Alfred, 69
Fallas, Carl (1885–1962), English sailor and writer of novels, travel literature,
    and autobiography. Fallas and RA met prior to 1914, and in 1916 they en-
    listed in the infantry together. 12, 151
Fallas, Florence (Mrs. Carl R.) (fl. 1912–62), wife of RA's long-time friend, 151,
    153
Fantasia of the Unconscious (Lawrence), 121
"Farewell to Europe . . . " (RA), 84
Farewell to Memories (RA), 147
Faulkner, William (1897–1962), American author and winner of the 1949 Nobel
    prize in literature is most famous for his series of works laid in Yokna-
    patawpha County, Miss. The "saga" includes, most notably, *The Sound and
    the Fury* (1929), *As I Lay Dying* (1930), *Light in August* (1932), *Absalom,
    Absalom* (1936), and *Intruder in the Dust* (1948). Dealing with all levels of
    Southern society, Faulkner saw the South as doomed by its exploitation of
    land and man. 98
"The Faun Captive" (RA), 21
Faust, Dorothy (Mrs. Frederick), 94
Faust, Frederick Schiller (1892–1944), an important figure in American popular
    literature. Publishing under twenty different names, of which "Max Brand"
    is the best known, Faust wrote an estimated thirty million words of fiction,
    creating such characters as Dr. Kildare. He was associated with more than
    seventy motion pictures. RA and Faust met in Hollywood where RA became
    Faust's closest friend. From Africa, Faust wrote his wife to telephone RA:
    "The thought of him is like an oasis in this desert." Faust died in Italy, a war
    correspondent accompanying an attack force there. 94
Fedin, Konstantin Aleksandrovich (1892–1977), Soviet novelist who tried to
    chronicle the evolution of the Russian intellectual under Soviet conditions.
    In the 1920s he was grouped with the fellow travelers, but gradually took a
    position more consistent with Soviet literary policy. In 1959 he was ap-
    pointed first secretary of the Union of Soviet Writers. He was one of the
    writers to host RA in Russia; this was fitting since Soviet critics cite Gorky's

letter to Fedin, 29 March 1932, as one of the starting points of RA's reputation in the Soviet Union. 153

"Feodor Sologub" (Cournos), 8

Fielding, K. J. (fl. 1961), a critic of RA's biography of T. E. Lawrence. RA wrongly considered this a pseudonym used by Liddell Hart. 146, 146 n. 11, 148

Fifteen Joys of Marriage, Ascribed to Antoine De La Sale, c. 1388–c. 1462, The (trans. RA), 42, 63, 101

Fifty Romance Lyric Poems (trans. RA), 63, 65, 101, 107, 110, 140

Finale of Seem (Lowenfels), 52

Finnegans Wake (Joyce), 26

Firbank, (Arthur Annesley) Ronald (1886–1926), English novelist who was greatly indebted to the literature of the 1890s, but his outstanding quality is his peculiarly fantastic and perverse brand of humor. Among his most characteristic novels are *Valmouth* (1919) and *The Flower Beneath the Foot* (1923). 127

Fire of Life (Barrow), 148

Fir-Flower Tablets (trans. Lowell with Ayscough), 25, 123

First Lady Chatterley, The (D. H. Lawrence), 62

First Satire of the Second Book of Horace, The (Pope), 40

Flanner, Janet (1892–1978), born in Indianapolis and educated at the University of Chicago. She went to live in Paris in 1921. On 10 October 1925, her first "Letter from Paris," signed "Genêt," appeared in the *New Yorker* and began a regular feature that continued into the 1960s. Flanner was author also of several books: *The Cubical City, An American in Paris, Petain: The Old Man of France, Men and Monuments,* and *Paris Journal.* 47, 51

Flaubert, Gustave (1821–80), French novelist, 71, 75, 117

Fletcher, John Gould (1886–1950), American poet who was one of the early Imagists. A friend of Amy Lowell, he contributed to her anthologies, *Some Imagist Poets,* 1915, 1916, and 1917. From Imagism Fletcher turned to regional poetry and eventually allied himself with the Agrarians. 6–7, 31, 52

Flint, F. S. (Frank Stuart) (1885–1960), English poet and translator associated with RA in the Imagist movement. He was also an important link between French and English poets, and, in addition to his literary work, was a successful member of the Ministry of Labour. Among his books of poetry were *In the Net of Stars* (1909), *Cadences* (1915), and *Otherworld* (1920). 4, 6, 8–10, 11, 12–14, 15, 29–30, 33, 35, 50, 52, 112, 120, 132, 136

Flint, Ianthe, 13

Folgore da San Gemignano (1270?–1330?), Tuscan poet; his poems tell of occupations for the months of the year and pleasures of the days of the week. RA translated his *Garland of Months,* which was first published by The Clerk's Press in Cleveland, Ohio, 1917. 14, 101

Fool i' the Forest, A (RA), 63

"For Armistice Day 1939" (RA), 82

Ford, Ford Madox (b. Ford Madox Hueffer) (1873–1939), English novelist, poet, essayist, and editor. He collaborated with Joseph Conrad, and was author of the Tietjens tetralogy, classic novels of World War I. As founder and editor of the *English Review* he encouraged literary talent by publishing the first work of writers such as D. H. Lawrence. Ford contributed to *Des Imagistes* (1914), and, for a short time, employed RA as a secretary. RA satirized Ford in a number of his writings. 4–5, 15, 29, 38, 47, 50, 52, 119, 136, 142–43

Forster, E. M. (Edward Morgan) (1879–1970), English novelist, short-story writer, essayist, and critic, 38, 111

Four English Portraits, 1801–1851 (RA), 110, 147

Fox, C. J., 53, 57

France, Anatole (pseud. for Jacques Anatole Thibaut) (1844–1924), French writer who received the 1921 Nobel Prize in literature; he was known for his lucid, graceful style: "A simple style is like white light. It is complex, but does not appear so." 31

Franco, Francisco (1892–1975), Spanish general who became head of the rebel government in 1936 and of the fascist Falange party in 1937. With the help of Germany and Italy, Franco won the Spanish civil war in 1939 and established his own government. Franco declared Spain a kingdom in 1947 and named himself its regent. He named Juan Carlos as his successor, but kept power until his death. 117, 134

Frauds (RA), 127, 131, 133

Frazer, Sir James George (1854–1941), Scottish classicist and anthropologist known primarily as author of *The Golden Bough*, 38

Frederick the Great, the Memoirs of His Reader, Henri de Catt (1758–1760) (trans. Flint), 13

French Comedies of the XVIIIth Century (trans. RA), 101

"French Literature and the War" (de Gourmont), 5

"French Revolution" (Wordsworth), 71

French Studies and Reviews (RA), 44, 63

Frere, Alexander Stewart (born Frere-Reeves) (1896–1984), English publisher with William Heinemann Ltd until 1964, when he retired as president. RA said of him, "He can always be relied upon to say the right thing at the right moment." 55, 57, 59, **61–62**, **65–69**, 72–75, 78, 82, 88, 90, 101, 106, 108, 111, 113, **116**, **121**, 124, **125**, 126, 128, 130–31, 133, 147

Frere, Patricia (Mrs. A. S.) (b. 1907), daughter of Edgar Wallace, a journalist. "Wallace," as she was known to her friends, was admired and held in fond regard by RA. She became Frere's second wife in 1932. 57, 66–67, 69, 72–74, 75, 88, 90, 108

Fresnay, Pierre (born Laudenbach) (1897–1975), French actor and theater manager who entered the Paris Conservatoire in 1914 and made his first appearance on the stage of the Comédie-Française in 1915. He served in the French army from 1916 to 1919. Besides many stage plays in France, England, and the United States, he appeared in over sixty films. 146

Freud, Sigmund (1856–1939), Austrian neurologist; founder of psychoanalysis, 105

Freytag-Lovinghoven, Baroness Elsa von (fl. 1920), sculptor, model, shoplifter, friend of the *Little Review* coterie and protégé of Marcel Duchamp. She was

House of Lords. A pioneer in the study of Scandinavian and French literature, he was knighted in 1925. 30, 42, 44

Gourmont, Jean de (1877–1928), French novelist (*La toison d'or* [1908]) and
critic (*Muses d'aujourd'hui* [1910]), who wrote of his brother in *Souvenirs
sur Remy de Gourmont* (1925), 44

Gourmont, Remy de (1858–1915), French novelist, poet, playwright, and critic,
important in the growth of the Symbolist movement. His fifty volumes are
mainly collections of articles; his work influenced Pound, Eliot, and other
Modernist writers. RA corresponded with de Gourmont just before World
War I, and, with Amy Lowell, helped him financially. In 1929 RA translated
Selections from All His Works, and, in 1931, *Letters to the Amazon*. 5–6,
11, 15, 31, 40, 44

Graves, Charles Parlin (1911–72), American author of children's books. He began his career writing for advertising agencies in New York and Hollywood. 131

Graves, Robert Von Ranke (1895–1985), English poet, novelist, and essayist. He
wrote *Lawrence and the Arabs* (1927), an account of Lawrence that RA
takes issue with in his *Lawrence of Arabia* (1955). 131, 138

Gray, Cecil (1892–1951), composer, music critic, and writer of a "somewhat
speculative" history of music and of books on his friend Peter Warlock
(Philip Heseltine), Gesualdo, Sibelius, and others. Gray was the father of
H.D.'s child, but neither H.D. nor the child is mentioned in Gray's autobiography, and RA receives only one mention. (See *Musical Chairs*, London,
1948, p. 140). Gray has been described as "heavy and silent" but acutely
aware of all that was going on despite his look of somnolence. 18, 20–24,
49, 77

Grazzini, Anton Francesco (1503–84), a Florentine apothecary who devoted
himself to letters. Grazzini edited collections of satirical verse and carnival
songs; he composed satirical and mock-heroic poems, seven comedies, and
a collection of comic *novelle*. He was a founder-member of the Accademia
degli Umidi, in which he took the name of Lasca. 59

Great French Romances (intro. RA), 104

Greek Songs in the Manner of Anacreon (trans. RA), 16

Green, Helen A., 1

Green, Steve, 51

Greenslet, Ferris (1885–1959), American editor and author. His books include
James Russell Lowell (1905) and *The Lowells and Their Seven Worlds*
(1946). He was associate editor of the *Atlantic Monthly* from 1902 to 1907,
and literary advisor to Houghton Mifflin & Co. from 1907 and director
from 1910. 6

Greenstreet, Sydney (1879–1954), British stage actor long in America. A sensation in his first film, he became a major star of the forties. Some of his films
released while RA was in Hollywood were *The Maltese Falcon* (1941),
Across the Pacific (1942), and *Between Two Worlds* (1944). 98

Greenwald, Constantin de, 131

Gregg, Frances Josepha. *See* Wilkinson, Frances Gregg.

Gribble, George Dunning (1882–1956), British writer, translator, and playwright who was a close friend of RA's from the days both lived in Berkshire; in Aldington's last years they also lived near each other in France. 104, 134, 136

Grigson, Geoffrey (Edward Harvey) (1905–85), English poet and critic. He edited the works of William Barnes, Walter Savage Landor, William Morris, and others. 131

Guarini, Giovanni Battista (1538–1612), Italian poet and author of *Il Pastor fido*, a pastoral dramatic poem that became very popular throughout Europe, and reflected and influenced the manners of the age, 101

Guneau, Maxim and Suzanne, 154

Guignebert, Charles Alfred Honoré (1867–1939), French historian and professional who wrote many books on church history. His contribution to the *Criterion* was "Concerning the Devil," which appeared in October 1923. 38

Guillaume, Catherine Aldington. *See* Aldington, Catherine.

Guinzburg, Harold Kleinert (1899–1961), American publisher long associated with Viking Press, 69, 94

"The Gullibility of the British" (RA), 136

Haden-Guest, Stephen Heden, second baron of Sailing (1902–74), British translator and editor of scientific works; with British Information Services New York from 1941 to 1945; with United Nations Information Office from 1943 to 1946. He married Barbara Ann Pinson in 1948; they divorced in 1954. 48–49, 74

Hagedorn, Hermann (1882–1964), American novelist, poet, and biographer whose books include *Poems and Ballads* (1912), *Edward Arlington Robinson* (1938), and *The Roosevelt Family of Sagamore Hill* (1954). Some of his poems were included in *The New Poetry* (1917, 1925). 31

Haggard, Lilias Rider (1892–1968), daughter of British author Sir H. Rider Haggard, author of *Norfolk Life* (1943), for which Henry Williamson wrote the footnotes, and *Norfolk Notebook* (1946). She edited *I Walked by Night* (1935) and wrote a biography of her father (1951). 131

Hailsham, Lord. *See* Hogg, Quintin McGarel.

Haley, Sir William (1901–87), editor of the *Times* (London) from 1952 to 1966 and, before that, director-general of the B.B.C. from 1944 to 1952. From the time when, as Joseph Sell, he wrote a column on books for the *Manchester News*, Haley was a friendly critic of RA's work. 80

Hall, Fitzedward (1825–1901), American orientalist who settled in England. Hall was the first American to edit a Sanskrit text. 85

Hamlet (Shakespeare), 27

"A Happy Pagan" (Campbell), 134

Hardy, Thomas (1840–1928), English writer who published his short stories and novels until 1895, when the hostile reception of *Jude the Obscure* caused him to turn to poetry, 30, 152

Hark the Herald (RA), 49

Harmsworth, Sir Hildebrand Alfred Beresford, second bart. (1901–77), member of a family that exerted enormous power and influence in English journalism, especially during World War I, 108

Harrison, Austin (1873–1928), English essayist, political writer, historian. He replaced Hueffer (Ford) as editor of *English Review* early in 1910. 25

Harrison, Jane Ellen (1850–1928), English classicist who applied archaeological investigation to studies of Greek religion, 38

Hartley, Leslie Poles (1895–1972), British author and critic who wrote literary criticism for weekly reviews beginning 1923. Publications include short stories and novels beginning 1944. His novel *Eustace and Hilda* (1947) won the James Tait Black Memorial prize. 78

Hawk, Harold (fl. twentieth cent.), rancher at Del Monte near Taos, 88

Hawthorne (James), 120

Hawthorne, Nathaniel (1804–64), American novelist and short-story writer, 120

Hawthorne, Raymond, 146

Haynes, Edmund Sidney Pollock (1877–1949), possibly the English solicitor and writer of this name who was a member of the firm of Hunter and Haynes, solicitors, 49

Hazard, Caroline (1856–1945), prominent New England civic worker, writer, and from 1899 to 1910 president of Wellesley College, 81

Hazard, Thomas Pierrepont (1892–1968), estate manager active in Rhode Island civic affairs and government, 81

Hazlitt, William (1778–1830), English critic and essayist, 90

"Hearthstone" (Monro), 6

Heart to Artemis, The (Bryher), 151

Hegel, Georg Wilhelm Friedrich (1770–1831), German philosopher whose writings influenced modern existentialism as well as the thought of Karl Marx, 71, 90

Heine, Heinrich (1797–1856), German lyric poet and satirist whose revolutionary sympathies were at odds with the commercial interests of his family. Heine's *Nordsee* poems influenced the free verse of the Imagists via Henley's *In Hospital*. 15, 143

Helen in Egypt (H.D.), 145

Hell! Said the Duchess: A Bedtime Story (Arlen), 71

Hemon, Louis, 132

Henderson, Wyn (fl. twentieth cent.), a typographer who worked with John Rodker at the Ovid Press and with Sir Francis Meynell at the Nonesuch. She founded the Aquila Press in 1929 and in the following year published Nancy Cunard's *Poems (Two) 1925*. The Aquila Press did not survive the depression. She took over the management of the Hours Press in 1930 when Nancy Cunard went to America to attend the Scottsboro Trials and then began work on her *Negro Anthology*. The last five books of the Hours Press were produced under Henderson's direction. Their association ended when she and Nancy Cunard quarreled. Later, Henderson worked as Peggy Guggenheim's secretary and helper in the organization of art exhibitions. 54

Jacobs, Mendel (fl. 1950s), South African bookseller and occasional publisher in London, 115

James, Henry (1843–1916), American novelist and critic and one of the most influential theorists of fiction in the English-speaking world. Although he wrote for more than half a century as an American, he became a British subject a few months before his death. He wrote twenty full-length novels, a dozen novelettes, more than a hundred short stories, essays, and travel notes. He employed a forerunner of the "stream of consciousness" technique in his fiction. 117, 120

James Joyce's World (Hutchins), 136

Jane Austen (RA), 99, 113

Jane Eyre [Screenplay] (Huxley), 97

Januarius, Saint (272?–305), Italian ecclesiastic and martyr; patron saint of Naples, 85

"Japanese Print" (Fletcher), 6

Jarry, Alfred (1873–1907), French writer whose "fiercely grotesque, antibourgeois farce" called *Ubu Roi* (1896) was one of the sources of Surrealistic influence on modern French poetry, 131

Jeremiah (fl. ca. 628–586 B.C.), an Old Testament prophet who preached in Jerusalem and in Egypt, 106

Joachim, Harold Henry (1869–1938), professor of logic, Oxford University; writer and translator. Contrary to RA's expectation he did not publish in volume 2 of the *Criterion*. 38

Job, Thomas (1900–1947), British-born naturalized American playwright and professor of drama, who was a screenwriter for Warner Brothers and Twentieth Century–Fox. Job's *Uncle Harry* was produced in New York in 1942. 98

Joffre, Joseph Jacques Césaire, 1

John, Augustus Edwin (1879–1961), British portrait and mural painter, etcher, and lithographer who did studies of many leading personalities of his period, 78, 139

John Keats (Lowell), 35

John O' London's Weekly (London, 1919–54), 80

Johnson, Malcolm (1903–58), American editor and publisher who became vice-president of D. Van Nostrand Company. From 1937 to 1934 he was employed by Doubleday. 73

Johnson, Willard "Spud" (1897–1968), member of Taos group, a friend of Witter Bynner, and editor of a small western periodical, *The Laughing Horse*, to which D. H. Lawrence contributed, 88

Jones, Elizabeth, 75

Jonson, Ben (1573–1637), English dramatist and poet, 28

Jordan, Viola (ca. 1880–?), lifelong friend of H.D., 107

Jouhandeau, Marcel Henri (1888–1979), extremely prolific French novelist. He published seventy works between 1921 and 1960. 49

Journals d'un Voyage à Paris en Septembre–Octobre, 1820 (Jessop), 48

Journals of Claire Clairmont (ed. Stocking and Stocking), 141

Journey's End (Sherriff), 98

Joyce, James (1882–1941), Irish-born novelist who lived most of his life on the continent. He appeared with RA in the first Imagist anthology, and RA was literary editor of the *Egoist* when Joyce's *Portrait of the Artist as a Young Man* (1916) appeared there. RA admired Joyce's writing but felt it would be dangerous to try to imitate it. 8, 26, 30, 32, 35, 39, 43, 45, 52, 132, 136, 139, 153

Joyce, Lucia Anna (1907–82), only child of James Joyce. She had a mental breakdown at twenty-five and spent most of her life in hospitals. 136

Joynson-Hicks, Lancelot William, third Viscount Brentford (b. 1902), solicitor and senior partner of Joynson-Hicks & Co.; member of Parliament from 1949 to 1958, 122, 124, 148

Joynson-Hicks, William, Viscount Brentford (1865–1932), solicitor, head of the firm of Joynson-Hicks & Co., and a member of Parliament almost continuously from 1908 to 1929. Joynson-Hicks held numerous prestigious government positions, among them that of home secretary from 1924 to 1929. The year after the home secretary's office tried to intervene in the sale of Harold Acton's translation *The Last of the Medici*, published in Florence by Pino Orioli, RA's friend, RA attacked Joynson-Hicks and his successor with an article in *The Referee*, 28 December 1930. RA often referred to Joynson-Hicks as "Jix." 124–25, 148

Jung, Carl Gustav (1875–1961), Swiss psychiatrist and psychologist, 96

Junner, Sarah. *See* Maden, Sarah.

Kahn, Gustave (1859–1936), experimental French poet, author of *Chansons d'amant* (1891), *La pluie et le beau temps* (1895), *Limbes et lumiéres* (1895), *Livre d'images* (1897), and studies of Boucher, Fragonard, Rodin, and Baudelaire, 34

Kangaroo (Lawrence), 85

Kataev, Valentin Petrovich (1897–1986), widely translated Soviet novelist and playwright who fought in the Revolution. He contributed to *Krokodil* and was chief editor of *Iunost*. 153

Keats, John (1795–1821), English poet, 33, 35, 90, 152

Keith, Arthur Berriedale (1879–1944), Scottish Sanskrit scholar and constitutional historian of the British Commonwealth and Empire. Keith was professor of Sanskrit and comparative philology at Edinburgh University from 1914 to 1944 and lecturer on the constitution of the British Empire from 1927 to 1944. He was author of numerous books. 38

Kennington, Eric Henri (1888–1960), English artist who was art editor for T. E. Lawrence's *Seven Pillars of Wisdom*. Kennington also made the bronze head of Lawrence at St. Paul's Cathedral, the Lawrence medal for the Royal Asian Society, and a number of recumbent effigies of Lawrence. 129

Ker, William Paton (1855–1923), professor of poetry at Oxford and of English literature in London; author of learned studies in literatures of England, Scotland, and Scandinavia, 38

Kershaw, Alister (b. 1921), Australian poet, historian, biographer, and journalist who came to France in 1947. He acted as Aldington's secretary for some

Little Book of Modern Verse, The (ed. Rittenhouse), 31

Little Review, The (Chicago, New York, Paris; 1914–29), edited by Margaret C. Anderson with Jane Heap, 1921–29, 6–7, 15, 32, 43

"Little Tales" (Sologub, trans. Cournos), 8

"London Day by Day: A Blurb—for Mr. Aldington" ("Peterborough"), 130

London Mercury, The (1919–34), edited by John C. Squire, 35, 45

Longus (fl. ca. A.D. 200), Greek poet and sophist; author of *Daphnis* and *Chloë*. 108

Lorenzo. *See* Lawrence, David Herbert.

"Lorenzo in Chaos" (RA), 136

Lorre, Peter (1904–64), highly individual Hungarian character actor who filmed in Germany and Britain before settling in Hollywood. Some of his screen credits of the 1940s are *The Face Behind the Mask* (1941), *The Maltese Falcon* (1941), and *Arsenic and Old Lace* (1942; released 1944). 98

"Los Angeles Book Fair a Big Success" (anon.), 95

Louis XV (1710–74), king of France from 1715 to 1774, 104

Love Among the Haystacks (D. H. Lawrence), 121

Love and the Luxembourg (RA), published in London as *A Dream in the Luxembourg*, 51–52, 54–55, 63, 120, 147

Love of Myrrhine and Konallis, and Other Prose Poems, The (RA), 25, 120

Love Poems of Myrrhine and Konallis, The (RA), 14

"The Love Song of J. Alfred Prufrock" (Eliot), 118

Loving, Edward Pierre (1893–1950), English writer and editor who was on the staff of the *New York Herald*, Paris, in 1925, and advisory editor to *This Quarter*, Paris, 1929. His *Monsieur de Balzac Entertains a Visitor* was a 1929 Washington University Chapbook, no. 28, edited by Glenn Hughes. 46

Lowell, Amy (1874–1925), American poet and leader of the Imagist movement in America. After associating herself with *Des Imagistes* (1914), the first Imagist anthology, she sponsored three more in 1915, 1916, and 1917 under the title *Some Imagist Poets*. RA was a principal contributor to the four anthologies, but Pound disassociated himself from what he called "Amygism" after the first anthology and tried to prevent the new group from using the title. In many ways Lowell's promotion of poetry in America (her own included) rivaled Pound's efforts, which helped to account for their mutual animosity. 6–7, 15–16, 21, 25, 29, 31–32, 35–37, 46, 112, 123

Lowenfels, Lilian (fl. twentieth cent.), wife of the poet Walter Lowenfels, 47, 51–52, 54

Lowenfels, Walter (1897–1976), American journalist, poet, anthologist, and editor. His wife, Lilian, typed the manuscript of *Death of a Hero*. Lowenfels shared the 1929 Richard Aldington award with e. e. cummings; he fought for civil and labor rights until his imprisonment during the McCarthy period. Henry Miller called him "probably *the poet* of the age." 47, 50–52, 54–55, 112, 139

Lowry, Howard, 91

Lucas, [?] (fl. 1958), the chartered accountant employed by the publishing companies with which Eric Warman was associated, 137

Marivaux, Pierre Carlet de Chamblain de (1688–1763), French dramatist and novelist, 104

Marks, Mrs. Lionel. *See* Peabody, Josephine Preston.

Marmontel, Jean François, 55, 74

Marsden, Dora (1882–1960), founder, editor, and leader-writer of the *Freewoman* (1911), which became the *New Freewoman* when Harriet Shaw Weaver bought an interest in the journal, and which was eventually renamed the *Egoist*. Marsden was an English feminist and philosophical essayist; she appointed RA assistant editor of the soon-to-be-renamed *New Freewoman* partly because she resented Ezra Pound's take-over tactics. 6

Marsh, Edward (1872–1953), editor of *Georgian Poetry* from 1912 to 1922, the organ for the movement opposed by Imagism. A patron of arts and artists, Marsh was private secretary to Sir Winston Churchill periodically between 1905 and 1929. 30, 32, 35, 131

Marx, Karl Heinrich (1818–83), a German philosopher of history and the most important figure in the history of socialist thinking, 71, 153

Mary, Queen of Scots (1542–87), daughter of James V of Scotland and wife of Francis II of France, and considered *de jure* queen of England by Roman Catholic Europe. After the death of Francis, Mary returned to Scotland as queen. Later, forced to flee to England, she was imprisoned by Elizabeth and, accused of plotting against the English queen, was beheaded. 42

Masséna, André, duc de Rivoli and prince d'Essling (1758–1817), French marshal under Napoleon I, 91

Masterman, Charles Frederick Gurney (1874–1927), English politician, author, and journalist. Elected to Parliament in 1906, he supported Lloyd George's national insurance plan. Masterman was a member of the Cabinet when war was declared in 1914; he directed Wellington House (propaganda department) from 1914 to 1918, and in 1918 was director of the literary department of the Ministry of Information. His most popular book was *The Condition of England* (1909). 5, 142–43

Mathews, Charles Elkin (1851–1921), English publisher who issued RA's *Images of Desire*. After running a bookstore for some years, he founded the Bodley Head Publishing Company with John Lane. *The Yellow Book* (1894–97) was published by "Elkin Mathews and John Lane." 25, 29

Matisse, Henri (1869–1964), French painter, 116

Matthiessen, F. O., 120

Mattingly, H., 9

"Le Maudit" (RA), 31

Mauerman, Mary Anne (b. 1927), American writer and educator, the daughter of Babette and Glenn Hughes. She is also a college teacher and codirector of a professional writing school. 45–46, 52

Maugham, William Somerset (1874–1965), English novelist, playwright, and short-story writer. Maugham is best known for his semiautobiographical novel *Of Human Bondage* (1915) and the play *Rain* dramatized from the short story. He based *Ashenden* (1928) on his experiences in the secret service during World War I. 134, 152–53

Mavrogordato, John Nicholas (1882–1970), a close friend of Norman Douglas. Nancy Cunard called Mavrogordato, who was associated with Exeter College, Oxford University, a "Greek of great literary culture." 48

McAlmon, Robert (1896–1956), American publisher and editor. He grew up in South Dakota. After wandering from there to California and New York (Greenwich Village), McAlmon emigrated to London and Paris. There, from William Byrd's Three Mountains Press, McAlmon published his Contact Editions, started in New York with W. C. Williams. He married Winifred Bryher, but the marriage did not last. 49, 151

McCarthy, Joseph R., 139

McClymont, J. R. (fl. 1920s), 2

McCulloch, [?] (d. 1938), Netta Aldington's father, a successful solicitor and also a socialist, 78

McGreevy, Thomas (1896–1967), Irish poet and critic; graduate of University College; English reader at the University of Paris in 1926; lecturer at the Ecole Normale Supérieure; and critic for the *Studio* in London during the 1930s. He settled in Dublin in 1941 and was appointed director of the National Gallery, from which position he retired in 1964. McGreevy was a friend of Joyce (later his executor) who in turn introduced him to RA. "One of the best beloved of the many friends made for me by *Death of a Hero*," RA wrote. They traveled together in Italy; McGreevy also wrote the first book of criticism on RA, *Richard Aldington: An Englishman,* and was an original member of the C.L.S. In his later years, McGreevy changed the spelling of his name to MacGreevy, but I have followed RA's spelling. 54– 55, 57–61, 67, 126, 137

Medallions in Clay (trans. RA), 63

Medea (Euripides), 53

Medici, Gian (Giovanni) Gastone de' (1670–1737), last of the younger branch of the Medici. He was fifty-three when he succeeded his father, Cosimo III. In bad health and worn out by dissipation, he had neither ambition nor aptitude for rule, submitting in turn to Spain and Austria. 139

"Meditation on a German Grave" (RA), 54

"Meditation" (RA), 31

"Meditation [2]" (RA), 31

"Meditations 3" (RA), 31

"Meditations 4" (RA), 31

Medley, Charles Douglas (1870–1963), British solicitor, formerly senior partner in the firm of Field Roscoe & Co, 62

Meinertzhagen, Colonel Richard (1878–1967), British officer who served in Africa, France, India, and Palestine. Meinertzhagen was a member of Great Britain's peace delegation in Paris, political officer in Palestine and Syria, and military adviser on the Middle East. He wrote about the birds of Egypt and Arabia (1930 and 1954) and published four diaries: *Kenya Diary 1902– 1906* (1957), *Middle East Diary* (1959), *Army Diary* (1960), and *Diary of a Black Sheep* (1964). 149

Meleager (fl. early first century B.C.), Greek epigramist whose *Garland* contained, besides his own work, that of fifty or more poets from earliest times

of the Museum Arlatan, a museum of Provençal artifacts, and he was founder of the Société du Félibrige, an organization for the promotion of Provençal as a literary language. Mistral is the subject of RA's *Introduction to Mistral* (1956), which won a special *Prix de Gratitude Mistralienne* in 1956 from the Félibrige. 126, 132

Mitchell, Margaret, 86

Mlle de Maupin (Gautier), 19

Moby-Dick (Melville), 113

"Modern American Poetry" (anon.), 31

"Modern Free Verse" (RA), 41

Modern Lover, A (D. H. Lawrence), 121

"Modern Poetry and the Imagists" (RA), 3

Moiseiwitch, Maurice, 95

"Moment at Sea, A" (RA), 75

Mondadori, Alberto (1914–76), Italian publisher and poet who was director of Mondadori Publishing House, Milan, Italy, when it issued a number of translations of RA's works. Mondadori was the founder and managing editor of *Tempo* and managing editor of *Epoca;* he published two volumes of poetry in 1957. 73, 135

Monro, Harold Edward (1879–1932), English poet, anthologist, and editor; he established the Poetry Bookshop; edited *Poetry Review* in 1912, *Poetry and Drama* from 1913 to 1914, and the *Chapbook* from 1919 to 1925. Although dedicated to poetry he was never narrowly sectarian, publishing in close succession *Georgian Poetry* and *Des Imagistes*. RA said Monro "had been the Marshal Joffre of contemporary English poetry—always ten minutes late and two divisions short," but, by his devotion to its cause, Monro did help to make modern poetry possible; he was the publisher of RA's first book of poems, *Images (1912–1915)*, and helped him to find a place in London's literary circles. 1–3, 5, 6, 9–10, 15, 33–34, 38–39, 41, 45, 52, 112

Monroe, Harriet (1860–1936), American poet and editor, the founder and for many years editor of *Poetry: A Magazine of Verse* (first issue, October 1912), which soon became the leading journal of its kind. Although she published several volumes of verse herself, she will be best remembered for the forum she provided for new poets and poetry. RA's "Choricos" and "To a Greek Marble" were published in the second issue of *Poetry*, signaling the start of the Imagist movement. Years later, RA wrote to Monroe that she could never know what her publication of his work had meant to a friendless and unknown boy: "I could have embraced you as my fairy godmother." 3, 6, 30–31

Montaigne, Michel Eyquem Seigneur de (1533–92), French essayist who was one of the few great writers to introduce a new kind of literature in his *Essays* (1580–88), 35

Montgomery, General B. L., 93

Moore, George (1852–1933), Irish novelist best known for his autobiographical trilogy, *Hail and Farewell* (1911–14), 48

Moore, Harry T. (1908–81), professor of English and research professor at Southern Illinois University. Moore's numerous works include *The Intelligent Heart: The Story of D. H. Lawrence* (1954) and *The Collected Letters of D. H. Lawrence* (1962). A few weeks before his death, Moore and Ian S. MacNiven's edition of the correspondence between Lawrence Durrell and RA appeared under the title *Literary Lifelines*. 117, 121, 132, **142,** 149

Moore, Marianne (1887–1972), American poet, was first published in the *Egoist* (1 April 1915) when RA was an editor; later Moore's first book of poems was published by the Egoist Press in 1921. Her 1951 *Collected Poems* won a Pulitzer Prize. *The Complete Prose of Marianne Moore*, edited and with an introduction by Patricia Willis was published in 1986. She served as an editor of the influential review *The Dial* from 1925 to 1929. 6, 118, 136

Moore, T. Sturge (1870–1944), Irish engraver, art critic, aesthetician, and poet. Moore was one of the first modern poets to attempt to reform poetic diction. A collected edition of his poems was published in four volumes in 1931–33. 26

Morel, Edmund D. (1873–1924), British author and journalist; founder of the Congo Reform Association, 1904; honorary secretary of the Congo Reform Association from 1904 to 1912; editor of the *African;* secretary and part founder of the Union of Democratic Control; editor of *Foreign Affairs;* and member of Parliament from 1922 to 1924, 142

Morgan, Louise (Mrs. Otto Frederick Theis) (1885–1964), literary journalist who settled in London after World War I. Using her maiden name, she began a series on writers at work with an interview with David Garnett in the 10 July 1930 issue of *Everyman*. RA was included in the series as the subject of "Writing a Best Seller in Seven Weeks," which appeared in the 21 August 1930 issue of *Everyman*. In 1931, Chatto & Windus published a volume of her interviews, *Writers at Work*, as Dolphin no. 11. In 1934 she became special correspondent for the *News Chronicle* until her retirement in the early 1950s. 47, 59

Morley, Frank Vigor (1899–1980), English publisher, editor, and writer who was cofounder of the British publishing company Faber & Faber and vice-president and editor at Harcourt, Brace. 87

Mornings in Mexico (D. H. Lawrence), 68, 85, 111

Morrell, Philip (1870–1943), Labour member of Parliament for South Oxfordshire from 1906 to 1910; for Burnley from 1910 to 1918. His wife, Lady Ottoline, was a famous hostess and patron of the arts; Morrell himself was a militant pacifist during World War I. D. H. Lawrence was a frequent guest of the Morrells, and their fictional counterparts appear in his *Women in Love* (1920). 59

Morris, Jane Burden (Mrs. William) (fl. nineteenth cent.), daughter of a butcher, married William Morris when she was about eighteen. Allegedly, she was at one time the mistress of Dante Gabriel Rossetti, who lived briefly in the Morris home in Kelmscott. 110

Morris, William (1834–96), English social reformer, craftsman, printer, designer, artist, and poet educated at Oxford. Morris set a new style in home decoration, finding inspiration for it in the Middle Ages, which were the setting, too, for his poems and prose romances. His final project was the Kelmscott Press. 110, 112

Morton, "Jelly Roll" (Ferdinand Joseph LaMenthe) (1885–1941), black American musician and composer of mixed African and French American ancestry. He played piano in the bordellos of New Orleans, traveled through much of the United States spreading his concept of ragtime and jazz, and recorded with his own band, the Red Hot Peppers, some of the finest examples of New Orleans Dixieland style. He published *Jelly Roll Blues* in 1915. 47

Mosella (Ausonius), 9

Movietones, Invented and Set Down by Richard Aldington, 1928–1929, 62

Moving Along; Just a Diary (Orioli), 66

"Mr. Aldington's Collected Verse" (anon.), 112

"Mr. Aldington's Poems" [Letter] (Campbell), 112

"Mr. James Joyce's 'Ulysses' " (RA), 44

Muggeridge, Malcolm (1903–90), English editor who wrote for a number of newspapers, including the *Manchester Guardian* and the *Evening Standard and Daily Telegraph*. He was rector of Edinburgh University from 1967 to 1968. 78

Murder in France (Kershaw), 132

Murdock, Kenneth B., 120

Murry, John Middleton (1889–1957), English critic, editor, and biographer who was the husband of Katherine Mansfield (1888–1923). He wrote *Son of Woman* (1931), one of the biographies of D. H. Lawrence that appeared shortly after D.H.L.'s death. Aldous Huxley called it "a curious essay in destructive hagiography." 59, 61, 85, 140, 142

"Music Starts a Geometry" (Pound), 45

Mussolini, Benito (1883–1945), Italian politician and journalist who founded the *Fasci di Combattimento* in 1919, formed the first Fascist government in 1922, and became Il Duce in 1925–26. Italian losses in World War II led to his downfall and execution in 1945. 64, 83, 107

Myers, Frederick William Henry (1843–1901), English essayist and poet, better known for his physical investigations and for helping to found the Society of Psychical Research in 1822. 112

My Friends When Young (Patmore), 47

"My Immortal Friends" (RA), 75

Nana (Zola), 120

Napoleon I (1769–1821), emperor of the French, 91

Nash's Pall Mall Magazine (London), 54

Nation (New York, est. 1865), 90, 133

Nation and Athenaeum, The (London, 1907–31), 25, 31, 42

Nature in Downland (Hudson), 152

Navone, Giulio (fl. 1880), Italian editor, 101

"Nazis Sank 17 Ships in Bombing of Bari" (Shalett), 96

on RA's satire of Nancy Cunard "Now Lies She There: An Elegy," published in *Soft Answers* (1932). 47–48, 52, 55, 74, 131

Patmore, John Deighton (fl. early twentieth cent.), the poet Coventry Patmore's grandson, who married Ethel Elizabeth Morrison-Scott, called Brigit, in 1907. For a time, Patmore was a successful businessman and, in a partnership with the financier Clarence Hatry, made a considerable fortune and then lost it in 1924. At about the same time, Patmore and his wife separated and, although not divorced, never lived together again. 55

Patmore, Michael (b. 1911), younger son of Brigit Patmore. His wife, Netta, left him in June 1937 to elope with RA to France. 47, 50, 54, 72–76, 81, 97, 107, 116, 124, 130, 143, 145, 147

Patmore, Netta. *See* Aldington, Netta.

Pattern for Murder (Warman), 89, 93

Pauchinskaja, Ludmila, 151

Paulhan, Jean (1884–1968), French essayist, critic, and from 1925 to 1940 editor of the *Nouvelle Revue Française,* 48

Payne, John, 101

Pearce, Charles A. (1906–70), American publisher who in 1939 founded Duell, Sloan & Pearce with Samuel Sloan and Charles Halliwell Duell. Pearce was editor in chief from 1939 to 1961; executive editor of Meredith Press from 1961 to 1963; executive vice-president of Cue Ventures from 1963 to 1966; and of publisher Abercrombie & Fitch from 1966 to 1970. 145–47

Pearson, Hesketh (1887–1964), English biographer, began as an actor, was later a journalist, and wrote his first biography, *Erasmus Darwin,* in 1930. Some twenty books followed, concluding with *Henry of Navarre* in 1963. 138

"The Perfect Critic" (Eliot), 37

Pergolesi, Giovanni Battista (1710–36), Italian composer, 154

Perronick the Fool (Moore), 48

Personae: The Collected Poems (Pound), 44–45

Pétain, Henri Philippe (1856–1961), French general who was revered as the "savior of Verdun" during World War I. France turned to him after the collapse of the French forces in World War II; he became chief of state from 1940 to 1944. After the liberation of France he was tried and condemned to death, but his sentence was commuted to life imprisonment by de Gaulle. 140

Peter I (1672–1725), traditionally called "The Great," czar of Russia from 1682 to 1725, 153

Petrarch, Francisco (1304–74), Italian poet who was the first humanist and the first modern lyric poet. His sonnets to Laura began a brilliant period of sonnet writing and influenced many poets of the Renaissance. 40, 146

Petrie, Sir William Matthew Flinders (1853–1942), English archaeologist who made many discoveries in Egypt and Palestine. 85

Peyre, Henri (Maurice) (1901–88), French-born American scholar, writer, critic, and university professor who taught at Bryn Mawr, University of Cairo, and Yale University. Peyre has written and edited numerous works. A distinguished scholar, he has been called "a humanist in the richest sense." 147

Point Counter Point (Huxley), 76

Polevoi, Boris Nikolaevich (born Kampov) (1908–81), Soviet author. He became chief editor of the journal *Iunost* in 1962. He also served in the Soviet-Finnish War of 1939–1940 and was a war correspondent for *Pravda* from 1941 to 1945. 153

Politzer, Ronald (d. 1964), long-time publicity director for the publishing firm, William Collins & Co. In his later years, Politzer was a director of the firm. 124

Pollinger, Lawrence (1898–?), literary agent who handled D. H. Lawrence's affairs for the firms Curtis Brown Ltd and, later, Pearn, Pollinger, and Higham. In his last illness, Lawrence asked Pollinger to look after Frieda Lawrence's finances. 59, 61, 116

"Pomona" (Morris), 112

Pope, Alexander (1688–1744), English poet, 40

Portable Henry James, The (ed. Zabel), 120

Portable Oscar Wilde, The (ed. RA), 100–102, 105, 127

Portrait of a Lady, The (James), 120

Portrait of a Rebel. The Life and Work of Robert Louis Stevenson (RA), 133–34, 136, 147

Portrait of the Artist As a Young Man, A (Joyce), 8, 26, 136

Portraits of Places (James), 120

Postran, Eileen Edna Le Poer (1889–1940), English historian and teacher who became professor of economic history at the University of London in 1931. Her chosen subject was the economic position of women in the thirteenth and fourteenth centuries, but she also lectured and published on other aspects of the Middle Ages. 44

Potocki de Montalk, Count Geoffrey Wladislas Vaile (b. 1903), New Zealand–born poet and translator and pretender to the throne of Poland. Often unconventional, Count Potocki was sentenced to six months' imprisonment in 1932 for "obscene libel." He has hand-printed and published under various imprints since 1923. The following RA works were published by Potocki under the imprint of The Melissa Press, Draguignan, Var, France: *A Tourist's Rome* (1960), *A Letter from Richard Aldington* (1961), and *Balls and Another Book for Suppression* (1962). RA helped Potocki to get the Melissa Press under way by soliciting funds and contributing himself toward the purchase of a printing press. 135, **139–41**

Potter, Stephen (1900–69), lecturer at London University in 1926. He joined the staff of the BBC in 1938, served as drama critic for the *New Statesman* from 1945 to 1946, and is the author of *D. H. Lawrence, A First Study* (1930). 65

Pound, Dorothy Shakespear [Mrs. Ezra] (1886–1973), daughter of Olivia Shakespear and wife of Ezra Pound. 3, 119

Pound, Ezra (1885–1971), American poet, essayist, and editor. Leaving a teaching position in America, he went to London in 1908, where he espoused the causes first of Imagism and then of Vorticism. In 1920 Pound left England for the Continent. During World War II Pound made some radio broadcasts for the Fascists for which he was arrested by U.S. forces as a traitor. He

would have been proclaimed chief of state had the assassination attempt against Hitler of 20 July 1944, succeeded. 93

Ronald Firbank. A Biography (Benkovitz), 127

Roosevelt, Franklin Delano (1882–1945), president of the United States from 1933 to 1945, 88, 90, 123

Rose, William, 41

Rosenberg, Janet, 125

Ross, John Hulme. *See* Lawrence, T. E.

Ross, Malcolm (b. 1911), Canadian-born and -educated professor of English literature at Trinity College, University of Toronto. Ross was author of several literary studies and, from 1957, general editor of *New Canadian Library*. In 1955, Ross was elected to the Royal Society of Canada. 132

Ross (Rattigan), 146–47

Rossetti, Dante Gabriel (1828–82), English Pre-Raphaelite painter and poet. With others he formed the Pre-Raphaelite brotherhood and in their journal, *The Germ*, published one of his best-known poems, "The Blessed Damozel." The manuscript, buried with his wife and then retrieved, contains some of his finest poetry, notably "The House of Life," a sonnet sequence. 110

Rossetti, Elizabeth Siddal (d. 1862), Dante Gabriel Rossetti's model, whom he married in 1860. In his grief at her death, he buried with her the manuscript originals of his poems. 110

Roth, Samuel (1894–1974), American poet, translator, and publisher whose dissemination of allegedly obscene material occasioned a Supreme Court definition of obscenity in 1957. He was jailed in 1928 when police seized the plates of *Ulysses* from his publishing company. 43

Rothermere, Baron Esmond Cecil Harmsworth, viscount of Hemsted (1898–1978), heir to the Northcliffe newspaper empire, 65, 108, 124

Rothermere, Lady (d. 1937), born Mary Lillian Share, the wife of Harold Sidney Harmsworth, first Viscount Rothermere, head of a publishing empire. *The Criterion*, edited by T. S. Eliot, was endowed by Lady Rothermere. 37

Rubens, Peter Paul (1577–1640), leading painter of the Flemish school who was much in demand in the courts of Mantua, Spain, France, and England. In London, Rubens painted the ceiling of Whitehall, a panorama of allegorical but voluptuous nudes. 146

Rudge, Olga (fl. twentieth cent.), American-born concert violinist, mother of Ezra Pound's daughter Mary, born in 1924. When Pound was arrested in Italy in May 1945, he and Dorothy, his wife, were living with Rudge in her Casa Seicenta in the hills by Sant' Ambrogio. 56

Rudomino, Margarita I., 153

Ruffo, Fabrizio, 96

Ruskin, John (1819–1900), English writer, critic, and artist who in 1869 was elected first Slade Professor of Fine Art at Oxford. RA's *Religion of Beauty: Selections from the Aesthetes* (1950) includes excerpts from Ruskin's work. 93, 110

Russell, Ada Dwyer (1863–1952), born Ada Dwyer in Salt Lake City. She went on the stage after attending Boston Latin High School. She married the British actor Harold Russell, but they were divorced after the birth of a daughter. She met Amy Lowell at a literary luncheon in Boston; a lifelong alliance ensued. 6

Russell, Bertrand Arthur William Russell, third earl (1872–1970), English philosopher, famous also for his unflagging championship of individual liberty and his pacifist views. His *Principia Mathematica* (written with A. N. Whitehead) is a major contribution to symbolic logic. Russell received the Nobel Prize in Literature in 1950. 35, 121, 142

Russell, Countess Elizabeth Mary Annette Beauchamp (1866–?), whose pseudonym was Elizabeth. She was born in Australia, went to live in Germany in 1890 after her marriage to Count Henning von Arnim, and then to England after his death in 1910. There she married the second Earl Russell. Countess Russell wrote highly successful novels in both Germany and England, but her most successful was her first, *Elizabeth and Her German Garden*(1898). 60

Russell, Hastings William Sackville, twelfth duke of Bedford (1888–1953), a keen ornithologist and a supporter of the Social Credit movement. He was well known and the object of much public animosity because of his pacifism in World War II. 140

Sacred Wood, The (Eliot), 27, 31, 37

Saddest Story, The (Ford), 143

Sadler (or Sadleir), M.T.H. (1888–1957), English publisher, writer, and translator. With Constable and Company for a time, he also published (with Beaumont) *New Paths* (1918), which included RA's "Soliloquy" and "The Blood of the Young Men." As a critic Sadler wrote for Oxford's *Blue Book* and on Emile Verharen in *Poetry and Drama*. He was one of the founders of *Rhythm* and translated Kandinsky's *Concerning the Spiritual in Art* (1914). 16, 67

Saint-Exupéry, Antoine de (1900–1944), French author and aviator, reported missing in 1944. His works include *Wind, Sand and Stars* (1939), *Flight to Arras* (1942), and *The Little Prince* (1943). 105

St. Mawr (D. H. Lawrence), 104

Saintsbury, George Edward Bateman (1845–1933), English man of letters who was Regius Professor of Rhetoric and English Literature at the University of Edinburgh. His editions of French classics and books and articles on the history of French literature made him the most prominent English authority of his day on the subject. Before RA resigned his post as reviewer of French literature for the *Times Literary Supplement* and left England, he had hopes of filling Saintsbury's shoes. 35, 37–38, 42

Salisbury, Lord, 70

Salome (Wilde), 102

Samsonov, Aleksander Mikhailovich (b. 1908), Russian publisher who was head of Academy of Sciences Publishing House. He is a historian who specialized in the history of the Soviet Union's role in World War II and the author of numerous books, including *Under the Walls of Stalingrad* (1952) and *The Great Battle on the Volga, 1942–43* (1963). 153

published RA's selection of Lawrence's poems, *D. H. Lawrence: Selected Poems* (1935), and *Apocalypse* (1932) introduced by RA. 31, 61, 121

Second Book of Modern Verse, The (ed. Rittenhouse), 31

Secret Life of Salvador Dali (Dali), 95

Secret Lives of Lawrence of Arabia, The (Knightley and Simpson), 148

Selected Letters of D. H. Lawrence (comp. RA), 111

Selected Letters of D. H. Lawrence, The (comp. Trilling), 136

Sell, Joseph. *See* Haley, Sir William.

Sentimental Education (Flaubert), 71

Seven Against Reeves: A Comedy-Farce (RA), 57, 75, 78, 80–81, 131, 152

Seven Pillars Of Wisdom, The (T. E. Lawrence), 122, 138, 147, 149

Sevier, Michel (fl. first half of twentieth cent.), English artist, 48

Shakespear, Dorothy. *See* Pound, Dorothy Shakespear.

Shakespeare, William (1564–1616), English poet and dramatist, 35, 61, 68, 120, 141, 145–46, 152

Shalett, Sidney, 96

Shaw, Charlotte Payne-Townshend (Mrs. George Bernard) (1857–1943). She met Shaw through Sidney and Beatrice Webb, activists in the Fabian Society. The Shaws were married in 1898. The relationship between T. E. Lawrence and the Shaws is explored in Stanley Weintraub's *Private Shaw and Public Shaw* (1963). 129–30, 138, 146–49

Shaw, George Bernard (1856–1950), British dramatist awarded the 1925 Nobel prize in literature. RA writes that his mother sent Shaw one of RA's early poems and that Shaw rewarded him with a guinea. 79, 130, 138, 146–47, 149

Shaw, T. E. *See* Lawrence, T. E.

"She and He: Recent Documents" (James), 120

Shelley, Mary (1797–1851), English author; wife of Percy Bysshe Shelley, 121

Shelley, Percy Bysshe (1792–1822), English poet, 16, 67–68, 90, 121, 141, 152

Shelley (White), 141

Shepherd's Life, A (Hudson), 152

Sheppard, Sir John Tresidder (1881–1928), classical scholar, provost of King's College, Cambridge, and senior fellow of Eton College (1933–54), 129

Sherriff, R. C. (Robert Cedric) (1896–1975), prolific British playwright best known for *Journey's End* (1930). As a screenwriter his credits include *Good-bye Mr. Chips* (1939) and *That Hamilton Woman* (1941). 98

"Ship of Death" (D. H. Lawrence), 68

Shorter, Clement King (1857–1926), English journalist, critic, and author. He was the editor of the *Illustrated London News* from 1891 to 1900 and founded and edited the weekly *Sketch* (1893) and the *Tatler* (1903). Shorter wrote a biography of Charlotte Brontë and edited letters and works of the Brontës and others. 23, 25, 31

Shrewsbury Edition of the Works of Samuel Butler, 131

Sidney, Sir Philip (1554–86), an English example of the Renaissance ideal of the perfect gentleman. He was a soldier, statesman, courtier, poet, and patron of

Swinburne, Algernon Charles (1887–1909), English poet, 27, 112, 120

Sydney Bulletin (Sydney, Australia; est. 1880), 140

Symons, Arthur (1865–1945), English poet and critic who helped introduce the French Symbolists to England. Symons was associated at various times with the *Yellow Book*, the *Savoy*, Beardsley, Wilde, Dowson, Yeats, and Nancy Cunard. 41, 149

Symposium (Plato), 16

Synge, John Millington (1871–1909), Irish playwright and director of the Abbey Theatre and thus an associate of Yeats and Lady Gregory. When Synge's *Playboy of the Western World* was presented by the Abbey Players in 1907, it was interrupted by an organized disturbance. 6

Ta Hio: The Great Learning (trans. Pound), 44

Tales (D. H. Lawrence), 61

Tannhäuser (Wagner), 66

Tasso, Torquato (1544–95), major Italian poet of the Renaissance whose best-known work is *Jerusalem Delivered* (1575), 119

Taylor, Rachel Annand (Banabhard) (1876–1960), British poet, journalist, and student of the Renaissance in Italy and France, 111–12

T. E. Lawrence by His Friends (ed. A. W. Lawrence), 122, 138

"T. E. Lawrence: Man or Myth" (Hart), 132

Temple, Frédéric-Jacques (b. 1921), French poet, critic, and translator. Director of programs for Montpellier's Radiodiffusion-Télévision Française, Temple writes on English literature; he coedited *Richard Aldington: An Intimate Portrait*. 130, 132, 134

Tendencies in Modern American Poetry (Lowell), 16

"The Tenderness of Dante" (RA), 33

Tertullian (Quintus Septimus Florens Tertullianus) (ca. 155–ca. 222), the earliest and, after Augustine, the greatest of the ancient church writers of the West, 32

That Hamilton Woman [Screenplay] (Sherriff), 98

Thatcher, David S., 41

Thayer, Scofield, 26

Theis, Mrs. Otto Frederick. *See* Morgan, Louise.

Theocritus (fl. ca. 270 B.C.), Greek poet, 2

Théodat (de Gourmont), 11

These Same Men (Warman), 154

Thesiger, Frederic John Napier. *See* Chelmsford, Frederic John Napier.

"They Come Back Different" (RA), 97

Thibaud, Jacques (1880–1953), French violinist, 58

Thibaudet, Albert (1874–1936), one of the foremost French literary critics of the first half of the twentieth century, and professor of French literature at the University of Geneva. His essays and reviews, mostly contributed to the *Nouvelle Revue Française*, were collected in *Réflections sur la Litérature* (1938–41). 31

Whistler, James Abbott McNeill (1834–1903), American etcher and painter, 96

Whitall, James (1889–1954), American author and translator who lived in England for fourteen years working for publishing houses. On his return to the United States, he wrote *English Years* (1935); during his career he translated more than twenty-five works from the French, including works by André Maurois, Leon Daudet, and Joseph Peyre. 10, 81

Whitall, Mrs. James (Mildred), 81

White, Newman Ivey (1892–1948), American scholar who wrote a definitive biography of Shelley as well as many other books about Shelley and his work, 141

White Peacock, The (D. H. Lawrence), 68, 111, 136

Whitehead, Alfred North (1861–1947), British-American philosopher and mathematician who collaborated with Bertrand Russell in writing *Principa Mathematica* (3 vols., 1910–13), 35

Whitman, Walt (1819–92), American poet who was an admitted major influence on RA, 2, 120, 152

Wickham, Anne (Edith Alice Mary Harper) (1884–1947), English poet whose best poetry is in *The Contemplative Quarry* (1915) and *The Man with the Hammer* (1916). Monro published her work in *Poetry and Drama* for June 1914, and issued *The Contemplative Quarry* as a chapbook in the same year he published RA's *Images (1912–15)*. Wickham was represented in *The New Poetry* (1917, enlarged 1923) by six poems. 6

Widdemer, Margaret (1884–1978), American novelist, writer, and poet. She began writing poetry as a child and published her last book at the age of 84. 83

"Wide Guiana Strike Called by Leftist" (anon.), 125

Wilde, Dorothy Ierne Wilde (Dolly) (fl. twentieth cent.), daughter of William Wilde, Oscar's brother, by his second wife, Sophie Lily Lees. Dolly was an intimate of Natalie Barney. 47

Wilde, Oscar (1854–1900), Irish writer who followed J. M. Whistler's "art for art's sake" philosophy. His novel *The Picture of Dorian Gray* (1891) mirrored this new aesthetic, and his successful plays staged his own paradoxes and witty sayings. One of the most prominent personalities of his day, Wilde was sentenced to two years' imprisonment with hard labor for offences under the Criminal Law Amendment Act; this ended his brilliant career. 15, 100, 102, 127, 131, 140

Wilderness of Zin, The (Woolley and T. E. Lawrence), 122

Wilkinson, Frances Josepha Gregg (Mrs. Louis) (1884–1941), girlhood friend of H.D., with whom she first traveled to Europe in 1911. Frances Gregg married Louis Wilkinson in 1912 and settled in Europe. Thereafter she wrote a number of poems and short prose pieces for English and American periodicals. H.D. wrote about her relationship with Mrs. Wilkinson in *End to Torment* (1979) and *Hermione* (1981). 13, 112

Wilkinson, Louis Umfreville (1881–1966), English novelist who also wrote under the pseudonym Louis Marlow. He was friend, biographer, and editor of the Powys brothers; he spent some years in the United States as a lecturer on English literature. 13, 14